Engaging Children in Science

SECOND EDITION

ANN C. HOWE
North Carolina State University

LINDA JONES
California State University, Northridge

Merrill,
an imprint of Prentice Hall
Upper Saddle River, New Jersey   Columbus, Ohio

Library of Congress Cataloging-in-Publication Data
Howe, Ann C.
     Engaging children in science / Ann C. Howe, Linda Jones.—2nd ed.
          p.   cm.
     Includes bibliographical references and index.
     ISBN 0-13-598343-6
     1. Science—Study and teaching (Elementary)—United States. 2. Education, Elementary—Activity programs—United States.   I. Jones, Linda II. Title.
     LB1585.3.H69 1998
     372.3′5—dc21   97-9209
                                                                    CIP

Cover photo: © Comstock
Editor: Bradley J. Potthoff
Production Editor: Julie Peters
Design Coordinator: Julia Zonneveld Van Hook
Text Designer: Mia Saunders
Cover Designer: Rod Harris
Production Manager: Patricia A. Tonneman
Electronic Text Management: Marilyn Wilson Phelps, Matthew Williams, Karen L. Bretz,
     Tracey B. Ward
Illustrations: Kurt Wendling
Director of Marketing: Kevin Flanagan
Marketing Manager: Suzanne Stanton
Advertising/Marketing Coordinator: Julie Shough

This book was set in Galliard by Prentice Hall and was printed and bound by R.R. Donnelley & Sons Company. The cover was printed by Phoenix Color Corp.

© 1998 by Prentice-Hall, Inc.
Simon & Schuster/A Viacom Company
Upper Saddle River, New Jersey 07458

Earlier edition © 1993 by Macmillan College Publishing Company.

Photo credits: Bettmann Archive, pp. 20, 21; Scott Cunningham/Merrill, p. 18; Harvard University News Office, p. 32; Ann C. Howe, p. 313; T. Hubbard, p. 65; Anthony Magnacca/Merrill, pp. 1, 44, 49, 93, 110, 114, 118, 127, 143, 149, 151, 171, 177, 184, 196, 214, 231, 248, 258, 279, 296, 304, 324, 328, 335; Ernie York, p. 70.

Printed in the United States of America

10 9 8 7 6 5 4

ISBN: 0-13-598343-6

Prentice-Hall International (UK) Limited, *London*
Prentice-Hall of Australia Pty. Limited, *Sydney*
Prentice-Hall of Canada, Inc., *Toronto*
Prentice-Hall Hispanoamericana, S. A., *Mexico*
Prentice-Hall of India Private Limited, *New Delhi*
Prentice-Hall of Japan, Inc., *Tokyo*
Simon & Schuster Asia Pte. Ltd., *Singapore*
Editora Prentice-Hall do Brasil, Ltda., *Rio de Janeiro*

Preface

Engaging Children in Science is a guide to an activity-based course in science teaching methods for both preservice and in-service teachers. Informed by constructivist theory, the book takes the view that neither knowledge of science nor knowledge of teaching can be acquired passively by absorption through the senses but only by active thinking and doing. Learners, both children and adults, reflect on their experiences to construct their own meaning and understanding of the world around them. When learning is viewed this way, it becomes clear that the teacher has a responsibility to provide the special type of learning environment and the experiences that promote the construction of knowledge.

A child's years in elementary school span a period of dramatic physical, mental, and emotional growth. The teacher's primary role is often seen as increasing students' knowledge, but the most effective teachers also play an important role in promoting the growth of their students' independent, responsible thinking and actions, or, to put it another way, their students' growth toward autonomy. Children need to know that they can think for themselves and that their own thoughts are worthwhile and valuable to themselves, their classmates, and their teacher. This book reflects our belief that teachers can promote autonomous thought and action by the way they teach and interact with their pupils, and that helping children become independent thinkers and learners should be an important goal for science teaching.

ORGANIZATION OF THE TEXT

After an opening chapter on the modern view of science, the book lays the theoretical foundation for constructivism by describing the positions of Dewey, Piaget, Bruner, Vygotsky, and Kohlberg. The next three chapters show how the best current thinking on such topics as inclusion of all children, classroom management, thematic unit planning, teacher expectations, and authentic assessment is applied to science teaching.

The central section focuses on specific instructional strategies for science teaching, beginning with direct instruction and moving through guided inquiry, with separate chapters for primary and intermediate grades, to group and individual investi-

iii

gations. These chapters provide step-by-step instructions and detailed plans for science lessons illustrating each of the instructional strategies described. Lessons in physical science, earth science, and life science are included. Some of the lessons may be used as professional development activities in the methods course, and all may be adapted for later use by students as they begin their own teaching careers.

The final three chapters treat the integration of science with other subjects, building thematic units in science, technology, and society and the use of computers as tools for inquiry. These chapters include unit plans, numerous examples of lessons and units that have been used successfully by teachers, and lists of resources for lesson and unit planning.

FEATURES OF THE TEXT

Teachers who use this book will gain experiences that enhance their ability to construct their own understanding of how children learn science and how they can implement strategies to capitalize on this knowledge. An important feature of the book is an extended case study that follows the interaction between an experienced teacher, Ms. Oldhand, and a teacher in training, Mr. Newman. Strategically placed descriptions of Ms. Oldhand's methods of teaching science will help readers visualize how the strategies described in the book are used in actual classroom situations as they "listen in" on discussions of the challenges of implementing strategies in real classrooms.

Other important features are the Discussion Questions and Activities for the Reader that are placed at the end of each chapter. These are not afterthoughts but are central to the constructivist approach of the text. The discussion questions are intended to stimulate independent thinking on the part of students who too often believe there is one right answer to every question. The activities for the reader provide firsthand experiences that can lead students to construct new knowledge and understanding about learning and teaching science. These activities have been designed to be used as assignments to assist the course instructor in modeling the constructivist approach to teaching.

NEW IN THE SECOND EDITION

Important developments in science education over the past five years have prompted significant revisions in the text. The influence of two new volumes, *Benchmarks for Science Literacy* (American Association for the Advancement of Science, 1993) and *National Science Education Standards* (National Research Council, 1996), can be seen throughout the book. New lesson plans have been added, and each lesson plan is now tied to one of the standards. The gradual shift away from emphasis on individual science processes toward the integration of process and content in the context of inquiry-based instruction is also reflected in changes in the chapters that make up the central section of the book.

A new chapter on using computers to promote curriculum goals takes into account some of the rapid changes that have occurred in the use of computers in the past few years. These changes may perhaps be best understood by considering that the World Wide Web was only a distant possibility when the first edition was completed. Another new chapter, on building thematic units in science, technology, and society, addresses the need to include education for responsible citizenship in the science curriculum at all levels.

Comments and suggestions of those who have used the text have led to less emphasis on mathematics and a greater concentration on science activities. A section on safety precautions, an important consideration in all classrooms, has been added.

Current interest in authentic assessment, reflective practice, inclusion of children with special needs in regular classrooms, and attention to diverse populations led us to increase the treatment of these topics and to move them toward the front of the book as background for the chapters on instructional strategies. Reference lists for these chapters have been updated to include recent research.

ACKNOWLEDGMENTS

We thank Sarah Berenson, North Carolina State University, for her suggestions and advice on the chapter on using computers in the classroom and we thank the many other friends and colleagues who have cheered us on in this endeavor. One of us also acknowledges with appreciation and gratitude the encouragement and support of her husband, Charles Howe.

We extend our sincere thanks to the students of California State University, Northridge, for their valuable suggestions on early drafts of the manuscript.

In addition, we thank teachers whose ideas for Science, Technology, and Society units are included in the text. These include teachers at Henry H. Houston Middle School, Philadelphia, and Benjamin Syms Middle School in Hampton, Virginia.

We extend special thanks to all those at Prentice Hall who have guided and supported us: to Brad Potthoff for his generous help and encouragement as the revision got underway and took shape; to Carol Sykes, who guided us through manuscript preparation and submission; to Julie Peters, who turned a manuscript into a book; to Anthony Magnacca, whose photographs captured what it means for children to be engaged in science; and to other members of the editorial staff, each of whom made special contributions. Thanks are also due to Luanne Dreyer-Elliott whose keen eye and red pencil edited out our mistakes and inconsistencies.

We also thank our reviewers, whose comments and suggestions were the basis for restructuring much of the book: Joel E. Bass, Sam Houston State University; Glenn D. Berkheimer, Michigan State University; Carol Briscoe, University of West Florida; Frances Lawrenz, University of Minnesota; and Greg P. Stefanich, University of Northern Iowa.

Contents

Science for Everyone

◆ Joe Newman, teacher candidate, was discussing elementary science with his cooperating teacher, Ms. Oldhand.

MR. NEWMAN: I don't feel very confident about teaching science. I loved science in elementary school, but I'm nervous about teaching it myself.

MS. OLDHAND: I'm glad to hear that you liked science in elementary school. What courses did you have in high school and college?

MR. NEWMAN: I had all the required courses, and they were OK, but science wasn't my main interest, so I concentrated on other things.

MS. OLDHAND: Well, it was about the same with me. Some of my teachers gave interesting lectures, but the theories weren't connected with anything I felt I had experienced. Fortunately, I later had some opportunities to learn about hands-on science for children. Now, I'm really enthusiastic about it.

MR. NEWMAN: That's great. What happened to make you so enthusiastic?

MS. OLDHAND: The children enjoy hands-on science so much. I use that built-in motivation to bring in as many other subjects as possible—it makes sense to integrate science into the rest of the school day. The experiences with materials are so meaningful for the children that they actually want to write about those experiences, read background material, and even use the computer for something other than games.

MR. NEWMAN: OK, I'm convinced you've made it work. Now I just have to convince myself that I can do it, too.

MS. OLDHAND: That's the first step. You know, you don't have to learn everything in one day. Watch me start a new unit this afternoon. Then I'll help you plan one of the lessons for next week.

MR. NEWMAN: You make it sound so simple.

Science can be the most exciting subject in the elementary school for both children and teachers if science is an active, hands-on subject that children learn through doing, not listening or memorizing. In elementary school, when science is taught at all, it all too often is taught with reading as the main source of knowledge. The cognitive result is what has been called dissociated learning—isolated facts having little or no connection to the learner's life. This often results in children having attitudes toward science that range from neutral to negative. In fact, children love learning when it is meaningful. Play is not just a "childish" pastime but the way children learn their world. We wrote this book about science learning and teaching to help teachers and future teachers open children's minds to the natural world—the world of plants and animals, rocks, water, and the sky.

Young children learn best when they experience things themselves and then have time to think about those experiences as well as talk about what they have seen and done. Observing, measuring, collecting, and classifying—some of the ways of learning that work best in science—come naturally to most children. When you help children learn about the world through their own activity and thought, you reinforce their natural interests and curiosity.

Perhaps your interest in science began as a child, and you are now anxious to pass on a love of the subject to your pupils. Maybe you had a teacher who kindled this interest, or maybe your parents shared with you their own interest in some area of science. To you, science is an exciting subject full of opportunities for exploring the world.

Or, maybe your science education didn't really begin until you took required science courses in high school and college. You may have no recollection of having had science in elementary school. Science has not always received a high priority in elementary schools, and sometimes it is left out altogether. High school and college science courses can seem quite abstract and demanding for those who have had no opportunity to build a foundation in elementary school. Students who lack confidence in mathematics may feel disadvantaged in science courses as well. If you fit one of these descriptions, you are not alone. We want to reassure you that we have kept you in mind and have not assumed that all readers have positive memories or feelings about science.

We believe, however, that everyone who wants to become a good teacher can learn to present science activities in ways that are natural, interesting, and fulfilling for pupils. You have only to believe in your own ability to learn new things and to open up your mind to the ideas in this book. You can help your future pupils develop positive attitudes about science and strong self-images as problem solvers. In the process you can begin to understand some things that you never fully understood before. If you already enjoy science and want to pass on your interest to others, this book will help you develop the skills needed to engender similar interest and enthusiasm in your pupils.

By the time an adolescent enters secondary school, specialization of interests and abilities has often occurred, resulting in the selection of some courses of study and the avoidance of others. If students have had negative science experiences before high school, they usually take only the required minimum number of courses, thus cutting themselves off from many science-related careers and from the scientific understanding needed by every citizen. In the elementary school, on the other hand, all students take science regardless of what they will study in the future. Therefore, a good science program makes sense at every grade level. In today's climate of job insecurity, students sometimes shun studies not directly related to career preparation, but the quality of people's lives depends on more than just economic factors. Science is about developing reasoning skills, mental outlooks, and an openness to new information. All citizens need these skills to lead a rich and fulfilling mental life, as well as to enable them to make independent decisions about important societal issues.

TRUSTING YOUR OWN ABILITIES

As you become a teacher, we expect you to learn to trust your own ability to learn and teach science. Richard Feynman, a Nobel laureate in physics, had this to say in a talk he gave to science teachers at a national meeting:

> You teachers . . . can maybe doubt the experts once in a while. Learn from science that you must doubt the experts . . . When someone says, "Science teaches such and such," he is using the word incorrectly. Science doesn't teach anything; experience teaches it. If they say to you, "Science has shown such and such," you might ask, "How does science show it? How did the scientists find out? How? What? Where?" It should not be "science has shown," but "this experiment, this effect, has shown." And you have as much right as anyone else, upon hearing about the experiments (but be patient and listen to all the evidence) to judge whether a sensible conclusion has been arrived at. (Feynman, 1968)

One reason all of you can become good elementary science teachers is that children love hands-on learning. That is the natural way to learn; your main job is to provide the situation and teach them how to function within its boundaries. In such a context, science ideas will be concrete rather than abstract, and your role will be to guide a learning experience rather than to tell about or explain concepts.

Another reason all of you could become good teachers is that this book—and your instructor—will help you construct the knowledge and acquire the skills you need to be successful. As you develop knowledge of how to guide students through activities and discussions of the kind described here, you will gain confidence in your own ability to have a positive effect on student learning.

Self-efficacy, the sense that what you do can make a difference, is one of the few teacher characteristics shown to be related to student achievement (Woolfolk & Hoy, 1990). To be effective, you must believe that what you do will have an effect. You must also show children that what they do will have an effect. Particularly with girls and with minority children, you will need teaching strategies that give each child a sense of self-efficacy—a belief in his or her own ability to learn science as well as the motivation to be an active and responsible learner.

BUILDING ONE'S OWN KNOWLEDGE

The kind of science program described in this book is one in which children build their own knowledge from their own experiences, from both doing and thinking. "Hands-on" must be accompanied by "minds-on." Having interesting things for the children to do is not enough; thinking and talking about what they have done must be part of the science program, too. In this way children build their own knowledge from their own experiences.

The idea that people must build their own knowledge from their own experiences and thought is called *constructivism,* the belief that real understanding occurs only when people participate fully in the development of their own knowledge. The learning process is seen as a self-regulated transformation of old knowledge to new knowledge, a process that requires both action and reflection on the part of the learner. Contrast this idea of learning with the opposite idea, that people learn by absorbing what they are told or that their minds are like blank pages on which teachers or others can write. The research of cognitive psychologists and science educators over the past decade has shown that what children learn greatly depends on what they already know. Knowledge and understanding grow slowly, with each new bit of information having to be fitted into what was already there.

Constructivism has been defined by Fosnot (1989, pp. 19–20) as having the following four principles:

1. "Knowledge consists of past constructions." Cognitive development comes about through self-regulation or adaptation to new circumstances or ideas.
2. "Constructions come about through assimilation and accommodation." We assimilate new information to an existing logical framework if we can; when the framework is contradicted or is insufficient, we develop a higher level theory or logic to accommodate the new information.
3. "Learning is an organic process of invention rather than a mechanical process of accumulation."
4. "Meaningful learning occurs through reflection and resolution of cognitive conflict and thus serves to negate earlier, incomplete levels of understanding."

You may be thinking at this point that there are certain things a pupil simply must be told and then asked to remember, and you wonder how the memorization of facts fits into this idea of learning. Undoubtedly, some things have to be committed to memory without explanation, such as your telephone number, the name of the street you live on, and the names of trees, birds, and flowers. We all need a mechanism for remembering and retrieving these kinds of numbers and words, and you will want your pupils to know things of this kind. But learning of this kind is a lower-level mental function; although some may be necessary, it should not be the main emphasis or even an important emphasis of your teaching. Science teaching should lead to a deeper understanding of relationships and interrelationships, of causes and effects, of how we know what we know and how we can find out more. These concepts require higher-level thinking and should not be treated as facts to be memorized. This is the kind of knowledge that all learners must construct in their own way.

For you, too, knowledge and understanding will grow slowly, with each new bit of information having to be fitted into what is already there. This textbook includes hands-on activities for you that can only be effective if they are accompanied by reflection, discussion, and independent thinking. Your ideas of what constitutes good teaching have developed over all the years you have been a student, and you may find that some of those ideas will change as you focus on trying to become a good science teacher. You may find, also, that some of your ideas about science will change as you think of science in a broader context than that provided in most of the courses you may have taken.

WHAT SCIENCE IS

Science is commonly thought of as both knowledge, or understanding, and a way of arriving at knowledge. Science is not the only way of knowing; people can also arrive at knowledge through other pathways, including intuition, art forms, and faith. Science cannot answer all questions; questions about values, about good and evil, about the meaning of life cannot be answered by the methods of science. What science can do, and has done, is to achieve an ever increasing understanding of the natural world, which includes us as human beings, and the rules that govern the patterns and interrelationships found in nature.

The desire to know more about the natural world has probably always been a part of human life and has certainly been present since the beginning of recorded history, but the systematic study of natural phenomena in more recent times has produced an explosion of scientific knowledge that has changed almost every aspect of the way we live and the way we think. Many ideas that once seemed farfetched and even ridiculous are now part of our general knowledge. For example, it would be hard to find a person today who does not believe that bacteria and viruses exist and cause disease or that it is possible to obtain energy from splitting atoms, but these ideas were hotly debated and denied by intelligent people a little over a century ago.

To study science is to learn about what other people have found out and to learn about the methods that allowed them to arrive at this knowledge and then to convince other people to accept it. To be scientifically literate, a person needs to have knowledge of concepts and theories of science and, in addition, to have some understanding of how this knowledge has been obtained in the past and is still being learned today. Some of the distinctive aspects of science are explained next.

Scientists' View of the World

Scientists believe that the world is understandable and can be understood through the careful, systematic application of human intelligence. A look back through the history of the last hundred years shows how much has been learned about all aspects of plant and animal life, the particles that are the basic forms of matter, the history and composition of the earth, the parts of our solar system, and the complex workings of the universe beyond. As scientific work continues to probe all of these areas, unexpected observations will surely force scientists to revise their current ideas and develop theories that give better explanations than the ones we now have. Science will never be a finished body of knowledge because new ideas and theories are always being proposed, new discoveries are being made, and some things that were taken for granted turn out to be different from what they were thought to be. Students sometimes get confused when they hear that scientific knowledge is subject to change and ask "Then why am I learning all of this science if it may not be true?" One answer is that *science* is not the same as *truth;* science is the sum of the best explanations we now have for all the complexities of nature. This knowledge has been built up over thousands of years, and most of what has been learned endures; change comes slowly, and major theories or principles may be revised but are very rarely overturned. However, we always have to leave a little room in our minds for the possibility that some new observation may force us to change our ideas or that a new theory will be a better explanation for old observations. As teachers, we try to introduce our students to the scientific world view of the time we live in.

Science as the Search for Knowledge

Scientists use many strategies and techniques in their search for greater knowledge and understanding, but at some point they rely on observations that can be repeated or verified by others. Scientists use their own senses and instruments—sometimes very complicated ones—to make the observations that form the data on which they base the theories and hypotheses that explain what they have found. When important new observations are published, other scientists will try to verify them. If the observations, or data, can't be verified, they aren't accepted. When the observations are verified, however, other scientists may or may not accept the original scientist's explanation for them, and arguments may go on for years about how to interpret the observations, since other scientists may propose different hypotheses to explain the observations.

The advancement of scientific knowledge depends as much, if not more, on the hypotheses or theories scientists put forth as it does on the data they collect. In fact, hypotheses and theories usually determine what data will be collected, since isolated facts by themselves can seldom be interpreted. It may work like this: A scientist is interested in something that is not well understood. So, by a combination of extensive knowledge, intuition, and imagination, the scientist thinks of a possible explanation; this is stated as a hypothesis, and the scientist determines what data will be needed to support or refute the hypothesis. The next step is to develop a careful plan for collecting the necessary data in such a way that others will be convinced that the data are reliable. When the observations have been made, the scientist examines the data to see whether the hypothesis has been supported; if so, the scientist publishes the results and offers the original hypothesis as the explanation for the observations.

The various branches of science tend to use different methods for collecting the evidence they need to support their hypotheses or theories. The popular picture of a scientist is of someone carrying out an experiment in a laboratory with an imposing array of esoteric equipment. That is one important way that observations are made, but that is by no means the only way. Astronomy, paleontology, and geology are some of the fields of science in which laboratory experiments are not possible, and our knowledge of animal behavior has been advanced by scientists who leave the laboratory behind and go to where the animals are. Scientists who cannot carry out experiments in a laboratory have to find other ways to collect evidence for their hypotheses; for example, astronomers make observations when stars or planets are in a certain position relative to each other, and geologists travel to places where rock formations "tell a story."

The Social Nature of Science

Very few scientists work alone or in isolation from other scientists; not all of them are surrounded by other people on a daily basis, but they stay in communication with colleagues all over the world. Scientists work in research institutes, universities, industry, government, and hospitals, and they can be found all over the world. Although scientists everywhere make every effort to be unbiased in their work and to hold to the same ethical standards, science, like all human endeavors, is influenced to some extent by the culture of the country where it is carried out. The subjects chosen for study, the freedom accorded scientists, and the prevailing views of the meaning and purpose of life all may have an effect on scientific endeavor. In our own country, for example, the cultural climate is reflected in the way the government allocates various amounts of money for research in space exploration, medicine, new weapons, and environmental science. As women have become more vocal in seeking equality, more funds have gradually been allocated to women's diseases. And as acquired immune deficiency syndrome (AIDS) has become a terrible health problem, money has been redirected to research in that disease. Although science is correctly said to be international, it cannot be said to be entirely culture-free.

Science and Technology

As science helps people to understand the world, technology helps people to shape the world. From the earliest crude tools of cave people to the Worldwide Web of our time, technology has been a force in the development of civilization. We tend to think of technology as applied science. In our own time we have seen the application of science in ways that profoundly affect our lives, from the control of infectious diseases to the pervasive use of computers, but that is too simple a view of technology. The relation between science and technology is not a simple one-way street. Technology, like science, is a complex human endeavor that has often made its own discoveries and advances without the benefit of scientific knowledge. We know that the ancient Egyptian and Mediterranean civilizations developed technologies that allowed them to preserve the bodies of their dead, extract metals from ores, and make beautiful glass without knowing the chemical reactions involved in these processes.

Today science and technology contribute to each other and are dependent on each other in many ways. The application of scientific discoveries, for example, has led to technologies for using atomic energy, the control of many diseases, improved methods of food production, and space travel. On the other side, the electronic computer, a marvel of modern technology, has led to scientific advances in understanding gene structure, weather, and other complex systems. Science and technology are inextricably linked together, and, although the emphasis in this book is on science, technology will also play a part in the science activities in your classroom.

KINDS OF KNOWLEDGE

Some science concepts come from direct experience or observation; these are often called *concrete concepts*. For example, a child can directly observe the life cycle of a butterfly. No sequence of logic or leap of insight is required to understand that interesting changes take place along the way from egg to adult. A child can also notice that beetles go through similar changes in their life cycle. At this point the child might overgeneralize that all insects have larval and pupal stages. This misconception could easily be refined by providing some additional insect cultures to observe, such as crickets or mantises. Notice that the refinement is also based on concrete experience.

Other situations appropriate for direct experience have aspects requiring abstract thought. An example is sinking/floating. Anyone can observe that some objects float and some sink when placed in water. Observing the sinking/floating behavior of objects is a concrete experience. Certain conclusions about sinking and floating also can be drawn at a concrete level. For example, metal things sink, wooden things float. But as more and more exceptions to these conclusions become apparent, the firmness of the early understanding begins to slip. For example, some kinds of wood sink, and waterlogged wood also sinks; but metal cups float. An aircraft carrier, weighing hundreds of tons, floats. An adequate concept of sinking/floating—one that will explain and predict any floating/sinking system—requires abstract thinking that coordinates the density (weight per unit volume) of the object to the density of the liquid. Not all elementary pupils will be able to understand sinking/floating in this way.

Some science ideas are quite abstract and are not easily presented in any concrete way. The growth of knowledge about the spherical shape of the earth is an interesting example of the use of explanatory concepts in science. Before anyone actually sailed around it, many thinkers had postulated that the earth was round, though everyday experience told them, as it tells us, that the earth is flat. Thinking of the earth as a sphere was at first a scientific theory that explained many puzzling things not explained by the flat-earth idea and that supported a variety of predictions. For example, Columbus predicted that he could get to the Orient by sailing west and that he would not fall off the edge, because a sphere has no edge. His voyages supported the second prediction, but the first prediction was not borne out until Magellan's crew sailed around the globe.

All of the thinking that originally went into formulating the idea of the round earth was based on indirect evidence. And even though the idea had proved to be correct, it was not until the last half of the twentieth century, some 500 years later, that the entire earth was actually seen in one glance. The famous photograph taken by the Apollo astronauts on their way to the moon was literally an eye-opener. Many people, including news commentators, remarked that they always knew that the earth was round, but they never really believed it until they saw that picture.

By the time children are old enough to go to school they have acquired an amazing stock of knowledge, not all of which has been acquired in the same way. For instance, we might say that a certain child knows the alphabet, knows that ice is cold, and also knows why shadows are longer in late day than at noon. We could also say that the child knows how to play with other children. The way the child has arrived at knowing is different in each of these cases. A child learns the alphabet by memorization, learns that ice is cold through experience, learns about relationships in the natural world through thinking about experiences, and learns about getting along with others through interaction with other people.

These four kinds of knowledge are described in more detail next. The terms used—as well as the basic idea of kinds of knowledge—are derived from Jean Piaget's work, though the terms are not exactly the same as he used. An interesting and useful discussion of kinds of knowledge can be found in Kamii and DeVries (1978).

Arbitrary Knowledge

Knowledge is arbitrary in the sense that someone, at some time, decided that this is the way it would be. Included in this category are names, symbols, conventions, rules, and procedures. These have been defined by other people—or the society as a whole—and are learned from other people, either directly (by being told) or indirectly (by reading or from watching television). An easy way to understand this concept is to think about languages; what English speakers call a *house* is called *maison* in French, *casa* in Spanish, and *ie* in Japanese. All these words refer to the same thing. In some countries cars keep to the right, whereas in others they keep to the left. This is an arbitrary rule or convention.

Physical Knowledge

Physical knowledge arises from direct experience and observation of objects and events. People really know that ice is cold only if they have experienced ice. Examples of physical knowledge include the knowledge that rocks sink in water and wood floats, that water runs downhill, and that caterpillars turn into moths or butterflies. This kind of knowledge can be discovered by oneself and universally rings true. Learning experiences that lead to physical knowledge are the heart of science in the primary grades.

Logical Knowledge

Logical knowledge encompasses concepts, conclusions, and higher-order ideas derived from thinking about observations or experiences. This is the kind of knowledge that must be constructed by the learner. It cannot be acquired by observation alone, and it cannot be learned from being told; it has to be constructed in the mind of the learner. Young children think that a ball of clay broken into pieces will weigh more than it weighed before it was broken up. Weighing the clay before and after will not convince them; they think the scales are wrong. Eventually, however, they come to understand that, logically, the amount of clay cannot change when it is broken up and that the clay has to weigh the same.

Social Interactive Knowledge

Social interactive knowledge is gained through interaction with other people, including how to get along with others, how to understand the feelings of others, and how to work cooperatively. Children have to grow into the knowledge of others that allows them to see something from another's point of view. This is not the knowledge of rules of behavior but a deeper understanding of the ways of compromise and cooperation.

These four kinds of knowledge, or ways of knowing, are described and illustrated more fully in later chapters of this book, but an example here may be helpful. Consider an elementary science lesson about a balance beam. The names of the parts (arm, fulcrum, etc.) are arbitrary knowledge; the way the balance behaves when objects are hung on the arms is physical knowledge; the mathematical relationship between the masses of the objects and the distance from the fulcrum on a beam that is balanced is logical knowledge; knowing how to work in harmony with a partner is social knowledge.

SCIENTIFIC LITERACY AS THE GOAL OF SCIENCE EDUCATION

Scientific literacy for all students has been established as a national goal. To facilitate the achievement of this goal, several professional organizations have brought together scientists, teachers, and science educators to prepare guidelines and recommendations for what students should know and how science should be taught. Three of the publications are described here.

Science for All Americans

Science for All Americans (American Association for the Advancement of Science [AAAS], 1990) defines scientific literacy as (1) the awareness that science is a human enterprise with strengths and limitations, (2) understanding of the key concepts and principles of science, (3) a familiarity with the natural world and recognition of its diversity and unity, and (4) the ability to use this knowledge for individual and social purposes. The report recommends that schools teach less and teach it better and teach for broader understanding rather than to cover material. The authors of the report state their belief that elementary school science should enhance childhood; that is, science should be taught not only for some future benefit but also to make life richer and more rewarding for children as they experience it.

Science for All Americans identifies broad areas of knowledge that can be taught at many levels and in many ways. Details and facts are not important in themselves and are only useful to the extent that they lead to understanding of the principles involved. The focus is on depth of understanding and on using knowledge of science in the choices everyone makes in daily life. The recommendations are much broader than any list of topics could indicate, but some of the basic areas of knowledge are listed next along with our interpretation of how each might be translated into the elementary science curriculum.

Physical Science

The universe.   Children should become aware of the sun, the stars, and the planets and know that we are part of a very large universe.

The earth.   The shape of the earth, its motion around the sun, its climates, winds, oceans, and fresh water, and its changes through time are phenomena that children should gradually come to understand as they move through the elementary grades.

Forces that shape the earth.   Children should understand the effects of wind, water, animals, and plants.

The structure of matter.   Elementary science should include the study of observable states of matter—solid, liquid, and gas—and the changes brought about by heat and other forces but should leave atoms, electrons, and other invisible particles for study in later years.

Energy transformations.   Observable phenomena associated with heat, light, sound, electricity, and mechanical energy can form an experiential basis for later study.

Motion and forces.   Changes in speed, the action of magnets, and the pull of gravity should be observed by elementary children.

Life Science

Diversity of life.   The observation and study of the wonderful variety of living things should be an important part of elementary science at all levels.

Heredity.   Observation and discussion of easily observed inherited characteristics should be addressed in elementary science.

Cells.   Upper elementary children should begin microscopic and other exploratory activities associated with cells.

Interdependence of life.   Food webs, parasitic relationships, and ecosystems can be the basis for many interesting activities.

Flow of matter and energy.   Elementary science should include study of the effect of sunshine on plants and basic natural cycles.

Evolution of life.   This concept requires a level of abstract thinking that is beyond the reach of all but a few elementary children.

The Human Organism

Human identity.   The similarities that make us human should be discussed.

Life cycle.   Birth, growth, and death of human beings should be discussed.

Basic functions. Elementary school students should study the derivation of energy from food, protection from injury, internal coordination, and reproduction.

As you study this textbook, you will see many examples of lessons and activities that teach simple concepts related to these basic scientific ideas. These are not ideas that children, or anyone else, can learn by memorization or by listening to the teacher. People have to build knowledge and understanding gradually from their own experiences and from their own thinking.

Benchmarks for Science Literacy

Benchmarks for Science Literacy (AAAS, 1993) is a companion volume to *Science for All Americans* and breaks down the broad themes into specific science objectives for students of grades kindergarten through 2, 3 through 5, 6 through 8, and 9 through 12. An example from the book may help you understand how this is done. One of the goals of instruction is for students to learn about the structure of matter. *Benchmarks* recommends that by the end of second grade children should know the following things about the structure of matter:

◆ Objects can be described in terms of materials they are made of and their physical properties.

◆ Things can be done to materials to change some of their properties, but not all respond the same way.

By the end of fifth grade, children should know:

◆ Heating and cooling cause changes in the properties of materials.

◆ When a thing is broken into parts, the parts have the same total weight as the original thing.

◆ Materials may be composed of parts too small to be seen without magnification.

◆ When a new material is made by combining two or more materials, it has properties that are different from the original materials. (pp. 76–77)

Benchmarks continues in this way to list objectives for the nature of science, the physical environment, the living environment, the human organism, human society, and related areas. It was designed as a guide rather than a prescription for teachers and curriculum builders.

National Science Education Standards

National Science Education Standards (National Research Council, 1996) is the most recent of the publications to provide guidelines for science teachers, administrators, and curriculum developers. Produced by the National Research Council, it presents broad criteria for science education with a view toward reaching the goal of a scientifically literate society. Standards, or criteria, are presented for science teaching, the professional development of teachers, assessment in science education, science content, science education programs, and science education systems. In contrast to *Benchmarks,* the criteria are broad rather than specific, allowing more room for individual interpretation but giving less guidance in developing objectives.

An example will help you understand how this book is organized and allow you to compare it with *Benchmarks.* The Content Standard for Life Science for K–4 is as follows:

As a result of activities in grades K–4, all students should develop understanding of

The characteristics of organisms

Life cycles of organisms

Organisms and environments (p. 127)

These objectives are followed by several paragraphs of general comments about teaching life science to children and an explanation of the fundamental science concepts that underlie each of the parts of the standard listed. Thus, the reader is provided with general guidelines for teaching science in kindergarten through grade 4, grades 5 through 8, and grades 9 through 12, general recommendations for how to teach each subject at the different levels, and the basic scientific concepts that the teacher needs to know. As mentioned, there are also standards for teaching and for assessment. One of the most useful features of the *Standards* is the imaginative examples scattered throughout the book designed to show how the standards can be carried out in practice.

You will find the three books described to be useful guides in your own teaching and learning. We have drawn on them in developing ideas and activities for this book and have sought to make the material in this book congruent with their main ideas and themes.

GOALS FOR SCIENCE IN THE ELEMENTARY SCHOOL

Although details and specific lesson objectives may vary, there is remarkable agreement among scientists and educators about what an elementary science program should be and about the kinds of activities that children should engage in. From these sources, as well as from our own experience, we believe that the important overall goals for children in elementary science are to

◆ Develop and maintain curiosity about the world around them.

◆ Observe and explore their environment and organize those experiences.

◆ Develop the technical and intellectual skills needed to make further study of science possible.

- Build an experiential basis for understanding important concepts in science.
- Relate what they learn in school to their own lives.

Other goals are for children to enjoy science and to develop positive attitudes about school. Children who enjoy school and see their needs met there are more likely to become active learners and successful students.

TEACHING METHODS

This book will help you develop the knowledge and skills needed to carry out the recommendations and reach the goals in the preceding list. You will learn to

- Promote independent thinking.
- Encourage children's creativity and curiosity.
- Build on children's ideas.
- Reduce the amount of material covered so that more time can be devoted to developing thinking skills.
- Make connections between science and other areas of the curriculum.
- Start with questions rather than with answers.
- Focus on the needs of all children, including those from all ethnic groups and those with special psychological or physical needs.

These methods are appropriate at all ages; they apply to your learning also. We hope that this book will promote your independent thinking, encourage your creativity and curiosity, stimulate you to build new ideas and knowledge on the basis of what you already know, and help you make connections between what you learn here with what you are learning in other courses. As you work your way through this book, you will find demonstrations that will help you see how to put these ideas into practice.

◆ SUMMARY

You will find that children enjoy science and you will enjoy teaching it if you learn to guide children through activities that engage their hands and minds. Science is both knowledge of the natural world, including humans, and the way that this knowledge has been produced. Scientists believe that the phenomena and patterns observed in nature can be understood though the application of human intelligence, and they work to make the world understandable by developing theories that explain observations made by themselves or others. Since science is a human endeavor, it is part of the culture in which it is embedded, and it both influences and is influenced by that culture.

When children come to school, they already know a great many things, but the knowledge they have has not all been acquired in the same way. Four kinds of knowledge are described: arbitrary knowledge, physical knowledge, logical knowledge, and social-interactive knowledge. It is important for a teacher to be aware of the knowledge children have as well the misconceptions they have acquired in order to guide them in constructing knowledge that will be meaningful to them.

National Science Education Standards, (National Research Council, 1996), *Science for All Americans,* (AAAS, 1990), and *Benchmarks* (AAAS, 1993) are three important guides that can be useful to science teachers and curriculum developers. These books encompass all areas of science and provide recommendations on what should be taught and how to teach it at different grade levels. Professional development and assessment are other areas included in the *Standards.*

Science goals for elementary school children are simple and straightforward and are not designed to intimidate a future teacher. The purpose of this book is to help you have a better understanding of science and how to teach it so that you will become an enthusiastic and effective science teacher. In the next chapter, you will find some ideas that will help you understand how children's minds develop and how they learn. The succeeding chapters explain practical ways to work with your pupils to help them become active, responsible learners.

◆ QUESTIONS FOR DISCUSSION

Write your answers to the following questions and come to class prepared to discuss them with the whole class or in a small group:

1. How would you define science to someone from a totally different culture?

2. How could you incorporate four kinds of knowledge in a lesson? Give a simple example.

3. If you are going to explore the environment with children, you will be studying animals. Is there anything you are squeamish about? If so, how will you get over your squeamishness so as not to pass it on to your pupils?

4. What is your reaction to Feynman's statement to teachers?

5. What potential do you see for using science to help children become more responsible? In what ways, if any, is this potential different in science than it is in other school subjects?

6. Many children decide that they dislike science. Maybe you were one of them. What experiences might cause such an attitude? How might a person's life be different if a more positive attitude had developed?

7. Have you seen or do you have memories of different treatment or attitudes toward girls and boys in science class? If so, describe the incident and your reaction.

◆ REFERENCES

American Association for the Advancement of Science. (1990). *Science for all Americans.* New York: Oxford University Press.

American Association for the Advancement of Science. (1993). *Benchmarks for science literacy.* New York: Oxford University Press.

Feynman, R. P. (1968). What is science? *The Physics Teacher, 7*(6), 313–320.

Fosnot, C. (1989). *Enquiring teachers. Enquiring learners. A constructivist approach for teaching.* New York: Teachers College Press.

Kamii, C., & DeVries, R. (1978). *Physical knowledge in preschool education: Implications of Piaget's theory.* Upper Saddle River, NJ: Prentice Hall.

National Research Council. (1996). *National science education standards.* Washington, DC: National Academy Press.

Woolfolk, A., & Hoy, W. (1990). Prospective teachers' sense of efficacy and beliefs about control. *Journal of Educational Psychology, 60,* 327–337.

2

Children's Thinking and Learning

The study of children's thinking and learning has occupied some of the most original minds of the twentieth century and continues to be a subject of intense interest to psychologists, cognitive scientists, and teachers. This chapter gives a brief summary of the main ideas of five twentieth century thinkers who have influenced our thinking about how children learn science. All of them share the view that learning is not a passive activity but one that requires the active participation of learners in constructing their own knowledge. You may have studied in other courses some or all of the thinkers you will encounter here, but this chapter will help you understand how their ideas may be useful to you in teaching science and, thus, give you a basis for making instructional decisions. At the end of the chapter, a short section on recent research highlights several issues of current interest to researchers in science education.

JOHN DEWEY (1859–1952)

Although Dewey's life spanned the nineteenth and twentieth centuries and he cannot actually be called a constructivist (the term was not used in his time), he is included here because he believed, like constructivists of today, that "no such thing as imposition of truth from without, as insertion of truth from without, is possible. All depends upon the activity which the mind itself undergoes in responding to what is presented from without" (Dewey, 1956, p. 31). In his view, the schools of his day were too rigid and programmed with little opportunity for children to express their own interests and curiosity. Instead, he emphasized using the child's experience as the starting point for instruction, a process of "continuous reconstruction, moving from the child's present experience out into that represented by the organized bodies of truth that we call studies" (p. 11).

The Dewey School

In the 1890s, while a professor at the University of Chicago, Dewey founded a school that was used as a laboratory to test his ideas. The school was an expression of his belief that the curriculum should grow out of and deepen children's experiences; the lives and experience of children should not be sacrificed to follow a curriculum devised by specialists in the various fields of formal knowledge. Children's interests and activities, therefore, were the starting point that teachers used to guide their pupils toward greater knowledge and understanding. "If children can retain their natural investigating tendencies unimpaired" he wrote, "gradually organizing them into definite methods of work, when they reach the proper age, they can master the required amount of facts and generalizations easily and effectively" (quoted in Mayhew & Edwards, 1936, p. 34). The social value of having children work together as they carried out classroom activities was an important consideration in the overall plan.

Symbols or words are meaningful, Dewey believed, only when they represent something in the child's own experience. When subject matter is presented to chil-

John Dewey

dren as something known by experts but outside of their own experience, the words and symbols, whether in arithmetic, grammar, or history, have no meaning. They are like hieroglyphics, unrelated to anything encountered out of the classroom, and useless. Thus, the activities in school should be those that will help the child acquire experiences that can then be summarized or represented by symbols.

Dewey did not advocate basing the whole curriculum on children's current abilities and interests; these were only the starting points for development of knowledge and understanding of the subjects taught. He knew that some activities occupy children's time and interest but lead nowhere; nor were children to be left to their own devices to figure everything out for themselves without stimuli to guide their instincts and impulses into higher levels of thinking and understanding.

A practical application of these ideas can be seen in the description by a science teacher of the way science was taught to children in the school Dewey founded in Chicago. The guiding principle in selecting an activity, she explains, was its use in carrying the child on beyond the activity itself to an understanding of relationships. The important question about an activity was whether the processes and procedures to be carried out could be related in the child's mind to important general ideas about natural processes. For example, children learned at an early age to identify the notion of weight, which they already possessed, with the pull of the earth's gravity and to measure and control it. Observations of the effect of force of gravity on plants and animals began in kindergarten. The child's interest and curiosity about plant life and animal life led naturally, over the years, into a continually enlarging course of study dealing with the life processes of plants; with plants' relations to animal life; with the influences of moisture, soil, and environmental conditions; and with the influence of plants on environmental and geographic conditions. Leaves, stems, and flowers were regarded as important only in relation to function and processes. Observation and experiment were both important, and always, there was the teacher to stimulate children's thinking by asking questions, suggesting things to try, and helping them develop and learn to use the symbols and tools that would advance their thinking.

Piaget acknowledged Dewey's influence on his own thinking, and as you study the ideas of the other thinkers presented here, you will find many echoes of Dewey's philosophy of education.

JEAN PIAGET (1896–1983)

The person whose ideas have probably had the greatest impact in science education in the second half of this century is Jean Piaget. Piaget, who was born in Switzerland and spent most of his life there, was interested in finding out what goes on in children's minds as they try to make sense of the world around them. His research

Jean Piaget

method was simply to sit down with a child and ask a series of questions. The questions of most interest to us were designed to find out how a child thinks about or understands something encountered in daily life. Piaget showed that young children do not think logically by adult standards and that it takes many years for children to grow to think about things in a logical way. Of course, Piaget and his students and co-workers interviewed many, many children in the course of their studies. Their conclusions were based on patterns of thinking that they found repeatedly in the responses of children.

Although Piaget was not an educator, his work has been of particular interest to science teachers. The following classroom scene will help you understand how knowledge of children's thinking can improve your teaching of science and why teachers turn to Piaget for insight and help in understanding some of the problems they encounter.

◆ A CLASSROOM SCENE

Mr. Newman discovered that his first-grade children got very upset if they thought that he wasn't absolutely fair about everything. They got particularly upset if they thought that one person got more juice than another at juice time. After Mr. Newman had seen this happen several times, he planned a lesson to convince his pupils that he was always fair, even though it might appear that one child had more than another. He looked around his apartment and found five small glass jars of different sizes and shapes and took them in to school. The next day he set the jars in a row on a table and had the children sit on the rug where they could all get a clear view of the demonstration. He very carefully measured out 100 ml of colored water and poured it into the first jar. Then he called one of the children up to help him measure out exactly 100 ml of water and pour it into the second jar. Figure 2.1 shows what the children saw after 100 ml of water had been poured in each jar.

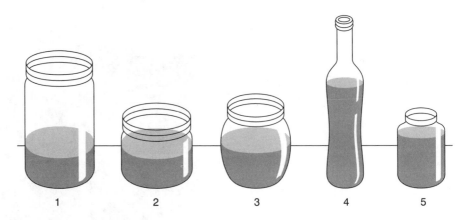

FIGURE 2.1   Mr. Newman's Jars

Mr. Newman explained that each jar had exactly the same amount because he had measured very carefully. Even though the amounts did not look the same, they were the same.

The children did not appear to be very interested in what Mr. Newman was trying to explain. Since they didn't ask questions or show much interest about the amounts in the jars, Mr. Newman thought it was clear and obvious to everyone that all the jars had the same amount of liquid. Actually, the children seemed to be more interested in the jars than in the amounts of liquid in them and asked questions about where the jars had come from and what they had originally contained.

Juice time came soon after this lesson, and Mr. Newman was prepared with two different kinds of plastic drinking cups and a measuring cup to portion out the juice. He could not believe his own ears when a big argument broke out between two children with different-sized plastic cups. One of the things that was most puzzling to him was that these were two of the brightest children in the class; both of them were reading well above grade level. The one with the larger cup started to cry because he thought he had less juice.

Mr. Newman was at wit's end over this episode and could hardly wait until after school to talk with Ms. Oldhand about what had happened. He just couldn't understand why the children didn't believe their own eyes when he thought he had made it all so clear and logical. He couldn't understand why his lesson didn't work.

Can you think of reasons why Mr. Newman's lesson didn't work?

When Mr. Newman found Ms. Oldhand and told her what had happened, Ms. Oldhand explained that Mr. Newman had presented the children with a task that is similar to one of the tasks devised by Jean Piaget to study children's thinking. She suggested that Mr. Newman would understand why his lesson hadn't had the outcome he had expected if he learned more about Piaget's ideas about children's thinking.

You will get a better idea of Piaget's work and how it relates to science teaching from examples of children's responses to the questions he asked when he interviewed them. In Chapter 1 we listed four kinds of knowledge that children may acquire—social-arbitrary, physical, logical, and social-interactive. In the following example, it is logical knowledge that is of interest.

Conservation of Quantity (Liquid)

The word *conservation* is used in science to denote the principle that a substance or an object remains the same, regardless of changes in form or appearance, provided nothing is added or taken away. For example, when a glass of water freezes, it changes in appearance, but the weight remains the same. A ball of clay can be flattened to the shape of a pancake, but it still has the same amount of clay. The following example, taken from *The Child's Conception of Number* (Piaget, 1965) summarizes responses from children who were asked questions about conservation of liquid, a concept that Mr. Newman assumed his children understood.

An interviewer shows a child two identical glasses containing equal amounts of lemonade and says that one glass belongs to Mary and one to Laura. The interviewer then pours the lemonade in Mary's glass into two smaller glasses and asks the child whether Mary and Laura still have the same amount of lemonade. Then the interviewer pours the lemonade from Laura's glass into two smaller glasses and repeats the question. As the interviewer pours lemonade back and forth between glasses of different sizes, the child is always asked whether Mary and Laura have equal amounts to drink (see Figure 2.2).

The typical reaction of a four-year-old is that the amounts are the same if the glasses are the same size and different if the glasses are of different sizes. As the liquid is poured back and forth, the child continues to say that the amounts are equal or unequal, depending on the size and number of the glasses, with no apparent awareness of any contradiction. Then there comes a transition period when the child is not quite sure; finally, usually around the age of six or seven, the child realizes that pouring the liquid back and forth, regardless of the shape or size or number of glasses, does not change the amount. When asked at this time, "How do you know?" the child answers "I just know. Once you know you always know."

One of the important things Piaget discovered is that children have their own reasons for thinking the way they do about the things they see happening around them; it is not easy to convince them to change their minds. Children construct their own realities, and there is a certain logic in the frameworks they construct. For young children, appearance is what matters. If something *looks* smaller, in the child's mind it *is* smaller.

Piaget believed that children's ability for logical thinking develops gradually, just as many of their other abilities do. We don't expect first graders to have the hand–eye coordination that will allow them to produce the kind of handwriting that we expect of sixth graders. In the same way, we should not expect the first graders to have the same degree of mental coordination that will allow them to "put two and two together" to arrive at a logical conclusion about the relative amounts of liquid in two glasses.

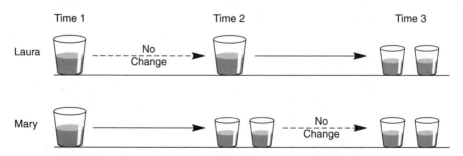

FIGURE 2.2 Mary's and Laura's Glasses

Piaget used the idea of "stages" to describe the way children's logical thinking progresses from infancy through adolescence. When Piaget's work first became widely known to science educators, they thought it was important to test children to pinpoint the "Piagetian stage" of each child. Today, however, the emphasis has shifted. Most educators and psychologists now believe that development tends to be a continuous process rather than one of stops and starts, although experience tells us that growth is more rapid at some times than at others. It is also recognized that what students can learn in any field or area depends on how much they already know in that area. Piaget's system of stages is now generally considered to be a useful shorthand for describing the capabilities that may be expected of children within a given age range rather than a rigid system with no exceptions or gray areas.

Piaget's central concern was with the question, "How do we come to know what we know?" His answer was that we must construct our own knowledge and understanding through logical thinking. Knowledge cannot be transmitted intact from one person to another. Children can memorize facts and be taught how to do many things, but they cannot really understand a phenomenon or a relationship except by thinking about it and putting the pieces together in their own heads. This is the essence of Piaget's theory of mental development and is the basis for the constructivist view.

In the preceding example, you saw how one kind of knowledge, logical knowledge, develops. The following example involves both physical knowledge and logical knowledge.

Children's Ideas about the Moon

This example is excerpted from *The Child's Conception of the World* (Piaget, 1951). Responses given by children of different ages to the same questions give insight into how children think about the things that they observe in the world around them.

Piaget asked children from ages 6 to 12 the question, "When you go for a walk at night, what does the moon do?" The interviews that follow contain responses that are typical of children at three stages of development.

Jac, Age 6 (First Stage)
What does the moon do when you are out for a walk?
It goes with us.
Why?
Because the wind makes it go.
Does the wind know where you are going?
Yes.
And the moon too?
Yes.
Does it move on purpose to go where you are going or because it has to?
It comes so as to give light.

Lug, Age 12 (Second Stage)

What does the moon do while you are walking?

It follows us.

If you and I were walking in opposite directions which of us would the moon follow?

It stays still because it can't follow two at the same time.

When there are a lot of people in the town what does it do?

It follows someone.

How does it do that?

It stays still and its rays follow us.

Kuf, Age 10 (Third Stage)

When you go out for a walk at night what does the moon do?

When you're walking you'd say that the moon was following you, because it's so big.

Does it really follow you?

No. I used to believe it followed us and that it ran after us (but I don't believe that any more). (Piaget, 1965, pp. 216–220)

In this example we can see a progression from (1) the idea that the moon's role and function are to be helpful to us to (2) an unresolved contradiction (the moon "follows us" but "always stays in the same place"). Finally, the child understands that the moon is independent of us, an idea that requires both physical knowledge and logical thinking. Since Piaget found that many children gave similar answers, he believed that these ideas arise spontaneously, based on direct observation and the child's own thinking.

This example of how children think about a natural phenomenon that all of us have experienced gives a science teacher a lot to think about. If children have these misconceptions or alternative frameworks about the moon, what do they think about the sun, clouds, wind, and rain? Is it possible to change their beliefs just by explaining things to them? We've seen that this didn't work in the case of the juice and the glasses. Is it any more likely to work in the case of objects as far away and as mysterious (to them) as the moon, the sun, and the wind?

From a Piagetian perspective, the task of the teacher is to provide the learning environment, the materials, and the tasks that will stimulate and encourage children to construct knowledge for themselves. Talking to children, or even demonstrating, will not teach them that the amount of water remains the same when it is poured from one container to another; they have to construct this knowledge for themselves through their own experience of acting on objects and through their own thinking. *Seeing* is not always *believing* for children; they have to experience things for themselves.

Piaget's work is no longer thought of as an infallible guide to teaching science, but it has inspired an almost overwhelming amount of research by others. Perhaps the most important outcome of research based on Piaget's work was stated by Confrey (1990) as "the belief that teaching is most effectively improved when the teacher learns to listen to students' thoughts and to interpret students' actions and thoughts from their perspectives as children" (p. 11). Our understanding of the importance of listening to children and to seeking their explanations for what they say and do is probably Piaget's most enduring legacy.

One way to construct for yourself a better understanding of how children think is for you to have experience in presenting Piaget tasks to children and hearing their responses firsthand. A representative sample of Piaget tasks is given at the end of this chapter.

JEROME BRUNER (1915–)

Piaget's chief interest lay in discovering the origin and nature of knowledge as it develops in the mind of the child, but he did not have much to say about what outside forces or experiences, in addition to natural growth and maturation, might propel a child from one stage to another. This is the problem tackled by Jerome Bruner. Bruner acknowledges a debt to Piaget, but he went beyond a description of stages to consider not only how children *think* but how children *learn* (Bruner, 1966; Bruner & Haste, 1987).

Problem Solving

Bruner noted that there are two kinds of problems children may encounter in school. The most important problem for many children is the problem of finding out what the teacher wants. When a child is confronted with a problem in arithmetic, for example, the first thing that pops into the child's mind is not "What is the best way to tackle this problem?" but, instead, the child thinks, "What did the teacher say about this kind of problem? How does the teacher want me to work this problem?" The child is focusing on pleasing the teacher rather than on solving the assigned problem.

Children who have never had experience in school with problems that require independent thinking are at first nervous and uncertain about how to proceed. The teacher has to reassure them that their ideas and suggestions will be accepted and that there are more ways than one to solve the problem. The teacher is not going to show them the "correct solution" at the end.

Modes of Representing Knowledge

Bruner identified three different ways of representing experience and knowledge. The child begins with the enactive mode, then develops the iconic mode, and finally the symbolic mode, but at all stages of life, we can and do use all three modes.

Enactive representation is experience translated into action. Anyone who has tried to teach a child to ride a bicycle or to play tennis, as Bruner points out, has become aware of the inadequacy of words. In those cases we represent what we know through action, not words. In many instances, the old axiom "action speaks louder than words" can be applied in teaching. Some things cannot be taught except by *showing* what we want children to learn. How to use equipment, such as a balance or a microscope, is one thing that comes to mind, but many things are best taught by action or example rather than words. We accept this principle in sports, music, and art education, but it applies as well in many aspects of science teaching.

Iconic representation depends on visual or other sensory means of organizing information. Just as many things are best taught by *showing how*, others are best taught by using a drawing, a picture, or a diagram. In science teaching, it is important to have children learn to use this method of representing their own experience. For example, children who have set up an electric circuit are more likely to remember what they have done and to understand it if they represent the system by making a diagram or drawing of it.

Symbolic representation is the use of words or mathematical symbols to express experience or ideas, the past, the present, and the hypothetical future. This is the most powerful as well as the most advanced mode of representation. Facility with language and mathematics is one of the chief goals of science teaching, but this is an ability that must be developed in children, and because of this, other forms of representation will be more effective for most of the science we teach in elementary school.

The Spiral Curriculum

In Bruner's view, the curriculum should involve the mastery of skills that in turn lead to the mastery of more powerful skills. This is in itself motivating and rewarding. He asserts that there is an appropriate version of any skill or knowledge that can be taught at whatever age one wishes to begin and that the curriculum should be built as a spiral; that is, the teacher and the learner come back again and again to the same topic, each time increasing and deepening understanding (see Table 2.1). Let's see how this might work in a science class.

Take, for example, the idea of acceleration, an important concept in physics. How do young children get the "feel" of acceleration? We can think of riding a sled or roller skating down a hill, or running down a steep bank or watching a ball rolling

TABLE 2.1 The Spiral Curriculum

Elementary	Middle School/Junior High	Senior High
Experiences with objects that float or sink	Measuring mass and volume; calculation of M/V	Calculation of specific gravity; Archimedes' principle
Observing changes in colors of acids and bases using indicators	Neutralization of acids and bases by mixing measured volumes	Titrations; using volumes, moles, etc.

down a hill, farther and farther out of reach. This is learning through the senses, in the *enactive* mode. As a teacher, you can ask the children to recall their experiences and talk about how it feels to go faster and faster. If there is a hill nearby, you can take the class outside to watch objects accelerate as they roll down the hill.

A few years later, the children will be given the materials for performing an experiment with cylinders rolling down an inclined plane. They will learn to measure how fast the cylinder rolls and be taught a way to represent that action on a chart, a means of *iconic* representation and a way to advance their understanding. They will now be given a word, *acceleration,* to describe what happens, so they will now have used enactive, iconic, and symbolic means to represent the same concept.

Now, step into a physics class in high school. Because of the spiral curriculum adopted by the school, the physics teacher is confident that pupils in the class have had experiences and performed simple experiments about acceleration, so now they are ready to carry out more complex, detailed experiments and to learn a formula expressed in mathematical symbols. After these experiences, they will have constructed an understanding of acceleration through Bruner's three modes—the enactive, the iconic, and the symbolic. But if, as often happens, acceleration is an idea that has never been discussed or represented in school, for most pupils, the formula will have little relation to the world of their experience. They will learn to work the problems by memorizing the formula.

On the other hand, for those fortunate pupils whose experience has included talking and thinking about and representing acceleration from time to time throughout their school years, the formula will represent a concept that can now be understood in a deeper and more meaningful way, because the new learning builds on what they have already learned. Some of them will turn and say to each other, "Do you remember when Ms. Oldhand took us out to the hill behind elementary school and showed us how a basketball went faster and faster as it rolled down the hill? I've always remembered that." Other examples of concepts that are returned to in this way throughout the years will be given in later chapters.

To carry out Bruner's ideas, the teacher has to be an active problem solver with an attitude of openness to pupils' ideas and the expectation that pupils will be active and enthusiastic learners. No formula or set of rules for inquiry teaching can capture the essence of Bruner. For him, the important thing is the process, not the product. The teacher as well as the children must become involved in the process.

LEV VYGOTSKY (1896–1934)

Lev Vygotsky was a Soviet psychologist who was born in the same year as Piaget but died when he was in his late thirties. His work was little known in the United States for many years after he died, but now that it has become better known, we can see that he had some very interesting and stimulating ideas that are relevant to science teaching. He was familiar with Piaget's early work and wrote one of his early books (Vygotsky, 1926) in response to some of Piaget's ideas about the role of children's language in mental development. Vygotsky, like Piaget, believed that the learner constructs knowledge; that is, that what children know is not a copy of what they find in the environment but is, instead, the result of their own thought and action, mediated through language.

Although both of these thinkers focused on the growth of children's knowledge and understanding of the world around them, Piaget placed more emphasis on the child's internal mental processes, and Vygotsky placed more emphasis on the role of teaching and social interaction in the development of science concepts and other knowledge. He also believed that language plays a central role in mental development. In this way, perhaps, Vygotsky had more in common with Bruner, and Bruner has, in fact, written that Vygotsky has influenced his own thinking (Bruner, 1985).

Development of Mental Function

Vygotsky believed that development depends on both natural or biological forces and social or cultural forces. Biological forces produce the elementary functions of memory, attention, perception, and stimulus–response learning, but social forces are necessary for the development of the higher mental functions of concept development, logical reasoning, and judgment. It is through social interaction, including the interaction with teachers, that children become conscious of their basic mental functions and able to use them in their growth toward self-control, self-direction, and independent thinking and action. As you will see in a later section, a good science program helps children develop the characteristics of self-control, self-direction, and independent thinking along with the knowledge of science concepts and processes.

The Growth of Scientific Concepts

Vygotsky studied the development of scientific concepts with the specific purpose of improving instruction in schools. He distinguished between the concepts that children develop on their own, which he called everyday concepts, and those learned in school, which he called scientific concepts. Everyday concepts are developed from experience and are tied to specific instances; scientific concepts are taught in school as part of a hierarchy or general theory and are remote from children's experience. Conceptual change is an ongoing process in which children integrate their everyday concepts into the system of related concepts that has been taught in school. For example, most children know a good deal about animals as pets and have seen other animals in the zoo or on a farm, but their knowledge is unorganized and random. When they are taught a hierarchical system for classifying and labeling animals, they have to fit what they already know into the system and give up their own classification schemes, which may label animals as those that are pets, those in the zoo, and those on the farm. This is a process that can only take place over time, starting with children's everyday concepts and helping them expand their concepts to be more inclusive, to apply to more cases, and to become integrated into a system (Howe, 1996).

Zone of Proximal Development

Vygotsky believed that children should have tasks set for them that are just beyond their present capability but which they can perform with guidance from a teacher or more advanced peer. He described a "zone of proximal development" (ZPD), an area just beyond a child's current level of ability. This is the area in which children need help at first to perform a task but gradually learn to do it on their own. At first, students must depend on the teacher to be shown what to do, but gradually they master the task and gain control over a new function or concept. Bruner suggested that this process is analogous to the process in which a builder constructs a scaffold to support the workers who erect a building. As the building takes shape, the scaffold is no longer needed and can be removed. Scaffolding in the context of science education refers to a process in which the teacher, parent, or tutor structures a task so that students are supported as they move from the beginning point to a higher point through a series of small steps.

It's easy to see how this works in teaching a physical skill, like riding a bicycle. The parent holds the child on and guides the bicycle until the child gets the "feel" of riding and gains confidence, then the parent lets go very gradually until the child can keep the bicycle up and guide it without help. The main point to remember is that the teacher has the responsibility to choose learning tasks that are just beyond students' current level but within their reach and then to help them move ahead to the new, higher level of performance. If tasks are too easy, children become bored and restless; if tasks are too hard, children become frustrated and anxious.

A Vygotskian perspective suggests a classroom where active exchanges between children themselves and between children and teacher are an ongoing part of daily life. Children have opportunities to work together, to give and receive verbal instructions, to respond to peer questions and challenges, and to engage in collaborative problem solving. The teacher sets tasks that are just beyond the learners' current levels of competence and provides the help that learners need to reach higher levels. From these exchanges and interactions, children construct meaning and knowledge.

LAWRENCE KOHLBERG (1927–1987)

Lawrence Kohlberg was another constructivist who built on the foundation laid by Piaget. His field of interest was the development of moral reasoning rather than logical reasoning. He, like Piaget and the others mentioned in this chapter, based his theory on studies of the responses of children and adolescents to questions asked during individual interviews. He presented situations in which a choice had to be made between conflicting ethical or moral values, a situation in which a person wants to do what is right but there is no way to avoid undesirable consequences. A simple example of a situation that children find themselves in is whether to report it if they see a good friend cheating on a test. From responses to situations of this kind, Kohlberg (1969, 1981) arrived at a developmental theory of moral reasoning.

Lawrence Kohlberg

By including Kohlberg in the short list of thinkers in this chapter, we are expressing our belief that science at the elementary level cannot be taught in a moral vacuum. The years in elementary school are a time of growth in all dimensions, including the moral dimension. The children you teach will live in a world of many real moral dilemmas, not a few of which will be brought on by the uses and misuses of science. They will be better able to make these hard choices if their moral development has kept pace with their increasing knowledge and understanding of science.

Stages of Moral Development

Kohlberg sought to show that children's development of a sense of right and wrong and the ability to make moral choices and to act on them are slow processes that take place over many years. He, like Piaget, defined stages of development, each of which has characteristics that differentiate it from the other stages.

In the preconventional stage, children accept the right of authority figures to exercise power and try to obey rules to avoid punishment. They are very concerned about fairness and may be quick to point out other children's infractions of rules. It is very upsetting to children in this stage if they think they have been treated unfairly or punished when someone else has escaped punishment.

In the conventional stage, children want to do what is right and try to live up to the expectations of parents and teachers. They want to be loyal, truthful, and honest. They may sometimes be torn between conflicts in values as, for instance, between telling the truth and being loyal to a friend.

Postconventional, or principled, behavior is based on awareness of the variety of opinions and values held by other people and recognition that most values and rules are relative to a group or culture. Finally, there is the stage at which a person believes in the validity of universal moral principles, including the equality of human rights and respect for the dignity of individuals, and has a sense of personal commitment to them.

Just as Piaget believed that children must construct their own logical knowledge, Kohlberg believed that children must construct their own moral knowledge. It was his view that children cannot become moral people by memorizing rules of behavior any more than they can become logical thinkers by memorizing ways to work problems. Trying to teach children to be "good" by admonishing them to obey a set of rules is equated by Kohlberg to giving them a bag of tricks to pull out at appropriate moments and is a method that has had notably poor results. Kohlberg's ideas can be put to practical use in several ways. Keep in mind that children are at a lower stage of development than you are.

They must pass through the earlier stages before they can reach the higher ones. Class discussions that center on what is the right thing to do in situations that may arise in the classroom must take account of the level of the children. Remember that they do not have an adult point of view, but you can help them to see things from other children's perspectives and to construct for themselves the rules that they will live by.

It is important to establish a classroom atmosphere in which each child is respected and where you as a teacher are scrupulously fair to all pupils. Fairness is extremely important for children in elementary school. They become uncertain and anxious in a situation in which they cannot depend on the adult in charge for fair treatment. Remember the classroom scene at the beginning of this chapter? The teacher was motivated to have a lesson on conservation because the children thought he was not being fair in giving out juice. When children are concerned and upset about lack of fairness, their attention is diverted from the lesson. Take care to be fair in assigning duties, in allocating equipment to groups, and in the amount of time you spend with individual children or groups. Fairness is an especially important consideration when a class is made up of children from different ethnic groups or has children with handicapping conditions. A more extensive discussion of this point can be found in Siegal (1982).

Kohlberg's ideas are important in the context of science teaching because of the guidance they can provide in establishing a classroom where the interactions between you and your pupils, both as individuals and as a group, are guided by moral and ethical considerations. One consideration is fairness: being fair and letting children know that you will be fair in all your dealings with them. Another consideration is respect: letting children know that you respect them and expect them to respect each other. Science cannot be well taught when children's social and emotional development are not taken into account. At a higher level, Kohlberg reminds us that the advance of science can lead to difficult moral issues.

RECENT RESEARCH ON CHILDREN'S THINKING AND LEARNING

Recent research has built on and extended the work of these thinkers and has brought new insights and ideas to the study of children's thinking. Three areas in which research has begun to influence practice are discussed in this section.

Research on Misconceptions

Researchers have uncovered children's spontaneous ideas about a great number of natural phenomena and have described efforts to design instruction that will bring their ideas more in line with accepted scientific knowledge. We have long known that children had "unscientific" ideas about many things. Years ago Piaget gave a description of Swiss children's ideas about living and nonliving things (Piaget, 1951), and this was followed by a similar but more detailed study of Canadian children's ideas about the same subjects (Laurendeau & Pinard, 1962). Studies of American children have shown that they also develop, on their own, many ideas about living things (including the human body) that might surprise their teachers. Examples include what happens to food once eaten, where various organs are located, and what is the nature of blood. Children develop their own ideas about physical phenomena as well as about living things (Carey, 1985; Eylon & Linn, 1988). Among the terms used to describe these ideas are *naive ideas, misconceptions, alternative conceptions,* and *alternative conceptual frameworks.*

Children's Ideas about the Earth

Several studies of children's ideas about the earth, carried out in different places, disclose some of their misconceptions, show how they may misinterpret what they hear in class, and how difficult it is to change their thinking. In the first of the studies, carried out at Cornell University (Nussbaum & Novak, 1976), children from two second-grade classes were individually asked a series of questions designed to elicit their beliefs about the shape of the earth. When first asked about the shape of Earth, all children said that, of course, the earth was round like a ball. On further questioning, it became clear that almost two-thirds of the children actually believed that the earth is flat. They had been taught in school that the earth is round "like a ball," but their experience told them that the earth is flat. Since what they were taught was contradicted by their own experience, they had to work out a way to reconcile the two opposing ideas. Subsequent studies conducted in Israel (Nussbaum, 1979), Nepal (Mali & Howe, 1979), and California (Sneider & Pulos, 1983) yielded similar results. Figure 2.3 illustrates what children in Nepal were thinking when they said the earth is round while actually believing that the earth is flat.

FIGURE 2.3 Children's Notions of the Earth

Source: Adapted from figure in "Development of Earth and Gravity Concepts among Nepali Children" by G. Mali and A. Howe, 1979, *Science Education 63*(5), p. 687. Copyright © 1979 by John Wiley & Sons, Inc. Adapted by permission.

These notions correspond with the numbered drawings in Figure 2.3:

1. The hills and mountains are round; that's why we say the earth is round.
2. The round earth is in the sky somewhere; we are on a different earth.
3. The earth is a flat disk, shaped like a pancake.
4. The earth has a flat plane through the center with the sky above and rocks, water, and dirt underneath.

Audiotutorial lessons were given to the children with the objective of changing their ideas, but at the end of the series of lessons, the number who still believed in the flat earth was almost as large as before instruction. Not only in this case, but in many others as well, researchers have shown that children hold onto their beliefs tenaciously, changing them only reluctantly and over a period of time. It's easy to see that telling children what you want them to learn will have little effect when the ideas they already have are strongly held. Adding a new fact to what they already know is not enough to bring about a conceptual change. To understand a new concept, children have to restructure their thinking.

Most children grow up with some cultural beliefs that they cling to even when those beliefs become untenable. Did you believe in Santa Claus when you were a child? If you did, it did not trouble you that Santa was supposed to go all over the world in one night and squeeze in and out of chimneys. When you noticed that not all children lived in houses with chimneys, you accepted your parents' explanation that Santa could just as easily enter houses through doors. Finally, you began to wonder how anyone could get around the world in one night, and you noticed some other very strange things as well. At this point you had what psychologists call cognitive dissonance. There were quite a few things that did not fit together, and you heard rumors from other children that Santa was not real. But you were not ready to give up the idea because it was an important part of your whole belief system. Eventually, you abandoned the idea of a Santa Claus. For most people, this is associated with some mental distress.

The conceptual change that takes place when children give up firmly held beliefs about the world as they experience it is somewhat analogous to giving up the idea of Santa Claus or the Tooth Fairy. Admittedly, giving up the idea of the flat earth may not be traumatic, but there are similarities in that it takes a long time and a lot of evidence to convince yourself that what you thought was true is not really the way things are.

The Role of Social Interaction in Learning

Recognition of the central role of social interaction in knowledge construction is bringing about a shift in emphasis in elementary science education. This owes much to the influence of Vygotsky but others have also contributed to this understanding (e.g., Moll, 1990). We no longer think of children as essentially solitary individuals trying to understand the world by applying logic to the results of their actions but as participants in an ongoing dialogue with children of their own age, with older and more knowledgeable children, and with parents and teachers. The importance of hands-on science is not in the manipulation of objects or the observation of phenomena but in the explanation and discussion of the experience that stimulates thinking and leads to understanding and knowledge.

Research in this area treats the classroom as a sociocultural system and studies the talk that goes on in the classroom between teacher and students and between students themselves as a way of understanding the development of knowledge (Forman, Minick, & Stone, 1993). The model is a classroom in which teachers use interactive teaching methods, scaffolding learning for students, supporting student's involvement in their own learning, and encouraging students to work and learn together.

Contextual Nature of Learning

Research has shown that learning is more dependent on context than science educators once thought it to be. That is, knowledge tends to be embedded in a specific situation, and the skills learned and used in one context may not be, and often are not, transferable to another situation or context (Rogoff & Lave, 1984). Young children may do poorly on memory tasks in a psychology laboratory but remember the names and location of objects at home without difficulty. Children who learn to make inferences or control variables in the context of a science lesson may not use these processes at all when confronted with a problem in their everyday lives. Teachers are sometimes baffled by children who have learned a skill in math class but can't use the skill in science. "That's math, not science" is what the teacher hears.

Recognition of the importance of context has also influenced our thinking about the importance of developmental stages in learning science. Many researchers have tried to show that specific science concepts can only be understood after a child has reached a certain stage of development and that, conversely, when a child reaches a certain stage, then the teacher can be assured that the child can learn concepts that could not previously have been learned. Research has failed to provide strong evidence for that point of view and suggests, instead, that multiple factors, including developmental level, play a part in what children can do and learn (Metz, 1995). What a child can learn at a given moment about animals, for example, depends on past experience with animals as well as on the ability to reason at a certain level (Inagaki, 1990). In one subject, you may operate at the concrete operational level and in another subject at the formal operational level (see, e.g., Linn, 1983; or Lawson & Wollman, 1976). Thus, research over the past two decades has gradually led science educators to place greater emphasis on the content and concepts of science. Developmental levels cannot be ignored, and science processes are still important, but they do not occupy the central place that they once did.

◆ SUMMARY

The common thread that ties everything together in this chapter is constructivism, the belief that meaningful knowledge must be built up, or constructed, by the learner. This concept is considered from different points of view by the people whose ideas were discussed in this chapter.

Dewey sought to free children from the intellectual constraints of a rigid curriculum that emphasized memorization and conformity. The curriculum he advocated emphasized various forms of constructive and practical activity that connected schooling to the children's everyday lives and served as the starting point for building knowledge and understanding. He is included among the constructivists because he believed that learners build knowledge through active mental involvement rather than through passive reception, and he showed how these ideas could be applied in schools.

Piaget described how children's ability for logical thinking develops partly as a result of natural maturation and partly through interactions with the objects and people in the child's surroundings. The developmental stages outlined by Piaget, if not rigidly interpreted, can be a useful guide to understanding children's abilities and progress in science. Remembering that learners must construct knowledge for themselves will help you be patient with your pupils as they try to absorb and internalize new ideas. The most important thing to learn from Piaget may be to listen to children's explanations for what they say and do and to take their ideas seriously.

Bruner examined ways in which instruction can promote the mental development that Piaget described. In his view, instructional materials should be structured and sequenced so that mental development is reinforced by a curriculum that returns to important concepts again and again throughout the school years, each time with a more sophisticated and inclusive interpretation.

Another important aspect of Bruner's work is his emphasis on the ways we represent what we know. He describes three modes of representation—the enactive, the iconic, and the symbolic—and points out their uses both as means of instruction and as ways for children to represent knowledge. Instruction, for Bruner, as well as for Piaget, should be a process in which the pupil is actively engaged with materials of all kinds and learns to represent the new knowledge through action, drawings, or words.

Vygotsky's main contribution to our understanding of children's learning is in the importance he attached to the role of interaction between the child and an adult or the child and an older peer and to the role of language as the mediator in these interactions. For Vygotsky, social interaction was the main force in learning of all kinds. He believed that children learn by being helped to do things that they are not yet competent to do alone but in which they can become competent with the assistance of another person.

Kohlberg's ideas on children's moral development help us remember that the planned curriculum is not all that is learned in the classroom. As a teacher, you will also be concerned about the moral climate of your classroom and about the moral as well as the cognitive development of your pupils. Learning will be enhanced in a classroom where the teacher shows respect for each individual and creates an atmosphere of fairness and trust.

Current research in science education has shown that children develop their own ideas about scientific phenomena and that instruction cannot be successful unless these misconceptions are recognized and dealt with. Other research has shown that a child's developmental level may not be as strong a determinant of what can be learned as was formerly thought to be the case; social interaction and the context in which a cognitive skill is learned and used are recognized as important factors in the construction of meaning.

Table 2.2 will help you put together the main ideas presented in this chapter.

TABLE 2.2 Constructivism in Science Teaching

Scholar	Major Ideas or Themes	Implications for Science Teaching
Dewey	Learning is meaningful to children when it grows out of their own experience. The school curriculum should be built around constructive and practical activities that extend children's experience and stimulate their thinking. Symbols are important as a means of representing experience and advancing thinking.	Establish a classroom environment in which children can express their own interests and curiosity. Select science activities that start with children's experience and lead beyond their experience toward larger ideas and concepts.
Piaget	Children acquire knowledge by acting and thinking. Knowledge is classified as physical, logico-mathematical, or social. Development of logical thinking is a maturational process. Understanding of natural phenomena depends on logical thinking ability.	Provide an environment to encourage independent action and thought. Distinguish between kinds of knowledge in planning instruction. Be aware of children's level of logical thinking.
Bruner	Children learn by discovering their own solutions to open-ended problems. Knowledge is represented in enactive, iconic, and symbolic modes. Appropriate ways can be found to introduce children to any topic at any age. The process of learning is more important than the product.	Use open-ended problems in science regularly and often. Use all three modes of teaching and testing for understanding. Emphasize processes of science. Teach concepts and processes that will lead to further learning.
Vygotsky	Children learn through interaction with peers and adults. Knowledge is built as a result of both biological and social forces. Language is a crucial factor in thinking and learning. Children need tasks just above their current level of competence.	Encourage pupils to work together and to learn from each other. Encourage children to explain what they are doing and thinking in science. Set tasks that challenge children to go beyond their present accomplishments.
Kohlberg	Children learn moral and ethical behavior by example rather than by teaching. Moral development is a slow, maturational process. Moral dilemmas that have no easy solution are part of life.	Set an example of fairness and honesty in your own behavior. Guide discussion of problems as they arise and allow children to suggest solutions. Include science-related societal problems in class discussion.
Recent research	Children bring many ideas and concepts to class; some of these can interfere with new learning. Learning is more domain-specific and less easily transferred from one area to another than was once thought. Social interaction and the context in which a cognitive skill is learned and used are important factors in the construction of meaning.	Probe to find out what misconceptions children bring to class. Expect greater competence in familiar topics than in unfamiliar ones. Recognize that developmental level is only a rough guide to children's abilities.

39

◆ ACTIVITIES FOR THE READER

1. A few representative Piaget tasks follow. If you have never had the opportunity to present these tasks to children and to reflect on their responses, we urge you to do it now. Find three children of different ages, and administer the tasks to each of the children. Record their answers and your observations, and come to class prepared to discuss them.

TASK I

CONSERVATION OF SUBSTANCE

Materials

Two equal-sized balls of modeling clay, about the size of ping-pong balls

Procedure

1. Let the child handle the balls of clay. Ask if the balls are the same size and, if not, how you can make them equal. Continue until the child is satisfied that the balls are equal.

2. Ask the child to flatten one ball out into a pancake shape and to leave the other ball unchanged.

3. Ask, "Does the pancake have the same amount, less, or more clay than the ball? Can you tell why you think that they are the same (or that the pancake has more or that the pancake has less)?"

4. Now press the pancake back into a ball, and ask the child to make a snake with one of the balls. Repeat the procedure and the questions that you asked about the pancake.

TASK II

CONSERVATION OF LIQUID AMOUNT

Materials

Colored water (orange and green)
Two glasses or beakers (100 ml)
One tall thin glass
One low wide glass or jar
Two smaller glasses or jars (25 ml)

Procedure

1. Fill the two glasses about half full, one with orange water and the other with green water. Make sure that the child believes that the two glasses have the same amount of liquid.

2. Ask the child to pretend that she has the glass of "orangeade" and her friend has the glass of "limeade." Pour the orange water into the tall thin glass, and ask the child whether she has the same amount to drink as the friend. If the answer is no, ask the child whether she can say which child has more or less. Ask the child to explain why she answered as she did and record the answer.

3. Pour the water back into the original container. Ask the child to verify that the amounts are the same again. Now pour the orange water into the low, wide dish, and repeat the questions and the request for justification. Record the answers.

4. Repeat the process, pouring the water into the two small containers this time. Ask the same questions, and record the answers.

TASK III

CONSERVATION OF AREA

Materials

Two sheets of green construction paper
20 to 30 identical one-inch cubes or squares
Two small toy horses (or cows)

Procedure

1. Show the child the pieces of paper, and say that they are the same size. Show the cubes or squares, and say that they, too, are all the same size. If the child questions this, or seems unsure, allow time for him to verify this.

2. Point to the pieces of paper, and ask the child to pretend that these are fields of grass and that the horses are grazing in the fields. There is the same amount of grass for each of the horses to eat. Now the farmer builds a barn at one corner of one field and a barn of equal size in the middle of the other field. Ask the child whether the two horses still have the same amount to eat. Ask the child to explain the answer given. Record the answer.

3. Repeat as in Step 2, adding a barn beside the first one in the first field and a barn away from the first barn in the second field. Repeat the question. Record the answer.

4. Repeat as in Step 3, adding the third barn beside the first two barns in the first field and at a distance from the first two barns in the second field. Ask whether the horses now have the same amount to eat. Ask the child to explain his answer and record the answer. If the child thinks the amount of grass is different after a few cubes are placed, you can stop. If, however, he thinks the amount of grass is the same, continue adding cubes. Children who are transitional in their ability to conserve area will often change their minds when more "barns" are added.

5. If the children in your sample are not familiar with horses or cows and their eating habits, the task can be changed in one of the following ways:

   a. The two fields become a sheet of cookie dough, and the barns are replaced by cookies that are cut out.

   b. The fields become lawns to be mowed, and the barns become flower beds.

◆ QUESTIONS FOR DISCUSSION

1. You have probably studied Piaget's and Vygotsky's theories, and perhaps those of Dewey, Bruner, and Kohlberg, in another course. How are the interpretations of their thought in this chapter similar to or different from your previous understanding of their ideas?

2. If you had to add a summary of one other person's ideas to this chapter, whose ideas would you add? Discuss other thinkers who have influenced your own thinking about something related to teaching.

3. In his book, *Toward a Theory of Instruction*, Bruner made the statement "there is an appropriate version of any skill or knowledge that may be imparted at whatever age one wishes to begin" (1966, p. 35). What do you think he meant by that statement? Try to defend or refute the statement with examples. Select one important process or concept in science, and discuss appropriate versions for primary children and for upper elementary children.

4. What does it mean to *create* an answer to a problem? Give an example of a problem that has more than one answer.

5. Give an example of and explain how you learned:

   a. Something learned in the enactive mode

   b. Something learned in the iconic mode

   c. Something learned in the symbolic mode

6. Can you remember a time when you felt that a teacher or other adult did not treat you fairly? Looking back on it, can you understand the adult's point of view, or do you still think the treatment was unfair?

7. Describe a misconception that you had at one time about a scientific or other concept. What made you change your mind?

◆ REFERENCES

Bruner, J. (1966). *Toward a theory of instruction.* Cambridge, MA: Harvard University Press.

Bruner, J. (1985). Vygotsky: A historical and conceptual perspective. In J. Wertsch *Culture, communication and cognition: Vygotskian perspectives* (pp. 21–34). Cambridge, England: Cambridge University Press.

Bruner, J., & Haste, H. (Eds.). (1987) *Making sense. The child's construction of the world.* New York: Methuen.

Carey, S. (1985). *Conceptual change in childhood.* Cambridge, MA: MIT Press.

Confrey, J. (1990). A review of research on student conceptions in mathematics, science and programming. In C. Cazden (Ed.), *Review of Research in Education* (pp. 3–56). Washington, DC: American Educational Research Association.

Dewey, J. (1956). *The child and the curriculum. The school and society.* Chicago: University of Chicago Press.

Eylon, B.S., & Linn, M. (1988). Learning and instruction: An examination of four research perspectives in science education. *Review of Educational Research, 58*(3), 251–301.

Forman, E., Minick, N., & Stone, C. (Eds.). (1993). *Contexts for learning.* New York: Oxford University Press.

Howe, A. (1996). Development of science concepts within a Vygotskian framework. *Science Education, 80*(1), 35–51.

Inagaki, K. (1990). Young children's use of knowledge in everyday biology. *British Journal of Developmental Psychology, 8,* 281–288.

Laurendeau, M., & Pinard, A. (1962). *Causal thinking in the child.* New York: International Universities Press.

Kohlberg, L. (1969). Stage and sequence: The cognitive developmental approach to socialization. In D. A. Goslin (Ed.), *Handbook of socialization theory and research* (pp. 118–140). Chicago: Rand McNally.

Kohlberg, L. (1981). *Essays on moral development* (vols. 1 & 2). San Francisco: Harper & Row.

Lawson, A., & Wollman, W. (1976). Encouraging the transition from concrete to formal operational functioning: An experiment. *Journal of Research in Science Teaching, 13*(5), 413–430.

Linn, M. (1983). Content, context and process in adolescent reasoning. *Journal of Early Adolescent Reasoning, 3,* 63–82.

Mali, G., & Howe, A. (1979). Development of earth and gravity concepts among Nepali children. *Science Education, 63*(5), 685–691.

Mayhew, K., & Edwards, A. (1936). *The Dewey school.* New York: Appleton-Century.

Metz, K. (1995). Reassessment of developmental constraints on children's science instruction. *Review of Educational Research, 65*(2), 93–127.

Moll, L. (Ed.). (1990). *Vygotsky and education. Instructional implications and applications of sociohistorical psychology.* Cambridge: Cambridge University Press.

Nussbaum, J. (1979). Israeli children's conceptions of the earth. *Science Education, 63*(1), 83–93.

Nussbaum, J., & Novak, J. (1976). An assessment of children's concepts of the earth using structured interviews. *Science Education, 60*(4), 535–550.

Piaget, J. (1951). *The child's conception of the world.* London: Routledge and Kegan Paul.

Piaget, J. (1965). *The child's conception of number.* New York: W. W. Norton.

Rogoff, B., & Lave, J. (1984). *Everyday cognition: Its development in social context.* Cambridge, MA: Harvard University Press.

Siegal, M. (1982). *Fairness in children.* New York: Academic Press.

Sneider, C., & Pulos, S. (1983). Children's cosmologies: Understanding the earth's shape and gravity. *Science Education, 67*(2), 205–221.

Vygotsky, L. (1926). *Thought and language.* Cambridge, MA: The MIT Press.

3

Creating a Learning Environment for All Children

Ms. Sanchez, a beginning teacher, was talking over a problem with her mentor, Ms. Oldhand.

MS. SANCHEZ: Ms. Oldhand, I need some help with one of the pupils in my class. Stephen's record shows that his grades have always been among the lowest in the class, beginning in first grade. He's a nice kid and has never been a behavior problem, but lately he doesn't even seem to be trying, and he is beginning to be a little bit of a show-off. I'm afraid that he'll start being a behavior problem as well as a low achiever unless I can do something to change his attitude.

MS. OLDHAND: Well, you have a good start on the problem because you assume that you can do something to turn the situation around. Would you like for me to sit in your class and see whether I can come up with some things for you to try?

MS. SANCHEZ: Yes, I think that's a very good idea.

The next day Ms. Oldhand observed the class.

MS. SANCHEZ: I'm glad you could observe my class this morning. You could see for yourself that Stephen is not interested in what's going on in class and that he tries to call attention to himself.

MS. OLDHAND: Yes, I did see that, and I agree with you that something needs to be done to help Stephen. I noticed several things that I wonder whether you are aware of. I noticed that when you asked Stephen a question—which was a very easy one—you only gave him a second to answer. When he hesitated, you turned to another pupil and asked her to give the answer. Why didn't you give Stephen more time?

MS. SANCHEZ: It seemed clear that he didn't know the answer, and I didn't want to embarrass him.

MS. OLDHAND: But when you asked a question of Rita—who is a very bright girl—and she hesitated, you gave her a clue and waited long enough for her to think of a reply. Why did you give her more time than you gave Stephen?

MS. SANCHEZ: I gave her more time because I knew that she could come up with an answer if she just thought about it.

MS. OLDHAND: In other words, you expected Rita to be able to answer the question you asked her, but you didn't expect Stephen to be able to answer the question you asked him. Stephen may not be the brightest student in the class, but he's smart enough to figure out that your expectations for him are very low.

MS. SANCHEZ: Are you suggesting that Stephen could do as well as Rita if I changed my expectations?

MS. OLDHAND: No, I'm not suggesting that. I am saying that I believe Stephen knows that you don't expect him to be able to master the work in this class, and that makes him think, "What's the use? Even the teacher doesn't think I can do this work." If he thought you believed he could do the work and expected him to do the work, he might try harder to live up to your expectations. That way he could get positive feedback and wouldn't have to try to get attention by showing off.

MS. SANCHEZ: It's hard for me to believe that my expectations influence the way I interact with Stephen, but I think I'll tape record the next question-and-answer session and listen to the tape to see whether you're right about this.

This chapter focuses on teacher attitudes and behaviors that are applicable at all grade levels and with all science activities. The purpose of the chapter is to stimulate your thinking about some of the challenges of science teaching and to help you become a thoughtful, reflective, competent teacher. Although we have maintained the focus on science teaching, you may have seen some of the ideas, particularly those on classroom management, in other courses; if so, you can move quickly through material that is familiar to you.

Before you begin this chapter, make a mental picture of what you would like a visitor to see and hear in your classroom in the middle of a science lesson. Choose a grade level, and think about what the children would be doing. Would the visitor see children sitting quietly at their desks? Would children be dashing about the room borrowing equipment from other students and bumping into things along the way? Would boys be doing an experiment while girls sit and watch? Would a child with a speech impediment be sitting all alone? Or would the visitor see all children busily engaged in an activity that you have planned as part of a series of lessons that lead to understanding of an important science concept?

PHYSICAL ENVIRONMENT

The way the classroom looks on the first day the pupils come to school—and every day thereafter—can play an important part in the way the teacher and the pupils feel about coming to school, teaching, learning, and being together all day. Certainly, a classroom should be a busy and happy place, perhaps even a neat and clean place. But there is still a great deal of variation in the way classrooms look.

Making the Classroom Attractive

Consider two classrooms, Room A and Room B. Room A has colorful bulletin boards, busy learning centers, a reading corner with soft seating, and neat storage of many kinds of materials. The double desks are arranged in pairs so that four pupils form a natural work group facing each other. The teacher's desk stands in the back of the room, and a carpet covers the floor near the front chalkboard for group lessons. Fish, animals in cages, and plants occupy various corners and nooks. Room B has individual desks in straight rows with all pupils facing forward toward the teacher's desk at the front. There are centers and bulletin boards, but no animals because the teacher thinks that taking care of animals makes extra work. All the children are at their desks.

In which classroom would you rather be a pupil? In which would you rather be a teacher? What do the differences say about the teachers' philosophies? Are there some reasons for selecting more features from Room A and other situations when it would be better to have a room more like B? Deciding how to arrange and provide for a classroom environment that enhances instructional goals is more complex than the either/or choice described here, but it is all part of creating an environment where children can learn to the best of their abilities.

Making the Classroom Safe

We have placed safety near the beginning of this chapter because of its importance in planning any science activity. Safety must always be considered in deciding how to arrange the classroom, what materials to use in science activities, and how to maintain an orderly classroom without restricting freedom to learn. Some science activities present situations that can be hazardous to children if you do not think ahead and take necessary precautions. It is impossible to plan for every emergency, but you can prevent most serious as well as minor accidents by forethought and planning. Familiarize yourself before school begins with your school or school district's policies and procedures and any other regulations that relate to school safety. Following are some of the main things to think about as you consider the children's safety.

Room Arrangement

Furniture and equipment should be arranged so that children can move about freely and have unobstructed pathways to the doors in case there is a need to evacuate the room. Make arrangements for assistance for any children with disabilities in case of an emergency. Electrical outlets should be unobstructed; connecting cords should be short and in good condition. No electrical appliances should be placed near water.

Fire and Heat

You can have an excellent elementary science program without the use of fire. If hot water is needed, tap water may be hot enough. If not, use a hot plate that you control or keep under your supervision (by fifth grade, most children can handle a hot plate with supervision). Avoid boiling water. At boiling temperature, water can cause serious burns because extra heat is given off as the water cools down on contact with the skin. Never leave a hot plate with red-hot coils unattended.

Chemicals

You can also have an excellent science program without the use of hazardous chemicals. Instead of thinking how to store hazardous materials, eliminate them. Be firm in setting rules for the use of all chemicals: no tasting, no touching, no fooling around. When these rules are obeyed, many commonly available materials can be used. If acid is called for, use white vinegar (acetic acid), lemon juice (citric acid), or a very weak solution of hydrochloric acid that can be obtained from a pharmacist. Rubbing alcohol, table salt (sodium chloride), baking soda (sodium bicarbonate), baking powder, a weak iodide solution, and weak ammonia water are others that can be used. Be aware that many household chemicals, such as chlorine bleach, drain openers, pesticides, and weed killers are *not safe*. The mercury in many thermometers is hazardous and should not be touched if the thermometer breaks; use thermometers with red liquid if possible. If you are not sure about the potential hazard of any chemical, ask a high school science teacher, a scientist, or a pharmacist.

Tools and Glassware

Beginning in kindergarten, children should be taught to use scissors. As they reach second or third grade, they can be allowed to use sharper scissors (the blunt-pointed scissors don't cut much) and other tools that require caution. Glassware should be handled with care; plastic containers and baby food jars can be used in place of beakers, sharp edges should be filed off of mirrors, and plastic tubing should be used in place of glass tubing if available. Be prepared to take care of minor cuts; they are seldom dangerous if handled promptly and treated to prevent infection.

Animals in the Classroom

We believe that an elementary classroom is incomplete without animals, including fish, but there are several things to keep in mind. You have to protect both the animals and the children. Animals need a good place to live and daily care, including care on weekends, and need to be free from harassment or teasing. Children need to be protected from bites, scratches, and animal-borne diseases. Purchase animals for the classroom from a reputable dealer to ensure that the animals are healthy, and teach the children how to handle each species. If you are not sure about keeping or handling animals, ask a veterinarian or someone from the Humane Society or zoo if one is nearby.

Plants in the Classroom

The main consideration with plants is to prevent students from coming in contact with plants that are toxic. Of course, you will not bring poisonous plants into the classroom, but some plants that seem harmless may cause an allergic reaction in some children, and some common houseplants such as philodendron and English ivy are poisonous. Caution children not to taste unknown plants and not to get sap on the skin. If you are unsure about a plant you want to use, you may get advice from an agricultural agent, a knowledgeable gardener, or, of course, a botanist.

Eye Protection

All students should wear goggles when any students are handling chemicals, even mild ones; sharp instruments; glassware; or other hazardous materials. A small cut on a finger from broken glassware is a minor problem, but a piece of glass in a child's eye is something you don't want to think about. Establish a routine for distributing, collecting, and cleaning goggles. *You must be firm about this and always wear them yourself.*

Emergencies

Keep a fire extinguisher in good condition, and know how to use it. Keep a well-stocked first-aid kit. Develop a plan for getting a student with any injury to the nurse or principal's office. (Will you leave the class to take the child yourself? Will you send one child with another?) You must also have a plan for calling an emergency number in case of a serious situation that calls for immediate attention. Do not forget that you will also be responsible for the other children, and you must plan to keep them

These children have learned to handle materials carefully and safely.

safe and calm. Make sure that children understand what to do in an emergency, but reassure them that they will all be safe. Once you have made these plans and have an emergency number close at hand, you can relax in the knowledge that you will be prepared for anything that may happen.

DEALING WITH COMPLEXITY

A beginning student teacher asked her university supervisor how to handle a particular situation. The supervisor replied that it depended on many factors and began to explain some of the various options. The student teacher grew restless and finally interrupted, "Don't confuse me with all that! Just give me the one-two-threes." The supervisor might have found a way to respond that would have been more directly relevant to the student teacher's needs; nevertheless, there are very few "one-two-threes" in learning to teach. Every successful teacher makes thousands of decisions every day. You may well respond, "That sounds impossible! How does anyone survive in that sort of pressure cooker?"

An Analogy

Consider an analogy. Almost every adult in the United States drives a car. Driving is a complex and demanding skill. The penalty for too many mistakes can be death or a whole host of lesser evils. Yet, we are usually able to function as drivers without being paralyzed by fear and indecision. Try to think back to when you learned to drive. It did not all happen at once. First you learned and practiced the mechanical aspects of operating the controls of the car. Later you learned the rules of the road and practiced driving in street traffic. Only after you had developed these skills did you dare to enter the freeway and tackle tricky interchanges at rush hour. What was happening to the early skills as you progressed to the more advanced ones? Are you consciously thinking about how to steer, accelerate, and brake (and maybe even shift) while you maneuver through a freeway interchange? Probably not; probably you are able to manage these early skills in an almost automatic way, a sort of mental cruise control. A similar process allows you to move through all kinds of skill hierarchies. There is one difference, however; it is human nature to forget very quickly what it was like not to know something just as soon as you learn it. You will be much more effective as a teacher if you can retain the memory of that preknowledge state, because retaining that memory makes you able to relate to the learning process in your own pupils.

Learning to be an effective teacher is complex but not too complex to learn. You just need to think about what you are doing and not let the mental cruise control become too automatic. Just as many driving decisions are made as you drive along, many teaching decisions cannot be made in advance but depend on unforeseeable circumstances. On the highway, your decisions depend on what is happening all around you; on a busy highway you have to be alert at every moment. In the classroom, your decisions will also depend on what is happening around you, and you also have to be alert at every moment. These in-progress decisions teachers must make include how to involve all the pupils, whether to interrupt the lesson to correct misbehavior, whether to use variations in language or to stress repeatedly the same words, whether to accept an incomplete pupil response or to take time to probe for more depth, whether to make a major excursion from the planned lesson in response to unexpected pupil reactions, and many, many more. As you see, most of these decisions involve being aware of what is happening around you, knowing and reflecting on what you are doing, and modifying your own thinking and actions accordingly.

INCLUDING ALL CHILDREN

One of the complexities of the classroom is the diversity of backgrounds, interests, abilities, and habits of the children you will teach. Although this is true in all classrooms, the complexity may seem even greater when your class includes children from different ethnic backgrounds and those with physical or mental disabilities. And, of course, you will have both boys and girls to add to the complexity. The following sections contain some very general suggestions and ideas about creating a learning environment for all children, whatever their backgrounds, physical or mental conditions, or gender. Each of the sections could be expanded to become a whole chapter, and, indeed, books are available on each of the topics.

The Multicultural Classroom

You will probably teach a multicultural group of children, since, in many parts of the country, almost all public school classrooms contain students of more than one race or ethnic identity; for some of these students, English is a foreign language. In addition to these cultural differences, there are often wide differences in family income and social status among the children in a class. Some see this diversity as a difficult problem, but we prefer to think of it as an opportunity to help children learn to live in a democratic society "with liberty and justice for all." Some of the children you teach may have been the targets of prejudice; others may have been brought up in homes where racial bias or antipathy to immigrants is considered normal. It will be up to you to create a classroom where all children are accepted and valued and all have equal opportunities to learn.

What can you do to prepare for this challenge? The following recommendations and some of the suggested activities at the end of the chapter are drawn from the work of Geneva Gay (1989).

1. Become aware of and reflect on your own attitudes and behaviors toward different ethnic groups. Find out how your behaviors and responses are perceived by students and what effects they have on students' self-concepts and academic achievement. Self-knowledge is the first step.

2. Learn to see the differences in cultural values and behavioral codes between yourself and those from other ethnic, cultural, or economic groups. Remember that there are vast differences within each of these groups; economic disparities often create greater barriers than ethnic or cultural differences.

3. Develop instructional skills that take into account the diversity in learning styles, life experience, and interests of pupils. The ability to employ a variety of teaching strategies, curriculum materials, modes of presentation, and assessment methods is essential.

4. Learn to communicate and interact with parents and other adults from groups that are different from your own. Remember that school is very intimidating to parents who have little command of English and may feel socially and economically inferior to their child's teacher.

5. Watch for cultural bias in textbooks assigned to your students, and take care to use curriculum materials, pictures, videos, and other materials that include representatives of minority groups.

6. Believe that the most important thing of all is for *you to accept all children.*

It is also important for the curriculum to reflect the multicultural nature of the classroom. Banks and Banks (1989) have outlined several approaches to the integration of ethnic content into the curriculum. The first and lowest level is the focus on persons who have made important contributions to American life and culture, including noted scientists and engineers of color. Holidays and special cultural elements are highlighted. This is the easiest approach, but it is limited in impact because students are apt to see it as an addendum or appendage to the "real" curriculum. This approach is further limited because young children are not much interested in and can hardly appreciate the contributions of major scientists of any ethnic group.

The second approach is what Banks and Banks call the additive approach. Examples are the addition of books about children from diverse groups or a unit on Native Americans. An example in science might be the addition of a unit on native medicines used in the Southwest or in Mexico. The second approach goes beyond the first, but it is still additive rather than integrative.

The third approach is called transformative and differs fundamentally from the first two. The emphasis is not on how different groups have contributed to mainstream culture but on how the common culture of our country emerged from the synthesis and interaction of the diverse cultural, racial, and ethnic groups that make up our society. Applications in areas such as social studies or music and art are more obvious than in science, but there are ways to recognize that the incorporation of diverse points of view, social customs, vocabularies, and experiences has become part of mainstream culture. For example, over the past two or three decades, our attitude toward the environment has moved closer to the Native American view and is moving slowly away from the view of the Europeans who took over the land. Many of the science activities suitable for elementary students are culturally neutral, but be on the lookout for opportunities to let the students know that the contributions that their diverse cultures have made to American life are recognized and valued.

Including Students with Disabilities

Legislation passed by Congress, called the Individuals with Disabilities Education Act (IDEA), requires that all students with disabilities be provided a free public education and that they be taught in the least restrictive environment. Another requirement is that schools collaborate with parents in designing educational programs for students with special needs. One result of this legislation is that many students who were once taught in special education classes are now enrolled in regular classrooms, a practice that is often referred to as *mainstreaming* or *inclusion*. It is estimated that about 15% of children have a disability of some sort, so the likelihood is high that you will have at least one child with a disability in your class. Children with a very severe disability may have an aide who accompanies them to class and works with them in whatever way is appropriate; most children with disabilities will receive some form of assistance, but, in practice, this may be minimal. This means that you, the teacher, will have to try to adjust the environment or the activities to meet the needs of children with disabilities without sacrificing the needs of the other children.

Children with visual, hearing, or motor impairment have one less avenue through which to learn about the world and are deprived of much of the incidental learning that other children naturally acquire. Every disability affects the way children learn and what they learn. Children with visual impairments or who are blind can see or feel parts but not the whole and do not have the same concept of space as children who see. Children with hearing impairments do not hear speech clearly and thus do not develop normal speech patterns. Children who have emotional disturbances or who have mental disabilities have their own special learning problems that often lead to difficulty in interacting with other children.

Science may be the curriculum area that is most amenable to adaptation for students with disabilities. Hands-on activities and group work, both a natural part of an elementary science program, provide opportunities that are seldom available in other subject areas. Science curriculum materials adapted or specially designed for children with hearing impairments, visual impairments, and mental handicaps have been shown to be effective in both regular and special education classrooms. Some of these are listed among the references at the end of this chapter. Adaptations include many commonsense ideas such as the use of motors or buzzers, rather than light bulbs, for students with visual impairments to test electrical circuits. For students with hearing impairments, teaching methods that emphasize communication through pantomime, pictures, and careful explanation of terms have been effective. For all types of disabilities, including learning disabilities and emotional disturbance, an activities-oriented curriculum is more successful than a textbook-based curriculum. Children with learning disabilities respond particularly well to activities that involve living things—but other children also respond to these activities.

Whatever changes or adaptations you make, the focus should be on the child's abilities rather than disabilities. There are also attitudes and strategies that are generally applicable, regardless of the specific disability. Some of these follow:

1. Show by your actions and words that you accept the child with disabilities as a valuable member of the class and that you expect all the children to accept this child also.

2. Encourage the children to offer help to the special child when needed but to allow the child to be as independent as possible.

3. Use group work and cooperative learning for science activities and place the child with disabilities in an appropriate group.

4. Give all explanations and directions clearly and explicitly. Be sure that the special child understands what is to be done and why.

5. Maintain contact with the parents, and work with them to provide the best learning opportunities for the child.

If you try these suggestions, you may find that they will help all your students, not only those with disabilities.

Gender Equity

In the early grades, most girls like science as well as boys do, but something happens to their interest and enthusiasm for science after elementary school; by the senior year in high school, science has become predominantly a boys' subject. Research over many years in many classrooms indicates that teachers pay more attention to boys than girls, wait longer for boys to answer questions, and reward girls more for obeying the rules than for having good ideas. When boys and girls work together on science activities, girls are often the recorders or the observers, while the boys set up the equipment and take the measurements. Another difference between boys and girls is that girls more often attribute their success in school to hard work or effort while boys attribute their success to their ability, even though the actual ability of the boys is the same as that of the girls (Howe, Hall, Stanback, & Seidman, 1983).

A factor that has contributed to the attitude that science is more appropriate for boys than for girls is the sex stereotyping that was found in many textbooks and other curriculum materials until recently. Pictures showed men as scientists and women as laboratory assistants, men as doctors and women as nurses, men as engineers, and women not even in the picture. With the single exception of Marie Curie, no women scientists' pictures found their way into science textbooks. This situation has changed over the past decade, and you will find that most up-to-date science textbooks for elementary students use illustrations that are balanced by gender and also by ethnicity.

Most teachers do not want to be biased in their treatment of students and are often shocked when they realize that they have treated boys and girls differently, usually in subtle ways. Becoming aware of the problem is the first step in correcting it.

Many teachers are now making sure that girls are actively involved in science activities, encouraging them to ask questions and share their ideas, to participate in science fairs, and to consider the possibilities of careers in science.

TEACHER EXPECTATIONS

All of us have expectations about what will happen in certain circumstances, and we often have expectations for ourselves and for other people. Most of us have felt at some time that we had to do something to live up to someone's expectations. This section presents some important ideas about teachers' expectations for themselves and their pupils as well as some possible outcomes of these expectations.

Before you read further, take a moment to write your reaction to the following statements. For each statement, choose from these possible reactions: strongly agree, agree somewhat, disagree somewhat, or strongly disagree.

1. All pupils can achieve success.
2. When you have a class of twenty-five children, dealing with pupils as individuals is not feasible.
3. Some children just don't want to learn.
4. Some children will disregard the rules no matter what the teacher does.
5. It is unreasonable to expect children from poor families to keep up with those from families that are better off.
6. If a teacher has high expectations for all pupils and communicates these effectively, all pupils will meet the expectations.

These statements were designed to help you increase your awareness of any unconscious assumptions that might influence your teaching behaviors. We will come back to these questions later.

In *Pygmalion in the Classroom*, Rosenthal and Jacobson (1968) reported the results of a research project in which researchers told a group of teachers that certain children in their classes were "late bloomers" and would make a spurt in achievement during the year. Actually, the children had been chosen at random, and the researchers had no objective reason to believe that they were different from any of the other children in the classes. But the teachers believed that those children were different and thus raised their expectations for the children. As a result (according to the authors), the designated children actually did achieve at a higher level than they had before. A valid conclusion seemed to be that when the teachers expected them to do better, the children did do better. The results have been questioned by other researchers and have led to some controversy, but the book was important because it focused attention on teachers' expectations and led researchers to ask how teacher expectations could influence pupil achievement. Now there is evidence that a teacher's expectations for a pupil affect the teacher's behavior toward that pupil, and

FIGURE 3.1 Pupil Achievement Affected by Teacher Expectations

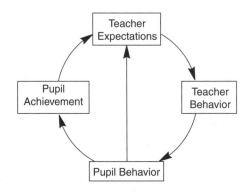

the teacher behavior has an effect on pupil achievement. Several popular television programs have been based on the idea that teachers who expect a lot from their pupils raise the level of achievement of the whole class. Figure 3.1 shows how the process might work.

Suppose a certain science teacher does not expect girls to be as interested in science as boys are and, therefore, does not expect girls to do as well in science. How might this expectation unconsciously affect the teacher's behavior? One thing a teacher might do would be to give different assignments to boys and girls when groups are formed. Girls might be assigned—or "allowed"—to be recorders while the boys do the experiments. This would give boys an active role and girls a passive role. Since children learn by doing, not by watching, the result likely would be that the girls would not learn as much as the boys, and the teacher's expectations would be confirmed. This is what is called a self-fulfilling prophecy—the teacher's behavior brought about what the teacher expected to happen. Suppose the teacher, taking a different tack, had thought, "Why shouldn't girls do as well as boys in science? I'm going to be careful to see that girls and boys have the same opportunities to learn in this class, and I'll expect all of them to do well." The teacher would organize the class so that all pupils had an opportunity to do some of the experiments and all took a turn being recorder.

It may seem natural for teachers to have lower expectations for low-achieving pupils than for high-achieving pupils, but this attitude can be discouraging and even damaging to the low achievers, who know they are being treated differently in class (Brophy & Good, 1986). Sometimes teachers assume that children with disabilities or minority children or those whose families are recent immigrants will automatically be low achievers. Therefore, in the following statements, one could think "presumed low achievers" as well as "actual low achievers."

Some of the ways that teachers treat high and low achievers differently include

Calling on low achievers to answer questions in class less frequently.

Waiting less time for low achievers to answer questions asked by the teacher. Since the teacher does not expect the pupil to know the answer, the teacher moves on quickly to someone else.

Dismissing low achievers' ideas. The teacher does not expect the low achievers to have good or useful ideas, though creativity and school achievement are not necessarily related.

Giving briefer answers to questions of low achievers. Since the teacher does not expect the low achiever to understand anyway, less time is spent explaining.

In all these cases, the teacher's behavior communicates to the low-achieving pupil that the teacher does not expect that child to know the answer, to have good ideas, or to be able to understand the learning task. These expectations can cause the pupil to become discouraged and lose interest, and the teacher expectation becomes a self-fulfilling prophecy. Some have suggested that teachers should neither look at pupils' previous records nor talk to other teachers about individual pupils in order to prevent forming negative expectations. Such denial seems unreasonable. What a teacher does with the information is the important thing. Information from the past can be useful in helping a teacher diagnose a pupil's problems and plan instruction that will meet the pupil's needs. Teachers should trust their own judgment and good intentions. All of us have unconscious assumptions and expectations that are often based on false premises. The way to avoid harmful expectations is not to restrict information but to become more aware of negative, unconscious assumptions and expectations and the behavior that signals these to pupils.

RESPONSES TO STATEMENTS ON TEACHER EXPECTATIONS

Now that you have thought about the effects of teacher expectations, we will return to the statements on teacher expectations and share our responses to these statements.

1. All pupils can achieve success. (Strongly agree)

Teachers should expect all pupils to meet minimum standards. These standards should be set so that all pupils who work hard at the tasks and assignments can succeed. Although all pupils cannot be expected to do equally well, a teacher can establish reasonable minimal objectives for everyone. Many pupils will be able to exceed the minimum, and the teacher should try to provide learning tasks that stimulate each pupil to go as far as possible.

2. When you have a class of twenty-five children, dealing with pupils as individuals is not feasible. (Strongly disagree)

As a rule, teachers should think, talk, and act in terms of individual pupils. This does not mean that teachers should not practice grouping or that terms such as "low achievers" should not be used. Teachers do sometimes lose sight of the individual, however. There are certain teacher behaviors to watch for as warnings that a stereotype has begun to structure the teacher's perception of a pupil. Among these behaviors are continual references in speech to group names to the exclusion of individual names ("the boys in this class" or "the kids from the projects") and an overemphasis on differences between groups. These warning signs are especially important when the groups in question are the more permanent ones of economic status, ethnicity, or gender.

3. Some children just don't want to learn. (Strongly disagree)

The teacher should assume that children enjoy learning, that each child wants to learn, is able to learn, and is hoping to learn. The teacher's job is to create the situation in which each child *can* learn. A teacher who does not realize this may act as if the pupils are expected to learn on their own with no help from the teacher. If a pupil does not catch on immediately after one demonstration, or doesn't do the work correctly after hearing the instructions one time, the teacher reacts with impatience and frustration. The real goal of teaching is not accomplished by giving information, although that is often a part of it, but by listening to pupil responses and observing pupil behaviors as sources of information and then using the information to design further learning experiences. A child is always ready to learn something; the art of teaching lies in finding out what each child is ready to learn and helping each child take the next step.

4. Some children will disregard the rules no matter what the teacher does. (Disagree)

The teacher should expect all pupils to follow the rules. Some teachers have a hand in creating serious discipline problems, usually by failing to establish and enforce appropriate rules of behavior. Adherence to rules is usually obtained rather easily by teachers who establish fair and appropriate rules, who are consistent in what they say, who say only what they really mean, and who regularly follow up with appropriate action whenever necessary. Appropriate action produces credibility and respect; the pupils are clear about what the teacher expects of them and know that they are accountable for meeting these expectations. Children are not born difficult; they learn that behavior if adults around them do not sufficiently respect their potential for growth and their current limitations. Children who have been taught to be difficult can usually be untaught. Exceptions to this generalization include children with certain learning disorders or intellectual disabilities. Until a problem child is diagnosed by a specialist, however, the regular classroom teacher should not hold lower expectations for that child than for any other pupil in the class.

5. It is unreasonable to expect children from poor families to keep up with those from families that are better off. (Strongly disagree)

Intelligence and motivation to learn are not distributed according to family income or according to gender, ethnicity, or physical condition. The teacher's expectations are especially important for children who come from families who are in difficult circumstances or are thought to be different in some way. It is true that children from poor families do not have the same opportunities for travel and some other experiences that children from middle- and upper-income families have, and for this reason, the experiences provided in school may be even more important for their future.

6. If a teacher has high expectations for all pupils and communicates these effectively, all pupils will meet the expectations. (Disagree)

Although positive expectations may go a long way toward improving student achievement, they are not magic. Some pupils will still have difficulty in meeting the learning objectives. To the extent that positive expectations initiate behavior that does lead to positive effects, they encourage students to work hard and do their best. All teachers, however, are sometimes disappointed; to expect perfection of yourself as a teacher or of your pupils is unrealistic.

CLASSROOM MANAGEMENT

Some of you may be thinking, everything in this chapter up to this point is fine, but how can I create and maintain a safe and stimulating learning environment when some children are constantly misbehaving and others are out of control about half the time? If that's what you are thinking, you can be assured that you are not alone. Although each beginning (and experienced) teacher wants to have a mental picture of a classroom in which all children are happily engaged in learning, many of us have had nightmares in which the classroom becomes noisy and chaotic, with several children running about and out of control just as the principal steps in.

Almost always, the major concern of beginning teachers is maintaining an orderly classroom and avoiding embarrassing discipline problems. Virtually all beginning teachers worry about classroom control. If you still have this early concern, take comfort in the notion that your feelings are quite normal and will begin to abate with experience. Once the early concern is accepted as normal, you can begin to gather potentially useful information. There are no absolute rules that always work in every situation, but there are some guidelines that will help very much most of the time. It is important to understand general guidelines for behavior management, even when one's own situation requires many exceptions to those guidelines. Otherwise, every solution to every problem would be unique and have no relevance for other applications. "Playing by ear" in every case is an extreme and unworkable solution. You would spend all of your time controlling each problem individually, and the pupils would be deprived of any opportunity to learn to take responsibility for their own behavior. The following sections should serve as starting points in learning to manage a classroom so that the classroom becomes a learning environment.

Why We Need Classroom Management

Many normal, acceptable home behaviors are disruptive when multiplied by thirty and packed into the confines of a small classroom. Thus, restrictions of freedom become necessary to provide an appropriate environment for learning. Each pupil has to give up some freedom of movement to gain freedom from disorder and disruption of learning. Although the obvious goal of managing behavior is to provide an environment conducive to learning, a subtle goal is for children to practice controlling their impulses and to develop consideration for the needs of others.

Good science instruction involves many materials and pieces of equipment that are naturally attractive to children and make it easy for them to forget the purpose of their activities and to lose control of their behavior. Even well-behaved children will test the limits and sometimes break the rules, but they want to know that they will not be allowed to go too far. Most children seem to know instinctively that they need adult guidance and protection and become uncomfortable and nervous if they feel that no one is in control.

Children know they are less effective in the world than adults. They yearn alternately to be more powerful and to be more secure. If they find no limits, or if the latitude of freedom exceeds their ability to manage on their own, they are likely to get into trouble. This generalization is closely related to the idea of overdoing in novel situations. Even while they are being disruptive or engaging in dangerous behavior, children are usually unconsciously asking for the security of adult control. They sense that they are not always able to control their behavior and that someone else needs to do so.

Preventing Inappropriate Behavior

Kounin (1970) and his associates conducted a pioneering series of research studies to examine how teacher behavior affects classroom management. A surprising finding was that when teachers who were successful at managing behavior were compared with those who were unsuccessful, no particular differences were found in the way they responded to pupil misbehavior. Later studies have verified and extended these results (Anderson, Evertson, & Emmer, 1980; Brophy & Good, 1986; Doyle, 1986; Emmer, Evertson, & Anderson, 1980). Researchers were determined to find out what made the difference between successful and unsuccessful classroom managers. If it was not the action taken by the teacher when a child misbehaved, what was it? The answer turned out to be prevention of inappropriate behavior. Teacher behaviors that prevent discipline problems have been summarized from the research and reported by Good and Brophy (1987). Four teacher behaviors that they found to provide the most prevention of misbehavior and class disruption are these:

◆ *Awareness of what is happening in the whole classroom at all times.* It involves use of ears as well as eyes to monitor noise level and take action when a crescendo is beginning to build. A teacher with this kind of awareness, and with a consistent history of intervention in potentially disruptive pupil behavior, conveys to pupils a sense of "with-it-ness" that prevents most problems from happening in the first place.

◆ *Being able to do more than one thing at a time.* This will allow you to keep an eye on learning groups while holding a direct lesson with others. This ability will let you respond to outside questions and manage routine jobs without seriously interrupting the main activity.

◆ *Maintaining lesson momentum.* This means being well-prepared and organized enough to avoid stopping to look at notes or backtracking after false beginnings. It means making judgments to ignore minor daydreaming but to intervene in situations that could escalate into disruptions. It also means minimizing the disruption to the lesson that such a teacher intervention itself causes.

◆ *Providing variety and challenge in independent work by assigning tasks that hold pupils' interest.* If the content is too hard or if the procedure is unclear, pupils will give up. If the task is too easy or overly repetitious, pupils will be bored. Either situation means wasted learning time and potential management problems.

In summary, appropriate pupil behavior is achieved by teachers who are flexible, businesslike, aware of potential trouble building up, and sensitive to pupils' needs and abilities. These traits cannot be developed simply by reading a methods book but require the experience of being in charge of a real classroom. Experience alone is not enough, however; also essential is understanding the needs and abilities of pupils and reflecting on your own behavior and the results of your actions. To find a workable middle ground between "don't-move-a-muscle" rigidity and "anything goes" anarchy, consider these generalizations about children:

◆ In addition to developing the essential teacher behaviors, a teacher must establish standards and consequences for guiding pupil behavior and must help the pupils understand why the standards are necessary.

◆ *Standards* are a set of general rules of conduct; *consequences* are what happens when a standard is violated. To begin, decide on a few absolute requirements that are not open to debate. Then, depending on the age and maturity of your pupils, you may decide to involve them in formulating additional standards and, possibly, more consequences. The number of each should be kept to a few, however. Do not emulate the first-grade teacher whose pupil went home after the first day of school and told her mother it was a boring day because "all we did today was listen to the teacher tell us all the rules." One way to involve children in the process is to discuss actual or potential disruptions and give them some alternative solutions to discuss and choose from. In any case, the pupils should be directly taught the few important standards that you will insist upon and the consequences of not meeting those standards. Instruction of this sort requires several interactive lessons at the beginning of the year, with frequent regular review and reminders thereafter.

When your class is made up of children from diverse backgrounds, you must be especially careful to help all children understand what the rules are and why they are necessary. Behavior expectations can be very different in different cultural groups; some of the behaviors you expect may go against the cultural norms of some of your children. For example, some ethnic groups teach their children never to look an adult in the eye, while others teach their children just the opposite. For one child to help another is cooperation to some and cheating to others. Children with handicapping conditions are another group who will need your careful attention to make sure that they understand the rules and that they are capable of following them.

Dealing with Minor Misbehaviors

When inappropriate behavior is not serious and stops on its own, it's best to ignore it. Two examples are momentary pencil tapping and brief talking. If these or similar potential distractions continue for a longer time, an emotionally neutral intervention is called for, such as establishing eye contact if that is appropriate, making a gesture, or standing near the pupil. With young children, a gentle touch often works, though this may be less effective with older pupils. Remember that the main idea is to continue the lesson or activity with a minimum of disruption. Calling on a pupil to gain renewed participation also fits here. None of these problems is serious and thus should not be the cause of embarrassment. Embarrassment of the pupil in question is noticed by the others and can itself constitute a disruption of the lesson. A simple redirection of attention is all that is usually necessary.

Applying Consequences in More Serious Cases

When inappropriate behavior goes beyond the minor type, you must intervene in a consistent, expected manner. If penalties are applied inconsistently, they will cease to be regarded as consequences, and discipline will collapse. Because it is hard to foresee every situation, some teachers are apprehensive about using a system in which negative consequences are invoked in a seemingly automatic way. Shouldn't exceptions sometimes be made? First, a clarification is needed: Not all negative consequences are punishments. In fact, punishment should be used only as a last resort; although punishment can control behavior, it has little or no effect in changing attitudes or in teaching acceptable behavior (Bandura, 1969). A series of consequences of increasing impact on the pupil can be used. The first offense could call simply for a reminder. For many pupils, a reminder is enough. A second offense by the same pupil could entail a short conference with the teacher, during which the pupil is required to describe the unacceptable behavior and identify the class standard that has been violated. The penalty for a third offense could be to have the pupil devise a plan for correcting the problem. Since this book is constructivist in its approach, you may wonder why we have used some of the principles of behaviorism in discussing classroom management. The reason is a practical one; we have found that these ideas usually work and that they prevent many of the problems that beginning teachers often face.

Preventing Behavior Problems

Some teachers use a comprehensive management system, that they have learned through in-service training or through their own reading or course work. All of these systems are based on the principles of behaviorism. As helpful as these approaches may be, it should be noted that many teachers have become excellent classroom managers without using any of these systems. Even though you may feel you need such a system in the beginning, you may find that you no longer need it after you have some experience in your own classroom. Whether you decide to use one of these approaches or develop your own, certain factors are common to all effective classroom management, sometimes referred to as the three C's: clarity, communication, and consistency.

Clarity in your own expectations is essential. If you are not sure what kinds of behavior to expect and what kinds you will not tolerate, then you will have to settle each problem on a case-by-case basis, a method that will not work for long. Advance planning is needed to think about the needs for general class rules of behavior—standards—and the consequences of deviating from them. In any case, you must decide ahead of time how to present the standards and consequences to the class. All of these decisions must be made, and your thinking on the matter must be clear.

Communication is essential to transfer your expectations to the pupils. Remember that children are not just little adults. They have limited capacity to make judgments. It is unrealistic to expect children to regulate their own behavior by judging its appropriateness. During the elementary school years, following clearly communicated standards is the first step and may be as far as some children can go toward the goal of responsible regulation of their own behavior. Remember that you learned in Chapter 2 that young children accept the right of authority figures to exercise power and try to obey rules to avoid punishment.

Consistency in applying consequences is essential. If children see or believe that their teacher lets some children "get by" with behavior for which they themselves have negative consequences, it is only natural that they will try to get by themselves next time. According to Kohlberg (1969), children at this age are very concerned about fairness and may be quick to point out other children's infractions of rules. It is very upsetting to children at this stage if they think they have been treated unfairly or punished when someone else has escaped punishment. When there are exceptions to enforcement, infractions continue and even increase in number. When children are not sure whether they can get away with something, they are tempted to test the limits of the system.

The secret to getting children to take responsibility lies in their learning a highly predictable sequence of cause and effect. The quickest and most humane way to teach responsibility while maintaining order is to enforce classroom standards by using prearranged consequences uniformly, immediately, and without exception. Remember that it is necessary to keep the number of standards to a few, or else you will be imposing sanctions too often and on too many children. Children should never feel that they are always in danger of breaking a rule.

Once you have gained confidence in your ability to prevent or handle problems, you may want to develop your own methods. But one way or another, you must have a classroom in which children can go about their work without continual or major disturbances. Principles of behavior management have been emphasized because that subject is almost always a concern of beginning teachers. However, the most effective way to prevent misbehavior and promote desirable behavior is to provide learning activities in which pupils will become completely and actively engaged.

Grouping for Instruction—Cooperative Learning

A teaching strategy generally referred to as *cooperative learning* has become very popular with teachers during the past decade. This is a way of structuring learning groups in the classroom so that children develop the ability to work cooperatively and productively with other children. Everyone has seen pupils working together in groups in which one person did most of the work; this happens in adult life as well as in school. In some groups, one child is effectively excluded and not given the opportunity to contribute. On the other hand, for other groups, the outcome is much better than anything that could have been accomplished by individuals working alone. Groups of the last kind are, of course, what you would like to have in your classroom.

Cooperative learning groups are formed by the teacher; that is, pupils are assigned to groups rather than choosing those they wish to work with. Groups of four or five pupils seem to work best. The groups should be as heterogeneous as possible. This means a mix of boys and girls, students with special problems, low-ability pupils and high-ability pupils, and, of course, pupils from the various racial and ethnic groups in your class. Research on the effects of using cooperative learning has shown that this strategy is effective in promoting better working relationships between boys and girls, between students with disabilities and those without disabilities, and between minority and nonminority children (Slavin, 1980). Children usually remain in one group for about six weeks; then the groups are changed. Groups work best when the whole group has one task that must be performed by the group. For example, in data collecting, each group will collect one set of data that "belongs" to the whole group. Each child contributes to the collection and display of data, but no child has his or her own set. Thus, if the observations are incomplete or the report is below expectations, the whole group has fallen down on its responsibilities. Conversely, a good result is something for all members to be proud of. Johnson and Johnson (1987), who have worked for years with teachers and pupils in many kinds of classrooms, have developed guidelines for the formation of cooperative learning groups. Details of how to set up cooperative groups are explained in Chapter 10. The important thing to remember at this time is that cooperative learning is a way to bring children together, across gender, ethnic, and social-class lines and to teach and promote the social-interactive skills that children need to be able to work effectively together.

Children learn to accept each other and work together in cooperative learning groups.

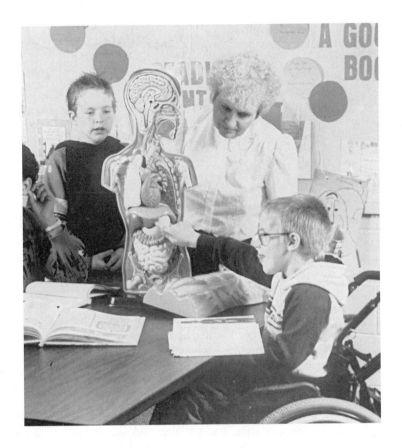

PUPIL ENGAGEMENT

When engagement happens, it can easily be observed by the teacher. Highly involved pupils are oblivious to things that normally distract them, because they are very busy and locked onto the task. Left to work on their own without teacher encouragement, they persist at the task much longer than at normal academic tasks.

Children who would not choose to spend their spare time at academic tasks may spend hours playing with construction sets, or watching bugs, or interacting with pets. Such activities are not just pleasant pastimes but important learning experiences of real and highly significant value to the child's mental and emotional development. Why would children voluntarily choose to educate themselves in this way? Because it is natural for children to be curious and to seek learning. Learning is only unnatural when removed from individual interests and curiosity. Individual teachers can make schooling more responsive to children's needs by trying to match the methods and activities more closely to children's natural interests. Figure 3.2 may help you think about how you can do this.

The learning activity types listed in Figure 3.2 are in the approximate order of difficulty children have in maintaining attention over time. Some qualifications and

FIGURE 3.2   Comparing Activity Types by Level of Engagement

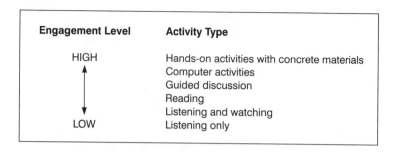

Engagement Level	Activity Type
HIGH	Hands-on activities with concrete materials
↑	Computer activities
	Guided discussion
	Reading
↓	Listening and watching
LOW	Listening only

exceptions apply to the sequence, but in general, the lower on the list, the harder it is for children to maintain lengthy attention. The activities higher on the list are more concrete. Another factor at work is interaction. In the bottom two activities, listening and watching and listening only, the pupil is essentially a passive receiver of information. Even in reading, children have some control of pace and sequence. In the top three activities, real interaction occurs; something happens in response to what the pupil does, and vice versa. Two factors, concreteness and interaction, are the main determinants of pupil engagement. Keep this chart in mind when you plan your science lessons, and always try to think of a way to meet the objectives by planning to use methods as high on the list as possible.

The kind of learning that children seek is through firsthand experience. A beginning teacher once asked, "Do you mean there are things that you can't learn from reading?" Yes, from reading you can't learn how a banana smells or what color the sky is, or how it feels to pet a kitten. You might learn the word *blue* from reading or from hearing spoken language, but unless you have previously had some firsthand experience with things that are blue, the word conveys no meaning. Words, after all, are a wonderful way to communicate when they cause the reader or listener to recall a firsthand experience. If no experience lends meaning to the words, no real learning can occur.

Teachers must constantly remind themselves how limited the experience base of a child is. A child now in kindergarten was born only sixty months ago. There just has not been time for a five-year-old to have had many experiences. Even older elementary-age children have amazing gaps in their experience that adults may not think to consider. For example, many children, even from affluent families, have never eaten or examined a fresh orange. This is true even in orange-growing regions, because many parents give their children frozen or ready-prepared orange juice. When teachers keep this limited experience base in mind, they are less likely to expect children to maintain attention for long periods of time during low-engagement activities such as listening. Without an extensive experience base, too many words and sentences seem meaningless. Extended listening is hard work even for adults; for children, even a very few minutes may be too hard.

Several ways are useful in minimizing the amount of time spent in low-engagement activities. First, modify activities to increase the level of engagement. Instead of continuous talking, break up the information with questions to check for understanding. Children can also be invited to ask questions or give comments. These changes move the engagement to a higher level. Any spoken information input should be carefully planned to avoid unnecessary details, as well as to keep things brief.

Second, spend more time in high-engagement activities. This book should help you learn to use these powerful methods with confidence and effectiveness.

Third, increase your own teaching efficiency. Learning time that is wasted waiting in line for supplies—or waiting while the teacher finds a piece of chalk—not only breaks the momentum and lowers the pupils' level of engagement but also sets the stage for inappropriate pupil behavior.

◆ SUMMARY

Science is for everyone and should be included in the school curriculum for all children. This chapter addresses a range of topics that need to be considered in creating a learning environment for all children.

The general appearance of the classroom and safety considerations need to be taken into account.

Teachers can successfully meet the challenge of working with all children, including those from many racial, ethnic, and cultural backgrounds, children with disabilities, and girls as well as boys.

High expectations are crucial in creating an atmosphere for learning. It is hard for children who are not expected to do well to have the motivation and incentive to succeed. This concept is particularly important for teachers to remember when they are relating to children who have traditionally been thought of as "different"—children with disabilities, minority children, poor children, or any others who may have been labeled as "problems." Sometimes girls are not expected to do as well as boys in science, because science has not been a traditional subject for women. While teachers increase their awareness of the role of expectations in pupil achievement, they also have to be realistic and not expect all children to have the same abilities and interests. Teachers can set reasonable expectations and work with children so that they can learn science.

The most common concern of beginning teachers is whether they will be able to establish and maintain a classroom in which children work productively and peacefully without rude or disruptive behavior. This is recognized as a legitimate concern because of the importance of providing an environment that is conducive to learning. Certain teacher behaviors and attitudes have been found to be effective deterrents to inappropriate pupil behavior. In addition, certain teacher behaviors are effective in handling minor problems and serious disruptive behavior, always with a view toward making the classroom a place where all children can learn and grow. The most important factor in management is good lesson planning, since many behavior problems will disappear when children become actively engaged in science lessons that provide new and interesting learning experiences.

◆ ACTIVITIES FOR THE READER

1. Make a diagram to scale of a classroom planned for twenty-five students. Include and arrange whatever furniture and equipment you think is necessary or desirable, keeping within a reasonable size. Specify the grade level.

2. If you are working in a classroom as an intern, a student teacher, or in another capacity, arrange to have a lesson or interaction with students videotaped. Use the videotape to analyze your own behavior. (This activity will be more helpful if done in pairs so that each person gets another person's perspective.)

3. Find out what cultural groups, other than the one to which you belong, live in your community. Are there any groups who arrived within the past ten years? What language is spoken? Is there a close-knit community or only isolated families?

4. Choose one of the following lesson activities, and write the directions you would give to pupils for doing it. As a group, critique your directions, paying attention to clarity and completeness.

   a. Collect leaves from different kinds of trees, and bring them to class. Compare and classify forms and patterns.

   b. Make a map of the classroom to scale of 1 m = 1 cm.

◆ QUESTIONS FOR DISCUSSION

1. What are your greatest concerns as a prospective or beginning teacher?

2. Suggest some ways not mentioned in the text that expectations could have an effect on the achievement of minority students, students with disabilities, boys, or girls.

3. How do you feel about mainstreaming children with severe disabilities? Do you believe they are better served in a regular classroom or in a special class or school? (This is a controversial subject, so you should feel free to give your honest views, provided they have been arrived at thoughtfully.)

4. If you have visited different elementary classrooms, you probably noticed a wide variety in the amount of pupil movement, the accepted noise level, and the general impression of order (or disorder). What are some factors that are involved? What do you think would work best for you? Why?

5. If you were planning to introduce science activities with concrete materials for the first time to your class, what are some safety considerations to keep in mind? Some behavior considerations to keep in mind?

6. What are some ways you might introduce behavior standards with a new class?

7. What are the differences among penalties, negative consequences, and punishment? If any of these are required, which are most effective for controlling behavior? For teaching responsibility?

◆ REFERENCES

Anderson, L., Evertson, C., & Emmer, E. (1980). Dimensions in classroom management derived from recent research. *Journal of Curriculum Studies, 12,* 343–356.

Bandura, A. (1969). *Principles of behavior modification.* New York: Holt, Rinehart & Winston.

Banks, J., & Banks, C. (Eds.). (1989). *Multicultural education: Issues and perspectives.* Boston: Allyn & Bacon.

Brophy, J., & Good, T. (1986). Teacher behavior and student achievement. In M. Wittrock (Ed.), *Handbook of research on teaching* (3rd ed.). New York: Macmillan.

Doyle, W. (1986). Classroom organization and management. In M. Wittrock (Ed.), *Handbook of research on teaching* (3rd ed.). New York: Macmillan.

Emmer, E., Evertson, C., & Anderson, L. (1980). Effective classroom management at the beginning of the school year. *Elementary School Journal, 80,* 219–231.

Gay, G. (1989). *Ethnic minorities and educational equality.* In Banks, J, & Banks, C. (Eds.), *Multicultural education: Issues and perspectives* (pp. 167–188). Boston: Allyn & Bacon.

Good, T., & Brophy, J. (1987). *Looking in classrooms* (4th ed.). New York: Harper & Row.

Howe, A., Hall, V., Stanback, B., & Seidman, S. (1983). Pupil behaviors and interactions in desegregated urban junior high school activity-centered science classrooms. *Journal of Educational Psychology, 75*(1), 97–103.

Johnson, D., & Johnson, R. (1987). *Learning together and alone: Cooperative, competitive and individualistic learning* (2nd ed.). Saddle River, NJ: Prentice Hall.

Kohlberg, L. (1969). Stage and sequence: The cognitive developmental approach to socialization. In D. A. Goslin (Ed.). *Handbook of socialization theory and research* (pp. 118–140). Chicago: Rand McNally.

Kounin, J. (1970). *Discipline and group management in classrooms.* New York: Holt, Rinehart & Winston.

Rosenthal, R., & Jacobsen, L. (1968). *Pygmalion in the classroom.* New York: Holt, Rinehart & Winston.

Slavin, R. (1980). Cooperative learning. *Review of Educational Research, 50,* 315–342.

◆ RESOURCES

Biological Sciences Curriculum Study. (1972). *Me now.* Boulder, CO: Author.

Hadary, D., & Cohen, H. (1978). *Laboratory science and art for blind, deaf and emotionally disturbed children.* Baltimore, MD: University Park Press.

Mastropieri, M., & Scruggs, T. (1992). Science for students with disabilities. *Review of Educational Research, 62*(4), 377–411.

National Science Teachers Association. (no date). *Safety Booklet.* Washington, DC: Author.

Available from the National Science Teachers Association, 1742 Connecticut Avenue, Washington, DC 20009.

Southern Poverty Law Center. (Biannual). *Teaching tolerance.* Montgomery, AL: Author.

Mailed to educators at no cost on request from the Southern Poverty Law Center, 400 Washington Avenue, Montgomery, AL 36104.

Turnbull, A., Turnbull, H., III, Shank, M., & Leal, D. (1995). *Exceptional lives.* Upper Saddle River, NJ: Merrill/Prentice Hall.

Wood, J. (1989). *Mainstreaming: A practical approach for teachers.* Upper Saddle River, NJ: Merrill/Prentice Hall.

4

Planning for Meeting Goals

In Chapter 1, you read a list of broad goals for elementary science. The goals on that list represent an ideal of what we would like to accomplish throughout the entire span of the elementary school years. To accomplish those goals, children need to have a consistent, coherent science program that builds, each year, on what has been learned in previous years. The purpose of setting goals is to guide planning and implementation of instruction to maintain focus and stay on track. In a dictionary, you will find that the word *objective* has about the same meaning as *goal*. In this book, a *goal* is a general statement of purpose; we also refer to the purposes of instructional units as goals. We define *objectives* as the expected outcomes of individual lessons. When all the objectives of the lessons in a unit have been accomplished, then the goals of the unit will have been achieved.

A science program should flow from the goals that have been set for it. A program that leads to meaningful and long-lasting learning requires thoughtful, purposeful planning and evaluation that are tied to both short-term and long-term goals. Without long-term goals as a guide, a science program can easily degenerate into a collection of "fun" activities that give the children some miscellaneous and unconnected ideas. A series of unconnected lessons, no matter how interesting or exciting, does not constitute a good science program.

TYPES OF GOALS

A general approach to articulating the goals of education, including, but not limited to, science education was developed by Benjamin Bloom, who is widely regarded for his leadership in classifying educational goals into domains and, along with others, for developing taxonomies of the domains (Bloom, 1956; Krathwohl, Bloom, & Masia, 1964; Harrow, 1972). Bloom's three domains are cognitive, affective, and psychomotor. We have expanded the list by adding the social domain, so that the list becomes as follows:

1. Cognitive domain: knowledge, comprehension, ability to use knowledge

2. Affective domain: feelings, attitudes, and values

3. Psychomotor domain: motor skills, such as small and large muscle control

4. Social domain: skills of getting along with others

For the purpose of planning instruction in elementary science, we include content and process goals in the cognitive domain. Each of these domains contains a hierarchy of educational goals. The lowest level is memorization of facts and words—that is, objectives that do not require thinking, only memorization. At the next level, children apply the knowledge they have gained to the task of solving problems. Higher-level goals include analyzing situations, synthesizing information, and applying critical thinking and evaluation skills to real-world problems.

There was a time when elementary science instruction focused primarily on processes of science rather than content. The goals were for children to learn such processes as observation, classification, and making inferences without regard to content. For example, one goal was to teach children to observe objects or phenomena closely and carefully with little attention to the significance of what was observed. The thinking about this has changed, and focusing on processes without regard to content is no longer considered sufficient at any level, even the youngest age group. Both scientists and educators recognize that the curriculum should be built around both important scientific concepts and processes of science. In practical terms, this means that such processes as observing, inferring, and experimenting are learned in the context of studying important ideas and concepts.

It is interesting to compare Bloom's goals of education with the Piaget-derived kinds of knowledge described in Chapter 1, since goals of education are tied to knowledge. Social-arbitrary knowledge and logical knowledge are in the cognitive domain, physical knowledge is probably in both the cognitive and psychomotor domains, and social-interactive knowledge is in the social domain. This comparison is made as a reminder that there are many ways to classify anything of interest, including goals of education.

Some cognitive scientists have classified knowledge as either declarative or procedural knowledge: Declarative knowledge refers to what a person knows about a subject, while procedural knowledge refers to the procedures used to solve problems or complete tasks. In the examples from the cognitive domain, the cognitive content goals are similar to declarative knowledge goals and the cognitive process goals are similar to procedural knowledge goals. The difference is sometimes explained as the difference between "knowing that" and "knowing how." In most of your science lessons, you should try to have both kinds of goals.

FROM GOALS TO OBJECTIVES

A practical example may help you see how the preceding ideas can be used as a guide in planning instruction. Consider how the goals from Bloom's taxonomy could be translated into objectives for a classroom science activity. As an example, consider a series of lessons on electric circuits. In this series of activities, children work in groups of four; each group is given necessary materials. The overall goal is for pupils to learn how to construct a simple electric circuit and to begin to build a concept of the characteristics of electric circuits. Although you may not be familiar with the actual content of the activities, reading over the objectives should give you an idea of how goals direct teacher thinking and planning as teachers translate broad and general goals into objectives for specific lessons. This is a partial list of objectives:

Cognitive Content Objectives ("Knowing That")

◆ Know the elements of a simple circuit and their arrangement.

◆ Know the effects of adding resistance to a circuit.

Cognitive Process Objectives ("Knowing How")

◆ Construct a simple electric circuit.

◆ Measure the brightness of a bulb with a simple meter.

◆ Make predictions about brightness of bulbs, and test the predictions.

Goals from the affective domain are not accomplished in isolation but simultaneously with the other goals of instruction. Part of your responsibility as a teacher is to model the behaviors exemplifying affective goals and to reinforce them as you observe evidence of their use among your pupils.

Affective Objectives

◆ Show persistence in constructing a circuit when the bulb fails to light.

◆ Show curiosity by testing different arrangements of batteries, bulbs, and wires.

Since hands-on activities are the heart of a good elementary science program, children need to learn to use equipment and apparatus with care and skill. This will be easier for some children than others, but the same can be said for cognitive tasks. As a teacher, you can have the expectation that all children—except, possibly, those with physical disabilities—will acquire increasing skill in the psychomotor domain while they also achieve the cognitive goals of a lesson.

Psychomotor Objectives

◆ Handle circuit elements and connectors safely.

◆ Develop skill in manipulating small pieces of apparatus.

It is essential to promote social goals when children are actively pursuing cognitive and psychomotor goals through active work, often in groups. If children are to learn from each other, they must be able to work together in harmony, at least, most of the time.

Social Objectives

◆ Share equipment equally among group members.

◆ Take turns in doing the interesting group tasks.

STANDARDS FOR ELEMENTARY SCIENCE

The preceding example illustrates how general educational goals can be translated into very specific objectives for daily classroom science activities. In this section, we consider the specific cognitive content and process goals of the elementary science curriculum. These are the main ideas and concepts that scientists and educators think children should understand by the time they complete elementary school. These are neither general educational goals nor specific lesson objectives but are, rather, what can be thought of as the overall goals for science in the elementary school. Most states have goals or objectives or a framework for elementary science, and, as mentioned in Chapter 1, several national groups of scientists and educators have defined goals for science learning as a guide for groups at the state and local levels. The content standards, or goals, set forth in *National Science Education [NSE] Standards* (National Research Council, 1996) for kindergarten through grade 4 and grades 5 through 8 are shown in Table 4.1. These standards outline what students should know, understand, and be able to do and thus can be thought of as goals. The standards as presented here are very general; the NSE standards elaborate on each of these and gives examples and guidance for implementing the standards. Throughout this text, you will find many references to the NSE standards in relation to the activities and experiments that will help you construct your knowledge of teaching science. As you see how basic and simple the NSE standards are, we hope you will gain confidence in your ability to teach science to children and that you will begin to think about the many interesting activities you can create to guide your students toward accomplishing these learning goals.

For other ideas on goals for elementary science, you may also find it useful to consult *Benchmarks for Science Literacy* (American Association for the Advancement of Science, 1993), mentioned in Chapter 1. This large volume explains what children should know at different grade levels about science, technology, and human society as well as associated values, attitudes, and thinking skills.

The lesson plans that you will find later in this book will all be tied to one of the guides to the standards listed in *National Science Education Standards* or, in some cases, to *Benchmarks for Science Literacy*. Most of the standards and benchmarks are broader than the objectives of a single lesson, thus, a lesson plan will describe a lesson that goes only part way toward meeting a standard or benchmark.

LONG-TERM PLANNING

One of the first things to do in planning a science program for the year is to look at the school calendar provided by your school or district. This will show the beginning and ending of the school year, the dates when grades are to be turned in, the teacher work days or conference days when pupils will not be attending school, and the holidays and vacation days. You will notice that the school year is divided into grading periods and that the grading periods are punctuated by the holidays and conference days. Thus, there are natural divisions within the year that should be taken into account in planning.

A year-long science program is more meaningful when it is planned as a series of instructional or thematic units. A unit is a sequence of classroom activities that have a central theme or topic and are designed to lead children toward increased knowledge and deeper understanding of the subject chosen. Instructional units have many advantages over stand-alone lessons. By staying with the subject of the unit for a longer time, pupils have more opportunity to experience and reflect, and the teacher

TABLE 4.1 *National Science Education Standards:* Content Standards for Grades K–4 and 5–8

Content Standards, Grades K–4

Unifying Concepts and Processes

Systems, order, and organization

Evidence, models, and explanation

Change, constancy, and measurement

Evolution and equilibrium

Form and function

Science as Inquiry

Abilities necessary to do scientific inquiry

Understandings about scientific inquiry

Physical Science

Properties of objects and materials

Position and motion of objects

Light, heat, electricity, and magnetism

Life Science

Characteristics of organisms

Life cycles of organisms

Organisms and environments

Earth and Space Science

Properties of earth materials

Obects in the sky

Changes in earth and sky

Science and Technology

Abilities of technological design

Understandings about science and technology

Abilities to distinguish between natural objects and objects made by humans

Science in Personal and Social Perspectives

Personal health

Characteristics and changes in populations

Types of resources

Changes in environments

Science and technology in local challenges

History and Nature of Science

Science as a human endeavor

75

TABLE 4.1, *continued*

Content Standards, Grades 5–8

Unifying Concepts and Processes	*Science as Inquiry*	
Systems, order, and organization	Abilities necessary to do scientific inquiry	
Evidence, models, and explanation	Understandings about scientific inquiry	
Change, constancy, and measurement		
Evolution and equilibrium		
Form and function		
	Physical Science	*Life Science*
	Properties and changes of properties in matter	Structure and function in living systems
	Motions and forces	Reproduction and heredity
	Transfer of energy	Regulation and behavior
		Populations and ecosystems
		Diversity and adaptations of organisms
Earth and Space Science	*Science and Technology*	
Structure of the earth system	Abilities of technological design	
Earth's history	Understandings about science and technology	
Earth in the solar system		
	Science in Personal and Social Perspectives	*History and Nature of Science*
	Personal health	Science as a human endeavor
	Populations, resources, and environments	Nature of science
	Natural hazards	History of science
	Risks and benefits	
	Science and technology in society	

Source: Reprinted with permission from NATIONAL SCIENCE EDUCATION STANDARDS. Copyright 1996 by the National Academy of Sciences. Courtesy of the National Academy Press, Washington, D.C.

has more opportunity to integrate the unit topic with other subjects and to the lives of the children. These enhanced learning opportunities are more than enough justification for selecting instructional units rather than relying on one-day lessons. There is another advantage, however, that should appeal to busy teachers. Teaching instructional units is easier for the teacher and much more efficient of both instruction time and evaluation time. The additional time and effort required to plan a unit is more than compensated by time and effort saved later, during presentation and evaluation. Because of the continuity of materials and ideas, start-up time for individual lessons is reduced. The materials, once collected, require little additional teacher preparation time. When pupils are taught to manage materials, the teacher's preparation time is further reduced. Little time is needed to focus or motivate once the unit is initiated, because enthusiasm and interest not only carry over but also actually increase from lesson to lesson.

As you study the school calendar, you will see that there are blocks of time within which to fit the instructional units, and you can estimate how many units to plan. A time frame of three to six weeks seems to work best for most units, with the shorter times for primary grade children and longer times for children in upper elementary grades. There will be time in the school year for perhaps six to eight units. Ordinarily, a unit can be planned to end just before a vacation or begin just after one. Holidays and vacations offer both opportunities and constraints on planning science units. Units about living things that need daily care should be scheduled so they are uninterrupted by vacation days. When interruptions are unavoidable, it will be best to plan a unit in which each lesson can provide a particular event without needing to hold over the actual setup for further observation on another day. The resourceful teacher always looks for ways to turn adversity into opportunity, however, and scheduling gaps are no exception. Slow changes that do not require daily attention are naturals for holiday periods. How much water will evaporate from an aquarium tank in two weeks? Which materials decompose most, or least, when buried in a terrarium? How much do various crystals dissolve when placed and left in water without stirring?

CHOOSING TOPICS FOR UNITS

When you have studied the school calendar and decided how many units to plan for the year and what the special timing constraints are, the next step is to choose unit topics or themes. These may have already been set by a required curriculum, by a required pupil text, or in some other way. If the topics have been set, you may or may not be able to decide when you will teach the units. If the choice of topics is left to you, it is easy to be overwhelmed by the idea of having to start from scratch all on your own. Until you have gained some classroom experience, it will be helpful to consult one of the resources listed at the end of this chapter and select topics for which there are activities that have been developed and tested by others.

Whether you are choosing a science unit topic or planning daily activities, always ask yourself, "What can these pupils learn by direct observation of real things, and what relationships and other ideas can they figure out based on those observations?" This book advocates a science for children that depends on real experience with actual objects and events as well as reflection on those experiences. Secondary materials, such as books, films, and speakers, should be used only to clarify and expand on direct experience. If a choice is open between two topics, the one lending itself more easily to direct experience should be selected. Topics that cannot be studied through direct experience, such as molecules, relation of planets to each other, or cell division, should be postponed until mental maturation makes the possibility of learning from models, photographs, and written explanations more likely.

Science will be more interesting both to the pupils and to you if you have a balance between topics in earth science, life science, and physical science throughout the year, remembering to plan so that activities are appropriate to the climate and seasons. All science involves change; the type and speed of the changes vary, however, and require some thought during the planning phase. Units about living things, such as plant growth or animal life cycles, usually involve slow changes. Children will make a series of observations over a period of days or weeks before the changes are complete. Studies of physical or chemical topics usually involve rapid changes. A popular unit for the lower grades is one in which pupils test common household powders (salt, sugar, baking soda, starch, etc.) with water, vinegar, iodine, and heat. The reactions occur immediately or within a few seconds. The child does something, and there is a quick result. Planning for this unit is different from planning for a unit on growing seeds in which the child plants a seed (or sets up a germination test on one day) and the results of this action become apparent days or even weeks later.

Both kinds of change—rapid and slow—are interesting and important for children to experience; each requires somewhat different planning considerations, however. Rapid-change topics are easier to plan in that there is immediate feedback to pupils on a particular activity. Data collection and data processing for a particular activity can occur during the same class period. A teacher can make a list of activities and plan to have a discussion about each activity before beginning the next activity. With slow-change topics, several activities may need to be scheduled before the observations on the first activity are ready to be discussed. This means the teacher must plan something similar to a three-ring circus, with several lines of activity taking place more or less at the same time. While waiting for seeds to grow or plants to mature, other lessons can be scheduled that involve shorter times frames, such as dissecting soaked seeds, examining roots in germination jars (set up earlier), or observing colored liquids moving up celery stalks.

Plan the units you will teach so that children have experience with both rapid and slow changes. Slow changes are especially useful for primary children as an aid to developing reversible thinking. When children keep daily records, especially in the form of pictures and simple graphs, they can look back over the records and mentally reconstruct the past events. By thinking about how a plant grew taller bit by bit and how it was at the beginning compared to the present, they practice thinking about a series of events both forward and backward in time. This valuable kind of thinking practice is often lacking in the curriculum. In addition to the scheduling needs and opportunities that depend on kinds of changes involved, some topics have other special considerations.

A unit on light and shadows, for example, involves relationships among light sources, object position, and shadows. Some activities are done with artificial light, and some are done outdoors using sunlight. It is important to have several indoor activities well-planned and ready in advance in case bad weather or heavy cloud cover makes an outdoor activity impossible on the day for which it was planned.

If all of this seems too complicated to be practical, you may be reassured by seeing one teacher's plan for one year. There are seven units, grouped by science discipline. In practice, the sequence is arranged to fit into the school calendar and the seasons of the year. Each of the units was selected in accordance with one of the NSE standards that children are expected to meet by the end of fourth grade. This science program for fourth grade consisted of units on the following topics:

Life Science

- *Living Things.* Differences between living and nonliving things, basic needs of living things, care of animals and plants, classification of animals and plants.
- *Mammals or Birds.* Habitats, observation of characteristic behaviors.
- *Plant Structures and Functions.* Observing and drawing cells under microscope, identifying functions of parts of plants, including flowers. Comparing plants grown in different environments.

Earth Science

- *The Sun and Moon.* Observation of times of sunrise, sunset, and moonrise for several weeks, observation of night sky, changes in shadows throughout the day.
- *Rocks and Minerals.* Rock formation, main classes of rocks, identification of rocks and minerals, and observation of rock layers and other geologic features in surrounding area.

Physical Science

- *Electric Circuits.* Constructing circuits, representing them in diagrams, experimenting with different arrangements and parts.
- *Sound.* Ways to make and record sounds, making simple musical instruments, and listening to and making sound patterns.

DEVELOPING A UNIT

When you have outlined a series of units for the year, the next task is to begin developing a unit. Start with the first unit, plan it in as much detail as you can, reflect on what is happening as you go along, and use what you learn from your experience to plan the subsequent units. You will collect ideas and activities for the whole year from whatever sources you have available, but it is likely to be overwhelming if you try to plan the whole year before you begin.

Although there are always decisions to be made on the spot while you are in the middle of teaching, other decisions can and should be made much earlier, during the planning stage. The lesson objectives, the specific materials to be used, the pupils who are to be involved, the time of day to introduce the lesson, and many more such decisions should be settled during planning. Later in this chapter, you will find some guidelines for selecting teaching methods to achieve different goals.

Virtually everything that can be planned ahead of time should be. Does this mean that a decision is locked into place once planned? Of course not. Once a lesson is underway, many contingencies of the real world may demand that the plan be modified. Whatever the purpose of a particular lesson, the main principle of instruction that always applies is this: Teaching is not merely transmitting information; rather, teaching is bringing together curriculum and the learner in a way that is appropriate to the learners' needs, thus enhancing meaningful learning. This principle means that the teacher must constantly assess the pupil's understanding and fine tune the delivery of the lesson as it unfolds. Occasionally, a teacher will discover part way through a lesson that the pupils are simply not ready for it. In that case, the best decision is to "abandon ship," or terminate the lesson. When the goal is understanding rather than information, this type of decision becomes possible.

A number of steps are involved in developing a science unit. Although there may be some variation in procedure, a common sequence follows:

1. Select a topic for the unit.
2. Set goals.
3. Outline a sequence of activities.
4. Try out the activities yourself with actual materials.
5. Write the lesson plans.
6. Provide continuity elements.
7. Plan an ending.
8. Develop a means of evaluation.

Selecting a Topic

The topic you select to start as the first unit sets the tone for the year and should be one that lends itself to many opportunities for active engagement with materials. Because you will be able to use the out of doors early in the year, and in most parts of the country that will not be possible later, topics from life science and earth science are often a good choice.

Setting Goals and Objectives

The goals for the unit may come from one of the sources recommended earlier, or you may set your own goals, remembering to include goals from all four domains. Although you may imagine that developing a set of lesson objectives would be the next task to tackle after choosing a topic and determining the goals for your unit, in fact most teachers think about the particular lessons or activities before setting down the objectives. This is fine. You will need objectives to guide your development of evaluation devices, so goals and objectives should come early in the development of the unit, but you may work back and forth between lesson ideas and objectives. As long as there is a close relationship between objectives and lessons, the exact sequence of writing them is not critical. Just because the development of objectives is described first in this chapter does not mean that you must develop your objectives completely before thinking about lessons, but you should have them clearly in mind before you begin to teach the unit. Remember to include noncognitive goals and objectives in your planning. What affective, psychomotor, and social goals can be achieved by the children as they carry out the learning activities you are planning?

Earlier in this chapter, you saw an example of lesson objectives from a unit on electricity. The unit from which those objectives were taken will be used as an example to help you get a better understanding of what is involved in developing a unit. The unit, which covers simple electrical circuits, is called Batteries and Bulbs; a source for this unit is listed in the resources at the end of this chapter. Since this unit can be used at any time of year and is based on rapid change, it can be scheduled in a straightforward way and makes a good place to begin in learning to plan units.

Outlining a Sequence of Activities

Whether the choice of topics for units is left up to you or determined by others, you will have to decide what activities you will use, how you will sequence the lessons, and how you will know whether the goals have been attained. If the principles of constructivism are used as a guide, you will plan the lesson or unit with as many opportunities as possible for the children to be engaged in activities that will stimulate their thinking and lead them to construct new knowledge for themselves. By the end of the lesson, they should understand something in a different way or know something that they did not know before. A unit should always have a variety of activities and may include lessons that integrate science with other subjects areas.

Batteries and Bulbs is a unit on simple electric circuits. It involves the use of flashlight batteries (D cells) and bulbs, as well as some additional simple materials. The eight lessons described next can constitute a coherent unit. Some lessons depend on others to establish prerequisite ideas, whereas other lessons may be interchanged in the sequence without causing problems. The short descriptions given are not to be thought of as lesson plans and are intended only to show how a unit may be put together so that one lesson leads into another as children develop understanding, acquire psychomotor and social skills, and are motivated to learn more.

Batteries and Bulbs Lessons

1. *Beginning Circuits.* In this lesson, each pupil is given three objects—a piece of wire, a battery, and a bulb—and then asked to make the bulb light. After a few minutes, children begin to find ways to light the bulb. Some will copy others,

and this is fine. They share ways that work and ways that do not work by drawing diagrams on the board. During the data-processing discussion, the teacher indirectly guides the pupils to identify the characteristics of a circuit.

2. *Holders and Added Elements in Circuits.* Pupils explore putting more than one battery, more than one bulb, and more than one wire into circuits. They become familiar with bulb holders and battery holders as tools to make circuit building easier.

3. *Bulbs and Their Innards.* Pupils examine bulbs with magnifiers and compare burned-out bulbs with functional ones. An optional activity is removing the glass from a bulb to see if and how the remaining parts function. The main objective of the lesson is to realize that there is a particular pathway inside the bulb that forces electricity to pass through the filament, which produces the light.

4. *Testing for Conductors.* Pupils make a circuit tester from a bulb and battery (each in its holder) and three wires. They use the tester to classify "junk" and other objects as conductors and nonconductors.

5. *Inferring Hidden Circuits.* Pupils use circuit testers to make observations on unseen circuits and generate inferences about possible wiring. Finally, they verify the wiring by opening the circuit boards and then discuss reasons for inferences that were verified and those that were not.

6. *The Secret Language.* Pupils learn to use standard electrical diagram elements in the place of realistic renditions of batteries and bulbs in their diagrams.

7. *Brightness Meter and Nichrome Wire.* Pupils construct and use a simple light meter composed of ten pages of white paper fastened together. The number of pages through which the light can be seen is the measure of brightness. The meters are then used to measure changes in light as increasing lengths of Nichrome wire (a poor conductor) are added to a circuit.

8. *Electromagnets.* Pupils explore electromagnets made from coils of insulated wire wrapped around soft iron cores (common nails) and placed in a circuit. Pupils decide how the number of turns of wire in a coil affects the number of paper clips that can be picked up.

Once the unit's activities (such as these eight) are selected, they must be placed in a logical sequence. Beginning Circuits is a good starter because it develops the concept of a circuit, which is basic to all the other activities. Holders and Added Elements fits well as a second lesson because it uses the ideas and materials from the first lesson and develops from there. The Bulbs lesson could have been placed later in the unit, but not earlier, because it needs both the basic concept of circuit and also uses holders. Testing for Conductors is needed before Inferring Hidden Circuits, because the idea of the circuit tester, which is used in Hidden Circuits, is developed in Testing for Conductors. The last two lessons could have been used in either order, but both depend on many of the concepts and techniques developed earlier. The Secret Language could have been placed anywhere near the middle of the unit. It depends on prior understanding of the circuit and on previous experience diagramming circuits with realistic drawing. You would want to place it before lessons in which standard diagrams are to be used. This group of lessons, sequenced as outlined here, uses interesting activities to lead from very simple ideas to a much deeper understanding of electric circuits and illustrates the value of a well-planned unit.

Trying Out Activities

In unit planning, it is crucial for you to try out the activities with the actual materials to be used in the classroom. A basic reason for this is to deepen your own understanding of the phenomena involved. Everyone tends to think that just reading about something provides understanding. But actually doing usually makes some aspects much clearer. Other reasons are to make sure the materials behave in the way we expected and to watch for any unexpected difficulties the equipment may cause.

There are many horror stories of lesson failures caused by equipment malfunction. One student teacher tried out all the activities in the Batteries and Bulbs unit she planned to present in class. This helped her write good lesson plans but was not enough. Shortly before beginning, she bought additional wire at a different hardware store. None of the pupils could light the bulb in the first lesson unless the cut cross-section of the wire was placed in firm contact with the appropriate circuit element. She discovered later that she had inadvertently bought wire that was covered with a thin film of transparent plastic, so that electrical contact was impossible except at the cut surfaces of the wire.

Other teachers have bought what they thought was iodine to use in a Mystery Powders unit as a test for starch (iodine causes starch to turn purple). When the expected dark purple color did not develop with starch, the "iodine" label was read more carefully. It turned out to be an iodide of some salt, that is, iodine that had already reacted with something else besides starch. It may have been fine as an antiseptic, but it no longer worked as a test for starch. Many teachers have tried out the activities of this unit at home in glass or ceramic containers, and then bought paper soufflé cups or paper picnic cups for pupils to use in class. Sometimes they found that in class everything—all of the powders—gave a positive reaction for starch! A bit of research revealed that it was the paper that was turning purple in the presence of iodine. In fact, many paper products are made with starch added to give extra stiffness. Nobody, including scientists, can know all the facts about things that can cause a problem. What you can do is test the actual materials in the way the children will use them in order to be sure everything is as it seems.

You may be lucky enough to avoid spectacular problems and still have problems with untested materials. Children sometimes find equipment awkward to hold or have other problems that adults may not have noticed. Always observe your pupils carefully when they are working with new materials, not only to monitor their learning but also to assess the adequacy of the materials for the purpose at hand. Minor problems can often be corrected before using the same or similar materials with the next class.

Writing the Lesson Plans

The next step in unit planning, writing lesson plans, is explained, with many examples, in Chapters 6 to 9 and is not explained here.

Providing Continuity Elements

Workbooks are a wonderful way to integrate language skills and provide a thread of continuity that unites the individual lessons. Workbooks can serve as data books and as journals. You will probably have some structured record sheets duplicated to make record keeping easier for pupils in some activities. Consider whether these should be pasted into the workbooks or whether they should be bound into a booklet along with blank sheets. You may not want pupils to see some worksheets before needed. Sometimes the worksheets give away the discoveries the pupils are supposed to make or perhaps cause other undesired effects. Regardless of whether and how you include structured record sheets, there should always be plenty of blank sheets for drawings and free description and other writing. If you have a computer and printer in your room, you could let pupils use a word-processing program to facilitate their writing and add a special element of motivation.

Planning an Ending

One or more activities should be planned to help pupils see how the individual lessons fit together into a big picture and relate to other subjects as well as to life outside of school. An important part of science is communicating what one has learned with others. You may choose to have a culminating activity that is developed into a regular lesson, or you may have other types of activities, including show-and-tell discussions. An example of a culminating activity for Batteries and Bulbs might be as simple as a class discussion reviewing what was learned in the unit and relating the learnings to life outside school. The Nichrome wire acted as a variable resistor; real-world examples are light dimmers, the volume control on radios, and fan speed switches. Burning out a bulb can provide good background experience for discussing fuses and circuit breakers. Short circuits can easily be demonstrated with simple equipment, as well as their potential danger by allowing a battery short circuit to heat the wire. Electromagnetic cranes for scrap metal are usually familiar to children, through television if not real life. Other possible culminations could involve a field trip to a power plant or other electrical facility, to a museum of science and industry, or to a scrap yard to see an electromagnetic crane in action.

Evaluation

Evaluation includes both assessment of pupil learning and assessment of the unit and should be an ongoing activity throughout the time that the unit is in progress. You will want to know whether the pupils attained the cognitive, psychomotor, affective, and social goals that were set and whether the unit needs to be kept as is, revised, or abandoned. These and other matters related to assessment are the subject of Chapter 5 and are referred to in other chapters as you continue to build your knowledge and skills.

DEVELOPING AUTONOMOUS LEARNERS

The preface of this book introduced the idea that a goal of science teaching is to develop autonomous learners. You may be more familiar with the use of the term *independent learners,* but we have chosen to use the word *autonomous,* which means "self-governing." To be autonomous means to be responsible for one's own actions, to think independently, and to arrive at one's own conclusions. Autonomy is related to science and science teaching because science demands that we each think for ourselves. Science includes facts and theories, but its real essence is the ability to consider evidence and draw a conclusion, and that ability requires independent, or autonomous, thinking. Teachers will shortchange children unless they guide children toward learning to think for themselves and know that their own thoughts are worthwhile and valuable.

Teachers can promote independent thought and responsible action, that is, autonomy, by the way they teach and interact with their pupils. Table 4.2 classifies three teaching methods according to goals of instruction and the level of pupil autonomy. These teaching methods are explained in detail, with examples, in Chapters 6 to 13, but the following explanations will give you the main outlines of each method.

Autonomy Level I

Autonomy Level I, the lowest level in the classification, is essentially teacher-centered in that the teacher has responsibility for all the instructional decisions. The teacher controls the source and flow of information as well as pupil movement and behavior. The pupils have little or no voice in determining the content, methods, procedures, or pacing of the lesson. This method of instruction may be appropriate for a short lesson at the beginning of a unit, such as a lesson on identifying rocks and minerals or on learning to use instruments that will be needed later. Some units cannot be started until pupils have mastered certain essential procedures or learned some essential information.

Most beginning teachers find learning to teach at Autonomy Level I easier than learning to teach at the higher levels, because there are fewer variables to keep in mind and fewer decisions to make once the lesson is in progress. Because pupils have fewer choices, they are less likely to get lost on sequence or procedure. This translates to fewer behavior problems for the beginning teacher to manage. There are, however, a number of limitations to teaching at this level, one of which is that it does not

TABLE 4.2 Autonomy Levels

	Level I	Level II	Level III
Goals for pupils	Learn and practice skills	Make skills automatic	Decide when and how to use skills
	Receive and remember information	Learn from direct experience	Design, carry out investigations
	Learn behavior standards	Internalize behavior standards	Cooperatively determine appropriate behavior standards
Type of instruction	Direct instruction	Guided inquiry	Group investigation
			Independent projects
Role of teacher	Provide knowledge, guide practice	Guide learning experiences	Motivate pupils
	Determine pacing and timing	Ask questions	Monitor progress
	Set and enforce behavior standards	Give students more responsibility for behavior standards	Assist with practical problems
			Monitor cooperative group behavior
			Plan and carry out learning activities
Role of pupil	Follow directions	Participate in learning activities	Devise questions to answer by investigation
	Answer teacher's questions	Ask questions, listen to others	
	Maintain expected behavior	Take responsibility for own behavior	Take responsibility for group behavior

promote the goal of increasing independence and responsibility as much as teaching at the higher levels.

Autonomy Level II

Teaching methods that introduce more flexibility into the lessons have been classified as Autonomy Level II. The goals of the lesson are for the pupils to use the procedures in further learning, to learn from their own actions and experience, to learn to work with others, and to learn to talk about what they have learned. Guided inquiry is an appropriate means to accomplish the goals. Now the pupils are given more responsibility and independence; they work in groups, talk to each other, ask questions, and decide how to divide up the work, how to tackle the problems they are given, and—to some extent—how to pace their own work. The teacher acts as a guide rather than a taskmaster.

To the inexperienced observer, Level II lessons look deceptively easy. The pupils seem interested and businesslike; the teacher seems to take a back seat in running the lesson. But that inexperienced observer is like someone who has entered a theater in the middle of a movie. The beginning of the movie would show how the teacher developed this amazing increase in responsibility by means of deliberate instruction done in carefully thought-out stages. Children can learn to behave responsibly, to manage materials effectively, and to become independent learners—if they are taught and have opportunities to practice those skills.

Autonomy Level III

A third level of pupil responsibility and independence comprises teaching based on individual and group projects, in which pupils have more choice in what they will investigate and how they will do it. The exact division between any two levels is arbitrary, but it is possible to illustrate each of the levels with descriptions of appropriate activities.

Autonomy Level III is the realization of the constructivist perspective in science teaching. At this level, children are well on the way to becoming autonomous learners who have confidence in their own ability to select questions to investigate, to decide how to investigate, and to construct meaning for themselves. This level of autonomy is the goal toward which you will have been aiming as you worked patiently to help your pupils develop the attitudes, habits, and skills that are needed to learn independently, to be curious and creative, and to have confidence and initiative. Instruction at this level does not exclude other kinds of instruction; it includes them, but it also goes beyond them. The processes that were once themselves the goals of instruction have become the tools for reaching other, more inclusive goals.

Comparing and Contrasting Levels

As you examine Table 4.2 and move across from Level I to Level II, notice how the role of the teacher changes from the role of one who provides information and guides practice to one who motivates, stimulates, and encourages pupils to do their own thinking and acting. The teacher's role also changes from setting and enforcing standards of behavior for individual pupils to assisting pupils in monitoring their own behavior and to setting standards for group behavior.

Notice, also, how the role of the pupils changes from answering the teacher's questions to asking questions and listening to other pupils' questions, and finally to thinking of questions to be answered through an investigation. The pupils' responsibility for their own behavior increases from simply doing what is expected and defined by the teacher to taking responsibility for that behavior, and, finally, to taking some responsibility for the group's behavior by reminding classmates when they are getting too noisy or disturbing others.

There are important similarities among the teaching methods at the various autonomy levels, as well as points of contrast. Concrete experience is always important. Real materials and firsthand experiences, as opposed to vicarious experience, should form the basis of initial learning whenever possible.

Each level is useful for certain types of learning or lesson goals. Methods at Levels II and III require a greater number of judgments and other complex teaching skills—much more is involved than just turning the children loose with materials. This book is intended to help you develop a repertoire of teaching skills and methods so that you can choose the method that will accomplish the goals of the lesson. Notice in Table 4.2 that in each section there is a progression toward self-reliance and responsibility for one's own learning. If you follow the goals across from Level I to Level III, you will see that the goal in Level I is to learn and practice skills, the corresponding goal in Level II is to make the skills automatic, and the goal in Level III is to decide when and how to use the skills.

Moving from Level I to Level III: Measuring Area

An example that concerns teaching children to measure area may help you understand how this progression works in practice. The first goal is to "learn and practice procedures" at Level I. You could plan a series of lessons in which children first measure area by covering a surface with paper squares. The number of squares could then be counted and area of the surface reported as so many area units. Later in the series of lessons, pupils could be taught to find the area of irregular tagboard cutouts by tracing them on square-centimeter grid paper and using a system for deciding which squares to count. If you look down Table 4.2 to the role of the teacher, you will see that the teacher should provide information, guide practice, determine the pacing and timing, and set standards of behavior. These are direct instruction lessons, so the pupil's role is to follow directions, answer questions, and follow the rules set by the teacher. Children stay in their seats, but they have lots of materials and time to handle them. The teacher guides their practice of the measuring skills being taught. Over the following weeks, the pupils have many opportunities to practice measuring area. These lessons are all directed toward the goal of "learn and practice skills."

If you look at the middle column of Table 4.2, Level II, you will see the goal "make skills automatic." Now the teacher's role is to guide learning experiences rather than just guiding practice. The pupils' goal is to use the skill to measure a variety of objects and in so doing to make the skill automatic. By practicing the measurement of area in many different contexts, pupils learn to make judgments more easily about which squares to count. They also come to understand which type of measuring device to choose for particular situations. For example, tracing a footprint on grid paper is convenient, but to measure area of a long and thin object, placing individual square unit models on the object may work better. Making the skill automatic takes time and practice. (Think back to how complicated it all seemed when you were learning to ride a bike or drive an automobile, and you will appreciate this point. What is now automatic once took a great deal of concentration.) As measuring area becomes an automatic procedure, accuracy and estimation become part of the process, so that care in measuring becomes automatic, and estimation ensures that a large mistake is noticed immediately. Since measuring is an integral part of many of the experiments and investigations that children will do later, this phase of learning is very important, as recognized in both the *Standards* (National Research Council, 1995) and in *Benchmarks* (American Association for the Advancement of Science, 1993).

If you look at the right column of Table 4.2, Level III, you will see the goal "design and carry out investigations." When measuring can be accomplished with little thought given to the procedures, pupils can then make decisions about what and how to measure as they plan their projects and experiments. By this time, they will have moved up to a higher grade and will be able to assume more responsibility in many ways. That is, they can devise procedures for measuring because they have learned the basic processes and can put their attention on the investigation rather than on the procedures themselves. For example, a group of pupils working together on a project may decide that they need to measure the area covered by the shade of a tree. To do this, they will have to devise procedures, since this is a new problem that requires the use of the skills they have learned but is not a problem they have been taught to solve. Now the teacher's role is to motivate, monitor progress, and assist where necessary. The pupils are assuming the main responsibility for their own work.

As you study Table 4.2 again, follow each section across from Level I to Level III. You will see that each section shows a progression similar to the example of measuring area. Look at the pupil's role. The second line shows the place of questions in science instruction. At Level I, the pupil answers the teacher's questions; at Level II, the pupil is allowed and expected to ask questions and listen to other pupils' questions; finally, at Level III, the pupil participates in the group as questions are devised to be answered by investigation. Questions and questioning provide a powerful means of teaching and learning science at all three levels, but the responsibilities of pupils and teacher are different at different levels. If you understand these differences and learn to teach science at all levels, you will have a repertoire for science teaching that will allow you to motivate and engage pupils in discovering the excitement of learning about the natural world.

◆ SUMMARY

A science program should be guided by both long-range and short-term goals, including goals in the cognitive, affective, psychomotor, and social domains. Examples of specific goals or objectives for lessons on electricity show how goals from each domain can be used in planning instruction. Cognitive goals, including both content and processes goals, have been formulated by a group of scientists and educators and published as *National Science Education Standards* (National Research Council, 1996). The standards set forth in this volume can be used as guidelines in setting cognitive goals, but the instructional means for meeting the goals is left up to teachers.

Classrooms in which children are highly involved in interesting and meaningful learning activities are the result of careful planning with attention to both the overall goals and the details of the daily activities. A year-long science program is more meaningful when it is planned as a series of instructional or thematic units with topics chosen from earth science, physical science, and life science, spread throughout the year. Developing each of the units requires careful thought and planning of many elements, including cognitive and noncognitive goals, sequencing lesson plans for a series of learning activities that build on each other, and evaluation that provides useful information to the teacher and the pupil. The teacher's goal throughout the planning and implementation is to engage children in learning activities that will help them build knowledge and understanding of science without neglecting their growth in affective, psychomotor, and social dimensions.

Three levels of student autonomy were described in terms of goals, type of instruction, role of the teacher, and role of pupils. A central goal of science teaching should be to lead pupils toward greater independence of thought and action, that is, toward becoming autonomous learners. Skill at teaching at all three levels allows the teacher to choose the most appropriate method for any situation.

◆ ACTIVITIES FOR THE READER

1. Make a list of behaviors you would look for as evidence that (a) psychomotor, (b) affective, and (c) social goals are being achieved.

2. Obtain a list of available publications from the following list of resources, and select materials you would choose to develop a science program for a specified grade level.

3. Outline an instructional unit for a topic and grade level of your choice. Determine the goals, and outline a series of lessons in a manner similar to that in the text.

◆ QUESTIONS FOR DISCUSSION

1. Should goals and objectives be the same for all children in a class?

2. React to this statement: "Science period should be for learning science. I don't see why I should be expected to teach children to get along with each other or to clean up after themselves at the same time."

3. How do teacher expectations, discussed in Chapter 3, interact with affective, psychomotor, and social goals?

4. "Science Is Fun" has been a popular slogan for some science educators. Do you think we should promote the idea that school science is fun? Why or why not? What does the word *fun* imply?

5. How much planning is enough? Should there be room for last-minute ideas and spontaneity? Explain your answer.

◆ REFERENCES

American Association for the Advancement of Science. (1993). *Benchmarks for science literacy.* New York: Oxford University Press.

Bloom, B. (Ed.). (1956). *Taxonomy of educational objectives: Handbook I, Cognitive domain.* New York: McKay.

Harrow, A. (1972). *A taxonomy of educational objectives: Handbook III, Psychomotor domain.* New York: McKay.

Krathwohl, D., Bloom, B., & Masia, B. (1964). *Taxonomy of educational objectives: Handbook II, Affective domain.* New York: McKay.

National Research Council. (1996). *National science education standards.* Washington, DC: National Academy Press.

◆ RESOURCES

The following list contains sources from which to obtain curriculum materials that may be used in building a science program. All of these sources supply teachers' guides for active lessons on a single topic that can be used to develop instructional units. Materials from this list can form the basis for excellent units, but additional planning is needed to develop lesson plans and a well-organized unit.

Science and Technology for Children.

Elementary science curriculum materials recently produced by The National Science Resource Center. Topics include butterflies, weather, organisms, soils, rocks, and minerals. Activities for children, teachers' guides, and kits of materials are available from Carolina Biological Supply Company in Burlington, NC 27215-3398.

Elementary Science Study (ESS) and Science Curriculum Improvement Study (SCIS).

Materials developed by these two national curriculum projects of the 1960s are now published by Delta Education, Inc., Nashua, NH 03061-6012. Teachers' guides, kits of materials, and/or lists of materials are available on a vast array of topics that includes Batteries and Bulbs, Mealworms, Clay Boats, Earthworms, Growing Seeds, Kitchen Physics, Microgardening, Mystery Powders, Optics, Pendulums, Structures, and Water Flow.

Great Explorations in Math and Science (GEMS). Lawrence Hall of Science, University of California, Berkeley, CA 94720. (415) 642-7771

Teachers' guides and lists of easily available materials for science activities on such topics as animals in actions; bubbles; earth, moon, and stars; animal movements; solids, liquids, and gases and others. (Not all are for elementary grades.)

Learning About Plants. LEAP. Cornell University, One Plantations Road, Ithaca, NY 14850.

Curriculum materials integrating classroom and field experiences for kindergarten through grade 6 on topics related to biology in general and plants in particular, including seeds, life cycles, energy for green plants, and others.

Science ⁵/₁₃. Distributed in the United States by Teacher's Laboratory, PO Box 6480, 214 Main Street, Brattleboro, VT 05301.

Teachers' guides, developed in Great Britain, for units of study in which children of ages five to thirteen investigate familiar materials and experiences. Topics include structures and forces, trees, working with wood, metals, colored things, and others. Many of the topics are presented at two different grade levels, allowing children to return to a subject after a year or two and study it at a higher level. Materials are usually simple and locally available.

Assessment to Promote Learning

MR. NEWMAN: I'm trying to write some test questions for the unit I'm going to teach, but I'm having a really hard time.

MS. OLDHAND: Maybe I can help. I'm very glad you are speaking to me about it now rather than after the you've finished the unit. The time to think about testing is before you begin rather than after the unit's almost over. Actually, most teachers don't think of it as "testing" like we used to do. What we want to do is find out whether students are making progress toward learning goals, and there are many ways to do that.

MR. NEWMAN: I think one reason I'm having trouble is that I always got very nervous when I had a big test coming up, and I never felt I could do my best or show what I really knew about the subject.

MS. OLDHAND: That's one of the main reasons we have changed our ways of measuring student progress. There are other reasons, too. Besides the anxiety that paper-and-pencil tests cause, there are so many important things that they can't measure that they give a very limited view of student progress and achievement. Come to my room after the last class today, and I'll show you some of the ways that I assess student learning.

Have you ever taken a course in which you felt that you learned a lot but didn't get the grade you thought you deserved? There are many reasons why that might have happened. Maybe your disappointment was due to tests and possibly a final exam that didn't tap into what you had learned. Or perhaps you weren't meeting the instructor's objectives all along, but you didn't get feedback to let you know that you weren't doing so well. You will be able to think of a number of other possible reasons. Whatever the reason may have been, it is likely that you have negative feelings about that course and/or the instructor.

The purpose of this chapter is to help you learn a variety of balanced and fair ways to assess student progress toward learning goals and how to let students, parents, and others know about the progress, or lack of it, that is being made. Assessment has a direct connection to goals and objectives and should be included in all planning for instruction. In later chapters, you will find many specific examples of ways to make assessment an integral part of your teaching.

FORMAL AND INFORMAL ASSESSMENT

Teachers who use activity-centered teaching methods are constantly making informal judgments about student learning as they move about the classroom from one group to another. Informal observation of this kind is not casual, and it is important, but it may not be equally discerning about the growth of each individual pupil and usually does not involve record keeping. This is what we refer to as informal assessment, a sort of careful looking around, with special questions when problems seem apparent.

Formal assessment, on the other hand, involves continuous, systematic data gathering and record keeping. It may include paper-and-pencil tests, but it does not rely solely on them. It may include observation of pupil behaviors in much the same way as in informal checking, but the teacher will keep a record of such observations and will be prompted by the record system to make observations of each pupil rather than observing pupils randomly or by chance. Systematic collection of many kinds of data will not relieve the teacher of having to make professional judgments about pupil progress or grades, but it will provide the necessary information on which to base a judgment and will provide understandable information about pupil achievement that can be communicated to parents and to the pupils themselves. The information you gather about student progress will also tell you whether the goals of the lesson or unit have been reached, and where the trouble spots are; so, as you assess student learning, you are also conducting a self-assessment as a teacher.

PURPOSES OF ASSESSMENT

Assessment should be closely tied to goals and objectives and should be an ongoing part of classroom life. The purpose is to assess pupils' achievement or behavior, not the pupils themselves as persons. Teacher assessment has a profound effect on students' growth, achievement, and self-esteem. Psychologists who have developed measures to indicate the factors to which students attribute their success or failure in school have found that students attribute success or failure primarily to either ability, effort, luck, or difficulty of the task. The challenge to you as a teacher is to develop and use assessment methods that will lead students to attribute their achievements in school to ability and effort rather than luck or the difficulty of the tasks. Differences in ability are real and are recognized by students themselves, but all students who put out reasonable effort should be able to succeed at accomplished school tasks and should know that they are succeeding.

The purpose of assessment is not to sort pupils out as "A students" or "B students," or as overachievers or underachievers, or into any other categories. Nor is the purpose to teach pupils to compete for grades. Everything you do, including assessment, should be directed toward helping pupils achieve the cognitive, affective, psychomotor, and social goals outlined in the previous chapter. Assessment and instruction are related to each other as two sides of the same coin.

Traditional methods of assessment have focused primarily on assessing the attainment of cognitive objectives and have relied on paper-and-pencil tests made up of multiple-choice, true–false, and completion items combined with problems and a few essay or free-response questions. Affective objectives have most often been measured, if at all, by statements to which pupils indicate levels of agreement or disagreement. These methods are limited in that they do not provide information about the attainment of many of the important objectives of science teaching and are more appropriate for older pupils than for those in elementary grades. The *National Science*

Education Standards (National Research Council, 1996, p. 5) recommend the following shifts in assessment:

◆ From what is easily measured to what is highly valued
◆ From assessing knowledge to assessing understanding and reasoning
◆ From finding out what students *do not* know to finding out what they *do* know
◆ From end-of-term assessments by teachers to ongoing assessment by students

It is often said that what is not tested will not be taught. This is not completely true, but it has enough relation to reality to give us pause. In the complex world of the elementary classroom, there is not enough time to do everything that one would like to do; priorities are set consciously or unconsciously. When the main mode of assessment is paper-and-pencil tests that measure a narrow range of outcomes, teachers tend to focus on those outcomes to the exclusion of some others that are equally, or more, important, including noncognitive objectives.

Quizzes and tests are sometimes treated as if they were accurate, objective measuring instruments, in the same class with thermometers or speedometers, but a moment's reflection will tell you that this is not so. Teachers use subjective judgment in choosing the questions to ask, in assigning weight to each item, and in evaluating answers. However hard teachers try to be objective, there is an unavoidable element of subjectivity in the test itself. Haven't you ever studied for a test and been disappointed that a question you were well prepared for was not on the test? The teacher was not singling you out but just didn't include every question that could legitimately be on the test. This is another reason not to rely solely on this method of assessment.

Authentic assessment is a term that refers to tasks that have some use or significance beyond the classroom, tasks that connect what has been learned in school to the lives and interests of students. Much of the information asked for in conventional tests is not connected to the real lives or interests of students. An interesting and instructive account of one elementary teacher's experience as she implemented authentic assessment strategies is provided by Kamen (1996). As the teacher gained a new understanding of what science teaching was all about, she shifted to a conceptually based constructivist model that allowed her to focus on what pupils had learned rather than what they didn't know. A variety of authentic assessment methods are described next.

WORKBOOKS

Beginning no later than fourth grade, pupils should keep a science workbook in which they record their activities in science class. This can be a primary source of information about student progress for you and of feedback for pupils. It is far preferable to a loose collection of papers and lab reports that get mislaid, mangled, and lost. At the beginning of the year, explain that each pupil needs to bring a small notebook and that the workbooks will be used only in science class and will be left at school. The workbooks should be handed out or picked up by pupils at the beginning of science class and returned to a special place at the end of class. This is one of the things that you should monitor or assign as a responsibility to one of the pupils, at the beginning and end of each science class period. Workbooks are the place where pupils write their interpretations, inferences, and plans for further experiments. The workbook can be anything you decide it to be. In all cases, it provides an ongoing record of the pupils' actions and thoughts about the unit topic. A workbook lets children see how their thinking has grown. When pupils need to remember what happened in a previous activity, the workbooks provide that information. They also give children a real way to apply writing skills. As children engage in a real application of skills that both makes sense and is useful, they learn to value writing in a way that no amount of disembodied practice can provide.

For each activity, pupils may write answers to the following:

◆ What I did:
◆ What I found out:
◆ Ideas for next time:

A page from a fifth-grade pupil's workbook is shown in Figure 5.1. Note that it is neat and carefully kept, though the child has corrected a few mistakes. Note also that this is a record of a rather simple experiment but one that fifth graders can carry out and understand without much explanation or help from the teacher. That is, the experiment is at their level of ability and understanding. The writing that is necessary is also quite within the ability of most fifth graders.

The open-ended form of responses allows pupils to express themselves freely and thus reveals more than you may have asked for directly. For example, misconceptions are sometimes apparent in children's responses: "I think the black stuff [in the aquarium] may be from the sand when they ground it up." Did you know that many children think naturally occurring sand is created by humans grinding up rocks? Length and style of a child's response can be indicators of interest and enthusiasm. You do not have to rely completely on reading between the lines, though. You can ask pupils to respond in their workbooks to specific questions and directives related to whatever activity is being used. Here are some examples from a unit on mealworms.

1. Draw a picture of your mealworm, and label the parts.
2. Did your mealworms seem to like one color more than others? What is your evidence?
3. Write a paragraph on:
   a. What you learned from today's discussion.
   b. What you liked or disliked most about today's activity and why.
   c. How your group is working out. Does everyone get along? Are you doing your part? What could be done to make things work more smoothly?
4. In what ways are you taking good care of the materials?
5. Write your suggestions for improving our cleanup system.

Our experiment was to find $ which materials could push what ~~wait~~ weights. Here is our table:—

Pushing

Weights	B. Cotton	alloy	Copper
5 g	no	yes	yes
50 g	no	yes	yes
10 g	no	yes	yes
20 g	no	yes	yes
100 g	no	yes	no
200 g	no	no	no
1 KJo	no	no	no
5 Klo	no	no	no

Conculsion

By looking at the table it shows that the cotton could not push any of the weights, so that means it is terrible at pushing. The Alloy and Copper did quite well but by looking at the table it shows that alloy is the best pusher because on the 1og Copper could not push it and alloy could.

FIGURE 5.1   A Fifth Grader's Workbook Page

98

Evaluating Workbooks

Workbooks are more useful to pupils and to you if they are collected weekly and returned promptly. If you have twenty-five pupils and take up five workbooks each day, you can review them and write appropriate comments rather quickly, or it may work better for you to take them all at once.

Rubrics, or criteria, for evaluating workbooks should be developed with pupil involvement at the beginning of the year. Rubrics define what is to be assessed and may define the levels of performance. Start with simple criteria, use them for a month or two, and reopen the discussion with pupils. Do they think the criteria are fair? Are there other things they would like to have assessed? Important criteria are completeness of information and observations, organization, and evidence of thinking. Since children's writing skills are in various stages of development, spelling and writing are best assessed in some other way; let the children be free to explain what they did and express their ideas without fear of losing points because of poor spelling. To serve as a basis for evaluation, the information you select should be summarized and recorded in some way. This could be in the form of a checklist combined with anecdotal records. Examples of such checklists for the first two questions in the preceding list for the unit on mealworms are shown in Figures 5.2 and 5.3.

FIGURE 5.2 Journal Summary for Question 1

	A	B	Comments
Susan			
Andy			
José			
Jared			
Kelly			

A: Drawing is realistic rather than fanciful.
B: Labels are complete and accurate.

FIGURE 5.3 Journal Summary for Question 2

	A	B	Comments
Susan			
Andy			
José			
Jared			
Kelly			

A: Shows understanding of the experiment.
B: States observations supporting conclusion.

As children become more experienced, you may decide to use rubrics that define levels of responses, but complex rubrics and grading systems are not appropriate at this level; keep it simple, ongoing, and understandable. To become independent learners, children have to be able to work on their own without constant adult guidance. For this to happen, they have to have science lessons based on activities, including writing, that they can manage mostly on their own. When science lessons become too abstract or too complicated—or the necessary record keeping and arriving at conclusions are too difficult—little meaningful learning can occur.

PERFORMANCE ASSESSMENT

Performance assessment in its purest form evaluates what a student can *do* as opposed to what a student *knows*. This difference has been explained as the difference between the written test and the road test that are required to obtain a driver's license. The written test shows what applicants know about rules and regulations, and the road test shows what they can do behind the wheel of an automobile.

Science is one area of the elementary school curriculum where performance assessment can fit in as a natural part of the learning process. This can be done in several ways. A behavior checklist, described next, records a teacher's observations of pupil performance and can focus on whatever seems most important at any given time; for example, how carefully a pupil or group follows directions, sets up apparatus, makes observations, and records them. If a teacher notices that many pupils are not performing some task as intended, the teacher can call for quiet, explain that each pupil or group is to set up a piece of equipment, for example, and the teacher can then walk around the room to check each setup. This is an informal performance assessment of a specific task that is intended to improve learning rather than assign a grade. If a formal assessment is needed, performance tasks can be used as a means of assessment at the end of a unit. How this might be done is explained next. You will notice that, although this is a form of performance assessment, it also depends on pupils' abilities to read directions and write or draw answers.

As an example of a simple performance assessment, we will use the unit on electricity outlined in Chapter 4, but these steps are applicable to any unit.

- Review the objectives for each lesson, and select those to be tested.
- Decide what you will accept as evidence of acceptable performance.
- Design simple sets of apparatus to test each objective and means for students to communicate their responses.
- Set up stations around the room.
- Work out a system for students to rotate among the stations.

If you refer back to the electricity unit outline, one of the first things you will notice is that it will not be feasible to test for all the objectives; therefore, as in all assessment procedures, choices of what to test for have to be made. We will use only three in this example, but you would probably choose four to six if you were conducting this assessment in a classroom. The objectives we will assess are these:

1. Pupil can use a bulb, a battery, and a wire to make an electric circuit.
2. Pupil can use a circuit tester to identify conductors and nonconductors.
3. Pupil can draw standard diagram elements to represent a given circuit.

Next you have to decide how pupils will communicate their responses and how you evaluate them. Since it will not be possible to observe each pupil unless you have an assistant to work with the other children, it will be necessary for pupils to write or draw their responses, and you will have to determine criteria for evaluating their responses. Examples of these criteria, or rubrics, as they are often called, will be given next. You are familiar with the idea of giving partial credit for answers that are partly correct; developing criteria, or rubrics, for assessing responses is a systematic way of doing this. The rubrics are developed in advance to make sure that the partially correct responses of all pupils are treated the same and that you know what you will accept as a correct answer. You will also have to have a classroom management plan for this assessment, since some students will be working through the tasks while others are engaged in other learning activities.

After working through all the steps just described, you will set up the tasks, each in its own cubicle. (If nothing else is available, you can make a cubicle by setting a large box, with its top cut off and open toward the pupil, on a table.) These tasks could be set up to assess attainment of the three objectives listed previously:

Station 1. A battery, a bulb, and a length of wire are placed on the table along with directions to use the materials to make a complete circuit, to explain how the student knows the circuit was complete, and to draw a diagram of it.

Station 2. A circuit tester, two conductors, and two nonconductors that were not used in the activity in class. The directions are to test each material, identify each as a conductor or nonconductor, and explain how that was determined.

Station 3. A complete circuit is set up with a lighted bulb and perhaps a switch. The directions are to draw a diagram of the circuit, using the standard method of representing electrical elements. A rubric to assess these tasks is shown in Table 5.1.

These rubrics have purposefully been kept simple and easy for you and your pupils to understand. Rubrics can be much more complex and are often tested ahead of time and revised before use, but that is not necessary in assessing children's performance on tasks of this kind. Assessment should be kept as simple as possible and viewed by children as a normal part of their classroom activities. When assessments become elaborate and time-consuming, the process fosters anxiety and competition for grades, both of which should be guarded against and, if possible, avoided.

TABLE 5.1   Rubric for Performance Assessment of Electricity Tasks

Task 1	Correct explanation (bulb is lit) and accurate diagram	2 points
	Either correct explanation or diagram	1 point
	Neither correct explanation nor diagram	0 points
Task 2	Correct identification of all materials and clear explanation	2 points
	Correct identification or clear explanation	1 point
	Neither of above	0 points
Task 3	Correct diagram	2 points
	Partially correct diagram	1 point
	No diagram or use of pictures instead of standard representation	0 points

Essays and Open-Ended Questions

Essay, or open-ended, questions ask pupils to write responses in their own words from their own knowledge without the prompts provided by multiple-choice, true–false, or completion items. They require organization of information learned in school or from everyday experience and reasoning or critical thinking that goes beyond information. Workbooks fulfill many of the functions in science of essay questions in other subject areas, but items of this kind can also be useful both as informal and formal means of assessment. They give pupils a chance to demonstrate what they know, and offer opportunities for relating experiences and knowledge from other contexts to science. Children too young to write responses can make drawings, which often reveal a great deal about their ideas and may give clues to their misconceptions and misunderstandings.

Assessment of open-ended questions, like assessment of performance tasks and workbooks, is based on previously developed rubrics. The emphasis in developing rubrics for these questions should be on the level of understanding and use of knowledge, and the items should be such that they can be answered in one paragraph. Questions of this type may also be used to help the teacher determine what understandings pupils have gained from a lesson or set of lessons. In that case, answers would not be scored but would be used as a guide in planning instruction or to identify pupils who are falling behind.

BEHAVIOR CHECKLISTS

Checklists can be used to make your observations of pupil behaviors during learning activities more systematic. Planning ahead which behaviors to notice and then listing them on a check sheet serve two functions: (1) to focus your observations and (2) to provide a convenient way to record them. The behaviors you choose to watch for will depend on your unit goals. Because goals are normally stated

FIGURE 5.4 Behavior Checklist for Persistence

	A	B	C	D	Comments
Susan					
Andy					
José					
Jared					
Kelly					

A: Continues after novelty wears off.
B: Completes task that others did not.
C: Records data spontaneously.
D: Repeats experiment despite apparent failure.

rather broadly, they are not good as checklist items by themselves. You will need to generate some behavioral indicators that could serve as evidence that the goal is being met. Although behavior checklists can be used in any of the goal domains, they are especially useful in the noncognitive domains, partly because these goals are more difficult to assess directly. For example, if one of your affective goals is for pupils to develop persistence, you might have a behavior checklist like the one in Figure 5.4.

This method can also be used to assess progress in the psychomotor goal mentioned previously: that is, handle circuit elements and connectors safely. What would you use as indicators for this psychomotor objective?

Checklists should be designed so that difficult judgment calls are not required. Rather than use a rating scale from 1 to 10, for example, simply use a check mark for satisfactory, a plus sign for especially noteworthy, or a minus sign for not observed. A checklist must be easy to use so that you can use it without drawing attention to it and so that a record is feasible on each behavior for each child.

PRODUCTS

Products made by the pupil can be useful in evaluation. The circuits constructed in the unit on electricity and other products that result from science activities give quick and reliable information about a child's understanding of involved concepts, as well as affective information such as neatness, creativity, care taken, and so on. Always be sure the product is judged in accordance with the unit goals. The same child's electric project could show an excellent conceptual understanding and yet be messy and unappealing visually. It is not useful to give an overall rating somewhere in the middle when both concept and appearance are original goals. Rate for each goal separately.

PORTFOLIOS

A portfolio is a collection of student work, assembled over weeks or months, that gives an in-depth picture of achievement or progress. You may think of a portfolio as a collection of paintings or drawings that aspiring artists carry around to show prospective employers or gallery owners; a science student's portfolio is similar to this in some ways. A portfolio should allow pupils to display their best work, it should contain a variety of materials, and pupils should be allowed to choose at least some of the work to include. It is a "collection of evidence with a purpose" (Collins, 1992).

The development and assessment of portfolios require much time and thought on the part of both pupils and teacher and should be undertaken with a clear purpose in mind. Questions that should be answered before deciding to use portfolios as an assessment method follow:

◆ What is the purpose of the portfolios? Will they be used to motivate pupils, to help them learn to organize their work, to assess achievement, or to demonstrate progress?

◆ Will the portfolios be assessed as part of the grading system, or will they be used to showcase pupils' work? Will each portfolio be assessed as a whole, or will each entry be evaluated separately? In either case, if they are to be formally assessed, clear criteria must be established at the outset.

◆ What will be included in the portfolios? Responsibility for this decision should be shared with pupils, but without clear guidelines a portfolio can become a messy collection of miscellaneous papers.

One purpose of building a portfolio is for pupils to look back on what they have accomplished and reflect on their work. Fourth- or fifth-grade children can write brief statements, and younger children can express their thoughts orally. Some children are very perceptive about their own work if they are encouraged to share their thoughts to a nonjudgmental audience—but only if their reflections are not to be assessed.

SHORT-ANSWER TESTS

Paper-and-pencil tests that require short answers, such as multiple-choice, true–false, and completion items, may not be necessary. Generally, you can get the sort of information needed to assess learning in the various domains from other assessment devices. The main advantage of these tests is that they gather specific information from every child in a relatively short time. The quality of the information gathered may be rather low, however, especially if the questions are unclear or misleading to pupils. It takes some experience and perceptiveness regarding children's misconceptions to write really good tests. Objective tests that are both fair to the pupil and useful in picking out those who are not "getting it" are especially hard to write. Probably the best use for tests of this kind, if they are used at all, is to check understanding of concepts and ideas as you go along. In that case, the tests are not means of assessment but a way to let you and the pupils know whether the objectives of instruction are being met.

ASSESSMENT IN PRIMARY GRADES

Many of the assessment methods and ideas described previously involve reading and writing and cannot be used with children who have not mastered these skills well enough to apply them without undue difficulty in forming and communicating answers. The focus in the early grades should be on observation and simple classification of objects and phenomena, experiences with plants and animals in the classroom, and learning to work with other children in groups to carry out learning activities. Assessments can be carried out by giving oral directions and asking children to make drawings of their observations rather than written records or explanations. Behavior checklists are a useful and appropriate means of collecting data with the emphasis shifted toward affective, social, and psychomotor rather than cognitive objectives. It is more important to provide learning tasks, experiences, and an environment that foster growth in these areas and interest in science than to try to teach science concepts that are beyond the mental reach of the children. Children who have learned to work in groups, who know how to use such simple equipment as magnets and magnifying glasses, who can classify and observe with care, and who are enthusiastic about science are prepared to undertake the more demanding tasks of the upper elementary grades. Assessment should focus on these objectives.

ASSESSING ACHIEVEMENT OF STUDENTS WITH DISABILITIES

Assessment tasks can be modified as needed to be appropriate for students with physical disabilities, learning disabilities, or limited English proficiency. Individual interviews may be the most appropriate method of assessment for those who have a physical disability that limits the ability to write or who have limited vision. Assessment tasks that depend on oral communication will have to be modified for those who are hearing impaired. Let common sense and fairness guide you as you devise assessment tasks and methods that are appropriate for children who have special needs.

STEPS IN DEVELOPING EVALUATION

You were introduced to Batteries and Bulbs in Chapter 4, where it was used as the basis for a unit on electricity. With that unit in mind, consider the steps involved in developing an evaluation plan. It is unlikely that you would use all the methods described next, but you can see the variety of assessment methods that would be appropriate for this unit.

STEP 1 **Look at the list of goals. Jot down the types of evaluation that seem best suited for each goal. In the example, evaluation types are coded as follows: WB, workbook; WT, written test; BC, behavior checklist; PT, performance test; and I, interview.**

1. Cognitive content goals:
   a. Know the elements of a simple circuit and their arrangement. (WB, WT, PT, I)
   b. Diagram actual circuits using standard electrical symbols, and construct actual circuits from provided diagrams. (WB, PT)
   c. Know the effects of adding resistance to a circuit. (WB, WT)
2. Cognitive process goals:
   a. Predict and verify arrangements of elements that will cause a bulb to light. (BC, PT, I)
   b. Predict and verify the relationship of electromagnet strength to number of turns in the coil. (BC, PT, I)
   c. Infer pathways inside a mystery circuit board based on observed effects. (WT)
   d. Measure the brightness of a bulb with a simple meter. (WB, PT)
3. Psychomotor goal:
   a. Handle circuit elements and connectors with increasing skill. (BC)
4. Affective goals:
   a. Show curiosity and persistence in working with materials and related problems. (BC, WB)
   b. Behave responsibly during the use and care of materials. (BC, WB)
5. Social goal:
   a. Show cooperation and courtesy in group work. (BC, I)

STEP 2 **Regroup goals according to evaluation type.**
   Workbook: Goals 1a, 1b, 1c, 2d, 4a, and 4b.
   Written test: Goals 1a, 1c, and 2c.
   Behavior checklist: Goals 2a, 2b, 3a, 4a, 4b, and 5a.
   Performance test: Goal 1a, 1b, 2a, 2b, 2d.
   Interview: Goal 1a, 2a, 2b, 5a.

STEP 3 **Describe each evaluation method in general terms and how it will address each of its goals.**
   Workbook assignments will vary from one lesson to another to solicit responses useful in assessing the various goals.

Written tests for Goals 1a, 1c, and 2c can consist of simple questions to which pupils respond by selecting from diagrams already present, by completing partial diagrams, or by drawing entire diagrams themselves.

Behavior checklists are called for in assessing six different goals. Is it possible to put all behavior indicators for all of these goals on a single checklist? A judgment must be made. If too many behaviors are needed, two or more checklists should be made and used on alternate days. Remember to try to keep it simple.

Is it possible to do the performance test/interview for Goal 2a at the same time as the interview for Goal 5a? This should be fairly easy. Children are asked one at a time to construct a working circuit from materials and then asked some questions about how group work is coming along.

STEP 4 **Generate the specific questions, behavior lists, and so on, and refine them for use. Let's look at a few specific examples of items for the various types of evaluation:**

Workbook:

◆ Draw and label two diagrams of circuits that work and two diagrams of circuits that do not work. (Goal 1a)

◆ Tell how you measured the brightness of a bulb. Add a drawing if you like. (Goal 2d)

◆ Tell how you took care of your lab materials today. Why is this important? (Goal 4b)

Written Test:

◆ Given: pictures showing simple circuits with (1) copper wire only, (2) a short length of Nichrome wire added, and (3) a long piece of Nichrome wire, and the following written question:

Would there be any differences in the brightness of the bulbs in these circuits? Write a short paragraph to tell what you know about these circuits. (Goal 1c)

Behavior Checklist

For Goal 3a (Handle circuit elements and connectors with increasing skill), a checklist similar to those given for summarizing journals can be used. Make a checklist column for each behavior of interest. In the example in Figure 5.5, four behaviors are used.

Performance/Interview

Example for Goal 1a (Know the elements of a simple circuit and their arrangement.)

1. José, here are some materials to make a circuit. Would you please put them together to make the bulb light?

2. What is each part called?

FIGURE 5.5 Behavior Checklist for Goal 3a (Handle Circuit Elements and Connectors with Increasing Skill)

	A	B	C	D	COMMENTS
Susan					
Andy					
José					
Jared					
Kelly					

A: Uses clips efficiently.
B: Adjusts bulb in holder as needed.
C: Chooses to use holders when making complex circuits.
D: Is able to complete circuits without asking partner "for a hand."

Interview

Example for Goal 5a (Show cooperation and courtesy in group work.)

Questions should be individualized to probe for further information after using other means of evaluation.

In the case of Goal 5a, you would have some initial information from using a behavior checklist. In this case, you may choose to use to use the interview only with those pupils who may be having difficulty working in their groups. The questions should be used flexibly, building on and probing pupil comments when possible.

1. Do you enjoy working with your group? Why/why not?

2. Have you done your part of the work? Tell me about it.

3. What problems have you noticed?

STEP 5   After using your evaluation methods, decide whether the various items work as well as you would like. Then revise as needed and reuse if possible. If journals or behavior checklists don't work well, the opportunity to do them over may be lost when the unit ends. In that case, devise a written or performance test to salvage needed information.

STEP 6   Get ready for the next time you will use the unit. After taking the time to develop a science unit, you probably will want to use it with more than one group of children. If possible, revise faulty evaluation methods as soon as you recognize a problem. If you can't manage an immediate revision, at least make notes on what worked well and what needs rethinking and modification. If you are as specific as possible, your job will be easier when you come back to it. If results showed that a test was too hard, either fix the test or modify the instruction.

PUPILS AS PARTNERS IN ASSESSMENT

It may seem contradictory to consider pupils as partners in assessment, since assessment is usually thought of as something in which teachers are active and pupils are passive. It is true that teachers are responsible for assigning or "giving" grades at the end of each marking period. However, there are ways that pupils can participate without taking away the teacher's ultimate responsibility and authority. In the process, students will move a step further toward assuming responsibility for their own learning.

Some of the ways that you can provide for pupils to participate in assessment are these:

◆ Plan to have pupil input in development of rubrics for workbooks and lab reports.

◆ Allow pupils in cooperative groups to assess each other's work, to be reviewed by you.

◆ Have pupils critique, in their teams or groups, the project presentations of other groups.

When children understand the criteria for assessment, how the criteria are arrived at, and what is expected of them, assessment is no longer a mysterious process over which they have no control.

COMMUNICATING RESULTS OF ASSESSMENT

The final step in assessment is communicating the results to those who will use the data you have gathered. The primary users of assessment information are the pupils themselves, but parents have a vital interest in assessment of individual students, and school administrators and other officials have an interest in the overall assessment of your pupils.

Ongoing Feedback to Pupils

It is essential for pupils to have a clear understanding about what is to be assessed and how it will be assessed. They must know what is expected and how they can meet the standards. Equally important is knowing to what extent they have met the expectations and how they can continue to improve performance. When a teacher gives ongoing feedback, with explanations, on quality of work, pupils come to understand how they are evaluated, what the criteria are, and what growth is occurring. Informal opportunities for feedback occur almost constantly as the teacher listens and responds to pupils' explanations during classroom discussions, interacts with pupils as they are engaged in hands-on activities, and provides comments on their workbooks and other written class work. Feedback of this kind should be serious, thoughtful, and honest. It is not useful to accept all responses as if they were equal with comments such as "That's an interesting idea" or "Thank you for your comment, Richard." It is better to ask for evidence, indicate that a response shows logical reasoning or "needs further thought," and tell a pupil, when necessary, that you will not accept silly responses. One should never be harsh, critical, or unkind, particularly to children who are shy or less able than others, but all children deserve to have their ideas taken seriously and to receive honest but gentle feedback.

A conference should be held with each pupil when grades are reported. It need not be long, but it should give an opportunity for the pupil to ask questions about assessment methods and results and for the teacher to explain what assessments were used in arriving at a grade. Elementary teachers will be discussing grades in other areas as well as in science, but these general principles apply to all. When pupils know that assessment and grading are fair, when they understand the bases for assessment, when feedback is clear and timely, and when they have opportunities to discuss their progress with their teacher openly and freely, then assessment can achieve its most important purpose of promoting lasting learning.

Report Cards

Ongoing assessments that have been made during a grading period form the basis for reporting progress. Many schools do not use report cards that assign letter grades to children in the lower grades, using performance criteria, narrative statements, or other more descriptive ways to communicate progress and achievement in many areas. When a letter grade is required, it should be based on a variety of kinds of

Each child needs honest feedback in order to meet the teacher's expectations.

assessments, most of which have been communicated to students. The grade on a report card should not come as a surprise to a pupil; if it does, then the matter can be discussed during the conference held with each pupil.

For report cards to communicate effectively and to encourage rather than discourage students from striving for excellence, Stiggins (1994, p. 368) recommends a process that includes these steps:

◆ Begin each grading period with a clear vision of the objectives to be met.

◆ Translate targets into assessments, aligning assessment methods to targets.

◆ Use the selected methods to assess attainment of objectives and keep accurate records.

◆ Combine data collected over time into a composite index of achievement, assigning grades that can be interpreted and understood by pupils and parents.

Every effort should be made to have a conference with parents or caretakers of each child in your grade when report cards are issued. Parents need to know the basis for the grades, in what ways their child is making or not making progress toward meeting expectations, what the child's strengths and weaknesses are, and what they can do to help the child improve. Parents of children who are meeting expectations like to hear about their child's success and can be given suggestions about ways to broaden their child's interests and skills. The conference may include the child and can be short if there are no major concerns, but one cannot assume ahead of time that there will be no questions. If a face-to-face conference is not possible, try arranging to speak with the parent or caretaker by telephone. A sensitive and sometimes delicate approach is always needed when talking to parents or caretakers about their children. Remember that not all parents feel comfortable in talking with teachers, that other parents will be very assertive in demanding more attention to their child's needs, and that for all parents the report card is likely to be an emotional issue.

SELF-ASSESSMENT AS REFLECTIVE PRACTICE

The assessment process is not complete until you have taken time to reflect on the outcomes of a science activity and asked yourself, "How well did I plan for instruction, implement the plan, and assess the results?" The answers to these questions need to be recorded regularly and systematically in a journal. The moment-to-moment demands of teaching are so great that it is easy to let the days and weeks go by without serious reflection unless you have a systematic plan and the resolve to follow it. The sources of data that you use for student assessment also tell you something about your planning, implementation, and assessment procedures. If pupils did not attain the objectives, was it because the activity was at the wrong level, too long for the time allowed, or not of intrinsic interest? Was the lesson well planned but not implemented as planned? Did the assessment procedure assess the wrong things? What would I do differently next time? Would I use this activity again? If the lesson, or unit, went really well, what were the factors that led to that positive outcome?

Engaging in serious thought about your teaching and working toward your own growth as a teacher is called *reflective practice*. The most important source of feedback is your pupils; they will let you know in both overt and subtle ways whether they are engaged and learning and whether the classroom is a pleasant and productive place for them. The outcomes of pupil assessment will also provide important data. Feedback from parents and from observations of administrators or colleagues are also useful and should be taken seriously. Your reflection on and response to all of these can be recorded in your journal. The amount of time you spend on your journal will depend on your writing style as well as the time you can devote to it; notes can be as useful as well crafted sentences. The important thing is to do it.

◆ SUMMARY

All classroom activity, including assessment, should be directed toward helping pupils achieve appropriate cognitive, affective, psychomotor, and social goals. Diverse data collection methods are replacing the traditional reliance on multiple-choice and other short-answer tests because of the limited ability of the traditional methods to measure many important educational objectives. A number of appropriate methods are available for assessing growth and achievement in elementary science. Foremost among these is the workbook that records what students do, what they find out, and what they have learned from and think about the experience. Workbooks provide a means of feedback to pupils as well as a means of keeping the teacher informed about pupil progress toward meeting learning objectives. Performance assessment is another method of letting pupils show what they have learned and whether they can put knowledge to practical use. Other methods of assessment are portfolios and products. These methods can be modified as appropriate for students with disabilities or limited language proficiency. Including pupils in the assessment process in appropriate ways can help them to become independent learners who can take responsibility for their own learning.

Communicating results to pupils, parents, or caretakers and others is the final step in assessment. Ongoing communication with pupils lets them know whether they are meeting expectations and how to improve their performance if expectations are not being met. Grading for report cards should be a process that begins at the start of each grading period and includes setting and communicating clear objectives, developing ways to assess attainment of objectives, gathering data, and compiling it to form a comprehensive index of achievement. The final step in assessment is self-assessment, a crucial part of reflective practice. Assessment remains a demanding and complex part of teaching, and teachers still have to grapple with many unanswered questions.

◆ ACTIVITIES FOR THE READER

1. Develop performance assessments for three additional objectives in the electricity unit.
2. Develop a list of items to be included in a fifth grader's science portfolio, covering one grading period, or about eight to ten weeks.
3. If your instructor has not assigned portfolios as a means of assessment in this course, develop a list of items that you would include in such a portfolio, and design rubrics for grading the portfolio.

◆ QUESTIONS FOR DISCUSSION

1. Should effort be included as a grading factor? Assume two students demonstrate the same level of achievement, but you know that one had to work much harder to reach that level. Should they both receive the same grade?

2. Should homework be graded and included in the composite grade? We know that some parents do homework for their children, others help their children, and others leave the children to do homework alone. On the other hand, if homework is not graded and taken into account, children tend to ignore it. What is the fair way to handle this?

3. Should growth or achievement be the more important factor in assigning a grade?

4. On what bases would you like to be graded in this course?

◆ REFERENCES

Collins, A. (1992). Portfolios for science education. *Science Education, 76,* 451–463.

Kamen, M. (1996). A teacher's implementation of authentic assessment in an elementary science classroom. *Journal of Research in Science Teaching, 33,* 859–877.

Stiggins, R. (1994). *Student-centered classroom assessment.* Upper Saddle River, NJ: Merrill/ Prentice Hall.

National Research Council. (1996). *National science education standards.* Washington, DC: National Academy Press.

6

Direct Instruction

This chapter describes a method of planning and presenting lessons called direct instruction, also known as direct teaching and teacher-centered instruction. A direct instruction lesson comprises specific types of activity that are carried out in a specific sequence. Using this structure ensures inclusion of many important elements of lesson presentation. Because decisions about structure are made during the planning stage, the number of instructional decisions the teacher must make during the progress of the lesson is greatly reduced. Direct instruction works well for many lesson topics and is much favored by administrators for two reasons: It is relatively easy to learn, and it can be used effectively by beginning teachers.

Direct instruction is the use of the traditional methods of lecture, demonstration, seat work, recitation, and feedback. The method is sometimes referred to as teacher-centered instruction because virtually all the instructional decisions are made by the teacher. The level of pupil self-direction is low. Pupils are generally not free to pace their own learning, to move about the room, to discuss their work with other pupils, or to follow up interesting ideas they come across in the course of the lesson. When this kind of lesson is operating as planned, the pupils' attention is focused on the lesson objective as determined by the teacher. Thus, direct instruction constitutes a series of actions taken by the teacher to bring about a predetermined learning outcome. This method is not to be confused with simply talking to pupils or what may be called "discussing a topic" when all the discussion is actually teacher talk.

Research on Effective Teaching

Researchers have attempted to discover relationships between what teachers do and how well students learn. Many studies have used achievement (gains made by students on tests of content) as the indicator of learning; these studies are called teacher-effectiveness research. From this work, a consensus has emerged about the most effective behaviors for teachers to employ in teaching basic skills in the early grades. In a comprehensive review of more than 200 such studies, Brophy and Good (1987) summarized the findings as follows: At least two common themes cut across the findings. One is that academic learning is influenced by the amount of time students spend in appropriate academic tasks. The second is that students learn more effectively when their teachers first structure new information for them and help them relate it to what they already know, and then monitor their performance and provide corrective feedback during recitation, drill, practice, or application activities (p. 366).

The second theme implies these steps in a direct instruction lesson: review of previous related material, presentation of new skill or content, guided practice, independent practice, and closure. The specific sequence of these steps (described more fully later in this chapter) is called the *direct instruction model*. There is general agreement among researchers that using this model is more effective than using individualized or discovery methods for teaching basic skills in fourth grade and below

(Rosenshine & Stevens, 1987). Thus, explicit teaching is clearly appropriate when the objective is a straightforward skill and the pupil is young. A straightforward skill is one that can be taught in a step-by-step manner and reinforced by practice and application. In reading and mathematics, the subjects in which most of the teacher-effectiveness research has been carried out, basic skills are easy to identify. In mathematics, basic skills include multiplication facts (such as 5 times 5) and the use of a multiplication method, or algorithm, for computation involving numbers larger than 10. Some mathematics skills that are beyond the basics include estimating and problem solving. In reading, basic skills include word attack, as compared to comprehension, which is a higher-level skill. In science, identifying basic skills proves more difficult, because science is less hierarchical and sequential than either reading or mathematics. Many science educators would agree, however, on two areas of science instruction that could be called basic skills, and thus these two are taught effectively by the direct instruction model: (1) learning to use tools and equipment and (2) learning certain processes such as measuring or writing reports. Both of these are needed for later application in science activities.

Research shows that well-organized teachers are more effective than others. One of the most interesting and important studies of the relation of teacher behavior to pupil achievement was carried out in Texas in the early 1970s (Brophy & Evertson, 1976). Pupil achievement data for three consecutive years were obtained for a large sample of second- and third-grade teachers. Those teachers whose pupils consistently showed gains in achievement were studied through many hours of careful classroom observation as well as through individual interviews. Researchers found that these effective teachers were businesslike and task-oriented and that they demanded that their pupils spend their class time engaged in learning activities. They tended to maintain well-organized classrooms and to plan activities on a daily basis. Since their activities were well prepared, the class ran smoothly with few interruptions and little time lost in confusion or aimless activity. When some pupils found the activities too difficult or could not keep up, these teachers often prepared special materials for them. Likewise, the teachers provided additional activities for pupils who finished early. These teachers spent a minimum of time in getting the class started, in transitions, and in bringing closure at the end of the lesson. To sum up, these teachers were prepared to start on time, to move right into the lesson, to provide materials needed for pupils to engage in the learning activities, and to take care of special needs of individuals.

Time spent in preparation allows a teacher to spend class time in effective and productive teaching. Although this kind of preparation takes considerable time and energy, a well-prepared teacher is not as tired at the end of the day as one who is poorly prepared. Consider two teachers: one who is and one who is not well prepared. The poorly prepared teacher has to rush around at the last minute gathering materials and making copies of worksheets while pupils are left with nothing to do. The class is off to a poor start and nothing seems to work right. There are many behavior problems. This teacher goes home exhausted while the teacher who was prepared goes home tired but satisfied that the class is doing well.

PLANNING AND PRESENTING A DIRECT INSTRUCTION LESSON

As mentioned, the usefulness of direct instruction for science is limited, mostly to teaching specific, stepwise procedures—how to use equipment, for example. Learning to construct and use graphs is another example. There are also times when specific procedures for an activity or specific behaviors, such as how to clean an animal cage, call for direct instruction. Procedural learning of this type constitutes only a small percentage of instruction in any science program. Additionally, some science procedures may be less clear-cut, and these could be presented either directly or indirectly. Most science instruction should be more interactive and inquiry-based, but the direct instruction model has its uses. It is an excellent device for beginning teachers to learn how to plan a well-structured lesson. An understanding of the direct instruction model and the interrelation of its elements provides the beginning teacher with a reasonable basis from which to understand other more complex models that will be described later.

Several main parts make up a direct instruction lesson plan. Each will be briefly described. Then a structured lesson plan for the balance lesson will be described. Finally, the idea of each component will be explained in more detail. First, though, read a general description of one of Ms. Oldhand's lessons.

◆ MS. OLDHAND'S BALANCE LESSON

In this lesson, Ms. Oldhand's second-grade pupils learned to use an equal-arm pan balance, also called a beam balance. Although the balance is an interesting example of a lever, in this lesson, Ms. Oldhand mainly wanted her pupils to learn to use the balance as a tool. Later, the pupils will need to use the balance to compare and measure weights of objects.

To save space, the balances were stored disassembled in boxes. In this lesson, Ms. Oldhand wanted each pupil to learn to put a balance together, learn the names of the parts, and get the general idea of how the balance works when objects are placed in the pans.

First, she showed the class how to put a balance together, explaining each step and naming the parts as she did so. Next, she showed them what happens when objects are placed in the pans. Then she asked individual pupils to come to the front of the class to try doing these things themselves. They came one at a time, and their work was watched by the others and closely monitored by Ms. Oldhand. When a problem arose, the pupils were helped in some way so that each mistake was gently corrected before the next step was taken. Then all the children had a chance to practice the new skills at their desks. Today, Ms. Oldhand decided to have them work in pairs. As they worked, she circulated to help as needed—to encourage, to acknowledge accomplishments, and to provide special advanced tasks for those who finished early.

A teacher begins a direct instruction lesson by explaining what the pupils are to learn.

Lesson Plan Parts

A direct instruction lesson plan has eight main parts. As you read the description of each part, think about Ms. Oldhand's balance lesson. Can you decide what would be written for each of these parts?

1. *Objective(s).* Statement of what the pupils will know or be able to do after the lesson that they did not know or could not do before.
2. *Materials.* List of materials that must be prepared or assembled for the lesson.
3. *Motivation.* What the teacher does to create interest or focus attention at the beginning of the lesson.
4. *Learning activities.*

   a. *Presentation.* What the teacher does to give information on how to meet the lesson objectives. Presentation is usually accomplished by showing, telling, or both.

   b. *Guided practice.* What the teacher does to provide closely supervised practice on the lesson objectives with immediate feedback on correctness. Guided practice is normally done one pupil at a time, with the others observing both the practice and the teacher feedback.

c. *Independent practice.* What the teacher does to provide independent practice for all the pupils at once. Teacher supervision is individualized.

d. *Closure.* What the teacher does to close the lesson. For closure, a teacher may decide to review, summarize, relate to previous lessons, or otherwise pull the lesson together.

5. *Assessment.* What the teacher does to evaluate whether the lesson was a success.

In addition to these eight main parts for the direct instruction lesson plan, additional parts may be added for clarity. In Lesson Plan 6.1, given here as an example, the grade level, a descriptive topic title, and a materials preparation statement are examples of optional lesson-plan parts. Also useful for inclusion is a statement of the National Science Education (NSE) standard that the lesson will meet.

LESSON PLAN 6.1

LEARNING TO USE THE BEAM BALANCE

NSE STANDARD

Employ simple equipment and tools to gather data and extend the senses. Includes using beam balance (National Research Council, 1996, p. 122).

GRADE LEVEL: 2

STUDENT OBJECTIVES

By the end of these activities, the pupil will be able to:

1. Assemble a pan balance from provided components.
2. Identify and name the parts of the balance: base, support, fulcrum, beam, and pans.
3. Describe the general behavior of the pan balance when objects are put into and taken out of the pans, such as "When one pan goes up, the other goes down" or "You can make the beam even by adding to the high pan or taking away from the low pan."

MATERIALS

For the teacher:

Parts for one pan balance
Several one-inch cube blocks

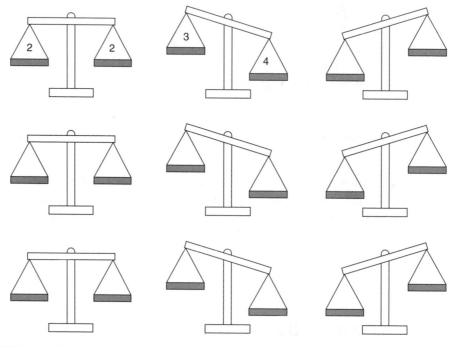

FIGURE 6.1   A Balance Worksheet

For each pair of pupils:

    Parts for one balance
    Ten one-inch blocks
    Two balance worksheets (see Figure 6.1)

MATERIALS PREPARATION

Place materials at each double desk during lunch or recess. When pupils return, have them sit on the front rug.

MOTIVATION

Ask whether pupils have ever played on a seesaw or teeter-totter. Ask what happened if a heavy child and a light child tried to seesaw together. "If you didn't know who was heavier, how could you find out with a seesaw? Today you will learn about a pan balance, a science tool something like a seesaw. We can use it to find out which things are lighter and which are heavier."

LEARNING ACTIVITIES

Presentation

1. Teacher demonstration: "Watch very closely while I show you how to put your pan balance together." Name the parts as you put the balance together (base, support, fulcrum, beam, pans).
2. When assembly is complete, hold a block over one pan. Ask, "What do you think will happen to the beam?" Take a few responses without comment, and then place the block in the pan. Continue adding blocks to alternate pans. Ask, "Who wants to predict what will happen when I put this on the pan?" Then, without comment, do it.
3. Write the names of the balance parts on the board, and go over them with the class.

Guided Practice

1. Take the demonstration balance apart. Hold up the parts one at a time, and ask for their names. Ask a pupil to come up and do a step of the assembly job and to describe the assembly activity using the correct names of parts. Continue by asking, "Who can show us the next step?" If someone has trouble, ask another pupil to help. As a last resort, do the assembly yourself, using the names of parts in clear, direct sentences.
2. Ask questions about the behavior of the balance, such as, "Who can tell how to make the balance go down on this side?" (Up on this side, down on the other side, etc.) Regardless of answer, have that child come up and do what he or she suggested.

   The balance will provide feedback. "Who can make the balance beam even? Is there another way to make the beam even?" Ask pupils to use the names of the balance parts as they demonstrate. Correct any incorrect naming of parts.

3. During part 2 of guided practice, begin drawing sketches of balances on the board to show the actions demonstrated.

Independent Practice

1. Prepare the pupils to return to their desks by giving directions for the seat work. Hand out a worksheet to each pupil, and explain how it corresponds to the diagrams drawn on the board. The worksheet consists of diagrams of balances in left-pan-up, right-pan-up, and even-beam positions (several of each). Explain that each student will work with a partner to put the balance together and then to make the balance look like the pictures by adding or removing blocks. They should record their work by writing a number in the pan of each diagram to show how many blocks were required to make the balance look that way.
2. Give a prearranged signal for the pupils to return to their seats. As they work, circulate to help as needed.

Closure

Give the signal for attention. Announce that time is up for the lesson and that more balance work will continue later in the week. Ask the pupils to take the balances apart and put the parts in the box. When this is done, the table monitors should collect the boxes.

ASSESSMENT

Informal observation during the independent practice and responses on the worksheets will provide information for deciding whether the objectives have been met.

Explanation of Lesson Plan

In this section, the parts of the lesson plan are explained in some detail, each part supported by research and expert opinion. The lesson-plan parts fall into two different categories: sequencers and organizers. Sequencers include motivation, presentation, guided practice, independent practice, and closure, all of which are bound together in a time sequence and occur one after another. Sequencers can also be called learning activities. By contrast, the organizers—performance objectives, materials, and assessment—are not together as a sequence; rather, they help the teacher organize thoughts about the total lesson. The performance objective and materials parts generally are not things the teacher "does." The assessment is something the teacher does, but the time in which assessment happens is not fixed. It may occur simultaneously with other lesson parts, afterward, or both. All the parts have a strong and necessary relationship to one another.

Objective(s)

The point of stating the objectives as pupil performance or behavior is to make them observable and therefore easier to appraise. Not all the behaviors that pupils do during a lesson, though, need to be significant new abilities. Many desirable pupil behaviors are simply procedural; that is, the behaviors do not indicate new abilities but are simply "housekeeping" actions necessary to the progress of the lesson. Examples of procedural (or nonsubstantive) behaviors in the balance lesson are

Sitting on the front rug

Discussing the activity with a partner

Taking the balance apart

Passing the boxes to the end of the table

All of these behaviors are important to the lesson's progress but are not in themselves new abilities acquired as a result of the lesson activities.

Materials

What materials would be most effective for your objectives? What quantities would be optimal? The ideal should be considered first. Then, if there are constraints, adjustments can be made with the conscious recognition of the compromise being made. In the balance lesson, Ms. Oldhand decided to have her pupils work in pairs because she wanted to encourage pupil-to-pupil interactions, not because there was a shortage of balances. Suppose she had decided that it was important for every pupil to work alone with a balance, but she had only ten balances. She could have chosen to do the lesson with successive groups of ten while the other pupils did something else. After you have decided what and how many materials you will use, list them in a way that helps you organize for teaching. You will find that designating the number of each material needed is a helpful way to plan. Notice how this was done in the balance plan.

The one-inch blocks used in the balance lesson were selected because they were simple, uniform, and available. Many primary classrooms have such blocks. If they had not been available, Ms. Oldhand could have used any uniform objects, such as washers, nails, or checkers.

Motivation

Some educators call this part motivation/review. Review is an important way to focus pupils at the beginning of a lesson that is one of a continuing series of lessons. The balance lesson example was the first lesson on that topic, so there was no preceding lesson to review. Instead, the teacher used two other techniques to focus attention and set a meaningful context for what was to follow. First, she asked the children to recall a previous experience. She figured there was a good chance that most of the children had played on a seesaw because their small town had seesaws in the public park. An assumption of this sort is becoming less and less certain, however. As the United States becomes more urbanized and the school population becomes more diverse socioeconomically and ethnically, it becomes harder to be sure that all pupils share any particular experience from outside school. Ms. Oldhand used another technique, just in case. She used an actual balance to show as well as tell.

In the example lesson, the use of a real balance for demonstration does not seem remarkable. Especially with young children, teachers use real objects often. In fact, in almost every lesson with learners of any age, real materials are highly effective as a motivational or focusing device. Many adults have a hard time remembering what it was like not to know about some common object or experience. For any new information to be meaningful, it must be "hooked on" to an older understanding. This is true even for adults, but adults have a rich store of previous experiences to form a context for understanding new information. The more removed from a person's past experience a bit of new information is, the harder it will be for that person to understand. Imagine how relatively poor a child's experience base is, compared to an adult's. There simply has not been time to build up many experiences. Because of a child's inexperience, a lesson is more effective if real things are used to provide a first-hand experience.

Once teachers know that all the children in their classes have had a certain experience, they can call up the pupils' memory with less tangible stimuli, perhaps even with words alone. In any case, the motivation part of the lesson should be short, and the pacing should be fast.

Learning Activities

Presentation. There are three characteristics of effective presentation: clarity, focus on the objective, and brevity (Smith & Land, 1981). One of the most consistent research findings is that students learn more when teachers give clear explanations than when teachers offer vague, fuzzy, and disconnected presentations. Teachers who interrupt themselves—who overuse "uh," "OK," "you know," and other such mannerisms—distract their pupils. The pupils shift their focus from the lesson objectives to the mannerisms. The following excerpt from a tape recording of a beginning teacher will illustrate the point:

> This lesson is—well—is going to be—about measuring liquids—some liquids, of course, not all liquids. We—well, actually, you, will measure the volume of liquids that—uh—I have prepared today. OK? First, though, I have to tell you what a liquid is—that is—if you don't already know.

Pupils cannot learn to do the lesson objective unless the teacher can create and maintain their focus on that objective. To do this, the teacher must focus on the new skill or concept that constitutes the objective. Digressions (jumping ahead and backing up) and ambiguous phrases distract pupils from the main point and confuse them.

Brevity is especially important. If the teacher remembers while planning the lesson to keep the presentation as short as possible, clarity and focus will probably be maintained. Attention span is almost always shorter than one might think—better to underestimate than overestimate it.

With primary pupils, brevity and clarity are even more important. The teacher should directly tell and show with a minimum of asking. The pupils do not know how to do the objective; thus, time and clarity should not be compromised on trying to elicit answers during the presentation. (If pupils can already do the objective, then the objective needs to be revised.) Instead, show and tell directly and briefly; then move into the guided practice. These guidelines, partly developed from a summary of research (Rosenshine & Stevens, 1987), may be helpful:

- ◆ Start with an example or a demonstration, not with a definition. A definition is meaningless until some understanding of the skill or concept has been attained.

- ◆ Use examples or demonstrations that are simple. Above all, they should not be harder to understand than the skill or concept you are trying to teach. Examples must be concrete and must already be familiar and well understood.

- ◆ Present material in small steps. Stop frequently to check for understanding.

Model the objective whenever possible—show your pupils what you want them to learn. Showing is always better than telling, though the combination of showing and telling makes things easier to remember than either showing or telling alone.

Guided practice. The main purpose of this part of a direct instruction lesson is to provide an opportunity for pupils to practice a new skill in a controlled environment, where mistakes can be corrected and gaps in understanding can be identified. Consider guided practice in a piano lesson: The piano teacher shows the pupil how a passage should be played, the pupil tries it out while the teacher watches, the teacher gives feedback and corrects any mistakes, the pupil goes home to practice, and the pupil finally comes back to the teacher to demonstrate that he or she has learned how to play the piece. Guided practice in science in a classroom may not look like this example, but there are a number of similarities. In one class, the teacher asks questions, gives cues or help as needed, and gently corrects errors. In another class, pupils work problems at the board under the teacher's guidance or come to the front of the room to try out a new skill while the teacher gives help and feedback. A secondary purpose of guided practice is to provide the teacher with feedback on how the presentation was understood, or rather, how it was misunderstood. By sampling the class for misunderstandings, the teacher can refine and modify the presentation to correct those misunderstandings. Identifying incomplete or otherwise faulty comprehension of the presented content is a positive and desirable part of the lesson, as much a part of the learning as any other component of the lesson.

One of the fine points of teaching is learning to judge the most effective way to give feedback and correct errors. On the one hand, the teacher must provide clear, unmistakable guidance—a pupil must not be permitted to leave this part of the lesson with an uncorrected error. On the other hand, the teacher must be sure that the pupils are not embarrassed to make mistakes and be corrected. They must be guided toward the objective skill or concept in a manner that will ensure a high success rate. The objective is practiced until the teacher is satisfied that most of the pupils can do the work on their own with a reasonable expectation of success. Only then does the teacher move on to independent practice. Guided practice should not be as brief as the preceding parts but should not be any longer than absolutely necessary, because pupil involvement in this part is relatively low.

Although the guided practice part is described separately from the presentation part, in actual practice, there may be some overlap between the two. Most lessons have more than one important point. The lesson should be organized so that one point is practiced and understood before moving on to the next step. This means that there may be several periods of guided practice, questions, and discussion within one lesson. Notice how guided practice was used in the balance lesson. Also, when pupil responses show misunderstandings, the teacher often chooses to repeat the presentation in a shortened and modified form to clarify particular points needing more emphasis.

Independent practice. Up to this point in the lesson, the pupil involvement has been relatively low. The teacher has been showing and telling, asking questions to the whole class (questions answered by only one child at a time), and having one pupil at a time perform guided practice. Independent practice provides a time for every child in the class to be involved to a much greater extent. To be effective, independent practice must provide each child opportunity to think about, try out, rehearse, apply, or otherwise internalize the new skill or concept set forth in the lesson objective. An independent practice that lets pupils practice the skill ten times is more effective than one that lets them practice it five times. Practice means multiple applications or trials.

Before setting the class to work on this part of the lesson, the teacher must give clear directions and be sure that everyone understands what is to be done and what kind of general behavior is expected. At all times during a lesson, all pupils should understand what they are supposed to be doing, and this is especially true during independent practice. Depending on the complexity of the task and on the maturity of the pupils, procedural directions for going about the task may be presented as a series of steps during the guided practice part of the lesson. The teacher who does not think through the planning of this part will have to interrupt the pupils after they have started in order to clarify the procedure and give further directions. This is another example of distraction from the main objective and should be avoided if at all possible.

An example from the balance lesson may clarify the difference between the substantive learning tasks and the procedural tasks of going about the independent practice. The substantive task (in every lesson) is to practice the new skills or ideas; in this case, it is to put the balance together, learn the names of the parts, and recognize how to produce certain positions by placing objects in the pans (see the lesson objectives). The procedural task is how to go about doing the practice. A portion of directions given by the teacher might be something like this:

> Listen carefully so you will know what to do. Stay on the rug until I give the signal. First, you will return to your seats. Then you will work with your partner to put your balance together. Look at my balance to see how it goes together. [Give each child a worksheet.] Look at the pictures. Your job is to find how many blocks it takes in each pan to make the balance look like each picture. When you find out, write the number on your paper to show how many blocks you used. Let's do the first one together. [Teacher shows with demonstration balance.] Now, how many blocks are in this pan? [One.] Fine. Now write a "one" there on your paper. How many blocks in the other pan? [None.] OK. Then write a zero on that pan. You may talk quietly with your partner, but please do not leave your seat. If you need help, raise your hand. Who remembers the first thing you will do? [And so on.]

In this example, the independent practice involved working with a partner using real objects. Sometimes the work will be only paperwork, and sometimes the work will be done alone or with larger groups. In every case, the level of engagement will be high. Each pupil will be doing things directly and actively—more so than at any other time in the lesson. For this reason, independent practice should get the lion's share of the lesson time.

The teacher is also active during this part of the lesson—walking around, noticing who is having trouble, giving advice as needed, providing a word of praise here

Independent practice on the equal arm balance engages children's full attention.

or there, and speaking to any pupil who is not being productive. Comments are made quietly to individuals and only as needed, without interrupting the whole class. The effective teacher knows when to be quiet and let the pupils work.

Closure. To bring closure means to end the lesson in an orderly way, usually with a short summary or reminder of what the lesson was about. Time should be allowed for materials to be put away by the children, for things to be turned in if necessary, and possibly for questions and comments from the pupils about the lesson. If there is to be a related lesson at a later time, the teacher may choose to mention this briefly. Closure functions to "clear the decks" for the next lesson or activity in a logical and orderly fashion.

Assessment

How does a teacher recognize a successful lesson? If, on the whole, the pupils can do the objective behaviors, then the lesson is a success. The importance of stating worthwhile objectives clearly becomes more apparent in this context. The clearer the statement of the objective, the easier assessment is. It is often not possible to make a thorough and systematic evaluation of each student during the course of a lesson. The main need at this time is to determine whether enough of the pupils "got it" to continue with the next lesson of the unit or sequence, or whether the lesson "bombed" and needs rethinking, replanning, and reteaching.

Lesson assessment is not so much evaluation of the pupils as it is self-evaluation by the teacher. If the lesson failed, what was the reason? Was it too hard for the pupils? Maybe it was too easy. Boredom with overly easy tasks can result in misbehavior. Was something overlooked? Were behavior standards appropriate for the type of activity? When a lesson fails, the teacher must take the responsibility to decide what went wrong and to correct the problem in the next lesson.

In the sample lesson, assessment was done by informal observation and by checking the worksheets. Informal observation can be done fairly easily when the pupils are working with concrete materials. Ms. Oldhand will notice which pairs are having trouble putting their balances together as she circulates during the independent practice. Seldom is it necessary to have an activity separate from the learning activities to decide whether the lesson was successful. In the balance lesson, Ms. Oldhand is appraising at the same time that the pupils are learning. In this case, her informal observations are augmented by checking the worksheets. The pupils' responses there will tell her who understands how to get the balance to do various things.

◆   Mr. Newman observed the balance lesson in Ms. Oldhand's classroom, and the two discussed it after the pupils left for the day.

MR. NEWMAN: I noticed that you laid out the balances on the desks before the children came back from lunch. Why didn't you just let them pick them up after the guided practice?

MS. OLDHAND: Well, I do want them to learn to manage their materials eventually. I just thought it would be too much for them to handle this first time. I did have them take care of cleanup. Next time we use the balances, I'll let them do the whole thing. Today, the lesson was just about the right length of time. Any more would have taken too long, and they might not have had time to finish.

MR. NEWMAN: Why did you have them come up to the front rug? Couldn't you show them just as well if they were in their seats?

MS. OLDHAND: Not really. These children are only seven years old, remember. They wouldn't have the maturity to ignore the materials on their desks while we did the first parts of the lesson. Something I learned the hard way was never to expect children to pay attention or listen when interesting materials are within reach. Come to think of it, that's pretty hard even for grown-ups.

A Postscript on Preparation

When a beginning teacher observes an experienced teacher conduct a lesson that flows smoothly with few interruptions and little off-task behavior, the novice is often unaware of the amount of planning and preparation that have gone into the lesson. Although experienced teachers seldom need the detailed lesson plans that student teachers are required to make, inquiry will reveal that the experienced teacher is clear about what to do, how to do it, and what the expectations for the pupils are. The student teacher, because of inexperience, needs to think specifically about all these details in advance, to reduce the number of unpleasant surprises during the lesson to a minimum. The lesson plan helps to structure this specific thinking. A well-designed lesson plan, backed up by well-prepared materials, gives the inexperienced teacher a feeling of confidence and of being in control that is communicated to pupils and prevents many of the behavior problems that new teachers dread.

◆ A LESSON ON LINE GRAPHING

Ms. Oldhand was planning a lesson for her sixth graders to introduce them to line graphing. Line graphs are a powerful means of displaying information. Patterns and trends that are difficult to discern by looking at raw data become immediately apparent when presented in graphic form. Learning to construct and interpret graphs is an essential element of scientific literacy, since graphs appear frequently in newspapers, magazines, television programs, and other means of mass communication.

The pupils in Ms. Oldhand's class had done many bar graphs and recently learned about circle graphs. Ms. Oldhand carefully developed the pupils' understanding of how to make and use these types of graphs, and when to select one over the other for a particular purpose. They knew, for example, that bar graphs are useful for showing distributions of things or events (e.g., how many of their birthdays fall on each month of the year) or for indicating which kinds of animals are most popular as pets. They also understood that circle, or "pie," graphs are useful to show the percentages of different parts that go together to make up a whole object, class, or situation. For example, one of the circle graphs they constructed showed the different percentages of pupils in the class who walk to school, who ride bikes, and who come by private car, by school bus, and by city bus.

In this lesson, Ms. Oldhand helped the pupils learn to make line graphs. Because this is the first lesson on line graphs, she didn't try to teach them everything there is to know about the topic. Many of the technical details were simplified by the way the task was presented. Ms. Oldhand didn't expect the pupils to learn how to figure a scale (how many units of measure to represent by one square on the grid). She didn't expect them to understand or remember the names for the kinds of variables (independent and dependent), and she didn't expect them to use the terms x-axis and y-axis at this time. Ms. Oldhand simply provided other details of this kind during this first lesson on line graphing, so that the amount of new material to master was not overwhelming. As sixth graders, Ms. Oldhand's pupils already knew a great many prerequisites for this lesson. In addition to knowing about other kinds of graphs, they were familiar with ordered pairs of numbers, number lines, and counting by twos, fives, tens, and hundreds. They also knew how to use the metric system for simple measurements.

In a recent science activity, the pupils collected data on how high balls bounce when dropped from certain heights. Ms. Oldhand used that experience to make the introduction to line graphing more concrete. Her main goal for the lesson was for the pupils to see and appreciate the line graph as a powerful tool for communicating information and predicting what would be shown if additional data were available.

Three different situations were used for graphing in this lesson. First, during the presentation, Ms. Oldhand showed the class how to make a line graph using data the pupils had collected earlier on the bounciness of a table-tennis ball. Then for guided practice, she showed them a setup for testing how much a rubber band is stretched when weights are added. With data previously collected on the stretching setup, Ms. Oldhand guided the pupils to make a class graph using the overhead projector. Finally, she distributed a worksheet for independent practice. It consisted of a labeled grid, a set of data for graphing, and some questions. The pupils were to graph the data on the grid and then use the graph to answer the questions. The subject of the graph, the growth of a plant, was new to the pupils.

The following lesson plan can be adapted as an in-class activity for professional development of preservice and in-service teachers.

LESSON PLAN 6.2

COMMUNICATING AND PREDICTING WITH LINE GRAPHS

NSE STANDARDS FOR GRADES 5 TO 8

Use mathematics to present, organize, and interpret data (National Research Council, 1996, p. 148).

GRADE LEVEL: 6

GOAL

Learn to construct and interpret line graphs.

STUDENT OBJECTIVES

At the end of this lesson, the pupil will be able to

1. Locate points on a grid to represent pairs of observations.
2. Connect the located points with a smooth line.
3. Describe an unfamiliar system from a graph of that system.
4. Make predictions using a line graph.

MATERIALS

For the teacher:

Overhead projector
Grid transparencies (labeled but not plotted)
    a. Bounciness (see Figure 6.2)
    b. Stretchiness of rubber band (see Figure 6.4)
Transparency marker
Two meter sticks
One table-tennis ball
A rubber band stretcher (see Figure 6.3)
Bounciness data (see Table 6.1)
Rubber band data (see Table 6.2)

For each pupil:

One plant growth worksheet (see Figure 6.5)
One worksheet with questions (see Figure 6.6)

MATERIALS PREPARATION

1. Tape two meter sticks to the wall vertically, one above the other, to measure distances from the floor. Both sticks should have the low numbers below the high numbers. (Add 100 to readings of the upper stick.)
2. Set up a rubber band stretcher as shown in Figure 6.3. Add weights and record data for the guided practice activity. Short rubber bands approach the limit of their elasticity sooner than long ones and are thus better for this lesson. This must be done well ahead of time, because this is where you get the data for making the transparency (see Figure 6.4). Use the same setup and the same rubber band for the class activity.

MOTIVATION

Explain to students, "Yesterday you collected data on how high different balls bounce when you drop them from certain heights. Do you remember that I asked you to use only those heights on the chart and not to do any extras? Well, today you will find out why. I will show you how scientists are able to predict the future. Then you should be able to do it yourselves! You will check out your amazing new powers by predicting how high a ball will bounce from some of those drop heights you didn't try yesterday, and then we will test your predictions."

LEARNING ACTIVITIES

Presentation

1. "We will be using a powerful tool called a line graph. The line graph is like the bar graph in some ways."

2. Turn on the overhead projector to show the grid labeled "Bounciness" (Figure 6.2). "I will show you how it works." Point to locations on the projection as they are mentioned. "A line graph has two number lines. The number line across the bottom here includes all the values for the drop heights we want to consider. The other number line is a vertical one going up the left side. It includes all the bounce heights we are interested in, not only what we observed but also a range where our predictions will fall. Now take a look at this data table for the table-tennis ball. See how the observations go in pairs? For every drop height we observed, we also observed a bounce height. The line graph lets you show a pair of observations as a single point. To locate the point for this first number pair, we go across on the drop height number line until we come to 40 cm. Then we go straight up until we come to the line extending from the second number of the number pair, 27, on the bounce height number line. Where these two lines intersect is our point." Make a fat dot to mark the point. Continue in this manner for the other number pairs.

3. "When you find and mark a point like this, it's called plotting the point." Continue to show and tell until all the points are plotted. "The points are sometimes called 'plots.' Let's look at the points we've plotted. Do they seem to have any pattern or regularity?" Pause. "Let's connect them and see." Draw a smooth curve through the dots. "You know about the bouncing ball system because you collected the data. But just looking at the data, can you describe the system?" Take a few comments but move on rather quickly, because this is not the time for a real discussion. Mention the following generalizations if they are not forthcoming:

   a. The greater the drop height, the greater the bounce height.

   b. The line looks straight at the beginning, but begins to level off at the end. This means that the bounciness of the table-tennis ball stays steady for a while and then begins to decrease.

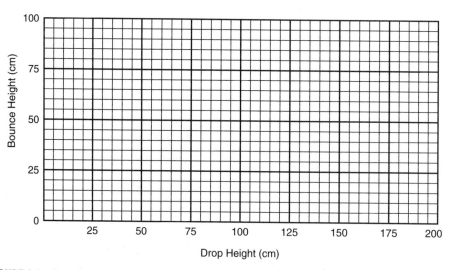

FIGURE 6.2   Bounciness of Table-Tennis Ball

TABLE 6.1 Table-Tennis Ball Bounciness Data

Drop Height (cm)	Bounce Height (cm)
40	27
60	40
100	54
120	63
140	72
200	85

4. Show them how to predict the bounce height for a drop height of 80 cm and 170 cm. "Find 80 on the drop height number line, from there go straight up until you reach the line we drew to connect plots, and then go directly left to the bounce height number line. The reading there should be the bounce height. Enter the drop heights in the blank spaces of the table of bounciness data [Table 6.1]. Then enter the values predicted from the graph on the table, but put parentheses around them."

5. "Now for the moment of truth! Will our prediction work?" Hold the table-tennis ball 80 cm from the floor (next to the 80-cm mark of the meter rulers taped to the wall), release it, and observe the bounce height. Repeat the procedure at the 170-cm mark.

Guided Practice

1. "Now we are going to try something new." Show the rubber band stretching setup (Figure 6.3). "I want you to see how this works. We have a rubber band attached to the support. There is a bent paper clip on the other end, so we can hook a paper cup onto it. Into the paper cup we'll put equal weights—in this case, washers. With no washers in the cup, I'll set the ruler so that zero is at the bottom of the rubber band. When I add a washer, the rubber band stretches down to [read measurement on the ruler]. I think you can guess that if I add more washers the rubber band will tend to stretch more and more. But I'm not going to show you all of the data-collecting procedure just now. Instead, I'm going to put up a chart [Table 6.2] with the results I got when I did it last night. Then we will all make a graph together using the data."

2. Project the transparency of the labeled grid (Figure 6.4) on the chalkboard. Lines and labels will be pale but visible. Ask a pupil to come up and plot the first ordered pair of observations on the projected grid by drawing on the chalkboard. Continue with other pupils for the remaining points. Be sure the pupils remember to move "over and up" and to locate points on lines rather than between them.

3. When all measurements are plotted, have the next pupil draw a smooth line to connect the points.

FIGURE 6.3   A Rubber Band Stretcher

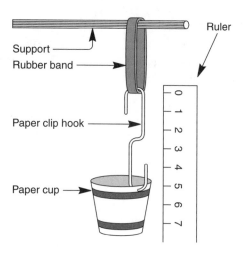

TABLE 6.2   Rubber Band Stretch Data

Number of Washers	Rubber Band Length (cm)
0	0.0
5	2.0
10	6.0
15	10.0
20	13.5
25	15.5
30	17.5
35	18.5
40	19.0

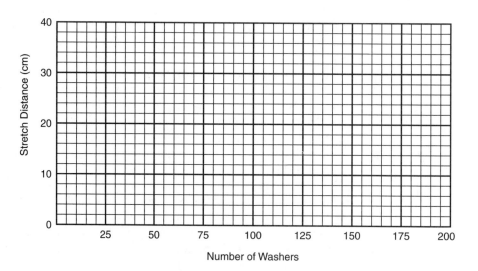

FIGURE 6.4   Stretchiness of Rubber Band

134

4. Get predictions from several intermediate points on the graph. Get a prediction for one point beyond the observations.
5. Discuss their predictions, and then check the predictions by demonstrating with the rubber band setup.

Independent Practice

1. Distribute the plant growth worksheet (labeled Growth of Mystery Plant, Figure 6.5), and give directions. Point out the days number line across the bot-

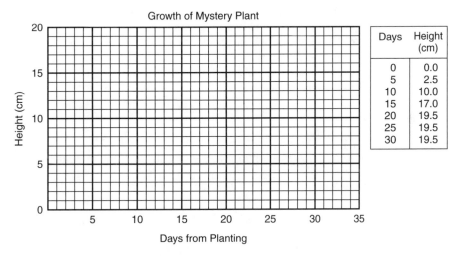

Days	Height (cm)
0	0.0
5	2.5
10	10.0
15	17.0
20	19.5
25	19.5
30	19.5

FIGURE 6.5 Worksheet Grid and Data

FIGURE 6.6 Worksheet Questions

1. A seed was planted on Day 0. What day did the plant come up? _____
2. How tall was the plant on Day 10? _____
3. How tall was the plant on Day 15? _____
4. Plot the points on your grid. Then use your graph to find how tall the plant was on these days:
   - Day 8 _____
   - Day 12 _____
   - Day 14 _____
   - Day 18 _____
5. Predict how tall the plant will be on Day 35. _____
6. Write a sentence to tell what happens to the plant's growth during the last two weeks shown on the graph.

tom and the height number line up the left side of the grid. Also distribute the worksheet with questions (Figure 6.6). "Your job is to plot the points, draw a smooth line to connect points, and answer the questions. You will have fifteen minutes to do the worksheet. At 1:45 we will stop to discuss your results and ideas."
2. Circulate and help as needed.

Closure
1. Compare a few results of the prediction questions. Emphasize a range of acceptable prediction values rather than a precise result, but try to identify the cause of any "wild" results.
2. Compare pupils' speculations about possible reasons for the shape of the curve.
3. "Next time you will learn how to choose useful number line values for the two variables."

ASSESSMENT

Informal observation during the discussions and checking the worksheets.

Ms. Oldhand asked Mr. Newman to study the lesson plan and decide whether he would like to actually teach it. After reading the plan, Mr. Newman had several questions.

MR. NEWMAN: I have studied your plan, and I understand most of it. I wanted to ask about the length, first of all. It seems kind of long. I'm afraid I won't be able to keep them interested that long.

MS. OLDHAND: Quite right. It is too long for one period. When I've taught it before, I have taken two or three forty-minute periods to do it all. And that's not counting the data collection. You look surprised.

MR. NEWMAN: I just never thought about a lesson being longer than a period. I guess I just thought lesson and period were synonyms!

MS. OLDHAND: Well, often they are, but they don't have to be. I find it makes more sense to keep all the learning activities with the set of objectives they go with and call the whole thing a lesson. I expect some people do it differently. There is no shortage of ideas on how to format a lesson plan.

THE TEACHER'S ROLE AND THE PUPILS' ROLE

Just as the nature of the teacher's responsibility is different when teaching a lesson from when doing other duties (e.g., lunch monitor or playground supervision), it is different for different types of teaching. The role of the teacher consists of one set of responsibilities when teaching a direct instruction lesson and another set when teaching an inquiry lesson. The nature of the pupil's responsibility differs in various types of instruction as well.

When considering the roles of both teacher and pupil in direct instruction, try to keep in mind that some responsibilities will be different when other instructional methods are used. In a direct instruction lesson, the decisions for the nature, direction, and pacing of the lesson are determined by the teacher. The pupils not only have little to say about lesson decisions but also are not given much latitude for movement or talking. More about pupil and teacher roles will be explained in later chapters, and comparisons of the differences and similarities, as well as the advantages and disadvantages between different ways of teaching will be drawn. Here are the roles of teacher and pupil in direct instruction:

Teacher's Role in Direct Instruction

- Set and enforce behavior standards and sanctions.
- Provide direct information by telling, showing, or by other means.
- Speak clearly and as briefly as possible.
- Listen carefully and check for understanding.
- Provide hands-on experiences whenever possible during independent practice.
- Estimate beforehand a time allocation for each part of the lesson.
- Plan carefully for smooth and efficient distribution and pickup of materials, involving children when possible.

Pupils' Role in Direct Instruction

- Follow standards at all times during a lesson.
- Pay attention when others are speaking or demonstrating.
- Follow directions.
- Ask for help if anything is not clear.
- Answer questions when called on.

BEHAVIOR MANAGEMENT

In Chapter 3, some general guidelines for establishing a pleasant and productive classroom climate were described. Those standards are the general standards used for most routine classroom situations, appropriate during most direct instruction, individual work, and classroom business. There are occasions, however, when the general rules need some amendments. One of these may be when pupils are working with concrete materials, as, for example, in the individual practice part of a direct lesson. If you have ever seen children given the opportunity to work with concrete materials, you know how keenly interested they become. This natural motivation can be harnessed to the benefit of both the lesson and the children's growth in responsibility. Simply explain, before the materials are distributed, how the materials are to be used, and perhaps give a few examples of inappropriate use. Explain that children who cannot manage their behavior while working with the materials will be separated from the materials until they are in better control. Then enforce the rule strictly, or all is lost.

MATERIALS MANAGEMENT

Using concrete materials adds some logistical concerns that must be carefully planned, like any other aspect of a lesson. It is an absolute must for you to try out ahead of time the demonstrations and activities with the actual materials to be used. Attempting to "wing it" with untried materials or with last-minute changes is one of the most frequent causes of lesson failure among beginning science teachers. The method of distribution and cleanup must be carefully planned as well.

VERBAL TECHNIQUES

Giving information and giving directions are important techniques in every teacher's repertoire. Although the two tasks may seem different, they have many similarities. Listening is hard work for children. The teacher should not rely on a child's being able to thoroughly understand from the spoken word alone. Here is a short list of tips for giving information and directions:

- Keep comments brief. Attention span for spoken language is very short.
- Be clear. Think and plan ahead for clarity.
- Ask children to repeat instructions or information back to you. This is feasible when the comments are as brief as they should be.
- Model procedural information as well as lesson content. Use props and body actions to help children understand.
- For all but the youngest, list key words of the directions or information for the children to read and refer to later.
- Establish an atmosphere in which it is safe to ask questions. Then be sure to solicit questions before assuming everyone understands.

In other words, directions as well as lesson content should be taught rather than simply told. In summarizing a large body of teacher effectiveness research, Brophy and Good (1987) described the actions of good classroom managers: Effective managers not only told their students what they expected but also modeled correct procedures for them, took time to answer questions, and, if necessary, arranged for the students to practice the procedures and get feedback. In short, key procedures were formally taught to students, just as academic content is taught (pp. 220–221).

In the context of this chapter, note that giving directions for a new procedure should be taught directly, using elements of the direct instruction model. For very young children, it may be necessary to prepare an entire lesson on the new procedure, with all of the lesson parts. Older children may be able to understand with just a few of the lesson parts. As a beginning teacher, you will need to decide how much teaching is needed for your pupils to learn a new procedure. Assuming that children will be able to carry out new procedures without special instruction is risky.

MODIFYING THE DIRECT INSTRUCTION FORMAT

Up to this point, only the standard model for direct instruction has been described and illustrated. The standard model is a useful starting point for beginning teachers. Once you get a feel for the function of each part, you can begin to consider modifications in certain situations. One way to modify the direct instruction model is to use an inductive rather than deductive presentation when the objective is a concept. In the usual presentation, the teacher presents the concept verbally, by stating a rule or generalization. Later, pupils are asked to give examples or specific applications for the generalization. In an inductive presentation, the teacher presents examples of the concept and then presents nonexamples of the concept. Usually, the name of the concept is also given. The pupils are then asked to generalize—that is, find the rule that characterizes the set of examples and distinguishes them from the set of nonexamples.

This distinction between inductive and deductive presentations has itself been presented deductively. The same distinction can be presented inductively. Consider two examples of presenting the concept of symmetry. Can you decide which presentation is deductive and which is inductive?

◆ PRESENTATION 1

"Today we will learn about symmetry. We can say a shape has symmetry when it has two halves that exactly match. One way to decide whether a shape has symmetry is to see if you can find a place to fold it so that the two halves exactly match." The teacher demonstrates with his two hands. "Let's see which of these paper cutouts has symmetry." The teacher folds several shapes, showing that some shapes have no symmetry and that some shapes have one or more lines of symmetry on which a fold results in two matching halves.

PRESENTATION 2

"Watch what I'm doing. As soon as you notice a pattern or can figure out what I'm doing, raise your hand." Without speaking further, the teacher picks up a piece of paper, folds it, and cuts out a shape. She then unfolds the shape, closes it, and opens it several times—demonstrating that the halves match—and places the paper on the left of her table. Then she takes another paper, cuts it, and then folds it. She opens and closes the fold several times to show that the halves do not match, and then places the paper on the right. She continues to fold first, cut, and place to the left, and to cut first, fold, and place to the right until most of the hands are raised.

If you picked Presentation 1 as deductive, or standard direct instruction, and Presentation 2 as the inductive modification, you are right. Think now about how this modified direct instruction model affects the other parts of the lesson plan.

Using the standard presentation, a teacher would have begun with some type of motivation. For example, a string of paper dolls or a paper snowflake might have been shown. The interest of the children would have been raised and a context developed to continue with the presentation. Although this same motivation could be used with the inductive presentation, it would have been less important because the puzzle-like presentation would have engaged interest and raised pupil involvement.

How do you think the other parts of the lesson plan differ in these two variations of direct instruction? You may be surprised to learn that the other components do not change at all. Guided practice should always be used by the teacher to make sure that most, if not all, of the pupils have the idea or understand the task. Independent practice is also the same in both cases.

Why would a teacher choose one method of instruction over another? What are the advantages and disadvantages? The advantage of the inductive modification is that pupils are more likely to be mentally involved right from the beginning. Instead of asking the pupils to watch and listen, the teacher begins by asking a question that requires figuring out a puzzle-like situation. Also, when learners figure something out for themselves, they are more likely to understand and remember it than when simply told. At least three points are disadvantages: (1) the inductive modification is not equally effective for all kinds of objectives, (2) its use requires judgment that may be beyond the beginning teacher's ability, and (3) it usually takes more time than the standard model.

The method in Presentation 2 involves learning a concept (symmetry), and such learning has been called "concept attainment" by Joyce and Weil (1996). For learning concepts, the inductive modification of direct instruction is widely recognized as effective. But the method works poorly or not at all for procedural objectives. Examples of procedural objectives are how to line up for cafeteria, how to draw a graph, and how to focus a microscope. For other kinds of objectives, such as simple association of names or use of systems of notation, there is no easy rule. An experienced teacher can usually make effective judgments about when and when not to modify the way direct presentation is made. A beginning teacher may misjudge in similar situations. A common difficulty some beginning teachers have is in trying to get pupils to "figure out" or discover names or procedures. Although the intention to have a discovery lesson is a commendable one, asking pupils to guess names or procedures ("It starts with a B") simply slows down a lesson without providing any of the benefits described. Furthermore, guessing names can be confusing to pupils because it emphasizes language rather than concept. The advantages of using the inductive modification of direct instruction for concept attainment generally outweigh the disadvantage of taking more time.

◆ SUMMARY

Basic skills such as psychomotor skills, facts, and some concepts not requiring deep understanding have been shown by research to be taught effectively by direct instruction. This research link is best established for the early grades; continuing research may show a similar relationship at higher grade levels. Some educators are reluctant to use the term teacher effectiveness for this body of research, because it looks only at pupil achievement and says nothing about affective and personal development, areas that are often included as educational goals.

The main strength of the direct instruction model is its systematic treatment of elements known to be important in basic skill learning. Inexperienced teachers increase their success rate by using this model because it reduces the number of judgments and complex teacher behaviors required. Teaching is a complex business under any conditions; the direct instruction model simplifies it a bit, with the result that new teachers have fewer lesson failures. With success comes confidence and the beginning of insight into the particular effects of particular teacher behaviors. With insight comes the beginning of conscious self-control of teacher behaviors to produce the pupil effects that are desired in a given situation. At that point, the teacher can begin recognizing some of the limitations of the direct instruction model and considering some of the alternatives.

◆ ACTIVITIES FOR THE READER

Some ideas for lessons are given here. Select one or more to develop using the direct instruction model described in this chapter. Then form a discussion group in class with others who considered the same idea. Finally, present to the whole class your group's pros and cons of various ways to present the lesson idea.

1. *Planet names.* Objective: The pupil will be able to name the planets in the order of their distance from the sun (Mercury, Venus, Earth, Mars, Jupiter, Saturn, Uranus, Neptune, Pluto). Use a mnemonic such as "My very educated mouse jumped suddenly under Nathan's pizza" (or make up your own). Include instruction to aid in remembering the order of the planets whose names have the same initial letter.

2. *Learning to read a thermometer and relate the reading to temperature as sensed by touch.*   Student objectives: The pupil will be able to (a) describe in words (cold/colder, hot/hotter, or cold/hot) the temperature of two objects of very different temperatures by touch alone and (b) describe the effect of change in temperature on a thermometer as movement up or down (e.g., when it gets hot, the thermometer goes up). Materials could be chilled water from a drinking fountain, warm water from the hot-water tap, and a thermometer with label tape over the numbers. The label could be marked to show change.

3. *Classifying.*   The first objective is to learn to pick a characteristic by which a set of objects can be sorted into two groups: those that have the characteristic and those that do not. The second objective is to reclassify the same objects by a different characteristic and to tell what the characteristic is. Materials could be unshelled peanuts, flowers, leaves, sea shells, or buttons—any set of things that has sufficient variety to permit multiple classifications. Pupils should be encouraged to use their own ideas for sorting but must be able to defend their categories without switching them during a sort. For example, a first sort of buttons could be into groups of two holes and more than two holes. A second sort of the same set could be into blue buttons and nonblue buttons.

◆ QUESTIONS FOR DISCUSSION

1. What are the differences between teaching by telling and direct instruction?

2. How can the degree of pupil engagement in a particular instructional activity guide the teacher's decision about pacing and time spent?

3. Explain differences between individual pupil evaluation and lesson assessment. Why not do thorough pupil evaluation for every lesson?

4. What are (a) signs and (b) possible causes of lesson failure?

◆ REFERENCES

Brophy, J., & Evertson, C. (1976). *Learning from teaching: A developmental perspective.* Boston: Allyn & Bacon.

Brophy, J., & Good, T. (1987). Teacher behavior and student achievement. In M. C. Wittrock (Ed.), *Handbook of research on teaching* (3rd ed., pp. 328–375). Upper Saddle River, NJ: Merrill/Prentice Hall.

Joyce, B., & Weil, M. (1996). *Models of teaching* (6th ed.). Boston: Allyn & Bacon.

National Research Council. (1996). *National science education standards.* Washington, DC: National Academy Press.

Rosenshine, B., & Stevens, R. (1987). Teaching functions. In M. C. Wittrock (Ed.), *Handbook of research on teaching* (3rd ed., pp. 376–391). Upper Saddle River, NJ: Merrill/Prentice Hall.

Smith, L., & Land, M. (1981). Low-inference verbal behaviors related to teacher clarity. *Journal of Classroom Interaction, 17,* 37–42.

Teaching Science as Inquiry

◆ Ms. Oldhand: Last week you observed the class while I conducted a direct instruction lesson. Today you will be able to observe a guided inquiry lesson.

Mr. Newman: Can you explain just what *inquiry* means and whatever happened to the processes of science that used to be the basis for science lessons?

Ms. Oldhand: You sound like my sixth graders, who always seem to ask me more than one question at a time! To answer your first question, *inquiry* is the process of asking a question, designing and carrying out an investigation, interpreting the results, and presenting the results to others. This could itself be called a process, but it is more involved than the processes we used to focus on, and it includes all of them.

Mr. Newman: How do the children carry out inquiry if they don't know the basic processes of observing, communicating, measuring, and so on?

Ms. Oldhand: As much as possible, we teach those processes in the context of learning science concepts, but we also teach skills separately, as you saw in the lesson on the balance [see Chapter 6]. In this lesson, you'll see how science processes are integrated into an inquiry lesson, and afterward we can talk about it.

You have already learned about a teaching method called *direct instruction*. The rationale for that method is that it is efficient and has been shown to reach the stated objectives. The method introduced in this chapter is called *inquiry-based instruction,* or, simply, *inquiry*. The rationale for this way of teaching is that learning is more meaningful and lasting if children are given opportunities to ask questions, explore materials, gather data, come to conclusions, and discuss results. It is not as efficient as direct instruction, but it leads to deeper understanding. This method does not follow exact procedures and requires more skill in classroom management and assessment of learning, but there are special reasons for choosing such a method that more than compensate for the difficulties. Inquiry-based science capitalizes on the child's natural curiosity about interesting objects. It results in a type of knowing that is not just disembodied words from a book but a fully integrated part of the learner. The difference between knowledge derived from active learning and knowledge derived from a book is the difference between knowing something as opposed to knowing about something.

Hands-on experiences are part of inquiry teaching in the elementary school, but inquiry is much more than just hands-on experiences. Other essential steps, even for children in the early grades, are asking questions and reflecting on the activity by comparing, looking for patterns, predicting, and making trial explanations. The

TABLE 7.1   Changing Emphases to Promote Inquiry

Less Emphasis On...	More Emphasis On...
Knowing scientific facts and information	Understanding scientific concepts and developing abilities of inquiry
Studying subject matter disciplines (physical, life, earth sciences) for their own sake	Learning subject matter disciplines in the context of inquiry, technology, science in personal and social perspectives, and history and nature of science
Separating science knowledge and science process	Integrating all aspects of science content
Covering many science topics	Studying a few fundamental science concepts
Implementing inquiry as a set of processes	Implementing inquiry as instructional strategies, abilities, and ideas to be learned

Source: Reprinted with permission from NATIONAL SCIENCE EDUCATION STANDARDS. Copyright 1996 by the National Academy of Sciences. Courtesy of the National Academy Press, Washington, D.C.

knowledge acquired from working with and acting on objects becomes the building blocks with which children construct knowledge and concepts that truly belong to them. Duckworth, Easley, Hawkins, and Henriques (1990) give an eloquent and practical description of this kind of teaching with examples taken from their work in many classrooms. The concept of inquiry-based teaching may become clearer to you as you study the two lists in Table 7.1, showing the changes recommended by the *National Science Education [NSE] Standards* (National Research Council, 1996) as the focus in science teaching shifts toward inquiry-based instruction.

GUIDED INQUIRY

Many attempts at using inquiry methods have failed because children did not receive the initial guidance they needed. In reaction to the excesses of traditional instruction in which children were passive receivers of information, enthusiastic teachers have sometimes overcompensated by giving children more freedom than they could handle. Guided inquiry is an attempt to avoid both of these extremes and to help children acquire the habits and ways of thinking that they can use later in independent investigations or full inquiry. Guidance is accomplished through the initial selection of materials, the type of data children will collect, and, most especially, through skillful use of discussion techniques. By indirect guidance and suggestions, the teacher increases the likelihood of outcomes that are both interesting and worthwhile.

An aspect of guidance that is essential to the success of guided inquiry teaching involves helping children become more responsible for their behavior and their own learning. Children who are accustomed to listening to the teacher, to reading, and to filling in worksheets as the main or only classroom activities will not automatically function well at this higher level of independence and responsibility; they must be taught how. Behavior standards provide children a means to decide for themselves whether a behavior is acceptable. Although children are not mature enough to judge without a standard, having a standard allows children to practice regulating their own behavior. Teaching new behavior standards can be done in a direct instruction format. Once the standards are learned, children practice applying them to their behavior in the limited freedom of the guided inquiry lesson. We explain how to do these things later in this chapter.

PLANNING AND PRESENTING A GUIDED INQUIRY LESSON

Guided inquiry lessons, like direct instruction lessons, can be structured into lesson plan parts, each with its specific function. Some of the parts are the same in both methods, but some are new, reflecting the special characteristics of inquiry. Content appropriate for direct instruction can be presented by direct means, such as telling and showing and having the children practice the new skill, but the skills of making careful and critical observations and accurate representation of observations cannot be transmitted through telling or showing. Although the objective of learning the parts of a mealworm could quite easily be presented by direct instruction, that objective is not very important in itself. There is, furthermore, a special motivational aspect in finding out something for oneself. That motivation is an important rationale for using an inquiry approach. The most important reasons for doing a lesson of the type described here lie more in the cognitive process, affective, and social domains than in the cognitive content domain.

COMPARISON OF DIRECT INSTRUCTION AND INQUIRY LESSON PLANS

In Chapter 6 you learned to structure a lesson for direct instruction. Guided inquiry lessons also need to be structured, but there are more options to choose from, based on the particular goals of the lesson. Consider a generic lesson-plan format:

All-Purpose Lesson Plan Format
1. Student objectives
2. Materials
3. Motivation
4. Learning activities
5. Assessment

Every lesson plan needs objectives, a list of materials, something to interest and motivate pupils, and a way to assess learning and evaluate the lesson. Every lesson plan also needs learning activities, but their type and sequence depend on the method to be used and the nature of the lesson goals. Now examine the differences in the type and sequence of learning activities in direct instruction and guided inquiry:

Direct Instruction	*Guided Inquiry*
1. Student objectives	1. Student objectives
2. Materials	2. Materials
3. Motivation	3. Motivation
4. Learning activities	4. Learning activities
a. Presentation	a. Questions
b. Guided practice	b. Data collection
c. Independent practice	c. Data processing
d. Closure	d. Closure
5. Assessment	5. Assessment

Description of Guided Inquiry Lesson Plan

Notice that everything in the two outlines is the same except for the central section of the learning activities. The new parts that make guided discovery possible are described in this section.

Question(s)

Inquiry lessons start with a question. It may be one that the teacher suggests or one that the pupils themselves ask. In the following example, Ms. Oldhand asked the children to see what they could notice. She asked the question herself because she was just getting the children started on a new unit, and, as she later said to Mr. Newman, she wanted to demonstrate that there are degrees of freedom for the children; a new teacher may have to ease into this way of teaching.

Data Collection

Data collection simply means gathering information needed to answer the question. The information may be recorded as a list of words describing an object or event or as numbers representing measurements. Data (the plural of the Latin word *datum*) may be recorded in many different ways, not only as words or numbers. Data can be collected as sound recordings, as pictures, as impressions in stone, or in countless other ways. In any case, data collecting involves making and usually recording observations. Data are records of observations, that is, information from the senses: sounds, feels, tastes, smells, and sights. In some situations, especially with younger children, data may not be physically recorded but simply reported during discussion. Guesses, predictions, speculations, inferences, conclusions, and other mental constructions go beyond observation and are, therefore, not examples of data.

Data Processing

Now that the data have been collected (i.e., the observations have been made), what happens to the data? Teachers must guide the children in using this information to arrive at inferences, speculations, generalizations, and other higher-level thinking. Guided inquiry needs to stimulate thinking that goes beyond simple observation. Once the observations are made and recorded, the pupils need guidance in thinking about those observations. Usually this is done through guided discussion. With younger children, the discussion may be limited mostly to describing and comparing the objects that were observed. Older children can begin to do more powerful thinking. Leading a discussion indirectly to help children think about observations and connect these observations logically with prior knowledge is a higher-level skill itself. The idea, after all, is for the children to reflect on their recent experience—not to "read" the teacher's face. Another way to think about this part of the lesson is in terms of the type of knowledge it is designed for. Data collecting involves acquiring physical knowledge; data processing should lead toward the construction of understanding and logical knowledge. Now look at Ms. Oldhand's lesson plan, and then see how she implemented her plan.

◆ MS. OLDHAND'S MEALWORM LESSON

"Today we will begin a new science unit," Ms. Oldhand told her pupils, "but first we must discuss behavior standards for science." She brought out a chart on which was written:

> **Science Activity Standards**
>
> 1. You may talk quietly.
>
> 2. Stay in your own seat.
>
> 3. Raise your hand if you need help.
>
> 4. Stop, look, and listen at the signal.

Ms. Oldhand explained the standards to her third graders and checked to make sure that each pupil understood. For standard 4, she said that when she needed to speak to them, she would sound the chime. This signal was already known by the class and had been used in similar circumstances. "Working directly with the materials is a privilege for those who are grown up enough to remember the standards," she said. "If you forget, I will have to take away your materials until you are ready to be more responsible."

Ms. Oldhand also explained that she would need some help in distributing and collecting materials and that she would appoint a helper, or monitor, at each table. "You will take turns being monitors," she said. "Each week, I will appoint a new monitor for each table, so everyone will have a chance to be a helper."

Ms. Oldhand took a mealworm from the container on her desk. "Look at what I have in my hand. It isn't harmful in any way, but it is a living creature with feelings, so we must be careful not to hurt it. It is called a mealworm, and each of you will have one to observe. See what you can notice. After a while, I will give the signal, and then we'll discuss what everyone noticed about their mealworms."

She passed among the children, placing a paper cup containing a mealworm on each pupil's desk. There was a great deal of interest, but some of the children seemed reluctant to touch their specimens. Ms. Oldhand did not insist that they do so, and after a few minutes of poking their worms with pencils, the reluctant children gradually became confident enough to touch and handle them directly. Ms. Oldhand walked among the pupils, sharing their excitement and listening to their comments.

The room was arranged in groups of four double desks, with eight pupils to a "table." After about fifteen minutes, she sounded the chime. Most of the class remembered to look up from their mealworms to see what she had to say. The

These children are happy with their mealworms.

others did so as soon as they heard her begin to speak. "Thank you for remembering the special science standards so well! Please take a minute to place all your mealworms in the paper cup, and then put the cup back in the center of your table." Ms. Oldhand then asked the table monitors to collect the cups and place them on her desk.

"What were some things you noticed?" Ms. Oldhand called on several pupils to share their observations. "Did anyone notice how many legs there were?" Some thought there were one number, some another. "Well! Do you suppose all mealworms have the same number of legs, or that maybe some are different? Let's think about how we could find out. Did anyone notice other things?" Discussion along this vein revealed that most of the children did not notice fine details but were more interested in how the mealworms moved and how they reacted to pokes and other stimuli. "What are some things you'd like to investigate with your mealworms next time?" Ms. Oldhand asked. Several ideas were offered, and Ms. Oldhand listed them on chart paper. "Fine," she said. "Let's be thinking about how we might find out some of these things. Tomorrow we will decide what to do next."

MS. OLDHAND: Mr. Newman, I wanted you to know that I included the strict behavior standards for your benefit. When I am just teaching my pupils without you here, I can be a bit more relaxed. I even let them move around the room. Student teachers usually need more structure, though.

MR. NEWMAN: Thanks. I appreciate seeing how you did it. I feel really insecure trying to think about how to present this method and how to prevent behavior problems at the same time.

MS. OLDHAND: [Smiling] You will soon internalize how to do that and forget that you ever needed this technique.

MR. NEWMAN: When I looked at what was happening as a pupil, it was fun, but when I think about teaching it, I get nervous because I don't understand how it works. Like the questions about the number of legs. If it's important for them to know, why didn't you just tell them, or settle it in some way? It seemed like a lot of questions came up that didn't get settled.

MS. OLDHAND: The main goal of this lesson was just to get started—to get the "new" off of the mealworms. In particular, I wanted everyone to get comfortable with handling the mealworms. Now they all know that the worms don't bite, and that they don't move suddenly. In fact, mealworms don't do much of anything that is very startling. Because the students know that from their own experience, they now will be able to turn their attention to more specific observations and tasks. Later in the unit, we will decide together how to answer some of the questions. What they find out by observing, like the number of legs, is less important than the act of finding out for themselves.

MR. NEWMAN: I'm not sure I know how to decide what's more and less important.

MS. OLDHAND: This lesson was more process than content. I wanted them to work on the skills of observing and communicating. You may understand better if you study my lesson plan for this lesson.

LESSON PLAN 7.1

GETTING TO KNOW YOUR MEALWORM

(Lesson 1 of Unit)

NSE STANDARD

Characteristics of organisms (National Research Council, 1996, p. 127).

GRADE LEVEL: 3

STUDENT OBJECTIVES

1. Gain confidence in handling a mealworm. (Affective objective.)
2. Describe the general appearance and behavior of a mealworm. (Cognitive objective.)

MATERIALS

For each pupil:

One mealworm in a paper cup

(Mealworms can be obtained for a few cents each at pet stores, where you can also obtain advice on their care and handling.)

MOTIVATION

"Look at what I have in my hand."

LEARNING ACTIVITIES

Data Collection

1. Give directions for data collection: "See what you can notice."
2. Allow fifteen minutes.
3. Collect materials.

Data Processing

Ask:

"What did you notice about your mealworm?"
"Did anyone notice something different?"
"What else would you like to find out about your mealworm?"

Write several of the ideas on chart paper.

Closure

"Tomorrow we will take a closer look at our mealworms."

ASSESSMENT

Informal observation.

◆ The next morning, Mr. Newman spoke to Ms. Oldhand before class began.

MR. NEWMAN: I have thought about the lesson I observed yesterday and how processes and content were integrated. Although I studied your lesson plan, I still don't understand exactly how to do this in a lesson.

MS. OLDHAND: Here is the beginning of my plan for the second lesson. I have the topic and a set of objectives. Why don't you try writing the rest of the plan? You'd better take a couple of mealworms and a magnifier with you tonight, too.

MR. NEWMAN: Really? Do I need to do that?

MS. OLDHAND: How much do you know about mealworms? You have about a two hundred percent better chance of planning a successful lesson if you have thoroughly experienced what you want the pupils to do and have tried out everything with the specific materials you plan to use.

Thinking About What Comes Next

The lesson you have just studied is the beginning of a unit that Ms. Oldhand planned. She wanted the lessons to relate to one another in a logical way, with the skills and concepts developed in the earlier lessons to be used and further developed in the later lessons. To begin thinking about lesson sequence and learning activities to provide instruction for given objectives, you are invited to try your hand at lesson

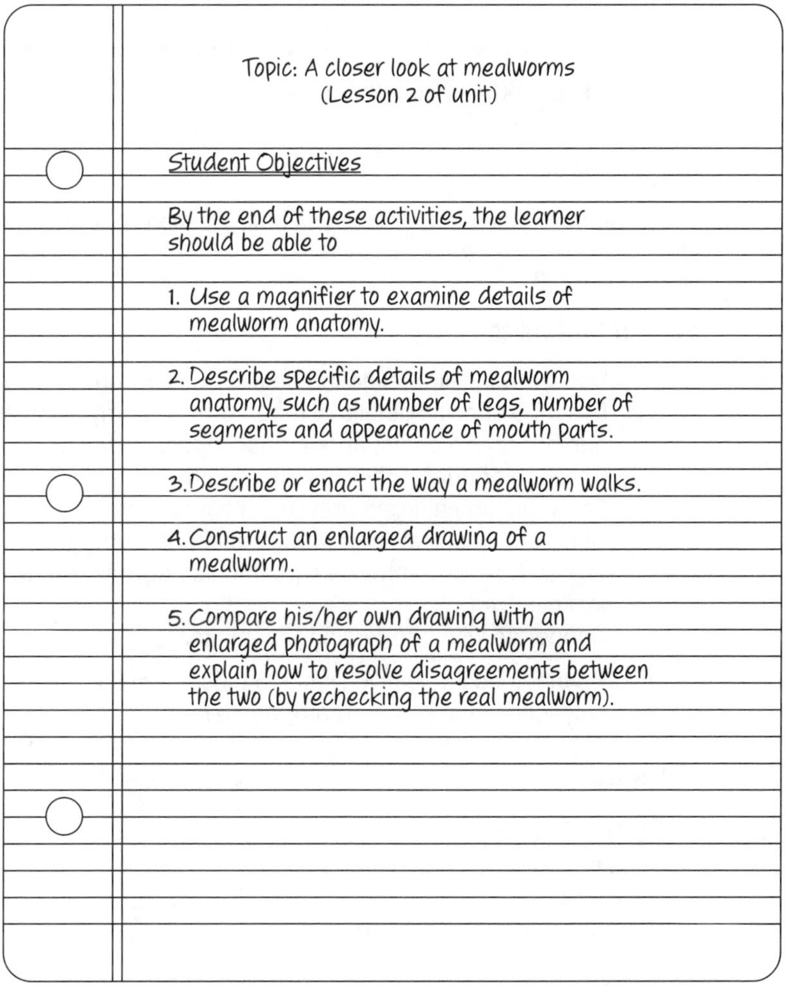

Topic: A closer look at mealworms
(Lesson 2 of unit)

Student Objectives

By the end of these activities, the learner should be able to

1. Use a magnifier to examine details of mealworm anatomy.

2. Describe specific details of mealworm anatomy, such as number of legs, number of segments and appearance of mouth parts.

3. Describe or enact the way a mealworm walks.

4. Construct an enlarged drawing of a mealworm.

5. Compare his/her own drawing with an enlarged photograph of a mealworm and explain how to resolve disagreements between the two (by rechecking the real mealworm).

FIGURE 7.1 Beginning of Ms. Oldhand's Plan for the Second Lesson of the Mealworm Unit

planning. Figure 7.1 shows the beginning of Ms. Oldhand's plan for the second lesson of the unit. How would you complete it?

Ms. Oldhand's plan for the second lesson follows. Compare it with the plan you developed for this lesson. Notice that it contains all the elements of an inquiry lesson plan as outlined previously.

◆ MS. OLDHAND'S SECOND MEALWORM LESSON

The following lesson plan can be adapted as an in-class activity for professional development of preservice and in-service teachers.

A CLOSER LOOK AT MEALWORMS

NSE STANDARD

Characteristics of organisms (National Research Council, 1996, p. 127).

GRADE LEVEL: 3

STUDENT OBJECTIVES

1. Use a magnifier to examine details of mealworm anatomy.
2. Describe specific details of mealworm anatomy, such as number of legs, number of segments, appearance of mouth parts.
3. Describe or enact the way a mealworm walks.
4. Construct an enlarged drawing of a mealworm.
5. Compare their drawings with an enlarged photograph of a mealworm, and explain how to resolve disagreements between the two (by rechecking the real mealworm).
6. Cooperate with partners and monitors.

(Notice that these objectives include those from the cognitive-process, cognitive-content, social, and psychomotor domains.)

MATERIALS

For each pupil:

One mealworm in a paper cup
One magnifier
One sheet of drawing paper

For each four pupils:

One set of crayons

For the teacher:

Enlarged photo of a mealworm

MOTIVATION

"Today we will be observing our mealworms with magnifiers."

LEARNING ACTIVITIES

Review Standards: Questions

"Here is the list of questions you had at the end of our last lesson. Does anyone want to add any other questions to this list?"

Data Collection

1. Give directions for data collection: "Look for answers to your questions, and see what new details you can notice."
2. Distribution of mealworms and magnifiers by monitors.
3. Allow fifteen minutes.
4. Monitors collect mealworms, magnifiers, and crayons.

Data Processing

1. (Description of findings.) Ask "What new details did you notice?" "How many legs?" "How many segments?"
2. Ask volunteers to act out how a mealworm walks. Discuss.
3. Comparing drawings with photo, ask pupils to notice discrepancies between their drawings and the photo. List these on chart paper to refer to at the next lesson.

Closure

"We will use this list next time as a guide to find out more. How do you think we will do it? Look at our real mealworms to decide."

ASSESSMENT

Behavior checklist, written observations and drawings in workbook (careful and accurate rather than fanciful), and description of pupil answers and comments during discussion.

◆ IMPLEMENTING THE LESSON PLAN

Ms. Oldhand picked up a magnifier and a mealworm from her desk. "Today we will look at our mealworms with magnifiers." She held the mealworm in the palm of one hand and used the magnifier to peer at it. The pupils watched with interest. Ms. Oldhand congratulated the pupils on what good scientists they had been. She thanked them for making science period pleasant by remembering the special behavior standards. She then reviewed the standards with the class and asked them if they remembered what would happen if they forgot to stay seated. "You have to lose your mealworm for a while," replied one child. "And what happens if you forget to keep your talking quiet?" she asked. In this way, she went through all the special standards with the children so they would have a better chance of remembering. Then she went on to give directions for the day's activity.

"The next thing we will do with our mealworms is something very interesting. Yesterday you noticed certain things about your mealworms, and you had some questions about other things you would like to know. I saved your questions and have put them on the chalkboard to help you remember what they were. Today, we will use magnifiers to help you notice new things. In a few minutes, I will also give you some drawing materials so you can record your observations by making a picture of your mealworm. Make your drawing big enough to cover most of the page. Your picture should be much bigger than the actual mealworm. Notice every detail you can, and show it in your picture. How many legs? How many segments? How does the mouth look? Look very carefully at your mealworm, and then draw what you notice. Then look again and draw what you notice. Keep looking back at your real mealworm, and then use what you see to make your picture more realistic. Compare your picture with your partner's picture. If they are different, look back at your mealworm to see if that will help.

"Now, before we begin, who can remember today's procedure?" Ms. Oldhand made sure that they remembered to make their drawings large and that they would include details in their pictures.

Before the lesson began, Ms. Oldhand had assigned one monitor from each table to hand out and pick up materials. "Would the materials monitors please come get the things for your tables?" She gave each of the monitors a box-lid tray with mealworms in cups and plastic magnifiers, which they then distributed.

The children went right to work, looking at the mealworms with their magnifiers. Ms. Oldhand then passed out the drawing paper and crayons without interrupting or interfering. As they worked, she walked around and answered questions that some children had.

After about fifteen minutes, she rang the chime for attention and asked the monitors to pick up the mealworms, magnifiers, and crayons. There were a few groans from the pupils as the mealworms departed.

"What new details did you notice today?" The discussion first involved comparing observations. "How many legs?" "How many segments?" "Shall we count the head as a segment or not? Let's decide, and then all use the same rule." Next, she asked about how the legs moved. This proved hard to describe, so she asked for three volunteers to come forward to act as the three pairs of legs on a mealworm. Several groups of three demonstrated their versions of the gait of their specimens. Afterward, they debated which rendition was the most realistic. Finally, Ms. Oldhand revealed a large photographic enlargement of a mealworm. She asked them to compare the photo with their own drawings and to notice any differences. Discrepancies the pupils pointed out were listed on a large chart paper. "Fine," she concluded, "We will use this list next time as a guide to find out more. How do you think we will do it? A look at the real mealworms would help us decide. Thank you for being such good scientists today. Please pass your drawings up, and let's get ready for lunch."

Working Toward Greater Pupil Freedom and Responsibility

In both of these lessons, the pupils were given only limited freedom, within specific bounds. They were not permitted to move freely about the room, and the activities were relatively simple without a great many choices for them to make. Ms. Oldhand was demonstrating for Mr. Newman how to begin a unit with third-grade children whose experience with inquiry learning is limited. To demonstrate techniques that could be used by a less-experienced teacher such as Mr. Newman, Ms. Oldhand was more conservative in allowing pupils freedom than she might have been otherwise. Nevertheless, she used several techniques intended to help the children increase their learning independence. They were allowed to talk quietly as long as they kept the volume down. In this way, they practiced being responsible by exercising judgment. The distribution and pickup of materials used in this case was easy and quick. Children were given the responsibility of being monitors; monitor duty rotates each week so that everyone has a chance to practice this kind of responsibility. In cases where more or messier materials are involved, every child participates more actively in cleanup.

GETTING STARTED WITH GUIDED INQUIRY

Each of the following steps has been or will be described in detail, either in this chapter or in others. You will find it useful to refer to this list from time to time as you gain experience and become more aware of the subtle aspects of guided inquiry.

1. Set or review behavior standards.

2. Do not tell pupils the objective of the lesson or present the concept.

3. Give clear, brief directions for the procedure to be used. Pupils should not be expected to invent their own procedures in this method. Directions for procedures should be made clear before the pupils begin working.

4. Introduce new vocabulary only as needed in context—that is, when it arises naturally in the lesson.

5. When pupils are working productively during the data-collecting part of the lesson, do not address the class as a whole. Don't interfere when they are doing what they are supposed to be doing.

6. Speak softly to children as needed, only to prevent serious boredom or terminal frustration. Mild, occasional frustration and limited boredom are to be expected in any worthwhile endeavor, including guided-inquiry lessons.

7. Separate pupils from materials before trying to hold a discussion.

8. During the data-processing part of the lesson, first ask pupils to report their data, that is, to describe their observations.

9. When possible, continue the discussion beyond description by asking for higher-level thinking such as inference, justification, generalization, and speculation about related systems not yet experienced.

10. Do not summarize the lesson for the pupils. Ask them to do it.

Facilitating Data Collection

It is important to try to give directions for the entire data-collecting part of the lesson, in addition to reminders about behavior standards and special directions for distribution and cleanup of materials, before data collection begins. Otherwise, you will have to interrupt when the children are concentrating on the most interesting part of the lesson. Some suggestions for this phase of the lesson follow:

◆ *Keep directions short and clear.*

◆ *Minimize interruptions during data collection.*   It is very hard to get children's attention to give more directions after they are engaged in hands-on activity. Try to give all the directions at one time, so that further announcements to the whole class are unnecessary until you are ready to conclude the data-collection activity. When they are doing what they are supposed to do, try not to interfere!

◆ *Plan materials distribution and cleanup carefully.*   An operation that took two minutes for you when you were trying out the activity at home may take an hour when multiplied by thirty children. Making children wait idly for extended periods while materials are being passed out usually leads to behavior management problems.

◆ *Enforce behavior standards strictly.*   Once a child or two start to lose self-control, chaos spreads rapidly to the whole class. Review the section on behavior management in Chapter 3.

◆ *Limit novelty.*   Whenever new elements of learning are to be introduced, find ways to limit the amount or number of new things that happen at the same time. New procedures, new locations, new ideas, new tools, or new objects to study should be introduced gradually. The trick is not to avoid novelty, but to spread it out in time so it does not all happen at once. Novelty is the essence of learning; to avoid it is to take the interest and life out of learning.

◆ *Allow time for exploration.*   Exploration is a preliminary examination in which a person finds out the general nature of the unknown object, place, or situation. Exploration reduces the degree of novelty to the point where children are not overwhelmed. Whenever a new physical object is present in a lesson, problems in management will be minimized by allowing some time for exploration. Before they are able to work systematically with or on the object, children must be allowed to play with it and "get some of the new off." Exploration also serves as a legitimate first step of investigation used by scientists and other adults in new situations.

◆ *Separate pupils from materials before a discussion.*   If you try to compete for their attention with attractive materials, you will probably lose. There are several ways to separate pupils from materials. Collecting the materials while the pupils remain seated is one way. Moving the children to a discussion area away from their activity tables is another. In extended units when pupils have time to get accustomed to the materials, you may be able to get by with the following: Each child or team has its own container for storing materials. If the container is small enough (and opaque), have them put materials in the container and move it to the center of the table, out of touching range. When pupils are mature enough to manage it, this method has the advantage of reducing the interruption of thinking between activity and discussion.

During data collecting, the pupil's role is to work with the materials, following the directions given earlier; the teacher's role is to refrain from addressing the whole class and to speak to individual pupils or small groups as little as possible. In other words, during data collecting, the teacher is supposed to keep quiet and let the children work. Learning to keep quiet and out of the limelight is one of the hardest things the teacher has to do in inquiry-based teaching. When a teacher uses a big voice, speaking to the whole class, pupils are placed in conflict. They know they are supposed to be working, but they also know that they are supposed to stop and listen to the teacher. Not only do the children have trouble shifting attention in this situation, but also the authority of the teacher is eroded. The way to avoid—or at least minimize—the need for interruption during data collecting is to give brief, clear, complete directions in the first place.

In addition to keeping quiet, the teacher's role during data collection involves noticing how pupils are doing. If a child is having trouble with equipment or has forgotten the directions, an indirect suggestion that leads the pupil to figure out the problem independently is best, for example, "What does the directions chart say to do next?" "What would happen if you fastened this connector here?" "Do you remember what we did about this problem yesterday?" Occasionally, you will find that a problem stems from faulty equipment or some other difficulty beyond the child's ability to solve alone. Simply replace or fix the problem when possible, or arrange for the pupil to work with another team. Sometimes you may find one or more children misusing or playing with the materials in nonproductive ways. If proximity control or other mild management techniques do not work, remind the children involved (with a small voice) of the behavior standards and the possibility of being separated from the materials.

Watching pupils work with materials is like looking through a magic window into the workings of their minds. They act out their thinking in concrete, observable ways. One way to get fully involved with a group's thinking is to sit or bend down with them at eye level and then simply watch and listen without speaking. You may ask questions or make indirect suggestions (in a small voice), but avoid correcting the children's misconceptions. The feedback coming directly from the materials is much more effective than anything the teacher could say and is emotionally neutral besides. Children revise their thinking when they are cognitively ready to do so.

In a task such as "Can you make the bulb light?" in a lesson on electric circuits, an intervention is necessary in the case of pupils who do not "get it" after a reasonable time. You might suggest that such pupils look around for ideas. An even more effective technique is to ask some pupils to draw diagrams on the board of circuits that "do work" and diagrams that "don't work." That way, everyone can be involved, and interesting arrangements that do not light the bulb are recognized. There should always be an open atmosphere of thinking and sharing ideas during guided discovery, never one of testing and "not cheating."

Although the situation is rare, you may sometimes find a pupil who is shy or seems uninterested in working with the materials. Often, placement in the right group is helpful in such cases, but occasionally you may want to sit with this child yourself and, in your best nonthreatening manner, try to kindle interest: "I wonder what would happen if I connect the wire here?" "Have you tried this one yourself?" Feigning puzzlement over something you know the child can figure out is often effective: "I could never get this circuit—Number 7—to work. Juan said he couldn't get it either, but Emily did!"

There is no magic formula for deciding when to intervene during data collection and when not to. The main guiding principle is that you cannot make a discovery for children; they must discover on their own. You can only facilitate, or arrange the environment so that the probability of success is increased. Most of the time, especially until you feel more at home with this new teaching method, the most effective intervention is none at all.

LEADING INTERESTING DISCUSSIONS

The material in this section is often included under the heading "Questioning Techniques," as if the main point is the questions teachers ask. That puts the emphasis on what the teacher is saying rather than on what the children are saying. In a discussion, as opposed to a question-and-answer session, everyone involved is getting new ideas, giving their ideas, and constructing new knowledge. The teacher has to be a participant, not just a question-asker.

Rowe, in her classic book, *Teaching Science as Continuous Inquiry* (1978), characterizes the difference between this kind of teaching and more traditional methods as "inquiry versus inquisition." Everyone is familiar with the traditional "discussion," where the main focus is reciting correct answers and getting lots of praise. Learners are often intent on studying the teacher's face for clues for whether answers are acceptable. Thinking has little or no place in this game. An inquiry-style discussion, by contrast, has everything to do with pupils' learning to think and with learning a whole new set of "rules" for doing well. These discussions are more like normal conversations about things that all parties, including the teacher, are really interested in. The teacher's role in inquiry is to stimulate and encourage thinking. But how?

One rule of thumb for beginners is to keep teacher talk to a minimum. Ask questions that elicit longer pupil responses. It is a good idea to begin with a few questions of description, such as, "How many legs did you count?" Begin at a fairly low level, but move on quickly to questions requiring more thought, such as, "What kind of food do you think mealworms like?" Open-ended questions are desirable for eliciting several different hypotheses quickly. Then, pupils can be asked to justify their points of view in terms of their observations: "What evidence do you have to support your idea?" "Have you noticed something that leads you to think that?" Fur-

A teacher gives her full attention to one pupil's answer.

ther investigations can be planned together to get more evidence for some of the ideas, such as by asking, "How could we find out about what mealworms eat?"

◆ MR. NEWMAN: I'm beginning to catch on to the way you get them started and then keep quiet while they are working, but I was wondering about the groans I heard when the materials were collected.

MS. OLDHAND: It's better to stop the activity while interest is still high than to wait until they are starting to get bored. The groans just show that they would rather work with actual things than have a discussion. That's natural; it's why I engineer the transition so carefully. Once they get into a discussion, they like it well enough.

Wait Time

Discussions that are more than rote drill require some silent time for thinking, both by pupils and by the teacher. Rowe's (1974) research in this area has identified two kinds of wait time. Wait time 1 is the time after a teacher asks a question and before anyone speaks again, either the teacher or a child. Wait time 2 is the time after a pupil speaks before anyone else speaks. Rowe found that teachers typically wait less than one second for pupils to answer a question. This does not give pupils time to form an answer unless it is something that requires no thinking, only something from memory. Many teachers—especially those who ask a series of rapid-fire questions—even interrupt pupils who are trying to respond by praising inappropriately or calling on another child. Some teachers answer their own questions before pupils have time to respond. With training and practice, teachers can learn to wait a few seconds for an answer after they ask a question. When teachers learn to extend their wait time to three to five seconds, the following things happen:

The average length of pupil responses is longer, indicating more thoughtful answers.

Pupils initiate more responses.

There are fewer failures to respond to the teacher's question.

The quality of pupil responses is greater.

Teachers become more flexible in their questions and reactions to pupil responses.

Previously "quiet" pupils participate.

Establishing an Inquiry Atmosphere for Discussion

The pleasant, mutually respectful, stimulating atmosphere of the inquiry discussion requires the establishment of an atmosphere that is psychologically safe for speculation as well as the sharing of thinking that is not yet finished. This open climate does not simply happen. It is not enough for a teacher to know how to avoid behaviors that reduce trust and how to use behaviors that favor inquiry. There must also be cooperation from the pupils. Because children are usually accustomed to classrooms with fast exchanges, they tend to respond to questions immediately, with short, superficial answers. If you want inquiry to succeed in your classroom, the pupils must be taught (directly) the procedure of the new discussion method.

The Learning-to-Discuss Cycle

Labinowicz (1985a) has described a way to teach children to function in a discussion in which thinking is valued more than correct answers. Many of the following ideas are taken from his book. Before beginning an inquiry discussion, inform the children of the reason for wait time through these sorts of comments:

Waiting time is thinking time. I will ask a question, and then I will wait for a while before I call on someone. I will not always call on a person with a raised hand. I am interested in how people think. It is important not to call out and not to wave hands, so that everyone has time to think. Different people will have different ideas. This is good because you will be learning from each other.

In later discussions, the children will need to be reminded of the wait-time procedures. The teacher can explain that when someone forgets and calls out an answer, any students who are still thinking about it will stop thinking. Students should understand that the idea that was interrupted could have been very interesting to everyone. Additional reminders will be needed for a while until waiting and respecting the views of others become habituated. The teacher can encourage pupils to tell whether they agree or disagree with another pupil's comment and to give their reasons. Hand signals can also be established to remind the impulsive or overeager child to wait quietly while thinking is going on.

Neither pupils nor teachers learn to function in an inquiry discussion overnight. To continue growing in the complex skills of leading inquiry discussion, the cycle of teaching and learning shown in Figure 7.2 is recommended.

A good class discussion in an inquiry (or discovery) lesson involves many advanced teaching skills. Rowe (1974) found that teachers tend to ask a barrage of questions—some teachers as frequently as ten questions per minute. Obviously, only the briefest and most superficial recall responses are possible in such rapid-fire exchanges. The pressure on pupils mounts during such a discussion.

Good and Brophy (1987) describe six characteristics of good questions. Good questions are clear, purposeful, brief, natural, adapted to the learners' level, and thought provoking. Clear questions are usually brief, and long questions are hard to understand. But not all brief questions are clear. "How about the habitat?" is vague and may be misleading. "What alternative paradigm might be applied?" contains words that might be unknown to children. Questions should have vocabulary and word order that are natural to the children. Some beginning teachers plan a discussion by simply thinking up every question possible that has anything to do with the subject. A much more effective practice is to plan a logical sequence of questions, all of which are pertinent to the gradual development of the lesson objectives.

FIGURE 7.2   Learning-to-Discuss Cycle

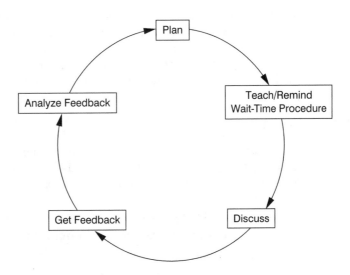

Praise

No teacher likes to be negative, and to many teachers, praise sometimes seems the only alternative to negativity. This may lead them to use praise too much, in the wrong way, or inappropriately. Praise is effective when it is genuine, appropriate, not overly dramatic, and directed to specific tasks or skills (Good & Brophy, 1987). Several research studies have reported that praise is often given for incorrect answers, especially when directed to low achievers. How can this happen? Teachers often use global praise—vaguely worded, random phrases that cannot readily be identified as praise of pupil, effort, or solution. When asked about specific instances of inappropriate praise, teachers report that they were attempting to encourage effort.

Pupils in a classroom where a great deal of praise is used are discouraged from learning to think for themselves. The probability of developing interest in the subject of discussion for intrinsic reasons is therefore reduced, and the primary payoff for the pupils becomes more praise. Like an addiction, praise tends to prevent normal development toward independent thinking.

Rowe (1974) concluded that overt verbal praise is effective in certain situations, but for establishing an inquiry atmosphere and encouraging higher-order, independent thinking, praise is actually counterproductive! In classrooms where praise was frequent, children showed lower confidence, as evidenced by inflected responses and checking the teacher's face. When verbal rewards were high, pupils tended to give short responses and incomplete explanations, show more hand waving ("Call-on-me!"), and listen less to other pupils' ideas. Discussions in classrooms where praise is frequent are more likely to resemble a game of competition for the teacher's attention than an interesting conversation. In contrast, when the frequency of overt verbal praise is decreased, these negative effects tend to diminish or disappear.

A Framework for Leading Discussions

Another approach to learning to lead good discussions has been explored by Watt (1996), who was interested in the questioning behaviors that are needed to develop a constructivist teaching philosophy in primary science. You may find this framework helpful as a guide in planning the questions you will ask as you lead children in discussions of the results of their investigations. The framework is shown in Table 7.2.

Planning a Discussion

This section contains some practical, everyday suggestions that will help you implement the preceding ideas and recommendations. As you plan a discussion, consider that you will first want pupils to report and compare their observations.

What did you notice about the detailed structure of your mealworm?

How many segments did the mealworms have?

Was this the same for everyone?

TABLE 7.2 A Framework for Teacher Questioning During Class Discussions

Social attributes of discussion

Level one: General management of discussion

Respond verbally to any answer with equal interest.

Use tone of voice in a manner which reinforces the interest in any answer.

Give a child ownership of an answer by using phrases such as, "What do you think…?" to begin a question.

Allow a child sufficient time to formulate a response.

Level two: Enabling greater participation in discussion

Cue a child to the cognitive level of response required by using phrases such as, "What do you think…?" to begin a question.

Invite an answer from every child who wishes to contribute.

Encourage children to respond to each other's views.

Cognitive attributes of discussion

Level one: Maintaining logical continuity in discussion

Seek clarification of a child's answer by repeating words.

Seek clarification of a child's answer by asking what s/he means.

Extend a child's answer by asking for a hypothesis or for evidence to support one.

Be sure of the area (rather than the specific content) of the discussion.

Ask questions according to a considered sequence.

Level two: Monitoring the development of ideas in discussion

Seek clarification of a child's answer by reflectively rewording her/his response.

Extend a child's answer by challenging her/his hypothesis.

Word questions so that the intention behind them is clear.

Listen to a child's answer and use it as the basis for the next question.

Source: From "An Analysis of Teacher Questioning Behavior in Constructivist Primary Science Education Using a Modification of a Descriptive System Designed by Barnes & Todd (1977)" by D. Watts, 1996, *International Journal of Science Education, 18*(5), p. 605. Copyright 1996 by Taylor & Francis Ltd. Reprinted by permission.

Should we count the tail as a segment? The head?

Which characteristics do you think would be the same for all mealworms, and which might be different?

Later in the discussion, you will want to ask for speculation on relationships or generalizations based on the observations.

Did you notice any patterns in the mealworm's behavior?

Which variables seem to make a difference in the swinging of the pendulum?

Did this remind you of anything people do on the playground?

Can you make a general rule to explain that?

Do you have an idea of what might have happened in this picture?

What are some possible explanations for that?

Planning questions is only one part of planning a discussion. You will also want to think about your reactions to possible pupil responses. During reporting of data, very little reaction from you is needed or desirable. Simply accept the responses without judging—instant judgment is not required. Remember the knowledge types described in Chapter 1. Observations are physical knowledge. The best feedback for questions of physical knowledge comes from the objects. If there is a discrepancy between observations of different children, the children will often raise a question themselves. If not, you could suggest that they check again to see if their observations can be duplicated. During initial reporting, you may wish to jot down the observations on the board, especially if you plan to refer to them later for comparison or analysis. This is a way of accepting without judgment. When children share their explanations, it is useful to probe for further thinking, regardless of whether the children are right or wrong. Remember, in discovery or inquiry science, thinking is at least as important as result. By asking for more ideas, you will not only get additional ideas already in place and ready to be reported, but you will also stimulate additional thinking.

Children's language is often imprecise; by asking for clarification, you help them develop more careful use of language as well as sharper thinking. Listen for "magic words" that children may use without fully understanding their meaning: *gravity, force, friction, density, photosynthesis, oxygen,* and so on. In addition, children often report inferences or other speculations as if they were observations. When that happens, ask for observations with questions such as

How do you know?

Did you notice something that supports your idea?

That's an interesting inference. What observations did you base it on?

What do you mean by *friction*?

Can you say that another way?

Please explain for everyone what that word means.

Is that anything like the term used earlier?

That's an interesting theory. Let's see if there are others.

Encourage pupils to listen and respond to one another. Avoid repeating pupil responses. Instead, ask a child to repeat so that everyone can hear, or ask another child to paraphrase. When you repeat a pupil response, you send two undesirable messages: (1) It is not necessary to listen to other children because the teacher will repeat it, and (2) a child's comment counts for nothing until it has been "authorized" by coming out of the teacher's mouth. Ask questions such as

What do you think of Kal's idea? Who would like to agree or disagree and say why?

Can you state Jennifer's idea another way?

How does Jeremy's idea relate to yours?

Tyrone, you also mentioned decomposition. Would you like to react to Felipe's idea?

Sometimes pupils get stuck in a blind alley with untestable explanations. Try to redirect them into a more interesting line of thinking by indirect suggestions:

Are other interpretations possible?

Are there any other ways to think about this?

Are there any other clues or observations that we haven't thought about? What other factors could be involved?

What would happen if we . . . ?

And if that were changed, what would happen then?

Learn to handle incorrect responses in a constructive way. Again, remember Piaget's knowledge types (see Chapter 1). Only errors in arbitrary knowledge need correcting by the teacher or some other authority, such as a dictionary. Physical knowledge (observations) is best corrected by further observation. Logical knowledge must be constructed in each learner's head; correcting logical knowledge only undermines children's confidence in their own thinking and makes them dependent on the teacher. Children's logical knowledge grows internally and at its own rate. Teachers must respect children's prelogical responses as a temporary stopover on the long journey of mental development.

◆ SUMMARY

Inquiry-based instruction is a method in which children ask questions, explore materials, gather data, come to conclusions, and discuss results. Science content and processes are integrated in lessons based on hands-on activities in which pupils use science processes to learn directly from interaction with the materials. Data processing often begins in a class discussion led by the teacher to guide the pupils to reflect on the experience they have just had. Discussions are begun with questions of a relatively low level to elicit description and comparison of the objects and events studied. Gradually, the teacher increases the cognitive level of the questions to help pupils construct higher-level ideas and deeper understanding.

Two lessons on mealworms were presented as examples of guided inquiry, a method in which the teacher guides pupils toward gradually increased independence and responsibility in their own thought and action. In the first lesson, children became acquainted with a mealworm through observation; in the second lesson, they started with questions they had generated, used magnifiers to observe in greater detail, and then represented their knowledge in drawings.

Teachers may need suggestions for how to get started in inquiry teaching, how to hold interesting discussion, and how to manage the classroom.

Because pupils must function more independently in guided discovery than in direct instruction, special, indirect teaching techniques are needed. To function and think more critically and more independently, children must learn to become more responsible. To facilitate growth in responsibility, the teacher must carefully plan management situations of limited complexity in which pupils can practice being responsible with a high probability of success.

The verbal techniques used in inquiry-based instruction differ from those used in direct instruction. Inquiry-based instruction requires a very different way of looking at teaching. One must realize that pupils can learn only social-arbitrary knowledge from the teacher's spoken word. For pupils to learn other, higher-order kinds of knowledge, the teacher must provide an appropriate situation and then allow the learners to do their own learning. For physical knowledge, the teacher provides objects and allows pupils to interact with those objects, essentially without interference. For logical knowledge, the teacher asks thought-provoking questions and then listens very carefully to the responses, often providing for additional thinking on the same idea before leaving it. Social-interactive knowledge as well as logical knowledge develops in an atmosphere of respectful give and take as ideas are compared and tested during group discussions. As for allotment of time, teachers using inquiry-based instruction seem to spend most of a lesson watching and listening. By thinking primarily about the children's learning and thinking processes, teachers allow the pupils to concentrate on the topic of study.

◆ ACTIVITIES FOR THE READER

The following activities can best be done in groups and then discussed by the class as a whole.

1. This activity will give you a firsthand feel for an inquiry lesson. The activity can be used with children or adolescents, but you will find it to be interesting and challenging. Your group will need some modeling clay, a good supply of small objects of uniform size and weight (coins, washers, tiles or something similar), and a sink or dishpan or other container of water.

   The first task is to make a ball of clay, and see what you have to do to it to make it float. After you have done that, see how many weights you can get in your clay object and still keep it afloat. That is, find out how many weights your object can hold and still stay afloat. Now find the shape that will carry the most weight.

   When this is done in a class, clay balls of equal weight are distributed, one to each group. The groups are challenged to make the clay float. Next they are told to get as much cargo (the weights) in their clay objects as they can. Finally, they are told to find the shape that holds the most weight and still stays afloat. Answers and ideas are displayed and discussed. This is an activity that engages the interest of students of all ages from about fourth grade up to adult level.

2. In the body of the chapter, you were asked to complete Ms. Oldhand's second lesson plan for the mealworms unit. Share and discuss your results with your classmates.

3. Examine an elementary science textbook on a topic such as insects. Try to list the main objectives of the section. Then classify the objectives according to kind of knowledge (cognitive, psychomotor, social, affective).

4. Select a small part of the insect (or other topic) section from the elementary science textbook, and develop a guided-inquiry lesson plan for it.

5. This activity was developed by DeTure and Miller (1984) and used in an unpublished teacher education videotape called *Teaching by Listening* by Ed Labinowicz (1985b). He reports that almost all teachers were able to achieve an average wait time of three seconds or more after only two practice cycles. For this activity:

   a. Select about ten children.

   b. Audiotape a discussion of about ten minutes' length.

   c. Choose a five- to seven-minute portion to transcribe verbatim.

   d. Record teacher talk and pupil talk on separate lines with space between.

   e. In blank lines, note wait time as type 1 or type 2.

   f. Time the wait time to the nearest second using a stop watch. If there is no wait time, record zero.

   g. Calculate averages for wait time 1 and wait time 2 separately.

   Tapes and written transcripts should be saved, since transcripts or tapes can also be analyzed for other verbal behaviors such as those suggested in the section on leading discussions.

◆ QUESTIONS FOR DISCUSSION

1. Describe your understanding of guided inquiry. Why should a teacher take the extra trouble to present lessons this way?

2. What is the difference between guided inquiry and guided practice?

3. What are the differences between hands-on science and inquiry science?

4. How would the mealworm lessons be different if all the objectives were to be achieved at the level of social-arbitrary knowledge?

5. Dinosaurs are a popular topic in first and second grade. Is it possible to have an inquiry lesson about dinosaurs? Explain why it is not possible, or outline a lesson plan for this topic.

6. With some children, especially the very young, it may be much easier for the

teacher to do the setting up and cleaning up of materials. How important is it for children to do these tasks?

7. In an earlier chapter on direct instruction, you read that during guided practice a pupil should be corrected immediately in case of an error. Why is it different when a pupil demonstrates an erroneous concept during guided discovery?

8. React to this remark: "Teachers like to praise. Children like it. What is the point of reducing or avoiding praise?"

9. Teachers need to let pupils know that they are listening to what the pupils say. What

are some alternatives to praise and mimicry? What is different about their effects?

10. Do all the following questions need the same amount of wait time? Explain. If you think not, which questions require more, and which less wait time?

   a. How many legs did you find on your mealworm?

   b. Do you think that all mealworms have the same number of legs?

   c. Have you noticed any patterns in what they do?

   d. Would any of these behaviors help a mealworm to survive?

◆ REFERENCES

DeTure, L., & Miller, A. (1984, March). *The effects of a written protocol model on teacher acquisition of extended wait-time.* Paper presented at the annual meeting of the National Association for Research in Science Teaching, New Orleans.

Duckworth, E., Easley, J., Hawkins, D., & Henriques, A. (1990). *Science education:: A minds-on approach for the elementary years.* Hillsdale, NJ: Erlbaum.

Good, T., & Brophy, J. (1987). *Looking in classrooms* (4th ed.). New York: Harper & Row.

Labinowicz, E. (1985a). *Learning from children: New beginnings for teaching numerical thinking.* Menlo Park, CA: Addison-Wesley.

Labinowicz, E. (1985b). *Teaching by listening: The time dimension* [Video series]. California State University, Northridge.

National Research Council. (1996). *National science education standards.* Washington, DC: National Academy Press.

Rowe, M. (1974). Relation of wait-time and rewards to the development of language, logic, and fate control: Part II—Rewards. *Journal of Research in Science Teaching, 11*(4), 291–308.

Rowe, M. (1978). *Teaching science as continuous inquiry: A basic* (2nd ed.). New York: McGraw-Hill.

Watt, D. (1996). An analysis of teacher questioning behavior in constructivist primary science education using a modification of a descriptive system designed by Barnes and Todd (1997). *International Journal of Science Education, 18*(5), 601–613.

Science Process and Content in Primary Grades

Are you, like Mr. Newman, confused about how to integrate content and process in teaching science? If so, you are not alone. This chapter and Chapter 9 have been designed to clear up some of the confusion by giving examples of inquiry lessons in which children use science processes as they learn science content. You will see that these lessons do not follow a rigid scientific method but do have a general pattern, regardless of the content or processes. You will also find some practical suggestions for the management of behavior and materials, since this is one of the keys to success when children are engaged in learning through inquiry.

Learning alternative ways of teaching can be confusing if all of your science classes have been taught by lectures and by the teacher "discussing" concepts. Those who have had models of better ways of science teaching will find it easier to adopt alternative models. It can also be confusing if you thought that you would learn the right way to teach science. The truth is, there is no one right way to teach. Experienced teachers can offer some suggestions and help you learn to be more critical in your thinking about the best methods for particular goals in certain situations. You must decide for yourself after experimenting with teaching methods. But remember that scientists do not form a conclusion on the basis of just one trial. This experimental viewpoint should help you feel less disturbed when something does not work out as planned. Instead of self-blame, you can chalk it up to experience and think about what can be done next time. That is a very good way to approach this chapter.

INFLUENCE OF AGE AND MATURITY

The essence of inquiry is captured in this question: What can children learn in and through their own actions on objects and through their own reasoning about those actions? You have been learning about guided inquiry, a method developmentally accessible to all pupils, including the youngest. The difference between primary-grade and intermediate-grade children will show up in several ways, however. Young children may need to stick to fairly simple procedures, whereas older pupils have the potential to keep a multistep set of directions in mind. The main difference between age groups shows up in the data-processing part of the lesson. Discussions with younger children should stress description and comparison of the objects and events they have observed. Older children should begin their discussions in the same way but are able to move into higher-level thinking skills, such as inferring, predicting from graphs, and even planning experiments. They can begin to use evidence to draw conclusions and support their explanations. Although even primary children can be asked to infer simple relationships and think about similarities and differences, older children can and should be asked to do a great deal more reasoning. As reasoning ability increases in the middle and upper elementary grades, critical thinking and analysis of the shared experience can be added to the simpler processes accessible to primary-grade children.

In this book, we use the term *primary grades* to refer to kindergarten through third grade and use *intermediate grades* to refer to fourth through sixth grades. The

National Science Education [NSE] Standards (National Research Council, 1996) does not use those terms and groups children in kindergarten through grade 4 and grades 5 through 8. *Benchmarks* (American Association for the Advancement of Science, 1993) uses yet another division, grouping children as kindergarten through grade 2, grades 3 through 5, and grades 6 through 8. These differences only illustrate that all such divisions are arbitrary and reflect the need to simplify and bring order to a complex subject.

BASIC SCIENCE PROCESSES AND ABILITIES

The modern elementary curriculum includes what scientists have found out (content) and what they do to find out (processes). Concepts, explanations, understandings, and theories constitute the content of science; the ways scientists make observations, try to explain the observations, and invent concepts and theories constitute the processes of science. As you study the guided inquiry lessons in this chapter, you will see that each is designed for pupils to learn how to use science processes as they learn about the subject of the investigation. Basic science processes have been identified as the following:

- *Observing.* Using one or more of the five senses to notice characteristics of objects or events.
- *Communicating.* Conveying information through language, pictures, or other means of representation. Using graphs can also be a means of communication.
- *Classifying.* Putting things into categories according to certain characteristics. Classifying includes creating and using new classification systems as well as using other people's systems.
- *Measuring.* Making quantitative observations by comparing things to one another or to a unit of measure.
- *Relating objects in space and time.* Using the relationships of space and time in describing and comparing shapes, locations, motions, and patterns.

The *National Science Education Standards* (National Research Council, 1996) does not make a distinction between content and process but has a standard for science as inquiry that includes, but is broader than, the processes in the preceding list. Expectations for children in kindergarten through grade 4 are that they should develop abilities to

- Ask a question about objects, organisms, and events in the environment.
- Plan and conduct a simple investigation.
- Employ simple equipment and tools to gather data and extend the senses.
- Use data to construct a reasonable explanation.
- Communicate investigations and explanations.

There is also a standard for science and technology that includes abilities needed to design a solution to a problem.

Expectations for children in kindergarten through grade 4 are to develop the following abilities:

- Identify a simple problem.
- Propose a solution.
- Implement proposed solutions.
- Evaluate a product or design.
- Communicate a problem, design, and solution.

This standard is meant to establish design as the technological parallel to inquiry. What this means in practice is that a science lesson can start with a question to be investigated or with a problem to be solved.

These lists can serve as guides as you plan and implement a science program for children in the early grades. To become an effective science teacher, you must understand how to guide children as they learn to use these processes in the context of learning science concepts. The lessons and activities in this chapter were designed specifically to help you gain this understanding.

For children in primary grades, it is important to remember that the question or the problem must be a simple one that leads to excitement and learning rather than frustration and loss of interest. The processes and abilities listed are *goals* toward which to strive; for children, understanding the meaning and use of science processes is developmental. Obviously, kindergarten children are very different from third graders in their attention spans, life experiences, mental development, and interests. The developmental level and interests of the children you teach will always be a major consideration in selecting topics and planning activities.

INTEGRATING PROCESS AND CONTENT

The first two lessons that follow are examples of inquiry-based instruction in which kindergarten and first-grade children learn to use simple science processes as a means of learning about the things around them. Science experiences in these years center on observation of natural events and objects, including living things, that are found in the children's environments. The kinds of natural events and the objects you use to develop children's powers of observation will depend on what you find where you are. The diversity of climates and landscapes in North America is so great that it requires you to develop your own powers of observation to look around you and find your own teaching materials. Look for things that will be interesting to children and that will provide opportunities for you to guide them toward developing new understanding or connections. Avoid trying to teach concepts that are not related to experience, either experience from their daily lives or experience provided at school. Children will often surprise you with their insights.

The lessons in this chapter are provided as examples for you to study and to use in your own teaching if they seem appropriate for the children you teach. The emphasis is on life science partly because young children are interested in animals and plants and partly because much can be learned about animals and plants by simple observation and discussion. Concepts that can only be explained or understood by mentioning atoms or genes or other nonobservable entities are not appropriate and should *never* be used at this age level.

By studying many examples and trying out some of them, you will gradually come to understand how to plan and implement inquiry lessons about any topic that you plan to teach. You will also see that science in the primary grades is based on very simple ideas and processes; it should not be complicated for either you or the children—but it should always be interesting.

◆ A LESSON ON NEEDS OF LIVING THINGS (ANIMALS)

While the teaching assistant was reading a story to half of the children in her kindergarten class, Ms. Grimaldi, who teaches science in the primary grades, asked the other half of the class to sit in a half circle on the rug around her. She had brought in a large clear glass bowl about half full of water with a large goldfish swimming in it. The bowl remained concealed with a cloth until she gathered the children; then she lifted the cloth and asked, "Who has a goldfish at home that you can tell us about?" After all who raised their hands had a turn, she continued, "Think of one word that describes something about this goldfish." She acknowledged each answer and wrote the words on a flip chart beside her.

She then commented, "We have a list of words that describe the fish. Now that we have all seen how beautiful and interesting the goldfish is, let's think about what the goldfish needs in order to stay alive and healthy. So let's make another list. This will be a list of what the fish needs to stay alive. Who can tell me one thing the fish needs?"

She wrote a new list on the flip chart and established that the fish needed food, clean water to swim in, and air to breathe. (This leads to mention of gills.)

Ms. Grimaldi then asked the children to compare the needs of the fish with their own needs. They immediately said that they need food and air and so does the fish. "What does the fish need that you don't need? And what do you need that the fish does not?" The concept to be established is that every living thing has needs and has to be in a place where its needs can be met.

Ms. Grimaldi closed the lesson by telling the children that they are going to have a place for fish to live (an aquarium) in their room, that she will help them plan what should go in the aquarium, and that they will all have a part in putting it together. (See Figure 8.1.)

Throughout the next few months, Ms. Grimaldi prepared lessons about other animals that were familiar to the children, including a hamster or other small animal to be kept in a cage in the room. In each lesson, the questions were, What are the animal's needs, how are they like my needs, how are the needs met?

FIGURE 8.1 Building our Aquarium

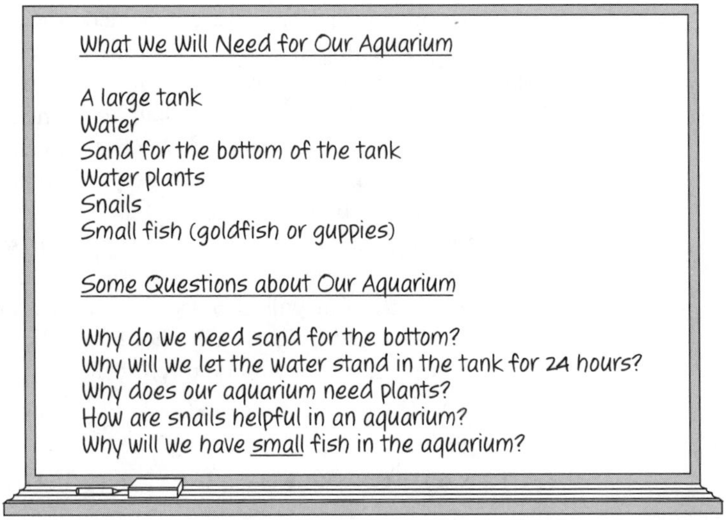

What We Will Need for Our Aquarium

A large tank
Water
Sand for the bottom of the tank
Water plants
Snails
Small fish (goldfish or guppies)

Some Questions about Our Aquarium

Why do we need sand for the bottom?
Why will we let the water stand in the tank for 24 hours?
Why does our aquarium need plants?
How are snails helpful in an aquarium?
Why will we have small fish in the aquarium?

LESSON PLAN 8.1

BASIC NEEDS OF LIVING THINGS

(Animals)

NSE STANDARD

The characteristics of organisms. All organisms have basic needs (National Research Council, 1996, p. 129).

GRADE LEVEL: KINDERGARTEN

STUDENT OBJECTIVES

1. Observe and describe a living thing (an organism).
2. Develop the understanding that organisms can survive only in environments where their needs can be met.
3. Develop an appreciation for the beauty and grace of a common organism (a goldfish) and for the variety of living things in the world.

MATERIALS

A goldfish in a large bowl
A cloth to cover the bowl

MOTIVATION/REVIEW

1. Questions about their own goldfish at home
2. Observation of goldfish to center attention

LEARNING ACTIVITIES

Data Collection

In this lesson, data collection is accomplished through recall of information from life experience.

Data Processing

Compare the needs of a fish to those of other living things that the children are familiar with.

Closure

Establish that the class is looking forward to preparing an aquarium.

ASSESSMENT

Reflect on whether children maintained interest. It is too soon to assess understanding.

Analyzing the Lesson

Kindergarten children are too young and cognitively immature to engage in full inquiry lessons, but they can begin to develop the abilities and learn to use the processes that they will need in later years for full investigations. This lesson helps

Observing life in an aquarium can lead to deeper understanding of living things.

them develop the ability to make careful observations and to express things they know from their own experience but may not have put into words before. Putting things into words helps children—and adults, too—clarify their thoughts and feelings.

This simple lesson addresses an important concept for kindergarten children. Piaget (1929/1965) showed that young children have a great deal of uncertainty about what it means to be alive. By the age of five, most children know that familiar animals are alive but do not yet have full knowledge of what that means. It is important to have animals, as well as plants, in the classroom and to provide experiences that will help the children clarify the differences between things that are alive and those that are not. Children understand that animals, especially mammals, are alive before they understand that plants, too, are alive. The following lesson reinforces the concept that plants are alive and focuses on one of plants' basic needs.

◆ GUIDED INQUIRY ON SOIL FOR GROWING PLANTS

Ms. Grimaldi started the investigation by showing the children in her first-grade class a handful of bean seeds she had brought to school. She asked all who had planted a seed and watched it grow to raise their hands. Many hands went up. "Who can tell me what a plant needs to grow?" Hands went up again. Ms. Grimaldi called on several children who said that plants need sun, water, and soil. Someone explained that too much water can kill a plant. Ms. Grimaldi asked whether the amount of sun makes a difference. Someone had grown a plant in a dark cabinet and explained the results. Throughout this part of the lesson, Ms. Grimaldi listened carefully to children's responses, did not repeat what they said but asked them to repeat if someone had difficulty hearing, made sure not to call on the same children over and over but to give everyone a chance to say something, and encouraged children to respond to each other, one at a time, of course.

Before children lost interest in this discussion, Ms. Grimaldi asked whether the kind of soil makes any difference in the way plants grow. No one had any experience to draw on to answer this question, so Ms.Grimaldi asked, "How could we find out?" From the children's suggestions and the teacher's guidance, a plan evolved to plant seeds in four different soils; sand, dirt from a yard, clay, and potting soil. What else would be needed? Pots, old newspapers to contain the mess, large spoons or small trowels to put the soil in the pots, and, of course, some seeds.

The next day, Ms. Grimaldi brought the materials to class and started the lesson by explaining how they would do their experiment. The class would be divided into two big groups. Each big group would be broken up into four smaller groups. Each small group would have soil, a small flower pot or container, and old newspaper to spread on their desks. Several trowels or large spoons were available if needed. There would be eight pots in all, two for each of the types of soil. She explained that the pots all belonged to the whole class; this was not a competition to see whose seed grew best but an experiment, or investigation, to find out what kind of soil is best for plants.

Ms. Grimaldi had planned how she would form the groups, so the children were soon in groups. She distributed the newspapers, waited until everyone had spread the papers on their desks, and then distributed the other materials. She had put samples of soil in plastic bags, ready to be transferred to the pots. The children went to work, planted one seed in each pot, labeled their pots (with Ms. Grimaldi's help), and cleaned up and threw away the newspaper. Ms. Grimaldi asked them to return to their seats and think about what to do next. She asked where the plants should be placed and what should be done about water for the plants. They told her that the plants should be placed on the windowsill where the sun came in and that they would need water. With a little guidance, they made a plan to water the plants with a measured amount of water each day, to inspect the plants daily, and record what they observed on a big chart. There was not enough time to work out the details of distribution of responsibility for watering and recording, so this was left for the following day.

On the following day, these responsibilities were assigned. The children also made predictions about the different soils, and these were recorded. From time to time over the following days, Ms. Grimaldi had to remind some of the children of their responsibilities, but she had expected this, and tried to teach children to

SOIL EXPERIMENT

Our Prediction: Best Soil _____ 2nd Best _____ 3rd Best _____ Worst _____

Our Observations:

SOILS

Week	Day	Sand	Dirt	Clay	Potting Soil
	1				
	2				
1	3				
	4				
	5				
	1				
	2				
2	3				
	4				
	5				

FIGURE 8.2 Chart for Soil Experiment

become more responsible by gentle reminders and a little help now and then. She would never let one of the plants wither or die to "teach a child a lesson." One child from each group made a report to the class each day, and observations were kept on the big chart (see Figure 8.2).

The final conclusions reached by the children were these:

1. Bean plants start to grow fast in sand and potting soil.
2. Bean plants grow very slowly in clay and are smaller.
3. Bean plants in sand stop growing sooner than in potting soil or yard soil, and they are thin and weak.
4. Potting soil is the best. Soil from the yard is next best. Clay and sand are poor soils for bean plants.

Finally, Ms. Grimaldi asked the children to explain the results. They thought that potting soil must have plant food in it because it is sold to people who want to grow plants. Ms. Grimaldi said that this was a reasonable guess but that the experiment only told them that potting soil was best, not *why* it was best.

LESSON PLAN 8.2

COMPARING SOILS FOR GROWING PLANTS

NSE STANDARD

Life science: The characteristics of organisms. All organisms have basic needs (National Research Council, 1996, p. 129).

GRADE LEVEL: 1

STUDENT OBJECTIVES

1. Participate in planning and carrying out an experiment
2. Develop understanding that plants can grow only in environments where their needs can be met.
3. Assume responsibility to do one's share of the work

MATERIALS

Bean seeds
Eight pots (small clay pots, tin cans, or plastic containers with holes in bottom) with saucers or plastic lids
Soil: sand, clay, potting soil, soil from an unfertilized spot

Old newspapers
Small trowels or large spoons

MOTIVATION/REVIEW

Questions about their experiences with growing plants.

LEARNING ACTIVITIES

Data Collection

Daily observation of plants recorded on a chart in the classroom.

Data Processing

Compare the growth of plants in different soils.
Were there differences between the two plants grown in sand? in clay?
Compare results with predictions.
Why do you think we got this result?

Closure

Record results on the chart, and display them prominently in the classroom.

ASSESSMENT

Informal observation during discussion; behavior checklist.

Analyzing the Lesson

This investigation combines the content goal of understanding the concept that organisms need a suitable environment with the science processes of observation, predicting, and inferring (that the potting soil contains more plant food) and the NSE abilities of asking a question about organisms in the environment, planning and conducting a simple investigation, using data to construct a reasonable explanation, and communicating results. Because the children were first graders, they needed careful guidance all along the way. The teacher has to monitor their behavior to see that they stay on task during the preparation of the pots and planting of the seeds and during the subsequent days, as they must remember to observe and water the plants every day and to record observations. Many children may need help in recording results, in which case, the teacher will have to work out a way to accomplish this.

Many aspects of this plan may need to be modified as the teacher considers the abilities, past experiences, and predispositions of the pupils in the class. If a teaching assistant is available, the management of behavior will be simplified. It may be appropriate for some of the soils and other materials to be brought from home by pupils. The investigation may be more appropriate at second grade than at first grade if children have had no experience in hands-on science. A teacher should never feel bound to a script for a lesson but should be free to make changes as needed.

THE PROCESS OF MEASURING

The following lesson requires children to make volume measurements, a process that was not required in the previous lessons. The process of measuring is basic in all areas of science and is not as simple to teach and learn as it may appear to be. Before beginning an activity that includes measuring, you should make sure that your pupils know how to do what is required.

Many short accounts of teaching measuring stop with measuring length and area and limit activities to those confined to the size of a desk top—or worse, a single sheet of paper. There are so many terrific, fun, and valuable activities possible that you should continue to search them out and to invent your own. Four resources to get you started are Cunningham (1976), Fuys and Tischler (1979, Chapter 6), *Match and Measure* (Elementary Science Study [ESS], 1985), and *Measurement in School Mathematics* (Nelson & Reys, 1976). The main theme of measuring and learning to measure is iterating (physically repeating, or placing over and over again) a unit until a mental picture of that unit is thoroughly established.

Another important idea in the learning and teaching of measurement is to avoid using shortcuts until the mental unit is established. Many shortcuts are used in real-life measuring, including indirect methods followed by computation and use of tools, such as trundle wheels. However, if the objective of an activity is to learn the concept of measuring or the concept of the quantity (e.g., area), then measuring should be done by reiterating the unit. It is important for you to have a good grasp of the underlying concept of measuring in order to guide your pupils toward ease and confidence in measuring a wide variety of variables. "Activities for the Reader," at the end of the chapter, include measuring activities for those who need practice in this important basic science process. Most of the activities there can be adapted to use in teaching children how to measure.

A LESSON ON ADDING WATER TO SAND AND SALT

This lesson, like the previous two, is simple in concept and does not require the teacher to have a high level of knowledge of science. The teacher does, however, have to understand how to conduct an inquiry lesson and has to be able to teach children how to use the simple filtration apparatus; the children have to be able to measure volume.

In this lesson, the children investigate what happens when water is added to sand and salt. It could be extended to other substances such as sugar, coffee, or iron filings. (Powdered substances such as flour and soda are not appropriate for this activity.) This lesson could be in a unit on water or in a unit on chemical and physical changes. Notice that the substances used are all harmless. Most children will be somewhat familiar with these substances and can use past experience or observation to make predictions.

LESSON PLAN 8.3

REACTIONS OF SUBSTANCES TO WATER

NSE STANDARD

Physical science: Properties of objects and materials (National Research Council, 1996, p. 123).

GRADE LEVEL: 3 OR 4

STUDENT OBJECTIVES

1. Understand that substances may react to water in different ways.
2. Make predictions based on past experience

MATERIALS

Sand
Salt
Sugar

For each pair or group of pupils:

A funnel on a stand
Filter paper
Beakers or jars
A graduated cylinder or arrangement for measuring

MOTIVATION/REVIEW

Ask children about their experiences with sand—on the beach, in a sandbox, or elsewhere. What is sand? (If no one knows, ask for a volunteer to find out and report the next day.) Have they ever poured water on sand or mixed water with sand? What happened? Is that the same thing that happens when water is mixed with salt? with sugar? How can we find out?

LEARNING ACTIVITIES

Data Collection

Children work in pairs or in groups of three or four if equipment and materials are limited. After discussion and explanation of how they are to proceed, each pair receives a small measured amount of sand (or, if it is feasible, have children weigh the same sand themselves) and a jar for measuring and one for mixing and access to water. Don't distribute the funnels until later. Children mix the sand with 100 ml of water, take care to mix it well, observe what happens, and record observations in workbooks. (If graduated cylinders are not available, pour 100 ml of water into a jar, and mark the top of the water with tape or a marking pencil. Repeat until there are enough for all students to have reasonable access to a marked jar. If a graduated cylinder is not available, use one measuring cup full of water as the standard. The important thing is for each pair of students to use a measured amount of water.)

After allowing time for mixing, observing, and recording, give a signal for attention, and ask the pupils what they observed. Then ask whether they could separate the sand and water, how this might be done, and whether they would they get all the water back if they could separate the mixture. Then demonstrate how to use a funnel and filter paper for filtration. Ask pupils to predict whether they will get all the water back after the mixture is separated. After predictions and a short discussion, ask the designated pupils to come up and distribute funnels (supported by rings on stands or some other way) and filter paper to the pairs or groups.

Recording data is an important part of an inquiry lesson.

Pupils filter the mixtures and measure the water and sand that are recovered. (Measuring the weight of sand is preferable, but measuring the volume is acceptable if balances are not available.) Results are recorded in workbooks.

Data Processing

"Could you separate the sand and water? How much water did you get back? how much sand? What do you think happened to the water that was not recovered? Does the sand weigh more or less than it did when you began?" Accept all answers, ask other pupils if they agree. "Was all the sand recovered? (We can't know the answer, but we can make an inference.)

"Would the same thing happen if we mixed salt and water? Sugar and water? Would it matter if the water were hot instead of cold? How can we find out?"

Closure

Pupils participate in planning for the next activity, which will be mixing water and salt. (In that case, the water will be allowed to evaporate to recover the salt.)

ASSESSMENT

Workbooks and behavior checklist can be assessed. Pupil responses in discussion are also important indicators of understanding.

INQUIRY INTO WHERE SEEDS COME FROM AND WHAT THEY DO

This lesson on seed sources is intended as the beginning of a unit on the life cycle of plants. Most children have encountered seeds in fruits but do not understand the relations among flower, fruit, and seed in the reproductive cycle of flowering plants. The question that drives this lesson is "Where do seeds come from?"

Ms. Grimaldi started the lesson by asking, "Who can tell me, where do seeds come from?" Hands went up, and children said that seeds come from trees, from the garden store, from fruits. Children were asked to react to these answers and were asked where the garden store gets seeds that are sold in little packages, what kinds of trees have seeds, and so on. After answers were noted and discussed, Ms. Grimaldi told the children that she brought some fruits that have seeds and that they can compare the seeds from different fruits. She held up a bean or tomato and said that this is one of the fruits she has brought. This elicited discussion of what a fruit is. Ms. Grimaldi introduced the idea that the part of a plant that has seeds is called a fruit by scientists. Then Ms. Grimaldi said that they will look for seeds in the fruits she has brought; they are to pick the seeds out, look at them with their magnifiers, and count the seeds in each piece of fruit. She said they should keep a record of how many seeds are in each piece; the seeds can be identified by writing the name or drawing a picture.

Children worked in pairs for this activity. With the help of pupils, Ms. Grimaldi distributed magnifiers, tweezers, and paper plates containing pieces of the following: tomato, cucumber, squash, green bean, apple, and orange. Each plate had a piece of each fruit on it.

As the children picked the seeds out of their pieces of fruit, Ms. Grimaldi walked around to answer questions, monitor progress, and remind any who had forgotten that they must keep a record. When most of the children had counted their seeds and made a record, she announced to the class that they had three more minutes to finish their work. Then they brought their plates to a designated spot and returned to their seats to discuss their results.

Ms. Grimaldi had prepared some questions to start the discussion: What differences did you notice between tomato seeds and apple seeds? Which fruit has the most seeds? The discussion established that there are differences in size and appearance between seeds and that some fruits have many more seeds than others. Then Ms. Grimaldi asked, "Which can produce more plants from one fruit, a tomato plant or a pea plant?" The children answered that the tomato probably could because it has more seeds. "If there was only a tiny bit of space for things to grow and a tomato and a pea pod fell in that space, which kind of plant would you be more likely to find next year?" This brought up the subject of size of seed and caused a great deal of discussion between pupils, which Ms. Grimaldi encouraged; she told them she did not know the answer and asked how they could find the answer. She ended the lesson with pupils still thinking about the question.

The next lesson was an investigation of what happens to seeds when they are planted. Each pupil planted several kinds of dry seeds in a small plastic container with a wet sponge, kept the sponge wet, and observed and drew a picture of the seeds as they germinated: First the root appeared and grew downward, then the stem appeared and grew upward, and leaves appeared on the end of the stem. These changes were observed with a magnifier and recorded by a series of drawings.

Ms. Grimaldi's lesson plan for the first lesson follows.

LESSON PLAN 8.4

SEED SOURCES

NSE STANDARD

Life science. Each plant has different structures that serve different functions in growth, survival, and reproduction (National Research Council, 1996, p. 129).

GRADE LEVEL: 2

STUDENT OBJECTIVES

1. Recognize fruits as the original source of seeds.
2. Identify any seed-bearing part of a plant as a fruit.
3. Observe variation in shape and size among seeds.

MATERIALS

Five or six different kinds of fruits, depending on locality and season (tomatoes, bananas, peppers, squash, cucumbers, apples, oranges, peas, green beans, pea pods, etc.). Some of the fruits should have many seeds; for example, tomatoes, squash, and cucumbers.

Paper plates
Paper towels
Hand magnifiers
Tweezers (toothpicks if tweezers are unavailable)
One knife (for teacher)

MOTIVATION/REVIEW

Ask "Where do seeds come from?" "What kinds of things have seeds?" Hold up a bean or tomato, and say that this is one of the fruits you have brought. Introduce the idea that scientists call anything with seeds a fruit.

LEARNING ACTIVITIES

Data Collection

Explain what the pupils are to do, and distribute the materials. Children pick seeds out of fruits, examine them with a magnifier, and count and record numbers of seeds in workbook.

Data Processing

"What differences did you notice? Which fruit has the most seeds? Which can produce more plants from one fruit, a tomato plant or a pea plant? If there was only a tiny bit of space for things to grow, and a tomato and a pea pod fell in that space, which kind of plant would you be more likely to find next year?"

Closure

Collect reports, and say that pupils will watch some seeds grow in the next lesson.

ASSESSMENT

The assessment of this lesson is informal, based on observation during the activity and on records. Records will be returned to pupils with comments.

How many ways can you classify these animals into two groups?

Rules: (a) There can be only two groups and (b) every animal has to be in a group. Label the groups and list the animals that belong in each group.

Hint: 1. Animals with fur and animals without fur.
2. House pets and not house pets, etc.

FIGURE 8.3 Classifying Animals

LESSONS ON COMPARING, SORTING, AND CLASSIFYING

Although we have not included them in this chapter, lessons on sorting, comparing, and classifying are often included in the curriculum at this level (see Figure 8.3). These processes are needed and used in many investigations and can be integrated with learning content in the context of an investigation that goes beyond the processes as such. For example, the point of the lesson on soils for growing seeds is to compare soils on a given criterion, the ability to produce the best plant.

Three important concepts involved in classifying are (1) classification is meant to be useful, (2) classification is arbitrary, and (3) any group of objects can be classified in more than one way. Because of the way classification is often taught, pupils sometimes get the notion that classification systems have some internal logic that was simply "discovered" by scientists of the past and is now passed on in school. Actually, systems of naming and classifying animals, plants, rocks, and other things were devised to make it easier for scientists to communicate with each other. The categories could just as well be classified by different criteria. In fact, many systems and names of things in science change rather often as new knowledge becomes available, as old knowledge is reconsidered, or as the animals themselves (or other things being classified) actually change.

MANAGEMENT OF BEHAVIOR AND MATERIALS

The suggestions in this section apply to inquiry-based teaching at the intermediate level as well as the primary level, but they are particularly important whenever children are introduced to inquiry-based teaching for the first time. These suggestions supplement those in Chapter 3, which are applicable to all teaching methods. The shift in roles from direct instruction to inquiry-based teaching means that pupils are expected to start learning to manage their own behavior and materials. Since the behaviors are new, the pupils must be taught how to do them. Teaching children how to manage for themselves is very much like the steps in a direct instruction lesson (though the time frame is much longer). The teacher gives motivation and then presents a procedure directly. The pupils practice, first with considerable guidance and later with less. Periodically, the teacher may call a class discussion to involve everyone in evaluating progress. One difference between direct instruction and guided inquiry is that pupils are expected to take greater responsibility for themselves in guided inquiry.

Noise

Some teachers are uncomfortable with any level of noise, either because they feel they are expected to maintain a quiet room or because they believe noise will lead to serious disorder. The amount of noise that is tolerable varies from teacher to teacher. Experienced teachers are acutely aware of noise and of their own tolerance levels. While there is no specific decibel level at which things always come unglued, too much noise can have a contagious effect that leads to disruptive behavior. In the past, many principals expected silence, but now—with newer methods such as cooperative learning gaining acceptance—most principals do not insist on totally noiseless classrooms. With experience, you will find a noise level that feels OK to you, that does not disturb other classrooms, and that is comfortable for the children.

Using Psychology Instead of Coercion

Children like to do hands-on science activities, and they usually like to work together. You can use this affinity to keep order. Explain that working freely with the materials is a privilege for those who can control their own behavior, and that if they forget, they will have to be separated from the work temporarily. (Because you need to tailor special standards each time the type of activity or materials warrants, you will need to remind the pupils of the standards occasionally—perhaps each day. What to include in the standards is up to you, but they should be specific and few. Some teachers like to include "Stay in your seat unless you are a monitor." Even if trips to the drinking fountain or pencil sharpener are allowed during other subject activities, you may want to try restricting them during science group work. Allowing both talking and walking around at the same time may be too much novelty to handle. If one table discovers something especially exciting, for example, their "oohs" and "ahs" may cause all the rest of the class members to leave their own work and crowd around that table.

A Signal

You will need some kind of nonverbal signal to regain attention after group work begins. This could be a sound, reserved especially for this purpose, that can be detected over the hum of busy group workers, such as a chime or bell. Some teachers flip the light switch off and on. Some just flip the lights off and leave them off until they get attention. Other schemes include rhythmic clapping (to which pupils join in) and simply raising a hand. Whatever signal you choose, talk it over with the pupils before using it—do not just expect them to know what it means automatically. Also, the signal may have been used for something different before you came. A student teacher once tried sounding a chime to get attention, and all the children stood up and sang "The Star-Spangled Banner"!

Another consideration for an attention signal is to use it sparingly. Consider a single science activity. After pupils begin group work, you will probably need your signal at least once, when it is time to stop working and begin cleaning up. In addition, you may need to use the signal to caution the class if you feel the noise level is increasing toward the "danger point." If such warnings happen more than once or twice, you should consider stopping the activity to review standards. A third use for the signal is when you find it necessary to give additional directions for the activity. Clearly, this last use is undesirable. The activity will go more smoothly if interruptions of this type, or of any type, are minimized. Still, interruptions will be necessary occasionally for some unanticipated problem, so having a pre-established signal is important. Remember to plan carefully to minimize the need for using the signal. If used too often, as with any frequent stimulus, it will lose its effect.

Distribution and Cleanup

Plan carefully for quick distribution of materials. A waiting child is not only wasting time but also getting restless and perhaps into trouble. On the first day of a new unit, some teachers like to set up all the tables while the pupils are out of the room, such as at lunch or recess. The problem of giving directions with materials already distributed can be handled by giving directions outside before the children come in or in a special discussion area of the room. After the unit is underway, a teacher should shift the setting-up and cleaning-up work to the pupils. They need to practice responsibility, and you need time to prepare your thoughts before beginning the lesson. A monitor system can be worked out, perhaps on a rotating basis—table captain of the week, for example. If necessary, special incentives such as extrinsic rewards can be used for groups showing responsibility in getting set up at the beginning and cleaning up at the end.

Dealing with Messes

Inquiry-based teaching is potentially messy. While careful planning and good directions will minimize messes, they can never be completely eliminated. So a child spills something—that is not the end of the world. The payoff from hands-on science is well worth an occasional mess. It is best to plan for the worst, though. Cover the tables with newspapers or towels, and have sponges, mops, and buckets handy just in case. If there is a potential for spilled liquids on the floor, restricting pupil movement around the room may be desirable to prevent slipping and possible injury.

Involving the Pupils at Home

Sending simple materials home with children has the potential for getting parents and others at the pupil's home involved with your science program. Although such involvement sounds good, there are some possible drawbacks to consider. Your pupil may not have control over what happens to the material once outside the classroom. Because materials may be lost or damaged, use caution in what you send home. For the same reason, if the material is sent home for the child to use in a homework assignment, do not penalize the child if the work is not done and do not depend on the work's completion as a prerequisite for a subsequent activity. Some teachers like to ask pupils to bring things from home. For example, if each child brings a working flashlight, you have most of the expensive materials for teaching electricity activities. Also on the plus side, you may have interested the parents in what is happening in their child's science program. On the minus side, some children will not be able to get a flashlight. Rather than penalize or call attention to those children, just have some extra flashlights on hand. Any time you ask for such materials, it is a good policy to send a note to the parents or guardians. Similarly, certain kinds of materials sent home should be preceded by a request to parents for permission slips. Any living things that require care or that might cause consternation should be sent home only after parents have given permission.

◆ SUMMARY

Children in primary grades can begin to develop abilities to ask questions about things in the environment, carry out simple investigations, use simple apparatus, and record and explain what they have done as they use such basic processes as observing, measuring, and classifying. Lessons based on activities with simple materials and simple apparatus allow them to have experiences from which they can make comparisons, see differences, and draw conclusions of their own. It is important to avoid activities that require lengthy directions for procedures and that are not based on observable phenomena. Lessons presented as examples show that teachers do not have to have sophisticated knowledge of science to be successful science teachers at the primary level. Important attributes for a teacher are to know what interests children and to be able to guide them through guided inquiry lessons.

Management of materials and behavior in inquiry-based teaching requires skills that are different from those often needed for other kinds of instruction. Noise created by purposeful activity, materials accidentally spilled, distribution of materials, and cleaning up after an activity are situations not encountered in a classroom where children do not have access to hands-on materials and the need to move about the classroom to accomplish their work. These situations can be managed by recognizing the kinds of problems that may exist and planning ahead to prevent as many as possible. Planning ahead is the key both to effective instruction and to effective management.

◆ ACTIVITIES FOR THE READER

1. Write a lesson plan for a lesson that will follow the lesson on mixing sand and water (Lesson Plan 8.3).

2. Plan a lesson in which children bring in small rocks, you combine them with rocks you have found or obtained from another source, and children classify the rocks first in one way and then in another way. One way may be according to size: rocks smaller than a peanut (or other object) in one group and all others in another. Another may be to base the two classes on whether a rock is darker than a large rock you bring in for a sample. (You will need a large assortment of rocks so that all children have enough to make the activity meaningful.)

3. The following activities on measuring may be done at home or in class. They were written for readers who may need practice in using metric units, but they can also be adapted for use with children.

MEASURING ACTIVITY 1

Cut a strip from an index card or similar material to match the length of the rectangle shown in Figure 8.4.

Then make a list of things in your home that are the same length or close to the same length. For example, you may notice that an electrical switch plate is very close to that length. Find other objects to bring your list to about ten items. Share your list in class. Which things named by your classmates did you also have on your list?

MEASURING ACTIVITY 2

Because of the way area is sometimes taught in school, it is often thought of as something figured out by multiplying linear measurements. This multiplying procedure is a shortcut for finding area, but it does not help in the understanding of the meaning of area or the meaning of measurement. Measuring Activity 2 is designed to make these meanings clearer. Area is the extent of a surface. Choose a surface whose area you will measure. A table or small "area" rug would be convenient. Next, choose an area unit, also for convenience. For a unit, choose something that possesses area itself. Also, you will want multiple copies of the unit. A string or a pipe cleaner will not do as an area unit, because each only has length. You could use playing cards, small index cards, little self-adhesive notes, or pages from a small tablet. First, look at the surface to be measured—say, a card table. Just by looking, estimate how many of your

FIGURE 8.4   A Rectangle of a Certain Length

units—say, playing cards—it will take to cover the table. Write down this estimate. Then check your estimate by actually covering the table with cards. Finally, count the cards. How else did you come to your estimate?

MEASURING ACTIVITY 3: METRIC SYSTEM

Select a group of containers in your kitchen. Here are some things you might easily round up: sauce pan, drinking glass, coffee mug, pie pan, mixing bowl, cereal bowl.

You will also need a measuring cup. It can be one-, two-, or four-cup capacity. Turn the cup around, and look at the markings on the side opposite the fractional-cup markings. Unless your measuring cup is an antique, you will find milliliter (ml) markings. Now follow these steps:

1. Look at the containers you have gathered. Which do you think will hold the most? Which will hold second most? Arrange your containers in the order you think will be from least to most volume. This may not be as easy as you think. Containers of different shapes may be hard to compare without pouring, but for now, do not do any pouring. List your containers on a sheet of paper in the order you estimated.

2. Check your estimated volume sequence this way: Fill with water the container you think is the smallest. Pour it into the next largest container. Did the second container still have room for more water? If not, rearrange the order. Continue in this way until you have checked all the containers and are sure that they are correctly ordered by volume.

3. Find another container that is smaller than the smallest container you listed. It might be a small paper cup, a spray can lid, or a demitasse. Make your list into a worksheet, as in Table 8.1. If your small additional container is not a lid, substitute its name in your worksheet.

4. In the estimate column under the heading "Lids," write the number of lids you think each container will hold.

5. After you have entered all your lid estimates on the worksheet, use the lid to measure each container. Pour and count the number of lidfuls necessary to fill each container to the brim. Enter your results in the worksheet.

6. Fill the measuring cup to the one-cup mark. Turn the cup around and notice the milliliter equivalent. If you have a larger measuring cup, fill it to two cups and four cups, noticing the milliliter equivalents.

7. Without pouring, look at the drinking glass (or whatever is first on your list), and estimate the number of milliliters needed to fill it to the brim. You may look at your milliliter measuring cup as a reference, but don't touch. Enter your estimated milliliters on the worksheet. Continue for each of the items on your list.

8. Now, measure the volume in milliliters of each container using your cup. Write your results in the far-right column. Are you getting better?

TABLE 8.1 Metric Worksheet

Container	Lids		Milliliters	
	Estimate	Measure	Estimate	Measure
drinking glass				
coffee mug				
cereal bowl				
pie pan				
sauce pan				
mixing bowl				

You may not realize it, but by virtue of having done Measuring Activity 1, you now have a mental picture of a decimeter. The strip of tag board you made to match Figure 8.4 is exactly 10 centimeters—1 decimeter—long. The purpose of the activity was to establish the beginning of confidence in you as a measurement teacher and a user of the metric system. Try to avoid translating metric units into units in the U.S. customary system (i.e., the foot–pound system). Because Americans grow up with the customary system, most already have mental images of many of its units. The way to feel comfortable with the metric system is to experience its units and build up mental pictures. It is much like learning a foreign language. If you have to translate word-for-word into and out of English, you will never approach fluency. Just live with the new language through firsthand experiences, and you will pick it up before you realize it.

You did this in the activity that involved covering a table with cards. It would have been more efficient to use a ruler and measure the length and width of the table and then multiply, but the objective was to learn, so you did it the hard way.

◆ **QUESTIONS FOR DISCUSSION**

1. React to this teacher's statement: "It is important for children to learn to listen; rather than worry about always keeping my telling and explaining short, I intend to teach my pupils to be better listeners."

2. What are some things that could go wrong when the teacher has not planned well enough in regard to using concrete materials? Perhaps you have a personal experience to share with your classmates.

How could the problem have been prevented?

3. Can "real science" be taught at the kindergarten level? Explain your answer.

4. Are all classifications arbitrary? What about night and day? male and female? animal and plant? mammal and bird? How does one determine how to place anything in a class or category?

◆ **REFERENCES**

American Association for the Advancement of Science. (1993). *Benchmarks for science literacy.* New York: Oxford University Press.

Cunningham, J. (1976). *Teaching metrics simplified.* Upper Saddle River, NJ: Prentice Hall

Elementary Science Study (ESS). (1985). *Match and measure.* Nashua, NH: Delta.

Fuys, D., & Tischler, R. (1979). *Teaching mathematics in the elementary school.* Boston: Little, Brown.

National Research Council. (1996). *National science education standards.* Washington, DC: National Academy Press.

Nelson, D., & Reys, R. (Eds.). (1976). *Measurement in school mathematics. NCTM Yearbook.* Reston, VA: National Council of Teachers of Mathematics.

Piaget, J. (1965). *The child's conception of the world.* Totowa, NJ: Littlefield, Adams. (Original work published 1929)

Science Process and Content in Intermediate Grades

Before you begin this chapter, take a moment to think about some of the differences between children in primary grades and those in intermediate grades. By fourth grade, most children can read with comprehension, can write without laboring over each word, and have developed basic skills in arithmetic. Although science instruction should always be based on active engagement with materials, some children will be interested in reading material related to science. Facility with writing allows written as well as oral reports, and basic skills in arithmetic can be used to advantage in science.

Along with those skills, children in intermediate grades have developed mental abilities that allow them to use more advanced science processes and build on the inquiry skills they have developed in primary grades. The basic processes described in Chapter 8 may be introduced with the youngest children and used in every grade thereafter. Each process, once introduced, should continue to be used in the subsequent years. The reason for this gradual introduction is to match the child's developing mental abilities. In this chapter, you will learn about using other, more advanced, science processes in lessons that lead to understanding of science concepts. Guided inquiry lessons that use these processes are presented so that you get a feel for using the processes in a natural way in the classroom. These lessons have a new element not previously developed in this book. In the data-processing part of the lesson, the teacher helps the pupils go beyond simply describing to applying higher-order thinking that approaches what is done by scientists.

Pupil autonomy should increase gradually through the school years. In other words, as pupils grow mentally and emotionally, they should be taught to take more responsibility for structuring their learning activities. Generally, this shift in the source of structure occurs as the teacher presents and guides practice in new methods of operating, just as teacher presentation and guidance are used to teach content. As pupils gain understanding and facility with the methods, less and less presentation and guidance by the teacher are needed. As teacher, your role is to decide how much outside structure your pupils need and how much structuring they are ready to manage for themselves in any particular activity.

SCIENCE PROCESSES AND ABILITIES FOR INTERMEDIATE GRADES

Science processes appropriate for developing in the intermediate grades have been identified as the following:

- *Predicting.* Using previous observations to make an educated guess about a future event or condition.
- *Inferring.* Making a tentative or trial explanation for a set of observations.
- *Controlling variables.* Identifying attributes or factors that could vary in a system and holding all but one constant.
- *Defining operationally.* Setting specific limits to the meaning of a term for the purpose of dealing with a particular situation.

◆ *Experimenting.* Applying all the science processes, as needed, to design and carry out as well as to interpret a test of a question or hypothesis.

The abilities necessary at grades 5 to 8 to do scientific inquiry are identified by the *National Science Education [NSE] Standards* (National Research Council, 1996) as the following:

◆ Identify questions that can be answered through scientific investigation.

◆ Design and conduct a scientific investigation.

◆ Use appropriate tools and techniques to gather, analyze, and interpret data.

◆ Use evidence to develop descriptions, explanations, predictions, and models.

◆ Think critically and logically to connect evidence and explanations.

◆ Communicate procedures and explanations.

◆ Use mathematics in all aspects of scientific inquiry.

Abilities related to science and technology are these:

◆ Identify appropriate problems for technological design.

◆ Design a solution or product.

◆ Implement a proposed design.

◆ Evaluate the completed design or products.

◆ Communicate the process of technological design.

As you study these lists, remember that they were developed for grades 5 to 8 and that many of the skills and abilities are not attainable until seventh or eighth grade.

INTEGRATING PROCESS AND CONTENT

The lessons that follow are examples of inquiry-based instruction in which children use science processes to learn some of the science concepts that are part of the science curriculum in most states and districts and that are incorporated in the NSE standards (National Research Council, 1996). Concepts from physical science, life science, and earth science are used in the examples. In some cases, children will need to learn a particular process or skill before they can begin an inquiry lesson. Direct instruction is often useful when that need arises. You have already seen that direct instruction was used to teach a lesson on the equal-arm balance (see Chapter 6). In the first example given in this chapter, the pupils need to have had some experience with graphing data before they start the lesson, but using graphing in the investigation strengthens their ability to make graphs and shows them the usefulness of that skill.

A LESSON ON PREDICTING THE SHORTEST DAY OF THE YEAR

The following lesson can be adapted as an in-class activity for professional development of preservice and in-service teachers.

◆ Ms. Oldhand started a discussion with her sixth graders. "Now that the year is getting along into November, have you noticed anything about the time it gets dark in the evening?"

Several children remarked that the time of sunset was getting earlier. One had noticed that for his after-school softball program lights were now needed, whereas a few weeks ago they were not. Another said her parents did not allow her to stay outdoors after dark and that her afternoon play time was getting shorter and shorter. Other students offered several more responses of this type.

"Have you noticed anything about the time the sun rises in the morning?" asked Ms. Oldhand.

Few children had noticed changes in sunrise on their own, but most agreed that they had to get up before it was completely light now and that last month this had not been the case.

"Does anyone know when the shortest day in the year is?" Ms. Oldhand asked. "There is a day that has the shortest time between sunrise and sunset. Before it comes, the days get shorter and shorter. After it is gone, the days begin to get longer again. The shortest day is called the winter solstice. Does anyone know the approximate date it falls on?" Several volunteered that it was late in December.

Continuing in this way, Ms. Oldhand established that the pupils had all noticed to some degree or other that the time of sunrise and sunset changes throughout the year in a regular and predictable way. Then she posed a problem. "I like to go for a walk after school. I walk a certain distance from my house through the park and back home again. It is about five o'clock when I get home. I have noticed that the sun is setting when I get home and that it gets dark very soon afterward. I don't like to be out walking after dark. Do you think I will be able to continue taking my usual walk throughout the winter, or will I have to cut it short in order to get home before dark? Will sunset continue to come earlier and earlier until the winter solstice?"

After some discussion by the class, Ms. Oldhand suggested a way to find out. "Let's see what patterns show up when we graph the data. First, let's look at this data sheet. I got the sunset time for three months from an almanac. Maybe that will help you decide whether I will be able to continue my evening walks." Ms. Oldhand provided the students with the data shown in Figure 9.1.

After a few days, the class had completed two different graphs, time of sunset and time of sunrise, as shown in Figure 9.2.

Then the discussion continued. They found that sunset got earlier for a while, then stayed the same for a few days around the end of November. Then in early December, sunset began getting later. Sunrises continued to get later until January

Sunrise and Sunset Times for Latitude 30°			
Date	Sunrise A.M.	Sunset P.M.	Daylight (Hrs, Min)
11–01	6:13	5:14	
11–04	6:16	5:12	
11–07	6:18	5:09	
11–10	6:21	5:07	
11–13	6:23	5:05	
11–16	6:26	5:04	
11–19	6:28	5:02	
11–22	6:31	5:01	
11–25	6:33	5:00	
11–28	6:36	5:00	
12–01	6:38	5:00	
12–04	6:40	5:00	
12–07	6:42	5:00	
12–10	6:44	5:00	
12–13	6:47	5:01	
12–16	6:49	5:02	
12–19	6:51	5:03	
12–22	6:52	5:05	
12–25	6:54	5:06	
12–28	6:55	5:08	
12–31	6:56	5:10	
1–03	6:56	5:13	
1–06	6:57	5:15	
1–09	6:57	5:17	
1–12	6:57	5:20	
1–15	6:57	5:22	
1–18	6:56	5:25	
1–21	6:55	5:27	
1–24	6:54	5:30	
1–27	6:55	5:33	
1–30	6:52	5:35	

FIGURE 9.1 Sunrise/Sunset Data Sheet

Source: The World Almanac, 1990, Mahwah, NJ, World Almanac Books. This and similar references give sunrise and sunset data for various latitudes; when using the information for a class, choose the times for the latitude closest to your location.

6th, when it reached 6:57 A.M. Then they stayed the same for several days, and on January 21st, they began getting earlier.

Ms. Oldhand asked how they could find the day with the shortest amount of daylight. Someone suggested finding the difference in the times of sunrise and sunset. She agreed that this would work, and they briefly discussed how to compute between A M. and P.M. times. She also suggested an easier way: "Hold your

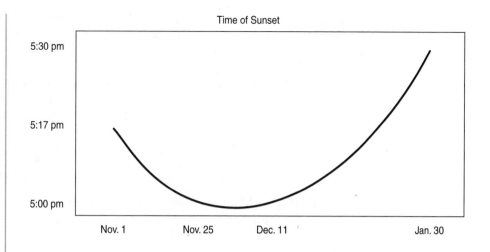

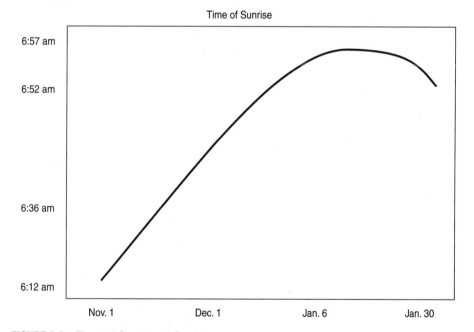

FIGURE 9.2 Times of Sunset and Sunrise

two graphs together, up to the light, so that the dates on the x-axes coincide. Then slip the papers up and down until you find where the two curves just barely touch." This placed turned out to be several days in late December (see Figure 9.3).

Then Ms. Oldhand suggested that they look back at the data sheet she had given them and actually compute the number of hours and minutes between sunrise and sunset for those days that "touched" on the graphs. When they did this, they found that December 22 was the day having the least sunlight, or the shortest day of the year.

To give everyone an opportunity to think about these discoveries, and to relate them to their own lives, Ms. Oldhand asked the children to write in their science journals, telling in their own words about the shortest-day lesson and what effect the changing amounts of sunlight had on them personally.

MR. NEWMAN: I really enjoyed that lesson, and I learned something, too. I always thought that the latest sunrise and the earliest sunset occurred on the December 21—and that was the shortest day.

MS. OLDHAND: That's a very common misconception and, fortunately, a rather harmless one. This lesson is one in which the teacher as well as the pupils can be a learner.

MR. NEWMAN: But how can I be a teacher and a learner at the same time?

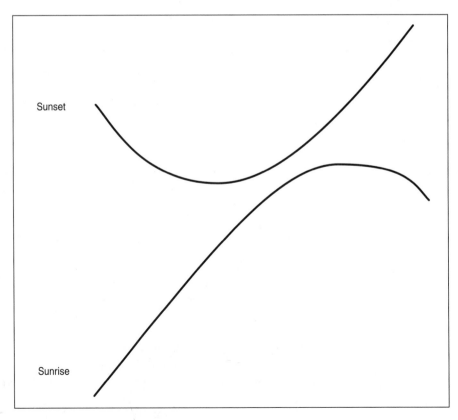

FIGURE 9.3   Sunset and Sunrise Composite Graph

MS. OLDHAND: That's an important question. It always concerns me when I occasionally hear a teacher say, "Oh, I'm learning science along with the kids." The teacher doesn't have to know everything — and can't know everything—but there are some things that a teacher must know.

MR. NEWMAN: Can you give me some examples?

MS. OLDHAND: A teacher must know how to plan lessons that will engage the pupils in learning and to guide pupils through the learning activities. A teacher must have a firm knowledge of basic science concepts that underlie the science curriculum and the processes involved in scientific inquiry. In the shortest day lesson, the teacher would have to have facility with graphing and know how to guide pupils in making and interpreting graphs.

MR. NEWMAN: There's so much to learn, it makes me wonder if I will ever become a good teacher.

MS. OLDHAND: There *is* a lot to learn. That's why good teachers never stop learning.

Now that you have seen how Ms. Oldhand guided her sixth graders through this lesson, you can study the plan she used for this guided inquiry lesson. Notice that this lesson continued over a period of several days and that Ms. Oldhand did not rush the children. (One of the skills that teachers need to develop is keeping activities at a steady pace without making the children rush through important steps.)

LESSON PLAN 9.1

PREDICTING THE SHORTEST DAY OF THE YEAR

NSE STANDARD

Earth and space science: Earth in the solar system (National Research Council, 1996, p. 160).

GRADE LEVEL: 6

STUDENT OBJECTIVES

1. Know that there are predictable patterns of the sun's movement.
2. Construct line graphs from provided data.

3. Predict from graphs the day with the earliest sunset, the day with the latest sunrise, and the day with the shortest period of daylight.
4. Describe effects of changes in time of sunrise and sunset on their lives.

MATERIALS

For each pair of pupils:

Sunrise/sunset data sheet (Figure 9.1)
Three sheets of graph paper

MOTIVATION/REVIEW

1. "Has anyone noticed when the sun is setting recently?" "How did you happen to notice?" Repeat for sunrise. Tell the name for the shortest day—winter solstice.
2. Pose a problem: "Can I continue walking after school, or will it soon be dark too early?" If the date of winter solstice (December 21 or 22) was mentioned earlier, ask, "Will sunset continue to get earlier and earlier until winter solstice in December? Let's find out."

LEARNING ACTIVITIES

Data Collection

(In this lesson, the data are not collected firsthand by the pupils but are presented by the teacher from a reference source. Because every child has experienced many sunrises and sunsets and because personal collection of three months of data would not be feasible, this procedure is acceptable.)

Pass out the data sheet, and discuss it briefly. Point out that only every third day is given. This does not affect the shape of the curve and will make constructing the graphs quicker. Briefly review graphing procedure. Have pupils work with a partner. One partner can read data from the data sheet, and the other can plot the points. Partners should alternate occasionally and check each other. Allow at least two days. Don't try to do all the graphing in one sitting.

Data Processing

1. Ask pupils to report the earliest sunset and latest sunrise (roughly, November 28 and January 9, respectively). "Are you surprised? Did you expect them to fall on the same day?"
2. "How could we find the shortest day?" (We could compute the difference between sunrises and sunsets on the data table.) "That would work, but even easier is this method. . . . " Explain how to hold the graphs up to the light, slide them up and down, and find where the curves touch. After finding days where the "touch" is located, ask pupils to compute the difference for those days only.

Closure

Ask pupils to write in their science workbooks (1) their results and (2) how the changes in daylight have affected their lives.

ASSESSMENT

Make informal observations during discussion, assess graphs, and read workbooks. (Pupils will be told that these assessments will be made.)

Analyzing the Lesson

Let's review Ms. Oldhand's lesson to see how processes and content were integrated in a guided inquiry lesson. The content, or science concept, that was the learning objective is the very basic knowledge that the movement of the sun is regular and predictable. You may be thinking that all sixth graders know that already, and in one sense they do, but this lesson reinforces that knowledge, makes it more real to pupils, and lets them see that they can use data to make predictions. This is an example of choosing a process, predicting, to emphasize a related concept, the concept that the sun's movement is predictable. Since not every science process is appropriate or useful for every inquiry lesson, it's a challenge, to match process to content, and it makes teaching more interesting.

You'll notice that graphing was an important part of this lesson and that the lesson followed the general pattern of an inquiry lesson. The lesson started with a question, in this case asked by the teacher, and continued with data gathering, putting the data in an interpretable form, interpreting data, and displaying and discussing results. In the next lesson, a different science process will be emphasized, but the pattern of an inquiry lesson will be similar.

A LESSON ON INFERRING HIDDEN CIRCUITS

The following lesson can be adapted as an in-class activity for professional development of preservice and in-service teachers. This lesson and the related activity that follows were designed as part of a unit on electricity.

◆ "Today we will continue with our electricity unit," said Ms. Oldhand. "Let's review what we have done so far." Hands went up, the main accomplishments were recalled and briefly reviewed. The pupils knew how to make simple circuits with one battery, one bulb, and one wire. They also had used simple holders for the batteries and bulbs and understood how those materials worked. The last thing they had done was to make circuit testers, as shown in Figure 9.4; they had

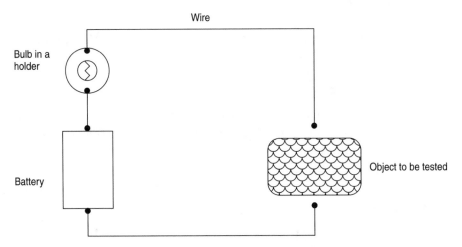

Wire

Bulb in a holder

Battery

Object to be tested

FIGURE 9.4 Circuit Tester

used the circuit testers to identify objects that would complete or would not complete a circuit. In other words, the pupils were able to decide whether an object was a conductor or a nonconductor by testing it. These understandings were essential prerequisites for today's lesson.

Ms. Oldhand clipped a large demonstration circuit board on the chart rack (see Figure 9.5). The circles on the outside of the circuit board were brads—brass paper fasteners. On the inside of the board, some of the brads were connected by copper wires and some were not. She opened the circuit board to show the wires inside. Figure 9.5 shows four such circuit boards.

"Our job will be to figure out how the wires are connected without looking at them directly," she said. "The boards you will be testing will be wired differently, and you aren't allowed to look inside. Scientists work on puzzles like this sometimes. First, let's review how the circuit tester works. What will happen when I bring the contact points together?" (The bulb should light.) She held the contacts of her circuit tester close together. "Let's see," said Ms. Oldhand. as she touched the contacts to demonstrate. "What if it doesn't light?" (Shows your tester isn't working.) "So it's a good idea to check the tester before using it. Yesterday, I saw someone trying to test an object by touching the tester contacts to the object, but the contacts were also touching each other. Is there a problem with this procedure?" (Yes, it only shows that the tester is working. The electricity is going through the tester wires only and is not forced to go through the object being tested.)

"This is how you can test for hidden connections," said Ms. Oldhand, as she placed her two circuit tester terminals on points A and B of the demonstration circuit board. "Aha!" said Ms. Oldhand, "the circuit tester light did not come on when the ends touched A and B. What does this tell us about a wire connection between A and B?" (There is none.) Ms. Oldhand wrote a negative sign after AB

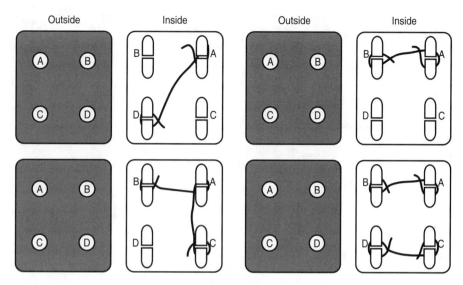

FIGURE 9.5 **Four Circuit Boards, Outside and Inside**

on the chart. "A negative sign means no reaction—no light." Ms. Oldhand then moved a terminal to point C, leaving one on point A. "Again, a negative result means no connection." For points B and D, she elicited the response that a positive result (light turned on) means that there is a connection. Ms. Oldhand continued in this manner until every possible pair of contact points had been tested and the result recorded. Figure 9.6 shows the results.

FIGURE 9.6 **Circuit Test Results**

Test Results for
Circuit Board "X"

AB –	BC +
AC –	BD +
AD –	CD +

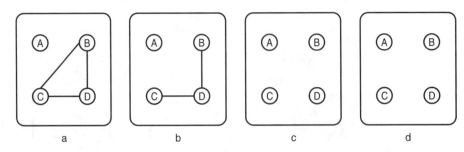

a   b   c   d

FIGURE 9.7 Wiring Diagrams for a Four-Circuit Board [There are four possibilities for wiring a four-point circuit board to give the results shown here. Can you find the other two?]

"Let's show the result by drawing a line between the points on the diagram," said Ms. Oldhand. She then made a diagram for the six results, drawing connecting lines between points when the data table showed a positive result. At the end, her diagram looked like Figure 9.7. "Does the real circuit board have to look like this . . . or could there be any other arrangements of wire connections that would give these same results?"

The pupils were not sure about this, and no one suggested any other arrangements. "What would happen if this wire were missing?" She put her hand over the connecting line between Terminal C and Terminal B on the diagram, making the diagram now look like Figure 9.7b. Then Ms. Oldhand touched points B and C again. "Would the circuit tester light up? Natalie?" After a few seconds, Natalie replied, "Oh! I see! Yes, the electricity doesn't mind turning the corner!" Ms. Oldhand smiled and said, "These are ideas you can check for yourselves."

"You will have some unwired practice circuit boards to test your inferences. If you are not sure that one of your inferences will work, wire up a practice board and test it. We will talk more about this later, but for now, I'll just say that several wirings will work. Try to think of as many as you can that will give the results you get with your testers, and record your inferences on the data sheet. Now," said Ms. Oldhand, "would table monitors please come up for your materials? When you have your supplies, you may begin working."

Each team of four pupils at a table received a duplicate set of three circuit boards and a data sheet like the one in Figure 9.8. The boards were made of corrugated cardboard with labeled brad heads showing on one side and wires connecting some of the brads on the other side. Pupils could not see the wiring, however, because another piece of cardboard covered the wires (making a "sandwich" held together with rubber bands). Team members worked together: testing with circuit testers, recording results, and trying to figure out all the possible wirings that might give those results.

As the pupils worked, Ms. Oldhand walked about from table to table, helping with procedural questions and equipment problems. Occasionally, a child showed her a data sheet with an inferred wiring and asked, "Is this right?" Ms. Oldhand always turned such questions back to the pupil: "How can you decide?" or "Have you tried wiring your inference on your practice circuit board?" or "Have you dis-

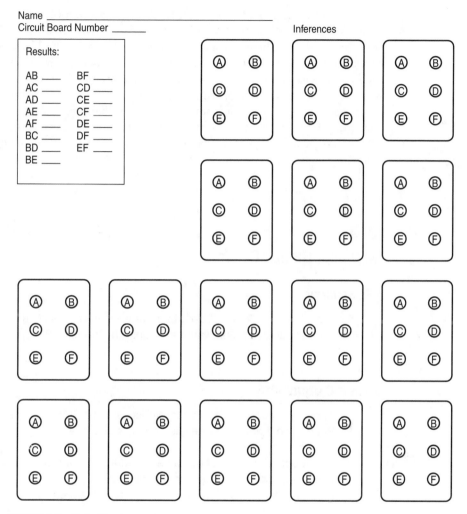

FIGURE 9.8 Data Sheet

cussed it with your partners?" or "Do your best for now, and we will talk about it in the whole group later."

When most of the pupils had finished, Ms. Oldhand signaled for attention and asked the monitors to collect the materials. Then she asked the class to get ready to discuss their results. Each of the circuit boards was discussed in turn. The results were reported, and volunteers checked with a tester to verify in cases of disagreement. The pupils then shared the various inferences they had made. Pupils explained why they thought some inferences would be impossible and came to the conclusion that there was no way to decide among the defensible inferences, given the limited materials of the activity. Finally, the insides of the three circuit boards were revealed.

Some teachers would choose not to allow pupils to look inside. This variation is quite similar to what scientists do in real scientific research. Such problems are called *black box problems.* There is usually no way to look into the black box in nature to check on inferences, so scientists build models of their inferences and then compare the models with the black box. Whether you allow pupils to open the circuit boards is your decision. Motivation runs high until the contents of the boards are seen. After that, the window of learning opportunity slams shut. Many science educators feel strongly that to simulate a real science situation learners should not be allowed to open the boards. This may seem hard, but consider the possible benefits of at least deferring the revelation for a day or more.

LESSON PLAN 9.2

INFERRING HIDDEN CIRCUITS

NSE STANDARD

Physical science: Electrical circuits require a complete loop through which an electrical circuit can pass (National Research Council, 1996, p. 127).

GRADE LEVEL: 5

STUDENT OBJECTIVES

1. Know the properties and characteristics of electrical circuits.
2. Recognize that a set of results can be logically explained by more than one inference.
3. Construct inferences of possible wiring to account for results of testing all possible pairs of terminals on a circuit board.
4. Distinguish between logical and illogical inferences.

MATERIALS

For the teacher:

A data sheet similar to Figure 9.8
One large demonstration circuit board
One circuit tester (Figure 9.4)
Prestructured transparencies for overhead projector (similar to pupils' data sheets)
Unwired circuit boards (three or four) (Figure 9.7c and 9.7d)
Copper wire and wire cutters

For each team of four pupils:

Three boards with hidden circuits

One unwired "practice" circuit board (Figure 9.7)
Six short insulated copper wires with ends stripped
Two circuit testers
Four data sheets (Figure 9.8)

MOTIVATION/REVIEW

Briefly review the previous activity on using circuit testers to distinguish conductors from nonconductors.

LEARNING ACTIVITIES

Directions (Direct Instruction Minilesson)

Using the chart (Figure 9.8), show how to test circuit boards for connections and how to record observed results on a data sheet. Lead a short discussion to establish that several arrangements of the wiring are possible for a single set of results. "What would happen if this wire were missing?" "Are there any other ways the wire could be connected to give the same results?"

Data Collection

Ask the table monitors to distribute the materials. Allow about twenty minutes, or longer if needed and time permits. Ask the table monitors to collect all the materials except the data sheets.

Data Processing

1. Ask pupils to report results for each hidden circuit board in turn. Record results on the overhead projector using prestructured transparencies. Ask whether anyone got different results. Ask for volunteers to come up and retest circuit boards that are disputed.
2. Ask pupils to report their inferences. Wire locations can be described as A to B, B to C, and so on. Record these on a prestructured transparency. Collect as many inferences as possible for each set of data. Ask, "Are all of these inferences possible?" "Are there any that just wouldn't work?" If there is any disagreement, ask volunteers to come up and test the inference by constructing the wiring arrangement on an unwired circuit board. Ask, "Is there any way we could decide which of these possible circuits is the one in the circuit board—without looking in and with only our circuit testers?" (No.)

Closure

Should we look inside the circuit boards?

ASSESSMENT

Informal observation during discussion and looking at the data sheets.

MR. NEWMAN: I see you're adding a section in your lesson plan called "Directions" just before the "Data Collecting." Should I start doing that all the time?

MS. OLDHAND: Only if you need it. I have learned the hard way that fifth graders need extra help with the idea of several possible wiring arrangements for each set of data.

MR. NEWMAN: To tell the truth, it was a new idea to me, too. Maybe I would have figured it out during the testing, but I'm not sure.

MS. OLDHAND: I have learned that when a procedure is complex or when a certain concept is important to carrying out the hands-on part of the activity, I add a little structure in this way. It is called guided inquiry, don't forget.

Analyzing the Lesson

The concept that was the underlying content objective of this lesson was the basic, and simple, concept that electrical circuits require a complete loop through which a current can pass. You are probably thinking, again, that all sixth graders know this, and they probably do, but this lesson reinforces that knowledge and goes beyond it. To answer the questions asked, pupils have to use their knowledge in a way they have not had to do before, and in doing so, they see the implications and the uses of the knowledge. Remember that conceptual knowledge grows slowly, over time, and each time pupils come back to familiar subjects, they learn a little more, gain a bit more understanding, and gradually master the concepts.

It's not hard to see why the process emphasized in this lesson, inferring, was chosen, since the immediate objective was to discover something hidden from view. Inferring means to draw a conclusion from indirect observations when the object itself cannot be directly observed. A great deal of scientific knowledge is based on inference rather than direct observation. We can't observe the center of the earth or an electron or dinosaurs, but we think we know something about all of them. The process used in this lesson is a very important part of scientific inquiry, one that should be used in other contexts as well.

A LESSON ON INVESTIGATING ANT POPULATIONS

The following lesson plan is, in contrast, based on direct observation. The activity outlined in Lesson Plan 9.3 may be part of a unit on insects, in which case the emphasis will be on close observation of the ants and differences between them. Alternatively, the activity may be part of a unit on distribution of populations, in which case the emphasis will be on differences in number and kind of ants found in various locations, results with different kinds of traps, investigation of an ant hill, and other related activities.

Before starting this activity, obtain permission from the principal or other administrator to take the children into the school yard to place and monitor ant traps.

LESSON PLAN 9.3

INVESTIGATING ANT POPULATIONS IN A SCHOOL YARD

Source: From *Investigating Ant Populations in the School Yard* (pp. 4–8) by N. A. Anderson, 1996, Raleigh, NC: SCI-LINK/GLOBE-NET, North Carolina State University. Copyright 1996 by North Carolina State University. Adapted by permission.

NSE STANDARD

Life science: Populations and ecosystems (National Research Council, 1996, p. 155).

GRADE LEVEL: 5

STUDENT OBJECTIVES

1. Develop knowledge of a population of ants.
2. Use the appropriate method to collect biological specimens.
3. Construct a graph to present data.

MATERIALS

Plastic container with lid for each pupil
Labels or permanent felt-tip pen for labeling
Squirt bottle for filling traps with liquid
Supersaturated salt solution
Wetting agent of kind used in dishwashers
Trowel or bulb planter
Cloth or plastic for flags to mark traps
Meter stick or measuring tape
White paper or plastic plates
Toothpicks
Forceps
Magnifiers

MOTIVATION/REVIEW

"Who has taken a really close look at an ant? What did you notice? Do you know where ants live when they are not visiting your picnic?" Explain that ants are found all over the world and that you are going to take a close look at some of those that live around the school.

LEARNING ACTIVITIES

Data Collection

The basic procedure is as follows: Small straight-sided plastic containers are filled with a salt solution and placed in the ground as ant traps. After twenty-four hours, the traps are collected, tops are placed on them, and they are brought back to the classroom. The containers should have straight sides; 35-mm film canisters and medicine bottles work well, but you may think of others. There must be a sufficient number of containers of uniform size, shape, and color for each pair of pupils to have one. (Pupils work in pairs for this investigation.) Prepare a saturated salt solution by adding table salt to hot water until no more salt will go into solution. Strain this through cheesecloth or a disposable dishcloth to remove solid residue. Add 4 to 5 ml of wetting agent per liter of salt solution. (This makes ants fall to the bottom rather than floating on top and perhaps escaping.)

Discuss with the students where the traps should be placed. You may place some in grassy areas and others in bare areas, or you may place them at varying distances from a walk or building. Traps in the same area (same site) should

Many kinds of data can be collected in the schoolyard.

FIGURE 9.9 An Ant Trap in Place

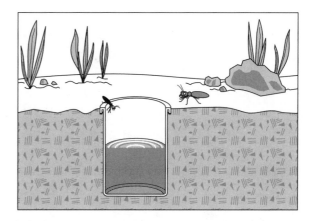

be placed about 2 meters apart. Take the pupils into the school yard to determine where they will place traps, and place numbered flags to mark the spots. Have students make a map or diagram for each area (site) to show where the traps are placed. (You may have to make a quick map for reference, depending on the age of the students, time, and other factors.)

Continue if there is time; otherwise, wait until the following day to continue. Do this on a day when no rain is expected for twenty-four hours. Now dig a hole with a trowel at each spot, set the dirt aside, away from the hole, and save it for replacement. Each pair puts a number, corresponding to the number on the flag, on their container and places it in the hole, with the cover on.

Traps are placed so that they are flush with the ground. Pack dirt under and around the trap to hold it steady. When a trap has been set properly, the lid is removed and the squirt bottle is used to fill the trap one-third full of salt solution. There should be little or no disturbance or leftover dirt around the traps (Figure 9.9).

Traps are collected after twenty-four hours; the covers are replaced, and the containers are taken to the classroom.

The contents of each container are poured onto a paper plate or piece of heavy white paper. Toothpicks and forceps can be used to separate the ants.

Data Processing

Pupils count the ants collected and record class data on a chart such as the one shown in Figure 9.10. Each pair can fill in their data. Engage the children in discussion of the data table later, after they have completed the table; they should record the data without interruption before the ants dry out.

Pupils now sort their ants into groups based on size and color. Small black ants go in one group, large red ones in another group, and others may be in a miscellaneous group unless there are several with similar characteristics. The numbers are recorded in their workbooks and used to make a graph similar to that shown in Figure 9.11.

FIGURE 9.10   Data Table for Ants Captured

	ANTS CAPTURED	
Trap Number	Number of Ants	Names of Students
1		
2		
3		
4		
5		
6		
7		
8		
9		
10		
11		
12		
13		
14		

FIGURE 9.11   Graph for Ants Captured

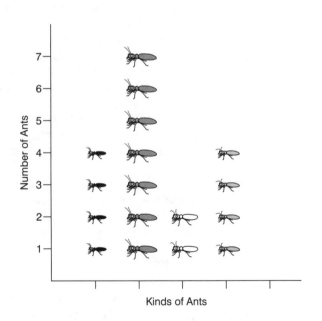

Closure

Display the class data and pupils' graphs. The direction of the discussion will be determined by pupil interests and the goals of the unit. Pupils will have many suggestions for further investigations, and you may use your judgment as to where to go with this. Finding other ways to observe and/or count ants, finding other ways to trap ants, making closer observations, and drawing individual ants are all possible follow-up activities. Many books on ants are available at all reading ability levels.

ASSESSMENT

Observation of pupils in the school yard provides the basis for the assessment of cooperative behavior. Workbooks and graphs can be assessed.

EXPERIMENTING

Inquiry-based instruction encompasses a broad range of student investigations, from simple observation and description of objects or phenomena to conducting real experiments. Most children below fifth or sixth grade have not developed the necessary skills and understandings to do complete experiments and can use their class time more productively in less complex investigations. Students who have developed inquiry skills through engaging in investigations throughout the earlier grades may be ready to undertake experiments and should be provided with the opportunity if it is appropriate. All or most of the various inquiry or process skills used in experimenting should be familiar to pupils before anything approaching fully autonomous experimentation is possible. We will explain and illustrate two of these processes—defining operationally and controlling variables—before we explain and give an example of experimenting.

Operational Definitions

Communicating clearly is not an easy job. Many words and expressions in the English language have several meanings, leaving considerable room for different interpretations. What, exactly, does it mean to "be a good girl," to "come home early," or to "mind your manners"? These are examples of terms that can have many interpretations. Sometimes a word carries one meaning in one context and another meaning in another context. For example, in tennis, a ball that falls on the line is *in*, but in basketball, a player whose foot is on the line is *out*. An operational definition narrows the possibilities of interpretation and provides a criterion in the form of an operation, or action. An operational definition sets specific limits to the meaning of a term for the purpose of dealing with a particular situation. It is a definition that everyone can understand and use for making decisions.

Operational definitions are often used in law. To make sure everyone drives at a safe speed, most states and cities have specific speed limits for particular stretches of road. You may feel inclined to argue with the officer who gives you a ticket for driving at an unsafe speed. You could try to make a case for driving quite safely. For example, if it is 3 A.M. and there is no traffic, you may be entirely safe driving at 40 mph. But if the law says that the safe speed for that stretch of road is 30 mph, you are legally unsafe.

Scientists use operational definitions to communicate exactly what some variable in an experiment is. Given a single question to be investigated, consider how different people might set up their experiments. The question is, "How does exercise affect pulse rate?" Investigator A has people take their pulses, do ten situps, and then take their pulses again. Investigator B has people take their pulses, run up a flight of stairs, and then take their pulses again. Each of the investigators has the subjects count pulses, but each interprets exercise in a different way. One uses situps, whereas the other uses running up a flight of stairs. Would it be valid to compare one of these experiments with the other?

◆ **ACTIVITY ON DEFINING OPERATIONALLY**

Mr. Newman observed Ms. Oldhand's class for several weeks, and now she asked him to plan and carry out a lesson on defining operationally. Mr. Newman had two friends who often argue over whether the college basketball team is as good as the football team this year. He asked them to let him audiotape part of one of their arguments to play for the sixth-grade class.

Mr. Newman started the class by telling the pupils he wanted them to listen to a tape and that they would then discuss it. After a few minutes, Mr. Newman stopped the tape and asked the pupils how the argument could be settled. Then he called on several pupils and wrote their answers on the board. He asked if anyone had an idea that was different from those on the board, and a few more hands went up. On the basis of pupils' answers, Mr. Newman developed the idea that basketball and football are different games and hard to compare and that the men on the tape need to define what they mean by "good." Then Mr. Newman gave each pupil a list of statements with instructions, which he had prepared and brought to class, to mark the words that would need to be defined to avoid "senseless arguments." Two of the statements were "A mother knows her children better than anyone else" and "You can have more fun in summer than in winter."

When the pupils had finished marking the statements, Mr. Newman led a discussion of each question and watched the faces of the pupils carefully to see whether they all seemed to understand. As the final activity for the period, Mr. Newman formed groups with four pupils in each group and gave them the task of writing an operational definition of a "good team." They were to finish by the end of the period and display and discuss their definitions the next day.

Controlling Variables

Controlling variables is one of the Piagetian tasks (Inhelder & Piaget, 1958) by which formal operational thinking is diagnosed. You might think that using this process would be too hard for all but a small percentage of sixth graders. In a sense, this is true, but with some careful structuring, even children younger than sixth grade can begin to think about controlling variables. As a result of past experience with games and contests, most children in the upper elementary grades have some concept of a "fair test" or "fair contest." Such background will go a long way toward understanding this and the other advanced processes. Before a teacher helps pupils think about how to plan an experiment, an example such as the following could help.

◆ Mr. Williams's sixth-grade class challenged Ms. Oldhand's sixth-grade class to a basketball free-throw contest. Each class chose its best shooter to represent it. Justin, from Mr. Williams's room, had ten shots and made six. Aaron, from Ms. Oldhand's room, was allowed only five shots, had to stand further from the basket than Justin, and had to use a ball that contained too much air. Aaron made four free throws. Who is the winner, Justin or Aaron?

At this point, there were plenty of complaints from the children in Ms. Oldhand's class. When asked to set up another game that would be a fair test of basketball skill, they mentioned factors such as these:

Both players get the same number of throws.

Both players use the same equipment.

Both players stand the same distance from the basket.

At this point, Ms. Oldhand pointed out that the factors they named—number of throws, type of equipment, distance from the basket—are all variables, factors that can be changed or varied.

To make a fair test of which boy is the better free-throw shooter, all these variables have to be the same for each. Ms. Oldhand also pointed out that there were two other factors to consider: the player (Justin or Aaron) and the scores they made. These two factors are also variables. In most experiments, the experimenter has two variables that are of interest, and usually the experimenter asks, "What effect does variable x have on variable y?" In the case of this contest, the question is, "What effect does the person who is shooting have on the score?" or "Does it matter who is shooting—Justin or Aaron—on the final score?"

Should all variables be kept constant? No. To have a contest, you control only one variable. All the others listed would need to be constant to have a fair test. The variable that you choose to vary—in this case, the person who is shooting—is called the *manipulated variable*. That is the variable that you manipulate or change on purpose. The variables that are kept constant are called *controlled variables*. You control them rather them letting them change at random. The score is a variable, too, called the *responding variable*. This is the variable that you will measure and record. Your pupils will not have to know these words, but they have to understand the three kinds of variables, and it is important for you to understand them, too.

The following activity will give you a feel for what it means to control variables. This activity has been written for you to do with a partner in class or at home. The equipment needed is simple and easily obtainable.

ACTIVITY ON CONTROLLING VARIABLES: PENDULUMS

Materials

Spool of sewing thread

Paper clip

Several washers of the same size

One ruler or short stick

Tape

One meter stick

Clock or watch with second hand

For this activity, you will investigate the behavior of simple pendulums to see if you can determine the effects of certain manipulated variables on how long it takes to swing from one point back to that point. This amount of time is called the period. Using the materials listed, make a pendulum like that in Figure 9.12. These are some variables that may be considered:

Period of pendulum

Weight of pendulum bob

Length of pendulum

Angle of release

Method of release

Nature of support

Can you classify these variables as manipulated, responding, and controlled? The period will be the responding variable, but which of the others is the manipulated variable will depend on what you are testing. If you choose weight as your manipulated variable, then length, angle of release, method of release, and nature of support

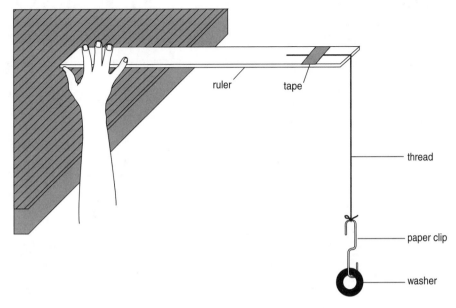

ruler   tape

thread

paper clip

washer

FIGURE 9.12   Pendulum Setup

will all be controlled variables. If you choose length as your manipulated variable, then weight, angle of release, method of release, and nature of support will be your controlled variables. Although you can certainly check all of these variables for their effect on the period, the last three are somewhat difficult to measure and are also difficult to manipulate consistently. At this time, simply control those factors, and test first weight and then length as your manipulated variables. To control the last three factors, use the following procedures:

Cut a piece of thread somewhat longer than a meter. Open a paper clip into a hook, and tie it to one end of the thread. Put one washer on the hook. Measure the desired length of the entire pendulum, from the bottom of the washer to the pivot point of the string. Tape the string at the pivot point to the end of a ruler or thin stick. Hold the ruler steady against a tabletop or other stable platform, with the thread hanging over the end of the ruler. This is shown in Figure 9.12.

Pull the washer back slightly—15 degrees or less from vertical. Release the washer so that it swings smoothly without bouncing. The pendulum may change the direction of its swing from parallel to the table edge to somewhat perpendicular. Don't worry about this; just keep counting. Count twice for each trial, to be sure everything is normal. If the two counts are different, continue trials until you get two that are the same.

To check for weight as the manipulated variable, keep the length constant, and simply add a second washer on the hook for the next trial. Continue for washers three and four. To check for length as the manipulated variable, keep the weight con-

Length Trials		Weight Trials	
Length (cm)	Swings/15 sec.	Weight (washers)	Swings/15 sec.
		1	
		2	
		3	
		4	

FIGURE 9.13   Pendulum Data Sheet

stant and vary the length for successive trials. It is easier to start with the longest pendulum and work toward the shortest.

To simplify the timing of the period, count the number of complete swings during 15 seconds and record your results in tables similar to those in Figure 9.13. It is easier if you have a partner to tell you when to begin and when to stop counting. The measurement you get is not strictly called the period, but it will have a regular, inverse relationship to the period.

STEPS IN EXPERIMENTING

An experiment is one kind of inquiry or investigation and, like other kinds of inquiries, starts with a question. The succeeding steps are open to some variation, but in general, an experimental procedure includes these:

1. Stating the question, sometimes called *the problem.*
2. Formulating a hypothesis (optional).
3. Identifying variables (using operational definitions as needed).
4. Designing a test of the question or hypothesis (using operational definitions as needed).
5. Setting up the test and collecting data.
6. Organizing and interpreting the data (tables and graphs).
7. Stating a conclusion in terms of the question or hypothesis.
8. Writing a report or making a presentation of the experiment.

In the following example experiment, each of these steps is explained.

AN EXPERIMENT WITH FERTILIZER

The question "Is this fertilizer any good?" is one that might arise spontaneously in conversation between gardeners. Before it can be tested, however, some critical thinking is needed. What is meant by "any good?" What is fertilizer expected to do? And how can you decide whether it does this function "well"? When people buy fertilizer, they must expect some kind of improvement in their plants—otherwise, why buy it? Actually, different kinds of fertilizer correct different kinds of plant problems or improve different aspects of plant growth. Consider one function for study, whether a fertilizer causes plants to grow faster. The question could be restated more specifically:

How does Fertilizer X affect the growth of corn plants?

A hypothesis is a formal statement of the experimental question. It is general in nature; that is, it includes all objects and events in the class of each main variable. And it is stated as a declarative sentence rather than a question. An example of a hypothesis for a plant study is

Corn plants treated with fertilizer will grow taller than untreated corn plants during the same length of time.

The experimenter does not know yet whether the hypothesis is true. The purpose of a hypothesis is to guide an investigation. If the corn grows taller with fertilizer than without, then the experimenter can conclude only that the hypothesis is supported. "Proving" that the hypothesis is true would entail testing every kind of corn plant with every kind of fertilizer. Obviously, that would be impossible. In fact, no one can ever say that a hypothesis is proven—only that it is supported or not supported. If lots of corn plants and lots of fertilizers are tested and the corn grows taller in every case, then the experimenter can have strong confidence in this hypothesis. Theoretically, it would take only one experiment in which the fertilized corn did not grow taller to disprove the hypothesis. Actually, when negative results occur, scientists usually use the new data to modify the old hypothesis rather than throw it out and start all over.

Formulating a hypothesis is more abstract than simply stating a question. A clearly stated experimental question is often sufficient to guide the relatively simple experiments appropriate for elementary children. You can be the judge of whether or not to include formulating hypotheses in your pupils' experiments.

Next, consider identification of variables. By stating the question clearly, you have already identified the manipulated variable (fertilizer or not) and the responding variable (growth of corn plants). Does either of these variables need operational definitions? You could decide to compare several different amounts of fertilizer, or you could compare plants with the amount of fertilizer recommended on the label to plants with no added fertilizer. For simplicity, do the latter. You have operationally defined fertilizer as Fertilizer X in the amount recommended on its label. What about "growth of corn plants"? Growth sounds like something that should be measured. How could this be done? There are a number of different ways, but since corn plants generally grow straight up and fairly stiff, it should be easy to measure the height of the plants with a ruler. If a different sort of plant had been chosen, you may have needed a different way to operationally define "growth of corn plants." For a vine or a shrubby branching plant, you might decide to count leaves or measure in some way the total surface area of the leaves. In any case, you would need an operational definition for growth.

Now think of other variables that you are not especially interested in, so that you can be sure that none of them is a factor in any plant growth differences you may see later. These other factors include amount of light, amount of water, temperature, type of corn plants used, type and size of containers for the plants, and kind and amount of soil. Your list may include other factors as well. Such a list is never complete, because there is no end to other factors that might be involved. The best you can do is to identify those that you think may be important and try to keep them the same for all plants. These are called *controlled variables*. The more variables you control, the more sure you can be that they do not influence any differences we may observe later in the growth of our plants.

The next step of the procedure is to design a test to answer the experimental question. There is no formula that tells how to design a test. You must consider the variables and make a number of judgments. How many plants are needed? What kind of containers, soil, and so on? How often should you water? How should the fertilizer be applied? Should you start with seeds, or could some corn plants be purchased at the nursery? How often should the seedlings be measured? Perhaps you can think of other decisions to be made.

Before deciding on the details of the experiment, keep in mind that one or more corn plants will receive fertilizer and one or more corn plants will not receive fertilizer. Conditions for both groups should be as much the same as possible—except for the fertilizer. All plants should have the normal amount of the other factors—water, light, and so on—because you want to test normal plants. If the plants were stressed by lack of water, for example, they might react differently to fertilizer. This means you need to know how to provide normal care for the plants. You might ask an expert or get information from a resource book about how to best maintain the plants in normal good health. Both sets of plants should receive all this good, normal care in exactly the same way, except for fertilizer.

Sometimes plants die for reasons no one can control. Also, plants receiving exactly the same care may not all grow exactly the same. It is usually a good idea to have several trials or multiple data to provide a more typical result by averaging. The following is one way to design the experiment; others could be equally valid.

Plant several shallow boxes (flats) of corn seeds—say, about 100 seeds. When the seedlings have grown to a height of about 10 cm, choose 20 seedlings that are as much alike as possible. Carefully transplant these seedlings to individual 1-liter containers, each having equal amounts of potting mix from the same bag. Place all the containers on the window sill, and water each, 100 ml. After three days, eliminate any plants that do not look healthy. Divide the remaining plants equally into the fertilizer group and the no-fertilizer group (also called the experimental group and the control group, respectively). Decide on a watering schedule—how much and how often will depend on what you learn from the resources you consult. All plants should be watered the same amount at the same time. In the water of the fertilizer (experimental) group, dissolve the recommended amount of fertilizer.

Set up the experiment physically in the way you have planned. Measure and record the height of each plant periodically—say, every Monday, Wednesday, and Friday for a month. Design a data table to record the measurements. Figure 9.14 is an example of a data table.

Construct a graph to show the pattern of growth for each of the two groups. Look at the overall growth of plants in the two groups. Figure 9.15 is a graph of the data in Figure 9.14.

Can you draw any conclusions? Do the graphs give any information not provided by simply comparing the final average heights of the two groups? The data table and the graphs show that there is no consistent difference between the growth of the two groups of plants. This conclusion could be stated in two ways, depending on whether it is in response to the question or the hypothesis. To the question, "How does Fertilizer X affect the growth of corn plants?" the conclusion could be stated in this way: Fertilizer X does not seem to have any effect on the growth of corn plants. To the hypothesis, "Corn plants treated with fertilizer will grow taller than untreated corn plants during the same length of time," the conclusion could be stated in this way: The hypothesis is not supported.

Writing a report on this experiment would be brief and easy if the previous steps were all taken. A report of an experiment should have the following parts:

1. Title of report
2. The question (or problem)
3. The hypothesis (if used)
4. Variables (manipulated, responding, controlled)
5. Design and procedure
6. Results (data, including tables and graphs)
7. Conclusions (Was the question answered? Was the hypothesis supported or not supported?)

An example of such a report is shown in Figure 9.16.

When an experiment gives negative results, there is just as much opportunity to think and learn as when the results are positive. When the results are unexpected (as in this case), it is a good idea to check that the procedure was carried out as originally stated and then to check for any possible measurement errors. If no such problems occurred, then the experimenter must examine whether the question or procedure needs rethinking. All of these steps are a part of real science and are valuable in practicing critical thinking. In this experiment, you might consider these two alternatives:

Day	Fertilizer	No Fertilizer
1	10	10
3	10	10
5	12	13
8	18	17
10	25	25
12	33	31
15	45	44
17	55	55
19	68	69
22	84	83
24	89	91
26	92	93
29	95	95
31	95	95

FIGURE 9.14 Average Height of Corn Plants (Centimeters)

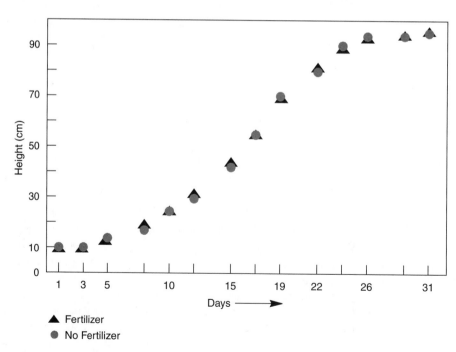

▲ Fertilizer
● No Fertilizer

FIGURE 9.15 Growth of Corn Plants

226

TITLE
A Study of the Effect of Fertilizer on Corn Plants

THE QUESTION
How does Fertilizer X affect the growth of corn plants?

THE HYPOTHESIS
Corn plants treated with fertilizer will grow taller than nontreated corn plants during the same length of time.

VARIABLES
manipulated = fertilizer or no fertilizer
responding = height of corn plants
controlled = soil, light, temperature, type of corn plant, type and size of container, water

DESIGN AND PROCEDURE
Twenty young healthy corn plants 10 cm tall were selected from a flat on basis of looking alike. Each plant was transplanted into equal volumes of planting mix in identical one-liter containers. Plants received normal care for three days, then unhealthy plants were discarded. The remaining 14 plants were divided into two groups. The experimental group received fertilizer (amount stated on label) in its water. Otherwise, all care was identical. Height of all plants was measured three days a week for one month. Average height for each group was graphed.

RESULTS
Data recorded in tables and graphs.

CONCLUSIONS
Added fertilizer appears to have no effect on the growth of corn plants. The hypothesis was not supported.

FIGURE 9.16   An Example Report

1. Fertilizer X is worthless, and people who buy it are being cheated.
2. Some important factor in our experiment was overlooked.

Consider the second possibility. What was different in the experimental procedure from conditions in real gardens? One obvious difference was the soil—commercial potting mix rather than ordinary garden soil from the ground. What if the potting mix contained added fertilizer? If so, then the control plants might have had enough nutrients to grow as fast as the plants grown with added fertilizer. In that case, you would modify the hypothesis to this statement:

When grown in common garden soil, corn plants treated with fertilizer will grow taller than untreated corn plants during the same length of time.

A new experiment based on the modified hypothesis might result in a graph like that in Figure 9.17.

Write a report similar to the example report in Figure 9.16.

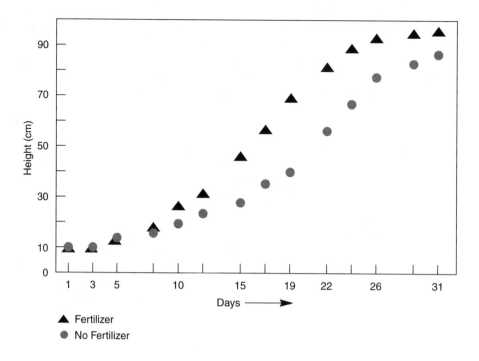

FIGURE 9.17 **Growth of Corn Plants in Garden Soil**

◆ SUMMARY

For purposes of presentation, the processes of science were divided into two categories, basic and advanced. Similarly, content standards have been divided into kindergarten through grade 4 and grades 5 to 8. In fact, there is no specific point at which to make such a division. The types of mental activity required and the knowledge and abilities to be acquired form a complex stream that is more like a continuum than two discrete groups. Individual science processes are also highly interrelated. Different writers have dealt with them in various ways. Science processes can serve as tools for the teacher in planning and carrying out science activities, and the standards can serve as guides. To interpret the processes or standards as individual packets of knowledge that must be transmitted to learners would be a misunderstanding of their purpose. They are only aids to thinking about science instruction.

Two lessons, one in earth science and one in physical science, were presented along with lesson plans and a detailed analysis for each. A third lesson, in life science, was described with analysis left up to the reader. These lessons illustrate how science content and process are integrated in the context of planned classroom learning activities. Experimenting is a special form of inquiry. The experimental activities supplied for the reader are designed to reinforce some of the processes and abilities that are necessary as a prerequisite to carrying out experiments. Experiments may have unexpected outcomes, which can also provide learning experiences.

◆ ACTIVITIES FOR THE READER

1. Observe a science lesson for an entire period. During or after the observation, formulate a question, related to what you observed that interests you. Determine what data you would have to collect to answer the question. Collect the data, answer your question, and write a report.

2. Design and carry out an experiment on the melting time of ice. Make a list of factors that might have an effect on melting time. Choose one of these as the variable you will change while you hold the other variables constant. Write a lesson plan, and present your results in oral or written form.

3. Write a lesson plan for the investigation of pendulums for fifth or sixth grade based on the activity presented in this chapter.

4. Reaction time is an interesting variable of humans. A simple way to measure reaction time is as follows: The experimenter holds a meter stick lightly by thumb and forefinger near the large number end so that it hangs with the small numbers down. The subject (person being tested) holds his or her thumb and forefinger wide apart on either size of the zero, or end mark, without touching. The experimenter drops the meter stick without warning, and the subject tries to catch it between thumb and finger as quickly as possible after it begins to fall. The experimenter should wait varying amounts of time so that the subject cannot anticipate the drop. The number gripped by the subject is a measure of reaction time. Using reaction time as the responding variable, design and carry out an experiment with classmates or family members. Possible manipulated variables include age, time of day, gender, and amount of time after heavy exercise. Perhaps you can think of others.

5. Different brands of paper towels make various claims and differ from each other in many ways. Make a list of claims you have heard (or can imagine). Can you derive an experimental question or hypothesis from each of these claims? Which of them would be the easiest to test? The hardest?

◆ QUESTIONS FOR DISCUSSION

1. What science processes and/or abilities listed in the first section of the chapter are used in the investigation of the ant population?

2. What elements should be included in an operational definition of each of the following?

   a. A good student

   b. A good course

   c. A good lesson

   d. A rich coffee

3. Would the experiment on fertilizer be suitable for use in the intermediate grades? Why or why not? If not, could it be adapted so that it would be suitable?

4. Should a teacher who never intends to teach fifth or sixth grade be excused from learning about the advanced science processes? Defend your position.

◆ REFERENCES

Inhelder, B., & Piaget, J. (1958). *The growth of logical thinking from childhood to adolescence.* New York: Basic Books.

National Research Council. (1996). *National science education standards.* Washington, DC: National Academy Press.

Group Investigations

◆ A BEGINNING TEACHER LEARNS ABOUT GROUP INVESTIGATIONS

Ms. Sanchez, a beginning teacher, had observed her mentor, Ms. Oldhand, several times during the year. One day she visited Ms. Oldhand's class and was surprised to see that the children, who had been in their seats carrying out directions on her first visit, were now spread out all over the room—some on the floor, some standing together in a corner, some talking excitedly in groups around their desks. The classroom was not quiet, but it wasn't really noisy either. It reminded her of a beehive: there was a low buzz of children talking, but no one voice rose above the others.

Ms. Sanchez walked over to Ms. Oldhand and remarked that this certainly looked different from the last time she had been in the class. "Oh, yes," Ms. Oldhand said, "The way I teach depends upon the goals of the lesson. When you visited this class before, I was teaching the children a specific skill that they needed to know in order to do other things later on. They were learning to use the balance, and they needed to practice until they had mastered the skill.

"Today the goals are different. I like to think that I am not actually teaching a lesson but giving them an opportunity to learn on their own. Today each group is working on its own, planning how to find out something that the children of the group want to know about trees. Children in each group have thought of a question about trees that interests them, and now they are planning how to collect data to help them answer their questions."

"This must be an easy way to teach," remarked Ms. Sanchez. "It looks as if the children are doing all the work."

Ms. Oldhand laughed. "Well it may look easy," she replied, "but actually, this kind of teaching is a real test of a teacher's skill. In the first place, the pupils have to be taught to conduct themselves appropriately and responsibly when they are working independently. Then an attitude of mutual respect and trust between pupils as well as between pupils and teacher has to be developed. The teacher has to plan very carefully and thoughtfully and then has to monitor the pupils' progress toward the goals of the day's work."

"I'd like to walk around and observe what the groups are doing to try to get a better idea of what's going on," said Ms. Sanchez.

This chapter describes a teaching style based on pupils working together in small groups to investigate different questions about the same topic. You have already seen examples in earlier chapters of an instructional style in which pupils start with a question and work in groups, but the style described in this chapter has some important differences. In guided inquiry, all groups study the same questions; in group investigations, each of the groups investigates a different question or set of questions, though all are related to the same general topic.

Chapter 11 also deals with children working in groups, but in that case, the pupils work on independent and group projects rather than on group investigations.

The line between an investigation and a project is not always clear, but you will understand why they have been separated after you study the two chapters.

The style of teaching called *group investigations* has its theoretical basis in the work of the thinkers discussed in Chapter 2. Dewey, Piaget, and Bruner stressed the importance of active participation and exploration in the construction of knowledge and meaning. Vygotsky stressed the importance of social interaction among peers in the process of learning. And Kohlberg's ideas of moral development can only be realized in a classroom atmosphere of respect and trust between teacher and pupils and among the pupils themselves. All of these ideas are put into practice in this teaching method.

Although you may never have experienced this way of teaching, it is by no means a new method. It was advocated in the United States by Dewey in the early 1900s and has been used successfully in other countries through the years. Of the science teaching materials published in the United States, those produced by the Elementary Science Study (ESS) in the 1960s are probably the most useful as sources of ideas for group investigations. The ESS booklets contain a wealth of ideas for investigations of topics of interest to children and adolescents. Some of those booklets are now available from sources listed at the end of Chapter 4.

Group investigations are a part of elementary science education in many schools in both Great Britain and Japan. Since the early 1970s, teachers in Great Britain have had available the Science 5–13 materials, a set of books produced by a government-sponsored team for children between the ages of 5 and 13 (Schools Council Publications, 1972). These materials help teachers help children learn science through first-hand experience. Each of the books in the series deals with a particular topic or subject area. Among the topics included are structures and forces, minibeasts, metals, working with wood, and science from toys. Each book contains suggestions and directions for a great number of investigations. Some of the titles in this series are included in a list of sources at the end of this chapter.

Japan is another country where group investigation is used as a method of teaching science in elementary schools. Its use there is particularly interesting in view of international comparison studies in which Japanese children have been found to have high levels of achievement in science.

Charron (1987), an American teacher who spent many hours in elementary science classrooms in Tokyo, reported that group investigations were used by all the teachers she observed as well as by all those who answered a questionnaire she distributed. In the classrooms she visited, children worked in groups as they planned investigations, obtained teacher approval for their plans, found the necessary materials and equipment, carried out their investigations, and described their procedures and results on worksheets or in workbooks.

Charron also observed that Japanese teachers had to devote little time to overt management of behavior, because pupils were busy and interested with their tasks. She made another important observation: Teachers spent the period interacting with students and asking questions focused on pupils' ideas, predictions, findings, and conclusions rather than on facts and memorization of information.

Her findings should reassure teachers who hesitate to try independent investigations because of a concern that pupils will not attend to their work or that they will even become loud and unruly. This chapter includes a section on cooperative learning that will show you how to set up productive groups.

PRACTICAL CONSIDERATIONS

The method of group investigations is most often used in the intermediate or middle grades, though children in the primary grades can learn to work in this way if the projects are not too ambitious and if guidance is provided. Younger children often become tired and frustrated on long projects, but fifth, sixth, and seventh graders who have learned the advanced science skills will thrive in a class in which they work in this way.

In this chapter, it is assumed that you have been with your pupils long enough to have worked out basic rules of classroom behavior and that the pupils understand what is expected of them. Some important things for pupils to remember (or be reminded of) are to

Interact courteously with one another.

Stay on task without constant reminders from the teacher.

Use simple equipment correctly.

Persist in a task until a "stopping point" is reached.

This teaching method makes high demands on both teacher and pupils. No one method can be successfully used for all instruction. The chapters in this book have been arranged so that each new level allows new instructional methods but does not rule out the use of methods previously described. The decision about whether to use group investigations depends on the goals of instruction, the teacher's experience in guiding instruction, and the pupils' ability to assume responsibility for their own behavior and learning.

If you review Table 4.2 on Autonomy Levels (see Chapter 4), you may gain a better understanding of the differences between this teaching method and the other two methods, by comparing the goals, the pupil's role, and the teacher's role across the three levels.

CHOOSING A TOPIC

Topics suitable for this style of teaching are those that can be studied through first-hand exploration of objects and materials that are readily available. The region where you teach and the time of year may be important factors. For example, you probably would not choose to teach a unit on trees if your school were on the edge of the desert or if you were planning to teach the unit during January in North Dakota. In both of those cases, you would have to depend mostly on books and films rather than on the pupils' use of materials available in their own environment. But you could have a unit on plastics and metals, for example, at any time or place that enough materials could be assembled.

An important consideration in choosing the topic is the potential of the topic for further learning. Careful thought should be given to choosing a topic that is broad enough and important enough to form the foundation for your pupils' further learning later on. The potential for further learning was stressed by Dewey and is the idea behind Bruner's spiral curriculum mentioned in Chapter 2.

Remember that most of these children still think predominantly in the concrete mode; that is, their thinking is still based on their own experiences with objects and events. Investigations should always be based on children's own experiences, although that does not mean that they can never use books or other sources of information to answer questions their own investigations have raised. When the needed knowledge is arbitrary knowledge, such as the names of different kinds of trees, then the use of books or other sources of information will be necessary. Such information will be more meaningful for children who have already had firsthand experience.

Questions to ask yourself when choosing a topic include the following:

◆ Is the topic broad enough to allow for many kinds of investigations at different levels of ability?

◆ Are materials available in this locality at this time of year?

◆ Are the materials safe for children to gather and handle?

◆ Can children find out interesting things through activities they can do on their own?

◆ Will there be opportunities to use a variety of science processes in their investigations?

GROUPING FOR INSTRUCTION: COOPERATIVE LEARNING

If you have decided to use group investigations and have chosen a topic, you will then consider how to organize the pupils to ensure a successful learning experience. Since the children will be working on their own much of the time and will have a great deal of responsibility to monitor their own behavior and their progress toward task completion, it is important that the groups work cooperatively. Cooperative learning, mentioned earlier, will be described here in detail because it is an essential component of this method of instruction.

Setting Up Groups

Groups of four or five pupils seem to work best. The groups should be as heterogeneous as possible, which means a mix of boys and girls, students with special problems, low ability and high ability, and the various racial and ethnic groups in your class. Research on the effects of using cooperative learning has shown that this strategy is effective in promoting better working relationships in the classroom between boys and girls, children with and without disabilities, and children from minority and nonminority groups (Slavin, 1980).

The first thing to do in setting up groups is to make a list of your pupils, ranking them from high to low ability. Use whatever information you have in ranking your pupils, and do not spend time worrying about fine distinctions; approximations are all you need. Next, divide this list into four sublists of equal or nearly equal size—the top fourth, the second fourth, and so on. These sublists are called quartiles. Now choose one from each sublist (quartile) to form learning groups of four pupils each. As you choose from the sublists to form the groups, balance the groups as well as you can by sex, race, and other individual characteristics.

To see how this works out in practice, consider a sample class of twelve pupils. Ranking them in ability from one to twelve, you will have a list like the one shown in the first column of Table 10.1. After you have made that list, go back and divide it into quartiles (fourths), as shown in the second column of Table 10.1. You will have as many groups as there are names in each quartile; in this case, you will have three groups.

Now, distribute the names in quartile 1 (the top-achieving fourth of the class) among the three groups, like this:

Group I—Judy

Group II—Bill

Group III—Joseph

TABLE 10.1 Formation of Cooperative Learning Groups

Ranking	Quartiles	Groups
1. Judy	1. Judy	Group I
2. Bill	Bill	Judy, Luis, Liam, Sam
3. Joseph	Joseph	Group II
4. Luis	2. Luis	Bill, Marta, Dolores, Amos
5. Marta	Marta	Group III
6. Takeisha	Takeisha	Joseph, Takeisha, Nabeel, Rita
7. Dolores	3. Dolores	
8. Nabeel	Nabeel	
9. Liam	Liam	
10. Amos	4. Amos	
11. Rita	Rita	
12. Sam	Sam	

Now distribute the names in quartile 2 (the next fourth) among the three groups, trying to balance the groups by ethnicity and sex as well as you can. For example, you could make a group based on ability alone that would be composed of Judy, Takeisha, Dolores, and Rita, but that would not be a good combination, because it would contain only girls. A better distribution is this:

Group I—Luis

Group II—Marta

Group III—Takeisha

Continue the process of group formation by distributing the names in quartiles 3 and 4 among the groups. Finally, you will have three groups similar to those shown in the last column of Table 10.1. These will be heterogeneous groups because of the way you put them together.

The same groups should not stay together for longer than about six weeks. If you continue to use groups for guided discovery, group investigations, or other kinds of lessons, the memberships of the groups should be changed by repeating the process described.

Johnson and Johnson's (1987) work is a good source for those who want to know more about cooperative learning; this chapter provides only enough information to get you started.

Teaching Cooperative Group Skills

Groups have two basic objectives: to complete a task and to maintain good working relationships among the members. To complete a task successfully, group members must obtain, organize, exchange, and use information. Members have to contribute, ask for help when needed, accept help when offered, and keep the objective of task completion in mind.

For the group to function well, members must encourage each other to participate actively and must learn to manage differences of opinion, ideas, and interpretations in a constructive way. Such differences are often what cause people to reassess their assumptions and give up misconceptions or deepen their understanding of important concepts. Part of your responsibility as a teacher will be to help your pupils develop these skills as they work together in groups. The groundwork has to be done before you start the unit. Here are some steps you can take:

◆ Explain that pupils will be working in cooperative learning groups. These groups will not be exactly like groups they have worked in before (unless they have already experienced cooperative learning groups).

◆ Explain that they will be assigned to groups and will be expected to work productively with everyone in the group.

◆ Ask for their ideas about the behaviors that will be needed for groups to be successful. Suggestions may include acceptance of other's ideas, sharing materials, showing trust for each other, trying to communicate clearly, listening to each other, and trying to see another's viewpoint. Take time to discuss each of these ideas.

Make it clear that you expect each child to work within the assigned group and that you will be available to help them work through any problems that arise. You cannot expect the groups to function flawlessly, but group skills are needed everywhere in life and can be developed through patience and firmness. You will probably find that you have to call the class together from time to time to review the basic principles of cooperative learning as well as to remind them of some of the things they may have forgotten.

DEVELOPING A PLAN FOR A GROUP INVESTIGATION

Previous chapters have described lesson plans designed to be used for one class period. Daily planning is always necessary, but day-by-day planning is not adequate for the instructional method described here. To accomplish the desired goals, a group investigation must be planned as a unit, a series of integrated lessons taking place over a longer period of time. As you learn to use teaching methods that give more freedom and responsibility to children, you will see the advantages of unit planning. The next section is a description of Ms. Oldhand's process of planning and implementing a group investigation, a specific kind of unit.

TABLE 10.2 A Unit Plan for a Group Investigation

Unit Part		Teacher Activity	Pupil Activity
1.	Goals	Determine expected outcomes	
2.	Motivation	Build interest and enthusiasm	
3.	Planning Activities	Work with pupils to identify questions and activities	Identify questions, and plan how to answer them
4.	Materials	Check pupil lists and help in securing materials	Develop lists of materials needed
5.	Group Activities	Monitor pupils' work	Carry out planned activities
6.	Closure	Work with groups to "pull it all together"	Present results to classmates
7.	Assessment and Feedback	Determine whether goals have been met, and inform individuals, groups, and parents	Receive feedback
8.	Reflection	Assess overall success and feasibility of unit	

Most of the parts of this plan are ones with which you are now familiar. The main difference is that in developing lesson plans the teacher does the planning, but in developing a plan for a group investigation, pupils are also involved in planning. Because this is a plan for a series of lessons over a period of two weeks rather than a single lesson, it may seem complicated, but an examination of Ms. Oldhand's unit plan shows that the parts of a lesson plan with which you are already familiar can be adapted to a unit plan. Table 10.2 shows an outline of her unit plan for a group investigation on trees.

Now return to Ms. Oldhand's class to observe the details of the planning and implementation of this unit over a period of about two weeks. Notice that the parts of the plan are not compressed into one day's lesson but are spread out over the entire series of lessons and activities.

◆ **GROUP INVESTIGATIONS IN MS. OLDHAND'S CLASS**

Ms. Oldhand began her sixth-grade unit by announcing the topic to the class.

UNIT PLAN 10.1

TREES

NSE STANDARD

Life science: Populations and ecosystems from *National Science Education [NSE] Standards* (National Research Council, 1996, p. 157).

GRADE LEVEL: 6

These lessons take place over a period of about two weeks. The parts of the plan are not compressed into one day's lesson but are spread out over the entire series of lessons and activities. Before she began the unit, Ms. Oldhand thought carefully about the unit's goals.

GOALS

Cognitive Goals

1. *Gain knowledge of trees.* Children are expected to learn many things about trees that they did not know before, but what they learn and how much they learn will depend on their own interests and activities. This kind of goal is very different from the goals of a lesson, in which pupils are expected to have acquired specific knowledge that has been determined by the teacher ahead of time. When you think about it, there is very little essen-

tial knowledge about trees that every sixth grader needs to know. It is more important at this age for children to become interested in trees—or whatever topic the teacher selects for a unit—and to develop the motivation, the confidence, and the skill to find answers on their own to questions that interest them.

2. *Acquire skill in use of science processes.* Most of the group investigations will require children to use these processes: (1) making, recording, and organizing observations; (2) recognizing patterns and relationships; (3) making inferences or drawing conclusions; and (4) representing and reporting results. In some cases, pupils will also carry out experiments to test their inferences and may seek information from other sources.

Affective Goals

1. *Build self-reliance and self-confidence in their own ability to think.* Children learn to believe that their ideas are valuable when adults value those ideas. Self-confidence grows when children are encouraged to plan and carry out a task through using their own ideas and initiative. When, on the other hand, science is taught as facts, formulas, and theories to be memorized or "experiments" to be performed by carefully following directions, pupils need to make no decisions and don't even need to think about what they are doing. In contrast, a teacher who uses group investigations assumes that pupils have their own ideas and interests and that these will be motivating and sustaining.

2. *Increase awareness of and interest in the subject of study.* Children learn to look at things more closely, to understand them better, and to value them more highly. Think about something you have studied or observed in detail—whether football or birds or automobiles—and you will realize that you have a greater appreciation for that subject than someone who knows little about it.

Social Goal

Learn to work cooperatively with others. This social skill is probably as important as any single skill a child can learn in school. This style of teaching gives children the opportunity to develop and practice the skills of cooperative group work under adult guidance.

Psychomotor Goals

1. *Practice care in handling materials.* Many things of interest to children are fragile and must be handled with care. This is particularly true of things that are alive or come from living materials. Flowers, insects, moss, and small plants are examples. Telling children to be careful is not as helpful as showing them how to exercise care and patience—recognizing that there are large differences in children's physical coordination. *Note:* The use of dangerous materials or equipment should not be allowed. The close supervision

needed to handle even minimally dangerous materials is not advisable in this method of teaching.

2. *Acquire skill in handling equipment.*   While every effort should be made to provide children with sturdy equipment, some items require care and skill in handling. As in the handling of materials, pupils cannot be expected to know how to handle equipment without instruction. Even when reasonable care is exercised, some breakage is inevitable.

3. *Learn to work in proximity to others.*   Everyone has seen children who cannot move around a room without bumping into other people, stepping on someone's materials, and knocking something over. These children will need help and patient guidance in developing spatial awareness and in learning how to exercise more control over their bodies.

MOTIVATION

Before the pupils began the work projects that Ms. Sanchez saw when she entered the classroom, they had already spent several class periods on the unit about trees. A day or two before Ms. Oldhand started the unit, she had arranged on the bulletin board several newspaper articles to stimulate pupils' interest and thinking. One article described the damage caused to trees in their state by acid rain. Another article described the destruction of the rain forest in the Amazon valley, showing large logs floating down the river. A third article was about a group of local people who were trying to save a large, old tree from being cut down to make way for a shopping mall.

On the day she began the unit, Ms. Oldhand brought in branches with leaves from five or six different kinds of trees. Ms. Oldhand had selected them to show contrasts in leaf size, shape, color, and type as well as contrasts in color and texture of tree bark. Some of the leaves Ms. Oldhand brought in are illustrated in Figure 10.1. She assigned pupils to groups, gave a branch and a short list of questions to each group, and allowed a few minutes for groups to decide on answers before she called on each group in turn.

The questions were simple enough that Ms. Oldhand thought at least one person in each group would be able to answer. Her questions included, What is the name of the tree that this branch came from? Where does it grow? What color do the leaves turn in the fall? Do they fall off in the winter? After each group had been given a turn to answer its questions, she called attention to the articles on the bulletin board. Then she called on a few volunteers to tell why they think trees are important or to tell about their experiences with trees. Ms. Oldhand allowed a few minutes for the children to talk and then brought the lesson to a close.

PLANNING ACTIVITIES

On the following day Ms. Oldhand moved into the next phase of the plan by asking the pupils to think of some things they would like to find out about trees. As

FIGURE 10.1   Samples of Branches with Leaves

the children thought of questions, they raised their hands. Calling on one pupil at a time, she wrote the questions on a transparency on the overhead projector. When she had written six questions, she asked the children who had not spoken to write their questions on pieces of paper and to save them for later. The questions she wrote on the transparency were these:

1. What kinds of trees grow in our town?
2. What kinds of fruits grow on trees? Do all trees have fruits? What is inside?
3. What happens when a tree dies?
4. What is the difference between an evergreen tree and a tree that loses leaves?
5. What is a tree like on the inside?
6. How is wood from one kind of tree different from wood from another kind of tree?

By then it was time to move on to another subject, so the questions were saved for the next day's lesson.

When Ms. Oldhand returned to her questions the next day, she said, "Now we will decide how we might find the answers to these questions. What data would we need? How could we collect them? Let's start with the first question and see what we can do with it." After fifteen minutes of skillful questioning and a few suggestions from Ms. Oldhand, this is what the children read on the overhead projector:

1. What kinds of trees grow in our town? How will we answer this question?
   a. Look around the area where we live, and identify all the different kinds of trees.
   b. Find out the names of the trees.
2. What happens when a tree dies? How will we answer this question?
   a. Bring a rotting log to school, and find out all we can about it.

At this point, Ms. Oldhand said, "Now that you have seen how we tackle these questions, it's time for you to do some of this on your own." She assigned children to groups of four or five and wrote these instructions on the board:

1. Decide on a question for your group. It may be one of the questions already identified, or it may be another question that your group likes.
2. Record the question.
3. Decide what you need to know or do in order to answer the question.
4. Write this down.
5. What materials or resources will you need? Which can you get yourselves and which will require some help?

After writing these directions on the board, Ms. Oldhand said, "I will come around to each group and hear your plans and answer questions. I am really looking forward to hearing all your ideas because I know they will be good ones. At the end of the period, I will collect your plans."

By the end of the class period, each group had a plan. The following is what each of the groups wrote.

Group 1

"Our question is, What kinds of trees grow in our town?

"We will each take an area close to our homes and make a survey. First, we will look for as many different kinds of trees as we can find. Each person will bring in a few leaves from each different kind of tree. If we can't reach the leaves, we will draw a picture. We will bring all those in to class and see which are the same and which are different. Then we will have samples of all the different trees that we found.

"We will identify the leaves by looking them up in a book from the library.

"If we have time, we will go back and look at the shapes of the trees and try to draw them, because the shape of the tree may tell what kind of tree it is."

Group 2

"Our question is, What happens when a tree dies?

"We will bring two pieces of wood into class. One will be a log that is solid and strong, and the other will be an old rotting log. We can find a good piece of wood from someone who has bought wood for their fireplace. For the rotting log, someone will have to find one in the woods or get one from someone who sells firewood and has an old piece that has been lying on the ground and has become rotten. A parent may have to help on this.

"We will compare the bark and the inside of the logs."

At this point, Ms. Oldhand came over to the group and heard their plans. She asked whether they thought anything might be living in the old log. With this suggestion, they added to their plans:

"We will put the log down on a big piece of white paper and watch to see whether anything crawls out. If it does, we will save it. Then we will dig into the log to look for insect eggs, cocoons, and other signs of life.

"We will need something to gently dig into the rotten log, a big piece of paper, and a container for insects (if we find any)."

Group 3

"Our question is, What kinds of fruits grow on trees? Do all trees have fruits? What is inside the fruit?

"We will collect nuts and other kinds of things that grow on trees in the neighborhood. First, we will make a chart to compare them for size, shape, color, and so on. Then, we will find out what is inside the nuts and fruits and seeds and compare them."

Group 4

"Our question is, Do all trees float in water after they have been cut down?

"We will get samples of wood from different trees and see whether they all float."

When Ms. Oldhand came over to this group, she suggested that they could expand their question. She thought that the group needed to dig deeper into the subject of floating than just determining that wood floats—which most of them knew already. They could ask whether all kinds of wood float the same way. Do some kinds of wood sink farther into the water than others? What else happens when wood is put in water? How could you make an experiment that would be a fair test of this? Her questions prompted them to expand their investigation.

"We will get blocks of the same size of different kinds of wood, put them in water, and mark the level of the water on each one. Then we will compare them. Next we will weigh them, put them in water, leave them there for three days, and then weigh each block to see if it changed weight. We will see if woods from different trees absorb different amounts of water."

Group 5

"Our question is, How are evergreen trees different from leafy trees?

"We will get branches from evergreen trees and from broad-leafed trees and compare them. Some of the things we will observe and record are

Bark
Shape of leaves or needles
How leaves or needles are attached
Smell
The kind of seeds on the tree or lying on the ground under the tree
Shape of the tree (we will have to go after school, observe the trees, and draw them if we can)
Anything else that comes to our attention"

Group 6

"Our question is, What is on the inside of a tree?

"We will get four different logs, if we can. Each person will observe and draw the cut surface of a log and then cut away the bark and observe what is underneath. We will also count the rings, because that tells how old a tree is."

At the end of the period, Ms. Oldhand collected the papers so that she could read them over and see whether she needed to make any further suggestions. She told the children that they would have several days to collect their materials in order to be ready to begin their investigations on Monday. This would give them a reasonable amount of time to enlist the help of their parents and find all the materials that they would need.

MATERIALS

Ms. Oldhand looked over the papers the pupils had handed in and noticed that there were very few things that she would have to provide for the investigations. She was pleased to see that the children were planning to find most of the things themselves. She made a note of the materials that she would have to assemble and planned to have most of them ready by Monday.

GROUP ACTIVITIES

On Monday the groups went to work, collecting data, making observations, and carrying out the tasks that they had assigned themselves. Each pupil kept a notebook to record what was done each day. Sometimes pupils recorded their observations by drawing a picture or making a chart.

Although the children were interested and busy, Ms. Oldhand did not relax. She moved about from one group to another, asking questions, answering questions, and keeping an eye on everything that was happening in the room. She was particularly watchful to see whether the children were using science processes appropriately. For example, she noticed whether children took variables into account when they made comparisons so that a test of an idea was a fair test. As she moved around from group to group, she asked these questions:

"Group 1, how can you find out which kind of tree is more abundant? Would you have to count all the trees in town? When you have thought of a way it might be done, let me know your idea so we can discuss it."

"Group 3, have you decided on categories for size, shape, and color? How will you agree on what category a seed belongs in?"

Ms. Oldhand also checked frequently to see that all children were keeping up their workbooks and required them to turn in their workbooks each Friday, so that she could take a look during the weekend. Sometimes a question from her helped children think again about how best to make an observation or test an idea.

During this time, Ms. Oldhand kept in mind the objectives of group investigations. She had made a notebook that contained the class list, with spaces beside each child's name for recording a bit of information each day. This was not the formal grade book that every teacher must keep, but her own way of appraising and recording performance. As she moved about the room, she

FIGURE 10.2   A Page from Ms. Oldhand's Notebook

Daily Record of Effort

Name	1	2	3	4	5	6	7	8	9	10
Adams	✓	✓	+	+	✓	✓	✓	+	✓	+
Berkonsky	−	−	✓	✓	✓	−	✓	✓	✓	−
Chavez	+	+	✓	✓	✓	+	+	✓	+	+
D'Amato	✓	✓	✓	✓	+	+	✓	✓	−	−
Edmister										
Fussell										
Goldsmith										

noted whether each child was on task and contributing to the group. At the end of the period, she put a plus, minus, or check by each pupil's name (see Figure 10.2). She used the plus to indicate extra effort, the minus to indicate too much time off task, and the check to show what she considered appropriate effort and behavior. She had a line in her book for each pupil. At the end of the group investigations, Ms. Oldhand used this as part of the assessment. This also helped her give feedback to parents about their children's participation and effort in science.

Ms. Oldhand was also interested in the science processes that the children were using. In the same notebook that contained the children's names, she had other pages for recording the use of science processes. This page listed the groups, rather than individual children, and had spaces for each of the processes previously listed as objectives in the unit plan. She had a separate space for each group. As Ms. Oldhand moved about the room, she watched for indications that groups were making observations, gathering data, and using other science processes. She made little checks in her notebook to record her own observations. The record for Group 1 is shown in Figure 10.3. Note that she kept a record like this for each group.

FIGURE 10.3 Ms. Oldhand's Record for Group 1

Daily Process Record

Group 1

Day	Observe	Organize	Record	Infer	Experiment
1	✓✓✓	✓	✓✓✓	–	–
2	✓✓✓	✓	✓✓✓✓	–	–
3	✓✓✓	✓✓	✓✓✓	–	–
4	✓✓	✓✓✓✓	✓✓	✓	–
5	✓✓✓	–	✓✓✓	–	✓✓✓
6	–	✓✓✓	✓✓	✓✓✓	–

Notice that Ms. Oldhand was actually using the science processes that she was teaching her pupils. She had made observations of pupil behavior, gathered data about their activities, and recorded data, and she would eventually draw inferences. She was modeling for her pupils the behaviors and thinking processes that she was teaching. When she had an opportunity, she pointed this out to them to show that what they were learning in science class has many useful applications.

The pupils and teacher continued to work in this way for the remainder of the week. When a group became satisfied with the answers to their questions, they began to plan how they would present their results to the class by means of charts, graphs, and illustrations.

CLOSURE

Ms. Oldhand reminded the class on Wednesday that they would have to bring their investigations to a close in time to present their results to the class on Monday. There was a great scurrying about to finish up. Some groups planned to meet on Saturday to complete their displays. On the following Monday, each group was given time to explain what they had done, and each group displayed their results for the class. Two of the presentations are described.

Children plan how they will present the results of their investigation.

Oak   Maple   Alder

FIGURE 10.4   Drawings for Poster on Local Tree Population

Group 1

Group 1 displayed a poster with labeled drawings of the trees they found. Under each drawing of a tree, there was a drawing of the corresponding leaf. Figure 10.4 shows some of the drawings they made to use on their poster. They had also made a map of the town, with their neighborhoods outlined and indications of the kinds of trees found in each area. Finally, they had made a bar graph to show and compare the number of trees of each kind. The group explained their posters and graphs and answered questions.

Group 2

Group 2 had found some interesting signs of insect life in their dead log. They drew pictures of what they had found and identified as many things as they could. They also had found moss and lichen, which they put into plastic bags and displayed on a poster. Another item of interest was some of the dead and rotted wood, also in a plastic bag, displayed beside a small piece of wood from a tree that had just been cut. This group, like the previous one, explained what they had found and answered questions.

ASSESSMENT AND FEEDBACK

Now it was time for the teacher to decide whether the objectives of the lesson had been met. Since Ms. Oldhand kept the objectives in mind all along, she had several things that could help her make an assessment.

The reports that the children gave were one indication of whether the cognitive goals had been met. Did the children learn anything about trees in their groups? And did they present what they learned in such a way that other children learned something, too? Because this style of teaching allows children to make many decisions about their own learning and because there was no predetermined information that all children were required to learn, Ms. Oldhand did not give a multiple-choice or fill-in-the-blanks test. Instead, she asked pupils to write answers in their own words to two questions.

"I'm going to give you two questions," she said, "and I want you to close your eyes and think about what you have been doing for the past two weeks. After you have thought about it, write the answers as clearly as you can. It is important to express your thoughts clearly. I want everyone's best answers." Her questions were:

1. List three important things about trees that you learned by working in your group.
2. List two things you learned about trees from other people's reports.

Ms. Oldhand did not expect everyone to have learned the same things. She wanted to know what the children would take with them for the future, not what they had memorized and would forget quickly.

The answers to her questions gave Ms. Oldhand some data about what the children had learned. Did they consider trivial facts to be most important, or did they learn something that they would take with them as the basis for further learning? Did the groups present their reports in such a way that other children understood what they had done?

Ms. Oldhand also had her record of the children's use of science processes to help her decide whether that objective had been met. And she had her record of daily performance to help her make judgments about an individual child's progress in becoming an autonomous learner. She would also use this information when she talked to parents about individual children.

Ms. Oldhand gave feedback to each group in the form of written comments, indicating the objectives that had been met and suggesting areas that remained to be worked on. She emphasized the positive outcomes, because her pupils were still learning to work in this way and she did not wish to discourage them. Besides, she always takes responsibility herself for much of what occurs in her classroom—if a group did not accomplish an objective, then she had not done her part in motivating and monitoring the pupils' work.

REFLECTION

Now it was time for Ms. Oldhand to reflect on the unit. She had to use her intuition and common sense to decide whether the topic and the activities captured and maintained children's interest. She asked herself some other questions. Did she allow enough time? Too much time? What would she do differently? Would she select this topic again? Ms. Oldhand reflected on these questions and then wrote her own assessment in her journal for her own future use.

GROUP INVESTIGATION OF INSECTS AND BUGS

This plan will not be explained in the same detail as Unit Plan 10.1, but the investigations would be carried out in the same general way. The teacher chooses a topic, the children think of questions, the teacher helps them organize their thoughts and ideas, and they then carry out group investigations and record and present their results. Assessment and feedback follow as in the unit on trees.

UNIT PLAN 10.2

GROUP INVESTIGATION OF INSECTS AND BUGS

NSE STANDARD

Life science: Diversity and adaptation of organisms (National Research Council, 1996, p. 158).

GRADE LEVEL: 4 TO 6

GOALS

Cognitive Goals

Gain knowledge of the topic.
Acquire skill in use of science processes.

Affective Goals

Build self-reliance and self-confidence.
Increase awareness and interest in the subject.

Social Goals

Learn to work cooperatively with others.

Psychomotor Goals

Practice care in handling materials.
Acquire skill in handling equipment.
Learn to work in proximity to others.

MATERIALS

Jars with lids
Butterfly nets
Cages
Magnifiers

MOTIVATION

Plan ahead to have some kind of interesting insect to bring into the classroom in a cage or terrarium. Starting with questions and observations about this example, arouse the children's interest in learning more about other insects and small creatures, such as isopods and spiders. If possible, plan a field trip for children to collect a variety of insects and other creatures that they will bring back into the classroom to study.

PLANNING

Planning for the field trip should include instructions in safety, discussion of some things to observe about insects in the field, discussion of how to capture the creatures that will be brought back, and development of questions pupils wish to ask about the creatures once back in the classroom. Children can begin keeping their logs by writing down some questions they have.

GROUP ACTIVITIES

In this group investigation, each group will first focus on the insect(s) or other creature(s) they find and observe in the field and then focus on those collected and brought back. Different groups may be asking the same questions, but they will have different answers because their insects will be different.

Children may need some suggestions at first for places to look for insects, slugs, spiders, and other interesting invertebrates. This depends to some extent on the time of year. As long as the weather is warm, insects can always be found in grass or weeds, and interesting creatures live under stones and logs. In the fall, insects will be found in fallen and rotting fruit, spiders will be found in webs in corners around buildings, and galls will appear on trees after leaves have fallen. In the spring, there are pupae in the soil under trees; then caterpillars can be found on leaves; later, butterflies can be found around flowers, and moths can be found resting on trees.

On the field trip, each pupil will take a small notebook so that observations can be recorded, including

Size and appearance: What color is it? How big is it? What special features does it have?

Habitat: Where was it found? Was the place dry or wet? Light or dark? How many were in one place?

Behavior: What was it doing? How does it move? Did it react if you touched it?

The easiest way to observe insects and other small creatures at close range is to keep them indoors in jars or petri dishes for a day or less. Most species will tolerate short periods away from food and normal surroundings. Short-term captives can be observed for general behavior, such as locomotion and grooming. With the help of a magnifying glass, structural features can be observed. Each child should try to draw his or her special bug. If the diet is known and can be provided, feeding behavior can be observed.

If the proper conditions are maintained, the captured creatures can be kept for longer periods in the classroom, allowing children to observe changes and carry out experiments. Some events to watch for are egg laying and hatching, eating, molting, mating, and life-cycle stages. Pupils can find out what foods are preferred, the effects of changes in light or temperature, and how the bugs react to various stimuli.

An important part of this project is the children's use of reference books to identify the creatures as well as to check their own drawings and information against what they find in books. Children who become particularly interested may want to learn how to catch and keep insects at home (Kneidel, 1994).

CLOSURE AND ASSESSMENT

Pupils should have an opportunity to display drawings, observations, and results of experiments. A special time for parents to visit might be arranged. As in Unit Plan 10.1, assessment will be designed to let each child say what was learned and what else he or she would like to know.

EXTENSION TO OTHER SUBJECTS

Writers and artists as well as naturalists and scientists have found insects, spiders, and other bugs to be endlessly fascinating. One of the favorite children's books of all time is E. B. White's (1952/1980) *Charlotte's Web*, a story about Charlotte (a spider) and a friendly pig. Drawings and paintings in art class, poems and stories in language arts, counting and estimating in math, and studying the habits and ways of social insects in social studies are ways to extend this topic to other areas of the curriculum. One class of younger pupils who studied caterpillars and butterflies made up a dance that represented butterflies flying over a field. When knowledge is represented in more than one way, it is more likely to be learned and remembered.

OTHER TOPICS FOR GROUP INVESTIGATIONS

Small Creatures Found in Water

Ponds and streams produce as interesting an array of small creatures as fields and woods. A field trip to a pond can produce both insects found around the edge and other creatures found in the water. Many of the questions asked about insects and other invertebrates can be asked about these creatures.

The Environment Around the School

The environment around the school is an interesting topic when the school is in a small town or rural area. What plants grow around the school? What insects, worms, slugs, spiders, and other creatures can be found? How tall are the trees nearby? What kinds of trash and refuse can be found? The activity on ants in Chapter 9 could be revised and extended to become a group investigation. Different groups could use different kinds of traps, place traps in different places, closely observe ants coming from and going to an ant hill, and observe other activities to answer questions that the pupils will suggest.

One popular activity is for each group to choose a square meter (which the group measures and marks) and then to count and label all the plants, insects, and other living things found in the square. Groups compare their findings, and the class discusses possible reasons for differences. What plants grow in sun, and what plants grow in shade? Where are insects likely to be found? What difference does dampness make?

Simple Machines

Each group chooses one kind of machine to observe and explore. Building models and demonstrating the uses of each kind of machine lead to learning experiences of more variety and depth than might be accomplished through other teaching methods. Since this is a topic that is a requirement in some state syllabi, sufficient time should be allowed at the end of the unit for each group to report and, in effect, teach the other pupils about its machine(s).

Extension to Other Subjects

The topic of simple machines lends itself to integration into a history or social studies unit. For example, a unit on simple machines could be extended to study buildings that were erected in the past, since simple machines were the only tools available to the ancient Egyptians who built the Pyramids, the Greeks and Romans who built Athens and Rome, and the medieval architects and artisans who built the cathedrals of Europe. There has been much speculation about how the ancient Britons moved the huge stones to Stonehenge and set them in place. Many books on these topics are available for intermediate- and middle-grade children.

Flowering Plants

In some parts of the country, flowers are in bloom for several months during the school year, making this a suitable topic for a group investigation. Pupils can identify flowers on a field trip and examine specimens in the classroom using hand lenses or the naked eye. The plants from which the flowers came should also be observed and described. Where does the plant grow? Is it in sun or shade? What parts of the flower can you identify? What is its name? Does it grow wild or have to be cultivated?

◆ SUMMARY

Group investigation is an instructional method that allows pupils freedom to choose what they will study about a topic that has been chosen by the teacher with input from pupils. Small groups of pupils, whose interest is aroused by the teacher, design investigations to answer questions that are of interest to them. The teacher is available to help in defining and refining questions as well as in planning. The teacher monitors pupils' progress toward finding answers to their questions and makes suggestions for further questions, plans for ways to bring closure to the unit, appraises pupil outcomes, and reflects on the overall outcomes of the unit.

This method fosters independent thinking and learning when it is planned around a topic that children can study through firsthand experiences and when the teacher has structured the classroom so that pupils understand the expectations and limits. The teacher's role is to provide an environment that encourages independent learning and responsible action. The teacher helps the children think about and understand the meaning of their experiences.

◆ ACTIVITIES FOR THE READER

1. Choose a grade level, and outline a plan for a group investigation. Select a topic, list objectives, and describe motivational activities for five possible group investigations, and then describe your method of assessment.

2. As a class project, divide yourselves into groups of five. Each group should choose a grade or several grades, depending on the number in your class. Each group then should develop an annotated list of books and articles that could be used at the chosen grade level(s) as sources of ideas for investigations. Share these lists by distributing copies to all class members.

3. Working with a group of four or five students from your methods class, plan, carry out, record, and display the results of an investigation that would be suitable for a grade of your choice. Report to the class what you learned that will be valuable to you as a teacher.

4. Make a list of five topics that are suitable for group investigations. Using the criteria in this chapter, explain why each topic is suitable.

◆ QUESTIONS FOR DISCUSSION

1. Choose a grade level, and list three problems you foresee in using the method of group investigation with that age group. What might you do to prevent each of the problems?

2. Describe in your own words the activities probably carried out by Group 1, as represented in Figure 10.3.

3. Compare methods of pupil assessment in group investigations, guided inquiry, and direct instruction.

◆ REFERENCES

Charron, E. (1987). *Teacher behavior in Japanese elementary science classrooms.* Paper presented at the annual meeting of the National Association for Research in Science Teaching, Washington, DC.

Johnson, D. W., & Johnson, R. T. (1987). *Learning together and alone: Cooperative, competitive and individualistic learning* (2nd ed.). Upper Saddle River, NJ: Prentice Hall.

Kneidel, S. (1994). *Pet bugs: A kid's guide to catching and keeping touchable insects.* New York: Wiley.

National Research Council. (1996). *National science education standards.* Washington, DC: National Academy Press.

Slavin, R. (1980). Cooperative learning. *Review of Educational Research, 50,* 315–342.

Schools Council Publications. (1972). *With objectives in mind. Guide to science 5–13.* London: MacDonald Educational.

White, E. B. (1980). *Charlotte's web.* New York: HarperCollins. (Original work published 1952)

◆ RESOURCES

Brockman, C. (1986). *Trees of North America: A guide to field identification.* New York: Golden Press.

A comprehensive guide with clear descriptions and colored illustrations of leaves, barks, and tree shapes.

Ennever, L., & Harlen, W. (1972). *With objectives in mind: Guide to science 5–13.* London: MacDonald Educational.

Available from MacDonald Educational, 49–50 Poland Street, London, England, W1. Now distributed in the United States by Teacher's Laboratory, PO Box 6480, 214 Main Street, Brattleboro, VT 05301-5480.

National Science Resources Center. (1988). *Science for children: Resources for teachers.* Washington, DC: National Academy Press.

A comprehensive annotated list of available materials in all areas of the elementary science curriculum.

Roth, C. E., Cervoni, C., Wellnitz, T., & Arms, E. (1988). *Schoolground science activities for elementary and middle schools.* Lincoln, MA: Massachusetts Audubon Society.

Available from the Massachusetts Audubon Society, South Great Road, Lincoln, MA 01733. A collection of ideas for projects that can be done on the school grounds by children from kindergarten through ninth grade.

Schools Council Publications. (1972–1973). *Science 5–13. Units for Teachers.* London: MacDonald Educational.

Available from MacDonald Educational, 49–50 Poland Street, London, England, W1. Now distributed in the United States by Teacher's Laboratory, PO Box 6480, 214 Main Street, Brattleboro, VT 05301-5480. The following titles, all from MacDonald, contain a wealth of information and ideas for group investigations:

Using the environment 1: Early explorations (1972)
Using the environment 2: Investigations (1972)
Science from toys (1972)
Trees (1973)
Minibeasts (1973)
Structures and forces (1972)
Working with wood (1972)

Smith, R. (1980). *Ecology and field biology.* Boston: Harper & Row.

U.S. Department of Agriculture Forest Service. (1970). *Forest insects and diseases.* Washington, DC: Superintendent of Documents. (Free)

U.S. Department of the Interior/Geological Survey. (1987). *Tree rings: Timekeepers of the past.* Washington, DC: Superintendent of Documents. (Free)

Young Entomologists' Society. *Insect identification guide.* Lansing, MI: Young Entomologists' Society.

Available from the Young Entomologists' Society, 1915 Peggy Place, Lansing, MI 48910. Detailed information to help teachers and students learn to identify insects.

Young Naturalist. *Nature education kits.* Newton, KS: Young Naturalist.

Available from the Young Naturalist, 614 East 5th Street, Newton, KS 67114. These include natural specimens, directions for hands-on activities, and a teacher's guide. The following kits are available: *What leaf is it? What seed is it? What crop is it?* (grades 1–12); and *Leaf and seed matching game* (grades K–3).

11

Individual and Class Projects

◆ Ms. Sanchez approached Ms. Oldhand after school.

MS. SANCHEZ: I've come to you for some advice. The principal has announced that our school is going to participate in a science fair. I know that your pupils win prizes every year, so you must have some secrets of success. Will you share them with me?

MS. OLDHAND: Well, I don't really have any secrets, but I will be glad to tell you how I help my pupils plan their projects and manage their time. I guess the most important thing is encouraging the children and helping them improve their ideas—but after that, it's just planning ahead and staying on schedule all the way to the end.

MS. SANCHEZ: I remember starting a project when I was in the fifth grade, but I ran out of time and didn't feel very good about the final result.

MS. OLDHAND: Independent projects require a lot of planning and monitoring. Otherwise, time can slip by, pupils lose interest, and the final days bring a frantic flurry of activity that leaves everyone—especially parents—exhausted and disappointed. Come by my room tomorrow, and I'll help you make a schedule and give you some ideas of the way I plan.

MS. SANCHEZ: Will you regret it if you help me and then some of my pupils win?

MS. OLDHAND: Of course not! To tell you the truth, I don't really like the competition. The important thing is for all the boys and girls to enjoy doing their projects and have a sense of accomplishment when it's over. As far as I'm concerned, all of those who make a real effort are winners.

INDIVIDUAL PROJECTS

Chapter 10 described projects that take place over several weeks, with class work supplemented by out-of-class activities that might be thought of as a kind of homework. This section also describes activities and projects that take place over a number of weeks, but these projects are different from those in Chapter 10. Although these projects may be discussed and planned in class, the students do most of the detailed planning and work outside of class. Projects for science fairs, for a parents' night, or for the culmination of a unit fall into this category. Although most of the actual work is done outside of class, children need guidance and encouragement as well as monitoring when engaged in these activities. The purpose of this chapter is to help you develop the skills and understanding needed to assist pupils in selecting, planning, and completing projects and then to guide pupils toward successful completion of the projects they have chosen.

Think back a moment to the group investigations described in Chapter 10. Those investigations take place mostly in the classroom and within a series of class periods. They begin and end at specified times, and they use all the class time allotted to science while they are going on. Another characteristic is that all the children in a class are investigating aspects of the same topic. Individual projects, in contrast, usually stretch out for several weeks and take place while other science topics are being taught in regular class time. Children may work alone, in pairs, or groups, though teachers should probably encourage children to work in pairs or groups more often than alone. Children who prefer to work alone have opportunities to do this outside of school, but for many children, school is the only place where they have the opportunity to work productively with other children.

A recent study on out-of-school science activities of third and fourth graders found that many children were carrying on little projects of their own without the help or even the knowledge of parents or teachers (Charron, 1990). For instance one fourth-grade girl said, "Sometimes I do stuff, but I don't really know that I'm doing science then. Sometimes I'll just follow an animal around and see what it does—like a worm" (p. 10). The wide variety of science activities of the children in this study makes plain that children are interested in science and that they have ideas that they would like to try. Individual projects give them that opportunity and also stimulate other children to think of things that they might like to do.

The overall goals of independent projects are similar to those of group investigations. The cognitive, affective, social, and psychomotor goals are the same as those listed in Chapter 10. The major difference between projects and group investigations is not in the goals but in the degree of independence and responsibility expected of the pupils. When pupils are doing much of the work outside of class—as they are in the projects described in this chapter—they cannot be monitored in the same way that they can when in the classroom under the watchful eye of the teacher. They are on their own more, and this independence requires them to be more autonomous and responsible.

As in group investigations, the particular knowledge to be gained by each pupil is not specified in advance by the teacher but is left up to the interests of the individual pupils. By allowing pupils to choose a project that interests them, the teacher is demonstrating that the pupils' ideas and interests are important and worthy of consideration. When pupils see that the teacher values their ideas and believes that they can learn on their own, they begin to believe it themselves. This is one of the most important goals of science teaching—for children to believe that they can learn on their own, that they can become autonomous learners. By working on projects of real interest to them, children are stimulated to make the mental connections that result in new knowledge and understanding; that is, they construct their own knowledge.

Successful independent projects require an overall plan that takes teacher and pupils through from the first day to the last. It is not accidental that some teachers' pupils produce interesting and successful projects year after year; this is usually the result of careful planning, encouragement, and monitoring on the part of those teachers.

Before embarking on independent projects, you will have to give serious thought to what is required for the successful completion of projects. The following are some questions to ask yourself before you decide to go ahead. You should proceed only if you can honestly answer yes to these questions:

Have the children developed the necessary skills and attitudes to plan and carry through?

Are the outcomes likely to be worth the necessary time and effort, or could the same objectives be met as well in other ways?

Are you willing to spend the extra time required?

SCIENCE FAIRS

This section describes a plan for independent projects for a science fair. Not everyone agrees that science fairs are appropriate for elementary children, but they are popular with parents and administrators. In addition, participation can be a positive experience for many pupils. If you plan for your class to participate in a science fair, you have the responsibility to make it a learning experience for all of your pupils. Here are some guidelines that may help you achieve that goal:

- Emphasize the learning experience rather than the competition.
- Do not use participation in the fair as a basis for the course grade.
- Let the activities supplement rather than replace the regular science classes.
- Insist that the children do the work themselves.

Children younger than fourth graders do not usually participate in science fairs, because of the difficulty young children have in sustaining interest and motivation over a period of time that is long enough to complete their projects. For younger children, shorter-term projects without competition are more appropriate. In the project plan that follows, the assumption is that all pupils will participate in the fair. There are arguments both for and against having everyone participate. The argument against having all pupils participate holds that children who are not interested in science are forced to undertake a project they have no real interest in. The argument for total participation holds that children who are not initially interested in science may develop that interest if allowed to choose a topic on their own. And since the objectives of the projects are broader than learning about a specific science topic, those who do not participate will lose important learning opportunities. Different viewpoints on participation and other aspects of fairs (along with many suggestions and ideas for projects) are presented in a useful booklet published by the National Science Teachers Association (1985).

Most projects for science fairs can be divided into three categories: (1) collections, (2) demonstrations, and (3) experiments. All three can be planned to include the use of science processes and should be expected to produce an increase in knowledge and understanding. These categories are described later in this chapter with suggestions of some things to keep in mind for each type of project.

As you study the following plan for projects for a science fair, notice how the parts of a lesson plan that are now familiar to you have been adapted for this purpose. You will see that the plan includes objectives, motivation, materials, learning activities, and assessment and feedback.

PLANNING FOR STUDENT PARTICIPATION IN A SCIENCE FAIR

GRADE LEVEL: 5

STUDENT OBJECTIVES

1. Plan a project.
2. Carry out a project.
3. Communicate the results.
4. Develop habits of independent work.

MATERIALS

Materials will depend on the projects and will be gathered as needed.

SCHEDULE OF ACTIVITIES

This schedule is for a five-week period preceding the science fair, which takes place on a Saturday. Other science lessons continue in the classroom during this five-week period, but time is set aside every Monday, Wednesday, and Friday for planning and discussing the pupils' projects.

First Week

Student Objectives: By the end of the week pupils, will have

◆ Decided whom they will work with and selected a project.

MONDAY (1)

Motivation: "You have done so well in all your science work this year that I think you are ready to take part in the science fair that will be held right in this school five weeks from last Saturday. Has anyone in this class ever been to a science fair?" The teacher explains that there will be three categories—experiments, collections, and models—and gives a short description of each category:

Experiments: Each experiment starts with a question that can be answered by collecting data and putting the information together in a meaningful way. The questions chosen have to be answerable by the pupils themselves from the data that they collect. To do this successfully, pupils should plan to control as many factors as possible and then vary only one thing (or one thing at a time) and measure the result. One way to help pupils plan their experiments is to give them a checklist to be filled in before the experiment is approved. An example of an experiments checklist is shown in Figure 11.1a.

FIGURE 11.1A Example of a Checklist for Experiments

Birds' Feeding Habits

The question we want to answer:

Will more birds come to a feeder hanging from a tree or to a feeder placed on the ground?

What we will do:

Get two similar bird feeders. Place one feeder on a wire and hang it from a tree limb and place the other on the ground. Observe both feeders for one hour each morning and evening and count the number of birds that come to each feeder.

The variable we will change:
Placement of the bird feeders.

The variables we will keep constant (unchanged):
1) Bird feeders are the same type
2) Time of observation
3) Length of time of observation
4) Kind of bird food

The variable we will measure:

How many birds will come to each feeder

How we will measure it:
Counting the number of birds

How we will report our results:

A bar graph that shows the number of birds that came to each feeder. We will also show how many came in the morning and how many came in the evening. (We may be able to keep a record of the number of each kind of bird, such as sparrows, blue jays, etc, but if there are too many kinds we will not be able to do this.)

Collections: Almost any natural materials that can be found locally and in some variety are suitable, including shells, leaves, rocks or minerals, nuts and acorns, insects, and flowers. Finding, identifying, classifying, and arranging for display are important processes for children at this age (Howe, 1987). Observations may also fall into this category, such as a record of sighting of birds or observations of the night sky over several weeks. Such observations would be interesting to some children and would provide data for conclusions about patterns. An example of a collections checklist is shown in Figure 11.1b.

Models: Some teachers have justifiably criticized the use of models, because so many of the same models have appeared over and over at science fairs. An example of this is a volcano model: a plaster cone with a center filled with a chemical that burns and gives off smoke and sparks. (This can be dangerous and should not be allowed.) The models that are most interesting and teach the most are those that demonstrate a scientific principle or show a cause-and-effect relationship. These models are ones children design and make themselves to illustrate a principle or to show how something works. Simple models with working parts can be fun to build—but they must be kept simple. If complicated pieces of apparatus are attempted, the children will become frustrated and either abandon the project or get their parents to step in. Anything that incorporates gears, pulleys, switches, or similar mechanisms is interesting and motivating. The construction of an object or a model that illustrates a principle or relationship requires knowledge of the principle or relationship and, in addition,

FIGURE 11.1B Example of a Checklist for Collections

> **Microorganisms in a pond**
>
> What we will collect:
> Samples of water from different places in a pond; then we will look at tiny drops under a microscope.
>
> Where we will find them:
> In a pond near one of our homes
>
> How we will identify them
> Using books in the school library (we have found the books we need)
>
> How we will classify them
> We will decide after they are collected
>
> How we will display them
> For each organism we will display a drawing, give the name, tell where it was found, and any other interesting information.

FIGURE 11.1C Example of a Check-list for Models

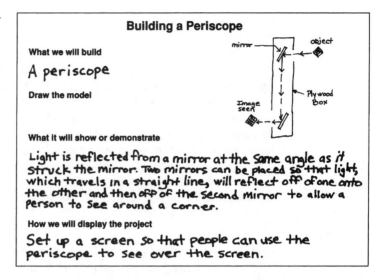

psychomotor skills and imagination. An example of a models checklist is shown in Figure 11.1c.

After a ten- to fifteen-minute discussion in which pupils are asked for ideas and the teacher mentions some possible projects, the teacher asks them to think about some things they might like to do and be prepared to talk about them on Wednesday.

WEDNESDAY (1)

Discussion: Discussion continues, with the teacher asking for ideas, reacting to suggestions, and guiding the discussion toward projects that are suitable and appropriate for the children in the class. Projects should be simple.

Assignment: On Friday, each group, pair, or individual will turn in a paper giving a brief, general idea of what they want to do. Questions about this are answered. Any who have not been able to think of a project that they really want to do can talk to the teacher, who is prepared to make suggestions as well as to help those who are ready to come to some closure.

FRIDAY (1)

Pupils turn in papers. Only a few minutes are spent collecting papers and answering questions.

Second Week

Student Objectives: By the end of the week, each pupil or group will have

◆ Developed a plan for a project.
◆ Made a list of materials and identified sources.

MONDAY (2)

The teacher approves and returns the plans or works with pupils to improve plans if necessary. The teacher has prepared a checklist for each category of project: experiment, collection, or model. Examples of a checklist from each category are shown in Figure 11.1a, Figure 11.1b, and Figure 11.1c. The teacher hands these out and explains how they should be used. Pupils respond to the items in the checklist with specifics about their projects. They will hand in their responses on Friday. They will also hand in a list of materials needed and how they may be obtained. (A strict limit should be placed on the cost of the materials. Pupils who need help in obtaining materials are advised to speak to the teacher. The teacher may need help from the PTA, a Mothers Club, or some other source for children who need assistance.)

WEDNESDAY (2)

Question and Answer Period: The teacher asks and answers questions but spends only a few minutes discussing any problems pupils are having.

FRIDAY (2)

Turn in Workbooks: A few minutes are spent collecting notebooks.

Third Week

Student Objectives: By the end of the week, the pupils will have

◆ Completed their models, experiments, or collections

Note well: This phase may take two weeks instead of one week. The teacher will revise the schedules if necessary.

MONDAY (3)

Discussion: Teacher returns workbooks with comments and suggestions and then gives opportunities for pupils to spend a few minutes talking about their plans, including what materials are needed. Now the pupils go to work in earnest on their projects.

WEDNESDAY (3)

Monitoring: The teacher takes a few minutes during the day to check on progress and answer questions.

FRIDAY (3)

Monitoring: The teacher continues to check to see that all pupils are working and keeping records. The teacher announces that workbooks are to be brought in next Monday.

Fourth Week

Student Objectives: By the end of the week, the pupils will have:

◆ Turned in their notebooks and given quick, informal oral reports.
◆ Learned methods of reporting results.
◆ Produced a plan for reporting results.

MONDAY (4)

Monitoring and Informal Reporting: Pupils turn in their notebooks and give quick, informal reports about their projects.

WEDNESDAY (4)

Direct Instruction Lesson on Reporting Results: For this lesson, refer back to Chapter 6. This will be a one-period lesson with a lesson plan that includes objectives, guided practice, and all the other parts of a direct instruction lesson. Ways to report results include bar graphs, line graphs, drawings, and written accounts.

Assignment for Friday: Bring in a plan for reporting your results.

FRIDAY (4)

Discussion of Ways to Report Results: This is a continuation of Wednesday's lesson but allows for pupils' input through questions and answers related to the assignment. Pupils can make changes in their plans if they decide to do so. Plans are handed in to be reviewed by the teacher over the weekend. (The teacher should set aside time over the weekend for this.) Pupils will collect materials that they anticipate needing.

Fifth Week

Student Objectives: By the end of the week, the pupils will have

◆ Completed a poster or other means of presenting results.
◆ Practiced explaining their project to their classmates.

MONDAY (5)

Reporting Plans Returned to Pupils: All plans for reporting should be approved by this time. The teacher will need to make constructive suggestions for those that need strengthening so that pupils can begin their charts, posters, and so on immediately. Class time will be allowed for working on project reports.

WEDNESDAY (5)

Continuation of Work on Reports

FRIDAY (5)

Final Touches on Reports: Pupils will form groups of four and take turns explaining their projects to each other.

ASSESSMENT AND FEEDBACK

Informal methods of assessment, similar to those suggested for group investigations (Chapter 10), are appropriate for projects. Questions that could be asked include

What scientific process or principle was demonstrated in your project?
How was that process or principle demonstrated in your project?
What was the most important thing you learned from your project?
What would you do differently if you could do it again?

The teacher will give feedback to each child, the method depending on the kind of project. When independent projects are undertaken for a science fair (as in the example plan), the winners will have feedback from judges, and all other participants will receive a certificate. The teacher will praise all of those who participated and perhaps point out to the class some aspects of the winning entries that were particularly good.

All pupils who completed their projects should receive positive feedback and encouragement. This kind of teaching is developmental and requires sensitivity, patience, and persistence on the part of the teacher.

The sources list at the end of this chapter may be useful if you plan to have your pupils participate in a science fair. Remember that projects of this kind do not have to be used as entries in a science fair. Shorter, simpler projects can be prepared for parents' nights, for a school fair, or to display one at a time on a science table. Requirements for planning and monitoring are the same, though simpler projects take less time. For example, one teacher assigned pairs of pupils to prepare projects for display in class throughout the year. The teacher did the first one, and then twice each month thereafter, a pair of pupils installed a new display or experiment. The children kept their projects a surprise until the day the project was unveiled and explained to the class.

CLASS PROJECTS

The projects discussed in this section to some extent defy categorization. These are projects that teachers over the years have found to promote development and learning in ways that more structured lessons and units may not. In general, these projects have broader and less well-defined goals than the projects described previously. Although cognitive objectives may be met, in many cases these projects are more effective in meeting affective, social, and (in some cases) psychomotor objectives.

These projects are carried out by the class as a group. They are similar to group investigations and individual projects, but they fall into a separate category because the children are working on a joint class project. In most cases, individuals or groups collect data or carry out other activities that will be assembled and displayed in some way when the observations have been completed.

These projects encompass activities that all children can participate in—including children who are less academically able, have disabilities, or simply have difficulty fitting in. Everyone can contribute. When children plant a garden and tend their plants, they will learn some things that you can identify ahead of time as instructional objectives, but they will also gain other important things from the experience that are intangible and would not be in your list of objectives.

These projects have a science focus, but other areas of the curriculum can be integrated easily and naturally. In almost all projects, things need to be measured and then graphed, providing an opportunity to use the skills that have been learned in mathematics. Written records must be kept, and pupils have opportunities for descriptive and imaginative writing. Drawing should not be neglected as a means of representation of observations, and geography can be a natural extension of many projects. Once you start to think about the interconnections of all areas of the curriculum, you will have many more ideas than you can find time to use.

Several projects are described briefly. Some are very low-key and easy to carry out; others require more planning and more time. The purpose of describing these projects is to give you some examples of simple learning experiences that children enjoy, as well as to stimulate you to think of similar projects for your classes. There are many, many projects—large and small—that will add to the interest of your science teaching. Actually, these are the kinds of things that children remember most about their science classes, so it is important to include them if you can.

EXAMPLES OF CLASS PROJECTS

A Garden

If you are fortunate enough to teach in a school that has a suitable climate and space for a garden, as well as a principal who understands—or can be convinced—that a garden can provide an important learning experience for children, then by all means take advantage of the opportunity. If you have never had experience with growing things outdoors, try to enlist the help of a parent, a friend, or another teacher. It will be helpful if you receive advice from someone who has grown plants in the area and knows what will grow easily, what time to plant, what insects to watch for, and similar information. Materials needed include seeds, small rakes and hoes, string, fertilizer, and small stakes.

You will have to arrange to have the garden plot plowed, or cultivated, as early as possible in the spring, and you should decide on a few vegetables and a few flowers from which children can choose. For example, in many parts of the United

States, lettuce, radishes, green onions, and peas grow easily and mature quickly; zinnias and marigolds are flowers that germinate quickly and bloom early. All of these are good choices.

An economical way to provide seeds is to allow each pair of children to choose several plants they wish to grow and place their orders for seeds. You can buy the seeds in bulk rather than in tiny packages and then place seeds in inexpensive envelopes to fill the orders.

A space 6 by 6 feet is ample for each pair of children. After the garden is divided into individual plots and the plots have been assigned, plan to spend one or two days a week outdoors, first working the soil and then adding fertilizer, setting strings out to mark the rows, planting, weeding, and, finally, harvesting. One way to keep motivation and interest high is to select each week the straightest rows or the plot with the fewest weeds, posting the name or giving a certificate to the week's winner.

An alternative to individual garden plots is a garden that is planned and planted cooperatively by the whole class. For a garden of this kind, the first step is the development of a plan—what to plant, where to plant it, and how to divide up responsibility for all the required tasks. The children can do much of this themselves, but you will have to help all along the way and be ready to step in when needed to keep the project going in the right direction. The National Garden Association has a comprehensive guide that will help you make this a lively learning experience (Ocone & Pranis, 1990).

Weather

Observations of changes in weather can be the topic for a class project at a wide range of grade levels. Younger children can make simple observations and keep very simple records, using symbols that are easily understood. Older children may make their own measuring instruments for a weather station, with groups taking responsibility for different aspects of recording and reporting weather changes. You may make this a major project or keep it simple, at any grade level, using it as an addition to the science activities going on every day in class.

In keeping such a class project simple, the basic idea is to keep a daily record of the weather over a period of four to six weeks and to use the weather data to look for trends and patterns. Begin the project by asking for volunteers to make a large weather chart. Place the chart on the wall, and ask all pupils to sign up for the days they will collect weather data. Two pupils collect data at the same time each day, and enter the data on the chart. For a simple weather chart, the data that might be gathered are temperature, sunshine, rainfall in twenty-four hours, type of clouds, and wind force.

For collecting temperature data, a centigrade thermometer should be located in an area that is protected from direct sun and is at a height that is comfortable for all the pupils to read. The amount of sunshine can be indicated simply by "sunny, light clouds, heavy clouds, rain" or some similar system. Rainfall can be measured by placing a Mason jar or a similar container in a protected place that is open to the sky and measuring with a metric ruler. You need not worry that this is not a really accurate measure; if children are interested, they will start checking their measurements with those published in the daily newspaper.

Clouds can be identified by reference to a book, or you can have a direct instruction lesson on cloud forms. Here again, accuracy is not a major concern; let the children decide among themselves what to record. Wind force can be indicated simply as "calm, mild, strong, very strong" and left up to the children to determine. If you wish to go into this in more detail, a weather vane can be used for wind direction, and a scale can be devised for force, but that is not necessary for this simple activity. Figure 11.2 is an example of a weather chart made by one fourth-grade class.

After several weeks, the class will have enough data to search for relationships between temperature and rainfall, between wind and clouds, and perhaps others. They can calculate average temperature, average rainfall, and days of sunshine and then graph the data obtained. Figures 11.3 and 11.4 are examples of graphs that pupils produced, using 1-cm graph paper. Such graphs can be used as the basis for class discussion of changes in weather and of various relationships. If your students have access to the Internet, this unit can be expanded to include the use of weather information from the Worldwide Web. Local, national, and international weather reports and satellite maps are available on many sites with almost constant updates.

Day

Weather	M 1	T 2	W 3	Th 4	F 5	–	M 8	T 9	W 10	Th 11	F 12
Temperature °C	19	17	14	15	18		20	22	18	17	15
Rainfall (ml)	200	120	10	0	0		50	100	10	0	0
Wind	2	1	0	0	0		1	2	1	1	0
Sunny/rainy	⫶⫶	⫶⫶	⊗	☀	☀		⫶⫶	⫶⫶	⊗	○	☀
Clouds	st	st	ci	cu	cu		st	st	st	st/ci	cu

Key:

Clouds
cu cumulus
st stratus
ci cirrus

Wind
0 calm
1 mild
2 strong

Sun/Rain
☀ sunny
○ overcast
⊗ cloudy
⫶⫶ rainy

FIGURE 11.2 A Weather Chart Made by a Fourth-Grade Class

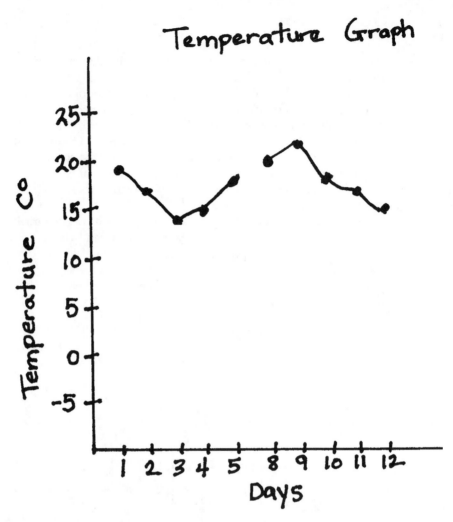

FIGURE 11.3   A Pupil-Produced Temperature Graph

FIGURE 11.4   A Pupil-Produced
Rainfall Graph

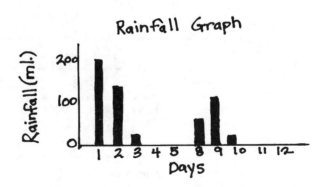

Square Meter of Earth (Grades 3 to 6)

The purpose of the Square Meter of Earth project is to develop understanding of the concept of ecosystem. The project requires an open area adjacent to or close by your school. It is more interesting if the spot selected has some variety in the amount of sunshine received or in the moisture content of the soil, but any spot will do.

Each pair of pupils measures off a square meter of earth, labels it with their names, and investigates this area intensively. They learn as much as possible about the plants growing there, the insects and other creatures there (or tracks or droppings), the soil itself, the rocks, the number of hours of sunshine the plot receives in one day, and any other characteristic that the pupils may think of. You may discuss these possibilities and suggest some things to look for, ways to measure, what they may collect, and some general ideas; but the details of deciding what to observe, measure, or collect are left up to each pair of pupils to plan cooperatively.

In deciding how long to continue the observations and collection of data, you will have to be guided, as always, by the age and skill of your pupils. The data will then be compared and combined, perhaps in a map of the area with predominant plants and insects superimposed on the map. If there is enough variety in the plots, pupils can note the relationship between amount of sunshine or moisture in the plots and the organisms found. It is important to pull the data together in some way to broaden and reinforce the pupils' understanding of the tiny ecosystem that they have studied. Chapter 13 describes an extension of this activity in which pupils used the information gathered one year to estimate the loss to the environment when part of the school grounds were torn up to make way for a road.

Moon Watching (Grades 1 to 6)

The Moon Watching project requires the cooperation of parents, since it takes place outside of school. The idea is simple. For about five weeks, children observe and record the appearance and location of the moon every evening at the same time and observe the moon rising when they can. Of course, the moon rises at different times during the lunar cycle, and whether they will be able to see the moon rise depends on the weather, the time of moon rising, and their own bedtimes. They bring their data to school, put their observations together, and discuss what they have observed. After the first cycle is over, they will see that their initial observations are being repeated. At this point, they make predictions that they then test by observation. This is enough for the younger children. Older pupils will be ready to study the relationship between the earth and the moon, including phases of the moon, eclipses, and other phenomena.

TEACHING AT AUTONOMY LEVEL III

In this chapter and the preceding one, you have studied examples of teaching at Autonomy Level III and have seen that the teacher's role and many of the responsibilities are different from those needed for direct instruction or guided discovery lessons. At Autonomy Level III, the pupils assume responsibility for some of the things that the teacher did at Autonomy Level I or II, but it is still up to you to see that standards are understood and that you enforce them resolutely and fairly when necessary.

Teacher's Role

Beginning teachers often worry that this kind of teaching will lead to children's spending too much time off-task. This may happen, but there are some actions you can take to prevent this or to deal with it if the problem arises.

1. Provide an environment that encourages children to work on problems that interest them. Their natural enthusiasm for their projects will keep them interested and busy.

2. Let pupils know that, once projects are chosen, they are expected to remain on task.

3. Remind pupils of behavior standards and sanctions that have already been set for your class, and discuss with the class why behavior standards are needed.

4. Guide pupils to see that additional standards are needed for working with materials and for working in groups, including an acceptable noise level.

5. Apply sanctions fairly and consistently, just as you would in any kind of teaching situation. This applies to deadlines for submitting plans for independent projects, for example, as well as to off-task behavior during classroom activities.

6. Move about and interact with groups as they work. Be alert for groups who are off-task or those having difficulty with the work.

7. Lead class discussions that allow interaction between students, the expression of different ideas, and explanations of different solutions to problems. Encourage open-ended discussions.

8. Set deadlines and time limits to manage pupils' use of time. Although most of your pupils can learn, with guidance, to control their own behavior most of the time, many of them will have more difficulty in learning to manage their time.

These teaching methods are possible only if your pupils are ready to assume responsibility for their own behavior. That is unlikely to be the case in the beginning of the year; it is more likely that you will have to work patiently and thoughtfully to help your pupils develop these skills. If you have started out by setting and enforcing standards as explained in Chapter 6—gradually allowing pupils to take more responsibility and gently guiding them toward acceptable behavior as explained in Chapter 7—they will respond by becoming more responsible for their own behavior and will help each other to maintain standards. Then they will be able to work independently, though they will always need monitoring and reminding. Ultimately, it is always up to you to see that acceptable standards of behavior are maintained.

One aspect of classroom management that you will have to monitor is the noise level. This has been mentioned before, so you may want to review the pertinent section in Chapter 8. It is normal for children to get carried away with what they are doing and to let their voices rise. You cannot have—and should not wish to have—a silent classroom or one in which children are talking in whispers; some noise is expected and is a healthy sign of interested children at work. But there will be times when the classroom noise level exceeds acceptable limits, and you will have to give a signal that is understood by everyone to mean "quiet down." The signal for lowering the noise level is up to you; just make sure that it is understood and that it does not have to be enforced too often. Remember that some noise is inevitable, expected, and accepted.

Be open to pupils' suggestions for changes in standards for behavior and materials management. After you have been teaching for some months, you should know your pupils and they should know you. If they have a reasonable suggestion for a change, you might agree to try it for a set period of time—two weeks, for example— and then evaluate the effects of the change. Whether you decide to make the change permanent is not as important as your pupils' seeing that you take their ideas seriously and that they can have some control over the conditions of their life in the classroom.

Pupils' Role

Pupils can be reminded that it is their responsibility to

1. Monitor and control their behavior.
2. Remind partners or members of their groups to maintain behavior standards.
3. Pay attention when the teacher or other pupils are speaking.
4. Move about the room quietly and carefully so as not to disturb others.
5. Ask for help when needed.
6. Help each other as much as possible.
7. Participate thoughtfully in class discussions.

Management of Materials

Children will be working with many different kinds of materials and will probably be carrying out some activities that you have not experienced. Remember, as described in Chapter 7, on guided discovery, you should try out everything beforehand. That is not possible with individual and class projects, but here are some general guidelines:

- Be sure that no dangerous materials are included when you check pupils' project plans.
- Enforce guidelines for management of materials.
- See that children obtain materials that they need. In some cases, children will obtain materials on their own or with help from parents; in other cases, you will have to help.

Management of Time

One aspect of management that becomes important in this kind of teaching is the management of time in the classroom and the scheduling of deadlines for submitting work completed outside of class. When all pupils are doing the same thing in class, as in a direct instruction lesson, they are led by the teacher from step to step, told when to hand in papers, and so on. In contrast, when they are doing many different activities and some of the work is done outside of class, the management of time and the monitoring of their work become very important parts of your responsibility. Be firm in setting deadlines, as explained in the example projects. Remember to remind students when the end of the class period is approaching, and be firm in insisting that they put away materials and clean up in good time.

◆ SUMMARY

Teachers can plan and carry out units of instruction in which the pupils learn about some part of their environment by conducting group investigations and independent projects. Both of these require a high level of independence on the part of the pupils and a high level of planning and group-management skills on the part of the teacher.

Group investigations are planned around a topic that can be studied by children through firsthand experiences. Small groups of pupils, whose interest is aroused by the teacher, design investigations to answer questions that are of interest to them. The teacher is available to help in defining and refining questions and in planning. The teacher monitors pupils' progress toward finding answers to their questions and makes suggestions for further questions, plans for ways to bring closure to the unit, appraises pupil outcomes, and reflects on the overall outcomes of the unit.

Independent projects are similar to group investigations in that pupil independence is required and the role of the teacher is the same. Major differences are that much of the work of the projects is done outside of class and that the projects may or may not focus on answering specific questions. Projects can include construction of models, forming collections, and other science-related activities that are of interest to children.

Remember this well: your pupils will not be able to have any of these interesting learning experiences until you have guided and helped them become responsible and independent learners who can cooperate with classmates and stay on task.

◆ ACTIVITIES FOR THE READER

1. Describe two appropriate independent projects for each of the three categories (experiments, collections, models).
2. Develop a set of criteria and procedures for judging an elementary science fair for grades 4 and 5.
3. Develop a detailed plan for a class project, using one of those suggested here or one of your own selection.
4. Develop a list of books and articles that could be used by fourth to sixth graders as sources of ideas for individual projects.
5. Write a lesson plan for a direct instruction lesson on reporting results (refer to Chapter 6 for guidelines of a direct instruction lesson plan).
6. Make a list of four topics that are suitable for class projects. Using the criteria in this chapter, explain why each topic is suitable.

◆ QUESTIONS FOR DISCUSSION

1. What problems do you foresee in using group investigations? What might you do to prevent some of the problems?
2. What are some pros and cons of science fairs? Do you think that all pupils in a class should be required to participate? Why or why not?
3. Do you think that the amount of monitoring suggested in this chapter is appropriate? On what have you based your answer?
4. How can you "cover" all the topics in the school curriculum using group investigations and class projects?
5. How are a teacher's responsibilities for group investigations and independent and group projects different from the responsibilities for guided inquiry and direct instruction? (See the section entitled, "The Teacher's Role and the Pupil's Role," Chapter 6.)

◆ REFERENCES

Charron, E. (1990). *Science activities children choose outside the school.* Paper presented at the annual meeting of the National Association for Research in Science Teaching, Atlanta, GA.

Howe, A. (1987). Collecting as a science activity. *Science Activities, 24*(3), 17–19.

National Science Teachers Association. (1985). *Science fairs and projects: Grades K–8* (2nd ed.). Washington, DC: Author.

Ocone, L., & Pranis, E. (1990). *Guide to kids' gardening.* Burlington, VT: National Gardening Association.

◆ RESOURCES

Cornell, J. B. (1979). *Sharing nature with children.* Nevada City, NV: Dawn.

Daab, M. (1990). *Science fair workshop.* Carthage, IL: Fearon Teacher Aids.

A step-by-step guide with pages that may be copied for individual or class use.

Grice, N. *Touch the stars.* Boston, MA: Museum of Science.

Forty-four-page astronomy textbook printed in Braille with eleven tactile illustrations of stars, solar system, galaxies, and constellations.

Macaulay, D. (1988). *The way things work.* Boston: Houghton Mifflin.

Explains the inner workings and principles behind all the things you use every day but don't usually think about. Many illustrations. Will soon be available on CD-ROM.

McMillan, B. (1991). *The weather sky.* New York: Farrar Strauss Giroux.

For children who enjoy observing clouds and learning about cloud patterns and other changes in the sky. Photographs, illustrations, and text for grades 3 through 8.

Mogil, H., & Levine, B. (1994). *The amateur meteorologist. Explorations and investigations.* Danbury, CT: Franklin Watts/Grolier.

Information and ideas for teachers and children in grades 4 through 8.

Morgan, S. (1996). *Weather.* San Francisco: U.S. Weldon Owen.

Photographs and text describing wind, temperature, clouds, weather forecasting, and climate change. Grades 3 through 8.

National Research Council. (1996). *National science education standards.* Washington, DC: National Academy Press.

Pages 131–133 have an excellent description of a year-long science activity of observing and recording information about the daily weather.

National Science Teachers Association. (1978). *Safety in the elementary classroom.* Washington, DC: Author.

National Science Teachers Association. (1985). *Science fairs and projects: Grades K–8* (2nd ed.). Washington, DC: Author.

Available from National Science Teachers Association, 1742 Connecticut Avenue N.W., Washington, DC 20009. A collection of articles including a range of opinions on fairs, guides for teachers planning fairs, and many ideas for projects.

Ocone, L., & Pranis, E. (1990). *Guide to kids' gardening.* Burlington, VT: National Gardening Association.

A guide for starting and maintaining a youth garden in your school and neighborhood, including experiments, activities, and projects for kindergarten through grade 12. A newsletter with ideas for teachers and pupils is available from the National Gardening Association, 180 Flynn Avenue, Burlington, VT 05401, and other information is available on the Worldwide Web at http://www.garden.org/edu.

Science in an Integrated Interdisciplinary Curriculum

Mr. Newman was nearing the end of his student teaching assignment and had just finished teaching a fifth-grade science lesson. He found that he was not able to finish what he had planned for the day, though the period had gone longer than scheduled. At the next opportunity, he talked about the lesson with Ms. Oldhand.

MR. NEWMAN: The children really enjoyed their science lesson today, and I think they learned a lot, but I feel very frustrated because there is never enough time for the children to do all that I want them to do.

MS. OLDHAND: That's a problem that we all have and one that I'm afraid you will always have to live with. The school day is never long enough for all the things that need to be done.

MR. NEWMAN: Well, you always seem to be able to get a lot more done in science than I can manage to do. When you teach, the children move along through the curriculum in math and language arts as fast as all the other classes, and you still have time for special science projects that I can't seem to find time for.

MS. OLDHAND: (Laughing) I can assure you that I sometimes feel frustrated, too, but teachers learn to become more efficient as they gain more experience. I certainly don't have any secrets that I'm keeping from you, but I think the one thing that has helped me the most is learning to build interdisciplinary units combining science with other subjects.

MR. NEWMAN: What does that mean?

MS. OLDHAND: That means taking one important idea or theme and using it as the basis for activities in several subjects so that what the children learn in one area adds to their understanding in the other areas. You know that we talked about integrating content and processes in science; building interdisciplinary units takes that idea a step or two further. There are many obvious ways to integrate two areas of the curriculum, such as using science books in reading and using examples from science when you make up word problems in arithmetic. A less obvious way to do this is to use the various science processes in other areas of the curriculum. After all, the processes of observing, measuring, communicating, and hypothesizing are not confined to science. Those skills are needed in all areas of the curriculum, as well as in everyday life. Actually, science is such an important and pervasive part of our lives that I find it just works its way into the curriculum all the time.

RATIONALE FOR AN INTERDISCIPLINARY CURRICULUM

In previous chapters, we have suggested many ideas for extending science lessons or units into other areas of the curriculum. In this chapter, we go a step further and demonstrate ways to develop integrated, or interdisciplinary, lessons and units to expand and deepen children's subject-matter understanding and skill development. *To integrate* means to combine things in such a way that together they form a unified whole; the aim when integrating subjects to build a unit is to interweave them so that children's understanding embraces several subjects as if they were one. Inquiry-based science teaching by its nature overlaps in many ways with other subjects. For example, writing in a workbook or journal reinforces skills learned in language arts, and making measurements and constructing graphs reinforces concepts and skills learned in mathematics. An integrated, or interdisciplinary, curriculum goes beyond this, however, in that neither subject is incidental to the other, but both, or several, subjects receive equal emphasis in setting objectives and other aspects of planning. Each contributes to understanding of a concept, building a theme, or learning a skill or process.

Building integrated interdisciplinary units will be easier for a teacher in a self-contained classroom than for one who teaches science as a special subject. In the latter case, the science teacher needs to work with classroom teachers to plan units and coordinate the integrated lessons taught by the science teacher with those taught by the other teachers. What makes the effort worthwhile is that "students' understanding within the subject matters can become deeper, their understanding of the relationships among the subjects can become sharper and their thinking can become more insightful and systematic, in school and out" (Jacobs, 1989, p. 3).

There are both practical and theoretical reasons for building units that incorporate science within the unit. Four good reasons follow:

◆ *Time pressure.* As Ms. Oldhand explained, a teacher has difficulty finding the time to do everything that needs to be done in elementary school, and science is sometimes the subject that gets neglected. By integrating science with other subjects when appropriate, the teacher can accomplish the objectives of the science lesson along with the objectives of one or more other subjects.

◆ *Fragmentation of the curriculum.* A rigid schedule—thirty or forty minutes for reading, followed by thirty minutes for math, followed by a lesson in writing, and so on throughout the day—does not help children see the connections between subjects and the purpose of learning the skills that they are taught. This can lead to what has been called *inert knowledge,* knowledge that can be delivered on request but that is not used spontaneously in solving real problems. For example, a pupil might be able to work exercises in addition and subtraction during arithmetic class but not be able to figure out differences in mileage between two points on a map during social studies class. In contrast, integration of subjects requires that children use their skills and knowledge in multiple contexts.

- *Pressure for the Three R's.* Some parents and others believe that teachers should spend most of their time on reading, writing, and arithmetic. Teachers who feel they are required to emphasize these subjects at the expense of all others can kill two birds with one stone by using science activities and concepts as the basis for work in other subjects.

- *The explosion of knowledge.* There is so much to be learned in science that no one can hope to teach everything children need to know. It is more useful if teachers can help them learn how to learn on their own. When subjects are integrated at the concept and process levels, children begin to understand how knowledge in one area is connected with knowledge in another area. This understanding will be helpful when they start to learn something new, because they will know that new knowledge can be tied into knowledge they already have.

CRITERIA FOR INTEGRATING SCIENCE WITH OTHER SUBJECTS

An integrated unit is one that integrates several subjects in a unified plan for a series of lessons with broad goals. Sometimes only two subjects are integrated to form a unit of study, and sometimes it seems best to focus on a science concept alone. Before you decide to teach an integrated lesson or unit, you should ask yourself these questions:

- Does the lesson or unit meet important goals or objectives in both science and the other subject(s)? It serves no useful purpose to include unimportant facts or something far outside of the science curriculum just to have an integrated lesson.

- Does the integrated lesson or unit do a better job than could be done in single-subject lessons? Does it lead to more understanding or a higher level of performance of a skill? If not, why are you doing it?

Whether you are in a self-contained classroom or working as a special science teacher, planning and gathering materials for any lesson take time and energy. It probably takes more time to plan integrated units or lessons than single-subject units or lessons. When you need to coordinate your work with that of other teachers, as you will if you are a special science teacher, even more time and energy are needed for planning. That is why you must ask yourself those questions and try to give honest answers. Unless you can answer "yes" to those questions, it may be best to teach a single-subject lesson or unit.

TYPES OF INTEGRATED LESSONS AND UNITS

Curriculum integration includes not just the interweaving of subjects, such as science and social studies, but also the interweaving of skills and processes that may be taught more effectively in relation to one another than separately. Three ways to integrate subjects or skills are first described and then illustrated by examples later in the chapter.

Topic-Oriented Units

Using topic-oriented units is probably the simplest way to integrate science with other subjects. Children explore a topic in science and look at the same topic in other areas of the curriculum. For example, you could have a unit on rivers in which content from earth science, geography, and literature are combined. To meet science objectives, children study how rivers are formed, how they change over time, and what the characteristics of flowing water are. To meet social studies objectives, children learn something about the major rivers of the world, where they are located, and how they have affected the development of civilization. Children's language skills can be developed through reading and discussing a book in which a river plays a major role, for example, *Where the River Begins* (Locker, 1994) or *Streams to the River, River to the Sea* (O'Dell, 1986).

In a unit of this kind, the pupils are not aware that one part of the unit is science and another part is social studies or literature. You, as the teacher, have planned the unit to integrate these subjects and meet the various learning objectives, but in the minds of the pupils, all the parts should come together to make the topic more interesting and meaningful.

Concept-Oriented Units

Many important concepts in science have counterparts or similar concepts in other subject areas. An example is the concept of network or web. In science this is an important ecological concept, used particularly in teaching about the interdependence between one life form and others. This is also an important concept in social studies, where children learn that peoples are interdependent and that they themselves live in a network. Such integration helps children acquire higher-order concepts that are applicable and important in more than one, and often in many, contexts. The value of both topic-oriented and concept-oriented integration of subjects to form a unit is that children may deepen their understanding of topics and concepts by seeing things from many points of view, making comparisons, and seeing connections.

Skills-Oriented Units

Important learning skills can be enhanced and made more meaningful when they are taught and used in several subjects. Skills to be integrated in this way include both symbolic skills and thinking skills or processes. Symbolic skills include arithmetic, writing, drawing, graphing, and mapping. When children watch a butterfly emerge from its cocoon and then write about it, the writing has immediacy and meaning.

Mathematics and science are often integrated at all levels because so much of science depends on the use of mathematics as a tool, and using mathematics in science brings abstract numbers on a page into the children's world. Writing should be a part of any science program, and drawing should not be neglected as a way to represent knowledge.

Thinking skills or processes include observing, classifying, inferring, hypothesizing, and various higher-order thinking skills, many of which have been discussed earlier in this book. Once you begin to think about using these processes in teaching other subjects, you will see many opportunities to reinforce their use. In a reading lesson with even the youngest children, you can read a few lines of a story and then ask, "What do you think will happen next?" and "Why do you think that?" When you ask those questions, you are asking children to form hypotheses based on evidence in the story, a process quite similar to forming simple hypotheses in science.

Classification is a basic and important process that can be used in all subjects—reading, writing, mathematics, social studies, art, and music. As children see that they can classify in all subjects, they will begin to consider this a tool for understanding and a useful way to think about the things they encounter in their daily lives.

In planning lessons for this kind of integration, your chain of reasoning may be something like this:

1. What are the content objectives of the lesson?
2. What activities will the pupils be carrying out?
3. What skills will they need to meet the lesson objectives?

Or you might follow this line of reasoning:

1. What skill will the pupils learn?
2. In what areas of the curriculum is that skill needed?
3. In what activities can the skill be used to meet content objectives?

In either case, the skill is taught and practiced as a tool to aid learning.

Since you have now had many examples and a lot of practice in developing lesson plans and designing units, all the details in the following examples are not spelled out. You should now be capable of using these outlines to write complete lesson plans that incorporate all the elements described and discussed in previous chapters.

A UNIT ON RELATIVITY

Possibly the easiest subjects to integrate in a unit are science and social studies because many concepts and processes used in science are also used in social studies. Both science and social studies are complex subjects that include many areas of knowledge within each one. Science includes biology, chemistry, physics, geology, meteorology, and other branches, each of which has its own history, methods, and traditions. Social studies include geography, history, economics, and other subjects, each of which also has its own history, methods, and traditions.

In earlier chapters, we introduced lessons that provide experiences designed to help children learn science processes, including observing, classifying, measuring, predicting, and inferring. Many of these and other processes are also applicable to social studies. Classifying, for example, is as useful to the historian and the geographer as to the biologist, the chemist, or the physicist. Classification is a thinking process that can be, and should be, used in many contexts and with many kinds of objects, characteristics, and ideas.

There is another very practical reason for integrating science and social studies (and teachers have to be practical). Because the elementary school curriculum is now focused so heavily on skills development, very little time may be allotted to either science or social studies. To fit these important subjects into the curriculum, many teachers schedule their class time so that science and social studies are taught at the same time on different days. For example, social studies might be taught at 1:30 on Mondays, Wednesdays, and Fridays, and science taught at 1:30 on Tuesdays and Thursdays. It is easy to see the advantages of building an integrated unit if you have that kind of schedule. Instead of teaching social studies two or three days each week and science the other days, the unit is taught every day.

The unit described in the next section is not only an example of such a unit but also an application of Bruner's (1966) ideas about what kinds of things to teach in science, social studies, and other subjects. As you saw in Chapter 2, Bruner advocates the teaching of important and powerful ideas in simple ways that children can understand and relate to. He believes that the curriculum should then return to those ideas in later years at a deeper level. Relativity is an example of a concept that will be understood at a deeper level later in a child's life, but here it is treated in a way that elementary children can understand.

The following unit plan can be adapted as an in-class activity for professional development of preservice and in-service teachers.

UNIT PLAN 12.1

RELATIVITY

NSE STANDARD

Position and motion of objects: The position and motion of an object can be described by locating it relative to another object or the background (from *National Science Education [NSE] Standards,* National Research Council, 1996, p. 127).

GRADE LEVEL: 5 TO 6

GOALS/STUDENT OBJECTIVES

This unit starts with a series of science lessons followed by a series of social studies lessons. The science lessons introduce the concept of relativity, a higher-order concept that is applicable both within and outside of science. The social studies lessons complement and extend the insights gained in the science lessons. The activities of the two parts of the unit are designed to provide experiences that will enable children to move beyond their natural egocentric viewpoint and take other perspectives as they view the world and themselves. The word *relative* will take on new meaning for them—and it may take on new meaning for you, too.

MATERIALS

Spacey (a cardboard figure, patterned after the illustration in Figure 12.1)
Graph paper
Large photographs of street scenes, landscapes, etc.
Appropriate stories or books

OVERVIEW OF UNIT'S SCIENCE ACTIVITIES

These activities are derived from ideas incorporated in *Relative Position and Motion,* a unit originally developed by the Science Curriculum Improvement Study (Berger, Karplus, Montgomery, Randle, & Thier, 1972). The basic concept is that position and motion of objects can be perceived, described, and recog-

FIGURE 12.1 Spacey

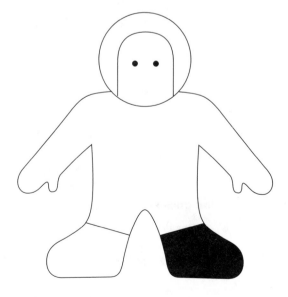

nized only with reference to other nearby objects. These other objects form the frame of reference, which is used to define the position of the original object.

Activities for this unit are outlined as Lesson 1, 2, and so on, but you should not assume that a lesson can be finished in one class period. That will depend on the detailed plans developed by each individual teacher.

Lesson 1

Begin with questions and games involving the location of objects in the classroom. Ask such questions as these:

The window is to my left. Juan, is it also on your left? If the window is on my left and on your right, is it really right or left?

The desk is in front of me. Tina, is it in front of you, too? How can the desk be between you and me and still be in front of us both?

Suppose you were a fly crawling on the ceiling. Would the ceiling be under you or over you?

Finally, introduce the term *point of reference.* The position of an object depends on the point of reference. You may call on children to stand in designated places and ask questions about locations of objects, using themselves as points of reference. In this way, children learn to use reference points in describing the location of objects. A certain chair will be "to my right" or "behind Jane's desk."

Lesson 2

In this lesson, you introduce Spacey, a cardboard figure who defines the position of everything in reference to himself (see Figure 12.1). Spacey does not say, for example, that he is standing on the table; he says that the table is under his feet. He sees the whole world from one point of view.

In this lesson, you will involve children in describing positions of objects relative to Spacey, who is first placed on a table. The children are asked to describe objects as if they were Spacey. They say "the window is to my left" or "the table is above my head." More complicated descriptions are then required, such as "to my left and higher than my head" or "behind me and to my left."

Lesson 3

When the children return from lunch or arrive in the morning, Spacey is turned upside down and hung from the ceiling; now the objects in the room are "over my head" and the ceiling is "under my feet."

Lesson 4

Introduce the concept of *frame of reference.* Children identify the position of objects by reference to landmarks. For this lesson you need photographs—preferably large ones—of familiar scenes. Children may bring pictures to share, which may be placed on the bulletin board. The photographs are used as the basis for identifying relative positions of buildings, automobiles, trees, and other objects, as well as the direction from which each photograph was taken.

If your pupils have had practice in making graphs, this section of the unit may be extended to include drawing graphs whose coordinates are labeled with reference to a zero point.

OVERVIEW OF SOCIAL STUDIES ACTIVITIES

In the social world, as in the physical world, each person's perceptions are structured by a frame of reference. The way one person relates to another person and is perceived by the other person depends on where the persons are in relation to each other. For example, a child may have a close relationship with an aunt or an uncle, but the relationship is not the same as a relationship with a cousin.

The first objective of these activities is to increase children's awareness of and sensitivity to other individuals who occupy roles unlike their own within their own reference group. The second goal is to help children learn to see things from another person's point of view and to be able to withhold judgment until other perspectives have been considered. The third and larger goal is to help children understand how membership in a group may determine their point of view and how the group appears to those on the outside.

Lesson 1

Introduce this part of the unit by saying that the class has studied relativity in the physical world; now they will think about relativity among people. Read a story to the class about an extended family. Many books are suitable for this purpose; choose one that you think the children will like and that has family members who can be identified by name; add family members and a few neighbors if more are needed. As you read the story to the class, ask questions as you go along and at the end.

Assign children roles from the story, and more if needed, and give each child a large name tag. Now you will play a game of introductions in which you assume the role of the mother, called here Ms. Chin. You and the children will role play a series of introductions roughly like this:

MS. CHIN:	Mr. Green, I want you to meet my son, Jack.
MR. GREEN AND JACK:	How do you do?
MS. CHIN:	Susie, introduce Jack to Mr. Brown, and say how he is related to you.
SUSIE:	Mr. Brown, I'd like you to meet my brother, Jack.
MS. CHIN:	(To the class) Is Jack a brother? I thought he was a son.
CLASS:	He is both.
MS. CHIN:	How can that be?
CLASS:	It depends.
MS. CHIN:	Depends on what?

Continue with the introductions—grandmother, classmate, uncle, cousin, and so on. You then say, "This is getting confusing. Tomorrow we will make a chart to organize these relationships."

Lesson 2

Remind the children of the story, and ask individual pupils to recall the relationships. Write names on the board. Draw a chart on the board, and ask the class to tell you what to put in the cells. For example, ask, "What is Jack's relation to Susie?" Or, you could ask, "Susie would say that Jack is her _____ ?" Continue in this way until the chart is filled in. (This chart must be based on the particular story you have used in introducing this lesson.) Table 12.1 shows a chart of an extended family.

Ask the children for a word that describes all of these people (relatives or relations). Then ask them to recall Spacey and compare the meaning of *relative* in the two contexts.

The assignment for the following day is for each child to choose four family members or friends and make a chart similar to this one. Children may bring in pictures of occasions, such as holidays, birthdays, or reunions, when the family is gathered together.

Warning: Make no assumptions about living arrangements of the families of your pupils. Accept as normal any arrangements that the pupils put in their charts. If a child says he or she has no family, say that sometimes other people are the same as family. A good friend may be the same as a brother, and the mother's friend may be like an aunt. If you find that you have homeless children in your class, you may not be able to do this as written but may have to modify it to suit the situation as well as you can. You must be sensitive on this issue.

When the charts are brought in, you can discuss them and let those who want to share with others do so. The pupils will paste their charts in their workbooks.

Lesson 3

Introduce the idea of different points of view in a conflict. The children will role play the resolution of a conflict that they might encounter. The objective is to see

TABLE 12.1 Chart of an Extended Family—"Relativity" Among People

Relatives	Jack	Susie	Ms. Chin	Mr. Chin	Ms. Parker	Mr. Parker	Tom Parker
Jack	self	brother	son	son	nephew	nephew	cousin
Susie	sister	self	daughter	daughter	niece	niece	cousin
Ms. Chin	mother	mother	self	wife	sister	sister-in-law	aunt
Mr. Chin	father	father	husband	self	sister-in-law	broth.-in-law	uncle
Ms. Parker	aunt	aunt	sister	sister-in-law	self	wife	mother
Mr. Parker	uncle	uncle	broth.-in-law	broth.-in-law	husband	self	father
Tom Parker	cousin	cousin	nephew	nephew	son	son	self

other people's points of view, or reference points. There are several ways this can be done. You can read a story that involves conflict, stop at a crucial point, and have the children act out what the characters would do. This can be accomplished by your choosing a few children to demonstrate, or—if they are used to working in cooperative groups—you can have the pupils move into groups and let each group act out the rest of the story. Each child assumes a role and explains the conflict from the point of view of the role assumed. Remind them of Spacey.

Another way to do this is to use an incident that is familiar to the children and have them take roles to act out the incident, showing how each participant has a point of view. However you do it, the point is to get children to see that a situation looks different to the different people involved in it and that they should try to see a situation from other people's points of view as well as their own.

One way to end the unit is to read a story about a child who was excluded from a group. Ask questions about how it feels to be on the outside rather than the inside of a group. It is better to leave children thinking than to have a neat wrap-up.

A UNIT ON EARTH MATERIALS

This unit integrates earth science, social studies, and language arts in an investigation that asks what kinds of rocks and minerals are found locally and how these materials are used in buildings, monuments, tombstones, walls, and other constructions in the local environment. Science objectives will include identifying local rocks and minerals, learning how rocks are formed, and finding out what forms are present in the local area. This will lead into identifying the stones used for various structures and finding out where they came from, why different stones are used for different purposes, how they are quarried, and how they have figured in local history. (You may wonder why we call earth materials "rocks" in science and "stones" when used for building. So far as we know, there is no reason other than custom.)

To make a unit of this kind successful, you will need to make certain beforehand that adequate sources of information are available. Work with your school librarian to ensure that resources are available for the children to use. It will be frustrating and unproductive to have children searching for information that is not available in any form or in any place to which they have access.

You could begin the unit with the lesson that follows, based on a simple activity that helps pupils learn the importance of choosing words carefully to convey the intended meaning to others. The teacher does not have to correct the children's language; the consequences of using imprecise words are built into the activity. This activity has some of the characteristics of a game, and children usually enjoy it. (You may want to use this activity at another time with other objects to lead into a unit on a different theme. Any interesting objects may be used, provided they are of the same category and that there are significant differences between the individual items.)

LESSON PLAN 12.1

DESCRIBING AND IDENTIFYING ROCKS

NSE STANDARD

Earth science: Properties of earth materials (National Research Council, 1996, p. 134).

GRADE LEVEL: 3 TO 6

STUDENT OBJECTIVE

Write a description of a rock that allows another person to distinguish that rock from other similar rocks.

MATERIALS

A collection of rocks
Paper and pencils

PROCEDURE

Distribute rocks, giving one to each child if there are enough to go around; otherwise, give one to each pair of children. Ask the children to observe their rocks carefully and to think of some words that could be used to describe them. Walk around the room to encourage children to attend to the task.

After a few minutes, go to the board and ask for raised hands from those who have thought of a word to describe their rocks. Call on a child, and write the word on the board. Repeat until six to eight words are on the board. If a child suggests "big" or "small," say, "Bigger than what?" or "Smaller than what?" You might suggest that they could use an egg for comparison and ask, "Is it bigger than an egg?" Continue until you have drawn out the idea that big and small, light and dark, and similar words are comparative.

Distribute half sheets of paper, and tell children to observe their rock carefully and to write a description of their rock, using any words that describe something about the rock. Direct them to write their names at the bottom of their papers and to fold the papers over when they are finished.

After they have had time to complete this task, pupils bring their rocks up to the front of the room and place them together on a table or in a space marked out on the floor. At the same time, they place their folded papers with descriptions in a container (a basket or box).

When all rocks and descriptions have been placed as directed, take the container with the descriptions around the room and allow each child to take one and read it silently. Then have the children come up in small groups, picking out the rock described on their paper. If a child cannot find the rock described on the paper, return the paper to the child who wrote the description and ask the child to improve the description. Once improved, the description is handed back to the other child.

When all rocks have been identified, spend a few minutes letting the children discuss what makes a good description and which words they found helpful or unhelpful. Explain that they will be studying rocks and minerals for the next few weeks and that careful observation will be very important. It will also be important to use precise words to describe their observations.

OTHER IDEAS FOR INTEGRATING SCIENCE AND SOCIAL STUDIES

Weather: Causes and Effects (Intermediate)

Weather is included in almost all lists of topics to be taught in science in the elementary school. A brief outline of such a unit is given in Chapter 11. This may be extended and enhanced by getting information from a newspaper, or over the Internet, throughout a period of days or weeks, about weather in other parts of the United States and the world. This can lead into an exploration—through books, films, and other media—of how animals and people protect themselves in extreme climates, such as the Arctic, the Sahara, and the Amazon rain forest. Field trips to a local park will add interest and knowledge, particularly if you can arrange several trips to the same spot at different times of the year.

Animal Habitats and People's Homes

The topic of habitats and homes is related to the previous idea but is not really the same. Animal habitats are included as a science topic in many sixth-grade curricula. This can be extended to a study of the houses people build and live in throughout the world—a topic that is also often included in social studies curricula. Provide materials and experiences that will lead the children to understand that both animals and people need safe shelters and that they use and adapt the materials at hand to meet their needs.

Simple Machines in the Ancient World

In Chapter 10 you saw that simple machines are a suitable topic for a group investigation. This topic lends itself easily to integration with social studies by extending the unit to include learning about the building of the pyramids in Egypt (Macaulay, 1981b), the cathedrals in Europe (Macaulay, 1981a), or other structures of the ancient and medieval world. Before the invention of the steam engine and, later, electricity, the only machines available were versions of those we call "simple machines."

Whether this unit is carried out as a group investigation or guided inquiry, it is essential to have a good supply of machines and tools. Strong hooks should be screwed into the ceiling so that pulleys can be attached and used for hands-on activities, including measuring the force needed to lift loads by various combinations of pulleys. Levers of several kinds should be available, as well as bricks or rocks to lift. Children will first learn about these machines by using them to lift real weights and by measuring forces and masses. This topic is often included in the prescribed curriculum or designated textbook for fifth grade, but you may wish to seek other sources (e.g., Macaulay, 1988; St. Andre, 1995) for hands-on activities. After pupils have had enough experience to achieve some understanding of how the machines work—and they should not be rushed—they will study the building of the pyramids as an introduction to life in ancient Egypt and, by extension, the ancient world. Building a model of a pyramid or other structure can be an interesting and worthwhile class project if several areas of the curriculum are integrated so that the learning objectives are kept in mind. Many opportunities exist for using mathematics in this unit, including the necessity to make careful measurements of the sides of the bases of the model of a pyramid. Drawing and drama could also be integrated into the unit. (There are so many available resources and so many interesting possibilities for this unit that some restraint will have to be exercised to keep it within a reasonable time frame.)

SCIENCE AND READING

As one of the three R's, reading has always consumed a major portion of the school day in the primary grades and has received serious attention all the way through the elementary school. Learning to read is a major developmental task for young children and of great concern to teachers and parents. If you are a teacher in a self-contained classroom, a good deal of your time will be spent on teaching your pupils to read, from early stages of emergent literacy, through skill at decoding and comprehension, and finally to the ability to use reading as a means of learning other subjects and understanding the world. Classifying, inferring, and hypothesizing—processes needed in science—also have a place in reading. As children get past the earliest stages of learning to read and begin to read for comprehension, these processes become important in their progress. Since reading consumes so much time in the elementary school, it seems sensible to integrate science and reading as much as possible. In the early grades, this is most easily accomplished by the use of science experiences as a basis for the experiential approach to teaching reading and, in intermediate grades, through the use of books as supplements to classroom science experiences.

Using Science as the Basis for Reading

Use of basal readers remains the primary means of instruction in beginning reading, but language experience and whole language approaches are other methods now in use (McGee & Lomax, 1990; Schickedanz, 1990; Stahl & Miller, 1989). These personalized, reality-based approaches encompass listening, speaking, reading, and writing, and children are encouraged and guided to use language in regard to a shared experience of the group. Both of these methods—similar in many respects—can use science experiences as the basis for narratives constructed by the children. In the older, language experience method, children tell their experiences to the teacher, either individually or in a group, and the teacher writes what they say. In the whole language approach, the children write their experiences themselves, spelling the words however they can. A science lesson on observing and classifying objects, for example, can form the basis for a language experience or whole language lesson.

The following example lesson is a simple activity that illustrates how a science experience can form the basis for a reading lesson or series of lessons. Almost any of the common topics of the kindergarten and first-grade curriculum—animals, parts of the body, the five senses, the seasons, shadows, magnets, floating and sinking, balancing—can be used as the basis for a language approach to reading.

LESSON PLAN 12.2

CLASSIFYING LEAVES

NSE STANDARD

Objects can be described by properties, and those properties can be used to separate or sort a group of objects (National Research Council, 1996, p. 127).

GRADE LEVELS: KINDERGARTEN TO 1

STUDENT OBJECTIVES

By the end of these activities, the learners should be able to:

1. Observe and classify leaves.
2. Represent their own experiences in writing, and read what they have written or dictated.

ACTIVITIES

When the leaves have begun to turn in the fall, the teacher brings a few leaves to class, shows them to the pupils, and asks questions to allow children to tell what they know about leaves, such as that some trees have leaves that change color in the fall and other trees stay green all year.

An alternative is to do this late in the spring after leaves have appeared on local trees. In that case, the questions are about leaves coming out in the spring. (If you are in an area where there are few trees, you may have to use some other local natural material.)

After a brief discussion, the children go for a nature walk on the school grounds or nearby where leaves can be found. All children should collect a few leaves to bring back. In the classroom, the children examine the leaves for color, shape, and size, perhaps with small hand lenses. Then they classify the leaves by color, shape, or other characteristics. In the next phase, the teacher draws out from the children a story about the walk (including what kinds of leaves they found) and writes that story on the board or on large paper, following the usual procedure for a language experience lesson. This could be the beginning of a unit on trees or on changes in seasons in which a series of related experiences forms the basis for a class book on the chosen topic.

Hatching Chickens

Hatching chickens is another science activity that can be used as the basis for writing and drawing. Watching chickens hatch is always exciting to children. This activity is usually reserved for kindergarten and first grade, but all children find it absorbing and fascinating. Eggs that have already been incubated can be bought from a hatchery and kept in the room for the final two or three days before the first cracks appear in the shells. Children watch the eggs and are allowed time to write their observations each day. The teacher leads discussions each day about what is happening, asking whether anyone has heard anything, noticed any differences, and so on. When the chickens hatch, the children will need little prodding to write about the experience and represent it in drawings. The chickens should be fed and given water for a few days. (In a rural area, it's easy to find a good home for the chicks. In a city, call the Humane Society.)

Effect of Diet on Mice

Another experience suitable for beginning readers and writers is a shared investigation of the effect of diet on white mice. Materials needed are two mice in separate cages, some advice about mouse nutrition, and a supply of food. (The National Dairy Council supplies information about good and poor diets.) After introducing the subject and explaining what each mouse will be fed—discussing how food affects our bodies and making whatever points seem appropriate—the teacher begins the investigation. The mice are fed at the same time each day, a good diet for one and a poor diet for the other. Children record their observations and read them back, or the teacher records them on the board if this seems preferable.

After about a week, the children will be able to see definite differences in the appearance of the two mice. After this has been noted and discussed, the ill-fed mouse is given the same diet as the other mouse. After another seven days, this mouse will look very similar to the other one. At each stage, the children record their observations in their own words. The experiment is discussed as it goes along, and sufficient time is allowed at the end to ensure that the children have understood the process and outcome.

Reading About Science

A wonderful variety of books on every imaginable science subject is available for readers of all ages. These range from books written at the lowest vocabulary level to detailed, accurate treatments of subjects of interest to those upper-elementary children who by this time are excellent readers and have a special interest in science. In between these two extremes are many science books that have wide appeal. All pupils should be required to read and report on, either orally or in writing, books about science subjects, along with works of fiction, history, and other areas of interest.

It is useless to require pupils to produce book reports unless you are willing to put thought and time into how they will carry out the assignment. To make the assignment is easy, but to follow through can prove difficult. There are a number of steps that pupils will have to take, and you will have to monitor their progress, including selecting a book (in this case, a book on a suitable science subject), having the book approved, reading the book and taking notes, submitting for approval an outline of the report, and getting the report in on time. In effect, the reports become independent projects, similar to those described in Chapter 11. You can determine whether writing a book report will be a growth-promoting process or a frustrating one for most of your pupils.

Readers can find a book on any science subject that captures their interest.

Books will also be needed for information on subjects studied in class, particularly in the case of group investigations and independent projects, such as for a science fair. School librarians are always ready to cooperate, within the constraints of their budgets, in securing books that children need for carrying out science assignments. You, the teacher, need to let them know ahead of time what your pupils will need for their science projects and assignments.

Although science must primarily be taught by means of an active, hands-on, experiential approach, that does not mean there is no place for books and reading. Reading can make experience more meaningful and can provide vicarious experiences that cannot be had directly. The problem arises when reading becomes the primary means by which children learn science. Reading should supplement experience, not take the place of it.

SCIENCE AND WRITING

Science and writing form an area in which skill and content can be integrated so that each is enhanced by the other. Writing shapes experience and helps in understanding it. This is as true for experience of the natural world as it is for other kinds of experience. Thus, writing should be an integral part of science instruction from the earliest grades. Science can be used as a basis for writing about observations, thoughts, and feelings. This practice is in keeping with the current interest in writing across the curriculum and the whole language approach in elementary school, both of which reject the notion that writing can be separated from experience and from other ways of learning.

Keeping records and describing observations and experiments are an essential part of science and should be considered as a normal part of a science lesson. The *National Science Education Standards* (National Research Council, 1996) state that students should be able to "gather, store, retrieve and organize data" (p. 145) and to communicate results to others.

Precision, accuracy, and clarity of expression are important characteristics of science writing and should not be neglected in elementary school. Analysis and theorizing (or hypothesizing) may begin to be encouraged toward the end of elementary school, but children first have to learn to communicate what they have done and observed in a way that others can understand. This emphasis encourages children to think of writing as a means of explaining to someone else what they have seen and done and, in the process, to understand it better themselves.

Several years ago, a pupil wrote this description of an accident: "I seen a reck at Main St. and Aurora Bldv. The blue car was dent and the white car was smushed." Although the pupil still had a lot to learn about grammar and spelling, these two sentences show that he was observant, since he remembered the street names and the colors of the cars, and that he could give the reader a graphic picture of the scene in a few words. This is what you want to encourage pupils to do as they learn to communicate their experiences and thoughts to others. Grammar and spelling are important, too, but their purpose is to aid communication, not inhibit it.

Keeping Workbooks

We advocated in Chapter 5 that, beginning no later than fourth grade, pupils should keep a science workbook or notebook in which they record their activities in science class. If you choose to grade the workbooks, you should grade them for completeness, organization, and evidence of thinking, but not for spelling or writing, since children's writing skills are in various stages of development. Whether you grade them or not, the workbooks should be checked to see that they are being kept up and that all important observations and information are included.

Refer back to Chapter 5, where a page from a fifth-grade pupil's workbook is shown in Figure 5.1. Note that the workbook in Figure 5.1 is neat and carefully kept, though the child has corrected a few mistakes. Note also that this is a record of a rather simple experiment, but one that fifth graders can carry out and understand without much explanation or help from the teacher. The writing that is necessary is also quite within the ability of most fifth graders. To become autonomous learners, children have to be able to work on their own without constant adult guidance. For this to happen, they have to have science lessons based on activities, including writing, that they can manage mostly on their own. When science lessons become too abstract or too complicated—or the necessary record keeping and arriving at conclusions are too difficult—children are forced to rely on adults and cannot grow toward autonomy.

Other Writing

Many scientists have written poetically and expressively about the beauty of science and their feelings about it. Children should also be given opportunities to write about their experiences in whatever way they wish. In most schools, children are more often given opportunities for expressive writing than they are required to convey information accurately and clearly. Science experiences can provide the basis for the development of clarity and accuracy.

SCIENCE AND MATHEMATICS

Mathematics is often taught as algorithms to be learned and problems for which there is one and only one right answer that can be arrived at by only one correct method. Doing mathematics is identified with searching for the unique solution to a problem that is stated in a uniquely acceptable way. Since mathematics is usually first taught in mathematics class and then applied in science class, it is often assumed that a problem in science must first be mathematically formulated and then the answer can be obtained by some means of automatic processing. Applying mathematics in science has come to be identified with writing down equations for end-of-chapter problems.

If mathematics and science are to be integrated in the elementary classroom, a different approach is needed, one that teaches and uses mathematics within the context of classroom experiences in science. Mathematics may then be considered a useful and necessary means of representing observations that have been made and working out problems that have presented themselves.

In a previous section, you read that pupils keep notebooks in which to record their observations, experiences, experiments, and conclusions. These notebooks should also contain notations of the mathematics associated with the work done in science, including measurements, graphs, and the calculations necessary to understanding their observations.

Mathematics as a Science

This section has focused on the use of mathematics as a way of representing and analyzing data collected during science activities. But do not be misled into thinking that these practical uses and representations of the physical world are all there is to mathematics. Mathematics is a science as well as a tool, and from the constructivist point of view, an understanding of mathematics does not depend only on experiences in the real world but also, and importantly, on logical thinking.

In the primary grades, mathematics and science merge in many ways, such as learning to identify shapes, understanding one-to-one correspondence, recognizing patterns in numbers as well as in objects, classifying numbers, and understanding concepts of area and volume. Learning activities associated with these processes and concepts are truly integrated, since mathematics and science are one at this level.

SCIENCE AND THE EXPRESSIVE ARTS

Music, art, and expressive movement are other subjects taught in elementary school that offer many opportunities for integrated lessons and units. Once you give up thinking about individual subjects and start thinking about ways to combine and integrate them, you will think of many ways to accomplish this. A bit of imagination and understanding of both science and the other subject are necessary, but you can find help among your colleagues, and perhaps some of them will join with you.

Visual Arts

There are many examples of trivial exercises planned in an effort to extend science lessons into other areas. In art, for example, teachers have been known to hand out "dittoed" sheets that are to be cut out and pasted together in some way to represent a small animal or plant. Other teachers give first-grade children outlines of dinosaurs or farm animals to be colored in. It only takes a moment to reflect that these activities do not meet the criteria provided at the beginning of this chapter and thus are appropriate for neither art nor science.

All styles of drawing and painting can be integrated with science lessons. Children can often represent more of what they know in a drawing than in writing and should be encouraged to include in their notebooks drawings of the animals, plants, and other things they have studied (Howe & Vasu, 1989). They can also be encouraged to express their feelings about other living things. You can imagine that the little girl mentioned in Chapter 11, who said she had followed and observed a worm, might be happy to express her thoughts and feelings about the worm in some art form.

Structural patterns found in nature have inspired artists through the centuries and can stimulate your pupils to respond in their own creative ways. For example, a science unit on insects can be extended to explore spider webs, honeycombs, or termite "castles" as stimuli for drawing, painting, or ceramics. For older pupils, optics is a topic that can be the basis for an integrated unit on light, color, and design.

Music

There are many areas of overlap between physical science and music. A unit can begin with the physical properties of sound and move into the relationship of sound to musical instruments. Children can make a number of different simple instruments that will produce a few distinct notes. Lessons on recognizing patterns in sound will use science processes in another context that will serve to increase pupils' understanding of the process.

Creative Movement

Chapter 10 referred to children's dancing to represent the flight of butterflies at the end of a unit on the life stages of insects. Other ways that children can use their bodies to represent the movements of animals include moving sideways like a crab, hopping like a kangaroo or rabbit, and walking like a bird, as well as too many others to list. These are often treated as trivial activities, more suitable for young children on the playground than for those in the classroom. Indeed, the playground may be the appropriate site; however, these activities are not trivial but are ways of taking another point of view and of increasing children's understanding and appreciation of the other creatures who share the earth.

◆ SUMMARY

Science may be integrated with other subjects in a variety of ways to increase understanding, make better use of time, and make schoolwork more meaningful for children. Subjects may be integrated by topic, by concept, or by using a skill from one subject in learning activities from another area. In all cases, it is important to identify objectives for both subjects and to plan the lesson or unit so that objectives in both subjects are met.

Social studies and science share many topics and concepts. One example was presented in the unit on relativity, which focused on relative position in the physical world and on relations between people in the social world. The integration of science and language arts may include using writing as a means of representing science experiences and using science as the basis for reading and writing. Science processes can be thought of in a broader sense as thinking processes and are applicable in reading comprehension. Although firsthand experiences are the primary way for children to learn science, many experiences are available only vicariously through reading. These can be memorable and valuable and should be a part of the science program in elementary school. Books of information are also required for a well-rounded science program.

Mathematics is an indispensable tool for representing and understanding science. Both geometry and arithmetic are so interwoven with science at this level that it is hard to separate them in a good science program. Although this chapter focused on the uses of mathematics in collecting and analyzing data, we recognize that mathematics is concerned both with applications to real-world problems and with ideas based solely on reasoning.

Integration of science with other subjects is an opportunity and a challenge for you to make science more meaningful to children. The world did not divide itself up into distinct subject areas; these divisions have been made by human beings who have classified and categorized what they found in the world in order to make it more comprehensible. Many simple, though important and even profound, ideas cut across disciplines. In fact, most powerful ideas are not confined to one subject but cut across the range of human experience.

In this chapter we have included many ideas or suggestions for lessons or units that were not fleshed out into lesson plans with objectives, lists of materials, activities, and evaluation. We hope that you will refer back to these when you are searching for ideas that you can develop and use in your own teaching. Your success as a science teacher will depend, in part, on how creative you are in taking a simple idea and developing it into a focused, activity-centered, goal-oriented unit of study.

◆ ACTIVITIES FOR THE READER

1. Outline a topic-oriented integrated unit.

2. Outline a concept-oriented integrated unit.

3. Outline a skill-content integrated unit.

4. Select suitable books to be used in the relativity unit, and give your reasons for each selection.

5. Outline a lesson for first grade that integrates reading and science.

6. Make an annotated list of thirty science trade books. Select five for each grade level from first through sixth grade, giving the correct citations for each. Write a short paragraph describing each book.

7. Design an interdisciplinary third-grade lesson integrating art and science or music and science.

8. Write a lesson integrating health and science.

◆ QUESTIONS FOR DISCUSSION

1. Consider the unit on relativity. Is this an example of topic-oriented integration, concept-oriented integration, or skills-oriented integration? Explain the reasons for your answer.

2. Many teachers hand out prepared sheets with blanks to be filled in rather than have pupils keep science workbooks. Their reasons are that pupils cannot write well enough, it takes too much time, pupils lose the workbooks, and workbooks take too much time to grade. What arguments can you give to justify the use of workbooks?

3. Explain and discuss the meaning of this statement: "Reading should supplement experience, not take the place of it." Do you agree?

4. Discuss the pros and cons of self-contained classrooms as opposed to having content specialists in elementary schools.

◆ REFERENCES

Berger, C., Karplus, R., Montgomery, M., Randle, J., & Thier, H. (1972). *Relative position and motion*. Chicago: Rand McNally.

Bruner, J. (1966). *Toward a theory of instruction*. Cambridge, MA: Harvard University Press.

Howe, A., & Vasu, E. (1989). The role of language in children's formation and retention of mental images. *Journal of Research in Science Teaching, 26*(1), 15–24.

Jacobs, H. H. (Ed.). (1989). *Interdisciplinary curriculum: Design and implementation*. Washington, DC: Association for Supervision and Curriculum Development.

Locker, T. (1994). *Where the river begins*. New York: Dial.

Macaulay, D. (1981a). *Cathedral*. Boston: Houghton Mifflin.

Macaulay, D. (1981b). *Pyramids*. Boston: Houghton Mifflin.

Macaulay, D. (1988). *The way things work*. Boston: Houghton Mifflin.

McGee, L. M., & Lomax, R. G. (1990). On combining apples and oranges. A response to Stahl and Miller. *Review of Educational Research, 60,* 133–140.

National Research Council. (1996). *National science education standards*. Washington, DC: National Academy Press.

O'Dell, S. (1986). *Streams to the river, river to the sea*. Boston: Houghton Mifflin. (paperback: New York: Fawcett Juniper)

St. Andre, R. (1995). *Simple machines and how they work*. White Plains, NY: Cuisenaire.

Schickedanz, J. A. (1990). Critique of Stahl and Miller's study. *Review of Educational Research, 60,* 127–131.

Stahl, S., & Miller, P. (1989). Whole language and language experience approaches for beginning reading. *Review of Educational Research, 59,* 87–116.

◆ RESOURCES

Cuisenaire Company of America, Inc. (P.O. Box 5026, White Plains, NY 10602) distributes many trade books for teachers. Two of interest are *Science and Language Links* by Johanna Scott and *Science through Children's Literature* by Carol Butzow and John Butzow.

Delta Education, Inc. (P.O. Box M, Nashua, NH 03061), now publishes materials originally produced by Elementary Science Study (ESS) and Science Curriculum Improvement Study (SCIS), including *Relative Position and Motion*.

All materials of the Elementary Science Study (ESS), Science Curriculum Improvement Study (SCIS), and Science—A Process Approach (S-APA) are now available on CD-ROM from Science Helper K–8, Knowledge Project in Science, PC-SIG/IASC, CD-ROM Publishing Group (1030E East Duane Avenue, Sunnydale, CA 94086).

Thematic Units: Science, Technology, and Society

◆ Mr. Newman was usually smiling and cheerful when he arrived at school, but one morning Ms. Oldhand noticed that he seemed concerned about something.

MS. OLDHAND: You seem to have something on your mind this morning. Is there anything I might help you with?

MR. NEWMAN: Well, I do have something on my mind, but there's nothing anyone can do. You know I live in an off-campus student apartment, not exactly the Hollywood Hilton. Until yesterday, we had a large tree on the lot that shaded the building and was a home to birds and squirrels. I really loved that tree, but when I got home yesterday I found that the tree had been cut down to make room for more cars in the parking lot. That made me really sad.

MS. OLDHAND: That seems like a shame. Did you talk to the owner of the building?

MR. NEWMAN: Yes, I did. He said that people who live in the building had gotten parking tickets for leaving their cars on the street overnight and that he had to provide more off-street parking. The only way to get more parking space was to get rid of the tree.

MS. OLDHAND: I, too, would be very sad about losing the tree. What has happened there is an example of how technology, in this case the automobile, has affected our lives in ways that no one foresaw when the automobile was invented. Later in the year, we will look at some other ways that science and technology interact with our lives in unexpected ways.

Science, Technology, and Society (STS) is the study of the relationships and interactions of science and technology in a social context. Environmental education is often included, since many of the most troublesome issues are those that affect the natural environment. As an introduction to STS and advance organizer for yourself, consider the following:

1. Vast amounts of energy are needed to maintain an industrial society and a high standard of living, but all sources of energy create problems. The burning of coal produces acid rain and other kinds of pollution; nuclear power is dangerous and produces hazardous wastes that are almost impossible to dispose of; the use of oil makes us dependent on foreign powers, and oil spills are devastating to life in the oceans. The coal, nuclear energy, and oil industries are all subject to federal regulation, which means that the government sets policies about them. Should the government allow coal mining on federal land in the West? Should the government encourage the development of nuclear energy? Should the government allow drilling for oil on fragile ecosystems? Who should decide?

2. The basis of agriculture in the United States is no longer the family farm but major business enterprises that do everything on a large scale. Fields of wheat and soybeans stretch as far as the eye can see; chickens, turkeys, and hogs are produced under factory-like conditions. One result is that food is plentiful and cheap, compared to food in other countries, and we have more than we need and export food to the rest of the world. However, the change from small, diverse farms to agribusiness has had other results. The huge fields require large amounts of pesticides and fertilizer that can be harmful to people. The animal farms spill waste into rivers and inlets, killing the fish, and making the water unsafe for recreation. What kinds of public policies should be established to deal with these problems?

In these, as in other cases, alternatives, risks, costs, and benefits have to be considered in determining public policies. Some of the questions that arise are listed in *Benchmarks* (American Association for the Advancement of Science [AAAS], 1993) as follows:

> What alternative ways are there to achieve the same ends and how do alternatives compare? Who benefits and who suffers? What are the financial and social costs, do they change over time and who bears them? What are the risks associated with using or not using a specific technology? How will a new technology and its waste products be disposed of and at what cost? (p. 57)

GOALS OF STS EDUCATION

One of the primary goals of American education is to prepare students to become responsible citizens of a democratic society. STS education plays an important role in meeting this goal because responsible citizenship in today's world requires knowledge and understanding of issues related to science, technology, and society that have profound implications for public policy. The way we approach the study and consideration of these issues is another important aspect of STS education and one that will contribute to the preparation for responsible citizenship. A social studies educator expressed the same idea as follows:

> The ability of citizens to make informed, rational decisions . . . is directly linked to understanding of public issues related to societal applications of science and technology. Ability to connect information and ideas within and between disciplines and to link different fields of knowledge is a key to understanding of social reality. (Heath, 1988)

In addition to these large societal concerns, there are issues and questions that affect the lives of elementary school children and their families. STS is not a distinct subject but a concept of building units around themes that cut across several curriculum areas and engage children in the study of real-world issues. One of the challenges of developing STS thematic units is to bring the larger issues down to the local level and study problems that are of concern and interest to children. A long-term goal is that experience in gathering data and discussing issues of public and personal concern will prepare children to confront the larger issues when they have the background and maturity to do so. In this context, the goals of STS education are for students to:

- Develop awareness and understanding of the interrelationships between science, technology, and society.

- Learn to recognize and deal with STS-related conflicts in their own lives.

- Master a body of fundamental knowledge of science that is needed to understand STS issues.

- Develop the intellectual tools and mental processes to deal responsibly with STS issues.

- Become aware of their responsibilities as citizens to influence public policies and outcomes.

GUIDELINES

For children in the primary grades, the best preparation for dealing with STS issues is to develop an appreciation of the natural world, to learn to care about other people, and to develop science process skills that are appropriate for their ages. Young children can become frightened and fearful if there is emphasis on the negative aspects of the world they live in. We were told by a scientist that his grandson was afraid to go out in the rain and asked his grandfather, "Haven't you heard about acid rain? That is very dangerous. I never go out in the rain." If you have a great idea for an STS unit for primary children, go ahead and develop it, but remember to keep it simple and avoid using ideas that might be frightening.

This chapter will focus on questions and problems that children in intermediate grades can investigate through thematic units that integrate science, social studies, and other curriculum areas. You have already seen many examples of integrated lessons and units, and you have studied how to plan and implement group projects and other inquiry-based instruction. The same principles apply in an STS investigation. The difference is not in methods but in the focus on an STS theme.

Some guidelines for developing STS thematic units follow:

- Identify a problem with local interest that is the result of the interaction of science and/or technology with some aspect of people's lives or the natural environment.

- Focus on personal impact that makes use of students' natural curiosity and concerns.

- Use local resources to gather information that can be used in studying the problem.

- Involve students in seeking information that is needed.

◆ Design the unit so that students use process skills only as they are related to the problem at hand.

◆ Resist the temptation to find the "right" answer. Bloom (1992) points out in an article about first- and fifth-grade children's study of earthworms, "As science educators in Western societies, it is difficult to divorce ourselves from the right (scientific) answer syndrome, which tends to see learning as positivistic and/or empirical in nature" (p. 412).

A THEMATIC UNIT ON ACID RAIN

Since you have seen many examples of detailed lesson plans, the lessons in this unit are described in general terms. Those who wish to pursue this theme and need additional details can consult the resources listed at the end of this chapter.

UNIT PLAN 13.1

ACID RAIN

NSE STANDARD

Science in personal and social perspectives: Human activities can induce hazards through resource acquisition, urban growth, land-use decisions, and waste disposal (National Research Council, 1996, p. 168).

GRADE LEVELS: 5 TO 6

GOALS

Children will learn what is meant by the term *acid rain,* how acid rain affects living organisms, what causes it, how we contribute to it, and some possible future consequences of current behavior and policies.

MATERIALS

Acids (weak solution of hydrochloric acid, vinegar, lemon juice)
Bases (ammonia, baking soda, antacid tablets)
Indicator papers (pH paper and others)
Radish or bean seeds
Potting materials
Prepared inventory sheets
Reading materials

OVERVIEW OF ACTIVITIES

Many of these activities are described in detail in *Acid Rain: Science Projects* (Hessler & Stubbs, 1987), available from The Acid Rain Foundation. This unit integrates science, social studies, math, language arts, and art, but it emphasizes the integration of science and social studies.

Lesson 1

Acids and bases, including vinegar, baking soda, antacid tablet, lemon juice, and other materials, are tested with pH paper and classified as to pH above or below neutral. (It is not necessary for pupils to know the definition of pH, only that it is a way of testing whether something is an acid, a base, or neutral.) Explain that children will be collecting rain samples to test for acid rain, and begin preparations for testing on the next rainy day. (Be prepared to deal with the possibility that the rain in your area is not, in fact, acidic.)

Lesson 2

Seedling response to acid rain is tested. This is a pupil experiment to be conducted as a controlled experiment. Radish or bean seeds are planted (two to a pot) and watered with water of varying acidity (pH from 3 to 6). Three weeks after the seeds are planted, pupils measure and record height, number of leaves, and leaf midrib length. (Other suitable activities are to find the effect of acidic water on leaves and on the tiny organisms found in pond water.) Their measurements should be carefully recorded and used to make simple bar graphs.

Lesson 3

Introduce the idea of acid rain and some information about its effect on trees. What is the evidence that acid rain has caused trees to die? This will lead them to search for sources of information. Your next questions should seek to relate the results of acid rain to social questions. How would it feel to live near a forest where the trees are dying? This could be an opportunity for creative writing or role playing.

Lesson 4

Where does acid rain come from? Ask questions about sources of air pollution. Questions and discussion follow about the meaning and origin of fossil fuels, what happens when they burn, and how they provide usable energy. (Children of this age all know something about dinosaurs and other prehistoric animals.) Pupils are assigned to collect pictures of sources of air pollution from magazines, newspapers, and other publications to bring to class. You or a committee will make these into a collage and add pictures as more come in.

Lesson 5

Sources of energy in the pupils' homes and in your city or town are addressed next. Begin by making a list on the board or overhead projector of machines and appliances pupils used before coming to school that day. Then discuss where energy comes from. Does the electricity in your area come from water power, coal, or another source? Pupils take a worksheet home and, with the help of parents, list all energy users in and around their home and what they think the source of energy is. These form a basis of discussion on the following day.

Throughout these lessons, don't neglect preparations for and actual collection of rain samples. When samples have been collected, they are tested to determine whether the samples are acidic. For this activity, have pupils work in pairs or cooperative groups; each group has samples of the water that has been collected, access to the available acids, bases, and pH and other indicator paper. They enter the results of testing in their workbooks, and the class discusses the results.

Lesson 6

Wrap up the unit by forming groups to discuss "What if?" questions that you will assign: What if we did not have any more fossil fuels? Would that be good or bad? What if we continue to pollute the air as we are now doing? What if our country makes laws prohibiting air pollution and other countries do not? What effects will that have on the environment and our relations with other countries? What if people have to pay higher taxes and lose jobs in order to lower pollution? Each group writes out answers on big sheets of newsprint, and these are read and discussed by all.

EXAMPLES OF STS UNITS

Integrated thematic STS units that engage children's interest and lead to meaningful learning usually grow out of local circumstances and depend on available resources and the interests of teachers and children. Detailed lesson plans that are useful in one location may not be applicable at all in other places. As an alternative to lesson plans, the following section describes interdisciplinary STS investigations that have been used in schools in different parts of the country. Many details have been left out of all of the descriptions; you will have to use your imagination to fill in the blanks.

RUNOFF OF WATER FROM SCHOOL BUILDING AND PARKING LOT

BACKGROUND

When rain falls on earth that is covered with vegetation, the water soaks into the ground and is available to support the life of the plants that live there, and these, in turn, support many forms of animal life. When the earth is covered with pavement or buildings, the rain that falls cannot soak into the ground but runs off into gutters or along streets or wherever there is a way for it to go. This has been happening ever since people began to build buildings and make roadways, but the pace of this process has increased rapidly in modern times, particularly in the amount of earth covered with highways. Runoff of rainwater and melting snow is a problem in many localities. A sixth-grade class in one school selected this problem as one to investigate.

QUESTION

What happens to the water from rain and snow that falls on the parking lot and roof of the school building? How does it affect the environment?

STUDENT OBJECTIVES

Increase awareness of how the needs of modern life affect the natural environment.

INVESTIGATION

The study began in the fall, soon after school opened. Immediately after the first substantial rainfall, the children noticed that water was rushing through a small stream close to the school grounds, and they saw that ditches and a culvert were leading water in that direction. On a day soon after this observation was made, pupils who had cameras brought them to class, and the teacher took the entire class out to look at the stream and to take pictures from spots that could be identified later. (Standing against a certain tree or a signpost, for example.) A few children made sketches of the stream, the banks, and trees nearby. A few small rocks and samples of dirt were taken back to the classroom.

When the pictures had been developed, the teacher assigned pupils to cooperative groups with the task of selecting a few photographs, from among the large number of those available, that gave the best views of the banks of the stream. These were put aside for later use. Several science periods were spent on identifying the earth materials (rocks and soil) that had been brought back and learning something about their resistance to erosion.

Meanwhile, the math teacher had assigned the sixth graders the task of determining the area covered by the parking lot and the school building. Later in the year, they determined the total volume of water that had fallen on that area. This involved finding out what the rainfall was from the date they began until the investigation was ended in May and multiplying the area by the rainfall, which is given in height. (Snow is converted to the equivalent amount of rain in official statistics.)

This investigation was carried out in an area that has a heavy snowfall every year and, therefore, has a runoff of water from melted snow in the spring. When spring came and the snow had all melted, the teacher took the pupils, with their cameras, back to the place where they had taken pictures in the fall. They were careful to stand in the same spots and use the same angles they had used when they took the photographs in the fall.

When they compared the two sets of photographs, they found that the banks of the little stream had been eroded, a result that did not surprise them when they considered the nature of the soil that formed the banks and total volume of water, much of which flowed into the stream.

The pupils made charts and graphs, mounted their before-and-after photographs on a foam board, and made a presentation at Parents' Night and to an assembly. There was no immediate action to be taken, but this investigation gave meaning to a topic in earth science (stream erosion) and increased the pupils' awareness of an STS issue.

WILDLIFE LOST TO ASPHALT

BACKGROUND

Any open space covered with vegetation supports a variety of kinds of plant and animal life. When the area is paved over, the plants are destroyed and the animal life is destroyed or has to find a new home. The impetus for this investigation arose as a new access road was built beside the school property to accommodate traffic into and out of the school grounds. In addition to the paved roadway, bulldozers cleared shoulders on each side of the roadway.

QUESTION

How much wildlife was destroyed or displaced when a road was built along the side of the school property?

STUDENT OBJECTIVES

Increased awareness of the trade-offs that are made as the population increases and urban areas reach farther into the countryside.

INVESTIGATION

The year before this unit began, fourth-grade pupils had carried out an investigation of the plant and animal life in an open space behind the school that sloped down to a marshy area. Each pair of pupils had marked off a square meter of earth and documented with great care all the plants and animals that they could find in their square. One of the purposes of this activity was to compare the plant and animal life found in a dry sunny square with that in a damp shady space.

Children enjoy collecting samples of plant and animal life near their school.

This activity had given them an appreciation of the great number and variety of organisms that can share a small space.

When they returned to school and saw that a road had been put in place over the summer, they asked whether they could use some of their science and math time to estimate how many organisms had been destroyed or displaced and then present this information to parents and other students. The teachers agreed that this would be a good way to reinforce math skills and to increase awareness of the trade-offs that must be made between preserving the environment and meeting the need for safe, efficient transportation. The children would plan the investigation and work in cooperative groups.

First, the pupils obtained a map of the school grounds. They divided the area covered by the roadway and the shoulders so that each group had approximately the same area to measure. One period was spent transferring the lines on the map to markers on the ground. When this had been done, the groups set about to measure the assigned areas. They soon found that the measurements could not be exact and that they would have to measure as well as they could but that the final figure would be an estimate. This increased their understanding of the use of estimation in solving real-world problems.

When all the areas had been measured, the results were added to give an estimate of the total area of the natural environment that had been destroyed. Using their previous year's results, they could now estimate how many plants, insects, worms, and other organisms had been destroyed or, in the case of some animals, forced to find another home. The teacher did not ask them to decide whether the road should have been built but left that as an open question.

STUDYING A CREEK THAT RUNS NEAR THE SCHOOL

BACKGROUND

Many streams that were once clear and full of fish have become polluted from runoff from farms, industrial wastes, and treated sewage that contains harmful chemicals. Awareness of the problem is the first step toward cleaning up the water.

QUESTION

What are the characteristics of the stream that runs near our school, and what changes occur over time?

STUDENT OBJECTIVES

Increase their knowledge and understanding of a stream and the area that surrounds and supports it; reinforce and improve skills in math, science, social studies, and language.

INVESTIGATION

A team of sixth-grade teachers took advantage of a creek that runs near their school to plan and carry out an interdisciplinary investigation that spanned the entire school year. The school is not in a rural area, as you might have supposed, but is in a large urban district. Some of the ideas for the investigation came from *City Science* (Perdue & Vaszily, 1991), a book of science activities that can be carried out in urban areas. Weekly walks to the creek, when the weather permitted, were part of the plan.

To arouse interest in the unit, a survey was taken to determine the views of pupils and their parents about environmental issues. The survey contained about twenty questions similar to those shown in Table 13.1, with spaces for pupils and their parents to indicate agreement or disagreement. After pupils wrote in their responses, they took the forms home and asked a parent to respond. The following day, the teacher put a transparency of the questionnaire on the overhead projector and asked for a show of hands of those who agreed and disagreed with each statement. She marked the numbers on the chart but did not indicate right and wrong answers, since the purpose was to get the children to think about the issues.

Plans for the first trip to the creek were discussed in several classes. In social studies, each pupil was given a copy of a map of the area through which the creek runs and a copy of a street map of the city. Before going to the creek, they plotted, on a separate piece of paper, the route that they would take to reach the creek area. After the walk to the creek, they worked in small groups to refine their maps and transfer them to grids. Historical sites, which had been discussed in class and pointed out on the walk to the creek, were marked on the maps. Later, the pupils learned to use topographical maps to relate or "match up" a map of the area to the actual features they could observe when they visited the creek.

On the first walk to the creek, the children made observations of the plants and animals that they saw in the creek or the surrounding area, took water samples, and measured the temperature of the air and the water. The pupils recorded these in their own logs, which were kept throughout the unit. These observations formed the baseline data for comparisons to be made later.

A Park Ranger accompanied the students for a geology walk along the creek. Pupils observed rocks in and along the banks of the creek and selected samples of rocks to take back to the classroom. On this trip, as on all others, they collected water samples, determined the temperature of the water and air,

TABLE 13.1 Environmental Survey

Myself			Parent	
Agree	**Disagree**		**Agree**	**Disagree**
		1. The United States has enough natural resources to last forever.		
		2. All pollution in our streams is caused mainly by business and industry.		
		3. Everyone is affected when the environment deteriorates.		
		4. Saving jobs is more important than saving a few rare birds.		
		5. The increasing amount of garbage is an environmental problem.		

TABLE 13.2   Air and Water Surface Temperature at Indian Creek

Month	Max. Air Temp. °C	Avg. Surf. Temp. °C
September	26.7	23.5
October	20.6	16.6
November	15.0	12.1
December	8.3	6.6
January	5.6	2.3
February	7.8	4.4
March	13.3	7.1
April	19.4	11.6
May	24.4	17.6
June	29.4	22.6

and recorded their observations, both in writing and in sketches, in their logs. Back in the classroom, they identified the rocks they had collected, using an identification key and comparing them to samples provided by the teacher. They learned that rocks may affect the water that passes through them or over them on the way to the creek and that the results may be beneficial or harmful to aquatic life. They found the pH of the water samples, using pH paper, measured the turbidity of the water, and recorded the water and air temperatures on a computer spreadsheet.

To investigate another aspect of water quality, the class collected samples of the insects and other invertebrates that lived in or on the water. The kinds of organisms that are found in a stream are bioindicators of water quality, providing information as to whether fish can live in it. The children collected fallen leaves from several kinds of trees and prepared mesh bags with an equal weight of leaves in each bag. These were labeled with waterproof labels, attached to a brick or rock, and suspended in the water. The bags were monitored each week

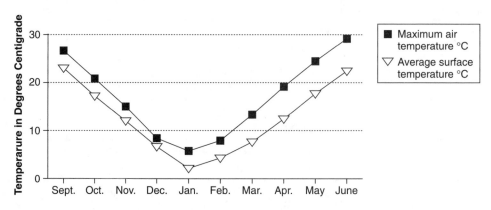

FIGURE 13.1   Air and Water Surface Temperature Change, September to June

and collected after six weeks. Then they were put in plastic bags, carried back to the classroom, and examined by scooping out the contents onto newspapers spread on tables. The children identified the organisms they found by using a chart provided by the teacher. The chart identified the various organisms as those that could live under various water conditions. A preponderance of certain organisms indicates good water quality, while others, including worms and leeches, indicate a high level of pollution.

By the end of the year, the sixth graders had a record of water and air temperature, pH, and turbidity, which showed the changes that take place as the seasons change. Table 13.2 shows a computer spreadsheet listing air temperature above the water and at the surface. The data collected by students were converted into graphs (Figure 3.1) and charts, to help students understand the changes. These could also be used in a presentation of results.

They had indicators of water quality, both the pH data and the bioindicator data. They had learned to make and use maps, and they had improved their writing skills in describing their observations and results of investigations. They had collected, analyzed, and interpreted data in geology, biology, and social studies. They were ready to present what they had learned to parents, other students, and administrators.

THE TRASH PROBLEM

QUESTION

What happens to the trash and garbage we generate? How can we reduce the amount of trash and garbage generated?

STUDENT OBJECTIVES

Learn about waste disposal in their community, and relate this knowledge to themselves; increase inquiry skills.

INVESTIGATION

The following unit was carried out in a middle school, but much of it could be adapted to fifth or sixth grade. A unit on recycling began with pupils making lists of the packaging materials used in the food that each pupil's family ate in one day (not including any fast-food packaging). This lead to a discussion of other consumer items. In addition to comparing packaging of food items, they compared packaging of different brands of pantyhose, fruit drinks, and toothbrushes. The City Engineer spoke to the class about waste disposal in their city and arranged for them to visit the modern sanitary landfill, drawing comparisons between modern methods with the old-fashioned town dump. They also visited a city park that had been built over a former waste disposal site. Students used data available from the city to calculate the amount of waste generated per person per day and per year in their city. Students made a "bathtub" model of a modern, sanitary landfill and placed in it various types of garbage (apple, orange, banana peel, cloth, paper, a leaf, a plastic spoon) and made daily observations for one month. At the end of the month, they drew conclusions about the decomposition of the various materials. They considered the placement of waste disposal sites, the NIMBY (not in my backyard) problem, and the question of whether waste disposal sites are more likely to be placed in poorer neighborhoods where residents have less political power. This was reinforced by a computer program (Intentional Education, Inc., no date) that provided data on four possible waste disposal sites and presented the problem, Where should the waste disposal site be located? At the end of the investigation, students organized and summarized their findings and prepared a presentation to school administrators and others with suggestions for decreasing the amount of waste produced at the school and recycling all possible materials.

Another investigation on a similar theme was carried out by a fourth-grade class that used the National Geographic Kids Network (1991) unit "Too Much Trash" as the basis for their investigation. They collected trash daily and categorized and weighed it. They entered their data in the Kids Network and found out from communications with other children nationwide that they had too much styrofoam in their trash. The culprit was the cafeteria trays. They talked with the cafeteria workers and found that reusable cafeteria trays were available but were not being used because the automatic dishwasher was not working. They talked with a restaurant owner, who told them the likely problem with the dishwasher was clogged water lines in the dishwasher due to minerals in the local water. They took all their information to school officials, suggesting steps that could be taken to remedy the problem of too much styrofoam in their trash.

INSTRUCTIONAL STRATEGIES FOR STS

In an STS unit, you may use any or all of the teaching methods and strategies that you have studied. Cooperative learning, which was presented in Chapter 10, is particularly useful, almost necessary, in carrying out an STS unit. Two additional instructional strategies that are often used are role playing and field trips.

Role Playing

One of the purposes of an STS thematic unit is to have pupils become aware that the interactions between science, technology, and society often lead to problems or situations that are undesirable but have no easy solution; where one person or group gains or benefits, another person or group loses or is damaged in some way. In the case of Mr. Newman—the tree and the parking lot—Mr. Newman and those who enjoyed the tree lost, while those who wanted a place to park gained. That situation might have had another outcome if people had cooperated to find another solution to the parking problem rather than cutting down the tree.

Role playing, as it is used in the classroom, is an activity in which pupils are assigned roles and take part in a dialogue or debate. Each person speaks and acts as the person whose role he or she has taken would speak and act. The point is to get children to listen to another person and to see the problem from that person's point of view. This can be very difficult for young children, who tend to be self-centered and see things only from their own perspectives. As children move into the intermediate grades, they gradually undergo a transition that Piaget (1966) described as follows:

> The child, after having regarded his own point of view as absolute, comes to discover the possibility of other points of view and to conceive of reality as constituted . . . by what is common to all points of view taken together. (p. 247)

Role playing can help children make the transition from seeing only their own point of view to seeing those of others as well.

Role playing can be used as part of any unit in which there is a controversy that is understandable and interesting to children. The controversy has to be one in which there is no villain, no obvious right or wrong side. The people on each side of the issue must have legitimate reasons for the stand they are taking. The case of Mr. Newman and the tree might be more salient for fourth graders if the tree had shaded their playground rather than an apartment building. To use role playing in this situation, a teacher might proceed as follows:

- Explain the situation. Lead a discussion for five to ten minutes. End with the idea of having children take sides and act out a debate in front of the class. You might say they will act as if they were presenting a case to the town or city council.

- Select six or eight children to take part. Have them draw straws to decide which side each will be on—the side of the children who want the tree to continue to shade their playground or the side of the car owners (perhaps teachers) who must have a place to park their cars. Their assignment is to think of all the arguments *for their side*. The other children are not involved at this stage but should be assured that they will have a turn at some time during the year.

- Allow the children to work on this overnight or, perhaps, for an additional day but no longer. (Everyone will lose interest if there is a long delay.) Set a time to meet with the children. *You will need to help them form their arguments.* Do not expect them to do this without help until they have had much practice. You are teaching them a new kind of activity that cannot be learned without coaching and practice.

◆ To prepare for the presentation, place chairs at the front of the room, have children take their places, and give children on each side time to make their arguments.

◆ After the presentations, lead a discussion with the entire class. The objective of the discussion is to bring out additional points, to allow children to react to the arguments, and to search for a solution that is different from what either side has advocated. Is there any way that the tree could be saved and the car owners get additional parking?

The objectives of role playing are directed toward both social and cognitive goals. The social objectives are for children to learn to listen to each other, to learn to take turns, to be considerate of others' views, and to argue without becoming angry. The cognitive goals are for children to weigh and evaluate arguments, to decide whether they are reasonable, logical, and, in some cases, based on sound scientific evidence. The situations or issues that are suitable for role playing in the elementary school are those that children can understand and that deal with something close to home. "How will it affect me?" is what children want to know.

Field Trips

A field trip is a trip away from school, usually on a bus or van that is provided by the school system, to a site that has some particular relevance to the theme or unit that the pupils are studying at school. A visit to an appropriate site can make classroom learning come alive and can be an experience that children remember all their lives.

Preparation for a field trip includes getting permission from the school administration, arranging for transportation, and getting written permission from the pupils' parents or guardians for them to go on the trip. You may have to secure permission to visit the site and set up a time for the trip. You will need to recruit several adults, usually parents, to help you keep the children together and to make sure that none of the children strays away from the group. If you will be away all day, you will have to make preparations for lunch.

Plan the time carefully so that you do not have more time at the site than you can use profitably. In most school districts, field trips are a lot of trouble to arrange, so you should not go to all the trouble unless you believe that the trip will provide your pupils with a learning experience that will be very worthwhile and one that cannot be gained any other way.

Preparation in the classroom is even more important for the learning value of the trip than making the arrangements explained here. A field trip may be the culmination of an investigation or unit, or it may come at the beginning of a unit or at any other time. Children should learn about the site, know what to expect, know what to look for, and know what they will be expected to do or report on return.

Preparation may begin with an announcement that the trip will take place, or it may be initiated by children who feel they need to visit a site to gather information for an investigation underway. A discussion of why you are going, what you may see or do, and how you will use the firsthand knowledge of the site may be the next step. Children may be assigned to find specific information about the site and report it or make it available to others in some way. Some teachers hand out a list of questions as a guide for making observations or collecting data. The goal is to prepare children so that they will know what to look for and what they are seeing when they are on site.

Whether the field trip comes at the beginning, the end, or somewhere in the middle of a unit of study, it should be treated as a means of making observations and collecting data. The discussion that follows the trip will be similar to a discussion you might lead during any investigation, and the suggestions in Chapter 7 for leading an interesting discussion are applicable. It is through talking about an experience and listening to others talk about it that children come to understand its meaning.

Using the School Grounds

Many interesting and useful observations can also be made on the grounds and within a short walking distance of many schools. This is a resource that should be explored and exploited if possible. At the beginning of the year, take time to walk around the grounds, observe the surrounding area, and think about the kinds of investigations, projects, units, or lessons that could be based on interesting things that are close at hand. If you are teaching in a self-contained classroom, you may find ways to use the immediate surroundings for social studies, mathematics, or language arts as well as or in addition to science. Always look for opportunities to connect schoolwork to the world beyond the four walls of your classroom.

◆ SUMMARY

Science, Technology, and Society (STS) is the study of the relationships and interactions of science and technology in a social context. By their nature, STS investigations that are appropriate for elementary children are interdisciplinary and are focused on a theme. Often, the theme is an environmental one, since many of the most troublesome issues revolve around the effect of science and technology on the natural environment, and changes in the environment often have an unexpected negative impact on the social fabric. The most fundamental goal of STS education is to help children become knowledgeable, responsible citizens who can participate in the democratic process of making policy decisions about the natural environment, the uses of science and technology, and the uses of public funds for the public welfare. Other goals are to understand the interrelationships between science, technology, and society; to develop the ability to deal with STS-related conflicts in their own lives; to master the knowledge needed to understand STS issues, and to develop the intellectual tools to deal with these issues.

The detailed unit plan for acid rain was followed by descriptions of interdisciplinary thematic units that are meant to suggest ideas for other, locally based, units to the reader. These units combine skills development and concept learning across the disciplines while they increase awareness and understanding of the STS issues.

Role playing is an instructional strategy that is often used in STS units, particularly when children can relate to a local issue that may affect them. Because STS units are based on local situations or opportunities, field trips are often included for formal or informal data gathering. The school yard can sometimes be used to good advantage and does not require the advance planning necessary for a field trip. Both role playing and field trips require careful planning and follow-up if the benefits are to be realized.

◆ ACTIVITIES FOR THE READER

1. Working within a group of six to eight fellow students, select one of the issues presented at the beginning of this chapter. Identify a role for each member of the group, evenly divided between the two sides of the issue. Follow the suggestions provided in this chapter for role playing, and make a presentation to classmates.

2. Working as a group, develop a plan for a thematic, interdisciplinary STS unit. Each member of the group selects a subject area of the elementary curriculum and focuses on that area, but all members work together to develop a focused, balanced unit. You will have a planned unit to take with you to your first teaching position.

3. Find out the procedure in a local school for getting permission to have a field trip. Make a detailed plan for a field trip, including a time line for following procedures, what you will do to prepare students to get the most from the trip, and how you will follow up.

◆ QUESTIONS FOR DISCUSSION

1. Planning for an STS unit requires much time and effort and takes up a sixth to a fifth of the time you have to teach the required curriculum. Under what conditions are the time and effort justified?

2. Do you think there is a danger that consideration of environmental and other problems may frighten children? What can be done about this?

3. What does the following quotation mean to you? "As science educators in Western societies, it is difficult to divorce ourselves from the right (scientific) answer syndrome, which tends to see learning as positivistic and/or empirical in nature" (Bloom, 1992, p. 412).

◆ REFERENCES

American Association for the Advancement of Science. (1993). *Benchmarks for science literacy*. New York: Oxford University Press.

Bloom, J. (1992). The development of scientific knowledge in elementary school children: A context of meaning perspective. *Science Education, 76*(4), 399–413.

Heath, P. (1988). *Science/technology/society in the social studies*. ERIC Digest EDO-SO-88-8. ERIC Clearinghouse for Social Studies/Social Science Education. Bloomington, IN: Indiana University.

Hessler, E., & Stubbs, H. (1987). *Acid rain: Science projects*. Raleigh, NC: The Acid Rain Foundation.

Intentional Education, Inc. (no date). *Environmental topics: Waste*. Acton, MA: William K. Bradford.

National Geographic Kids Network. (1991). *Too much trash*. Washington, DC: National Geographic Society.

National Research Council. (1996). *National science education standards*. Washington, DC: National Academy Press.

Piaget, J. (1966). *The child's conception of physical causality*. Totowa, NJ: Littlefield, Adams.

Perdue, P., & Vaszily, D. (1991). *City science*. Good Year Books.

◆ RESOURCES

The Acid Rain Foundation, Inc. (1410 Varsity Drive, Raleigh, NC 27606). Materials are available for teachers and pupils, including

Acid Rain: Science Projects
The Air around Us
Elementary Acid Rain Kit

Computers as Instructional Tools for Science

Webster's dictionary defines a tool as something "necessary in the practice of a vocation or profession" (Merriam-Webster, 1995), and that is what the computer has become for teachers who are aware of the computer's capabilities and who have learned to use it to achieve curriculum goals. The first approach to using computers in schools has been compared to the way movie cameras were used when they were first invented. If you have ever watched an old silent film with the camera aimed straight ahead at the set or seen one of the early "talkies" with its stilted language and overly dramatized movements, you can understand how far we have come in the use of film as a unique medium that can do what no other medium can. We are moving in the same direction in the use of computers in schools; that is, we are finding out what kinds of things computers can do that cannot be done by other means. When computers first became available in schools, programs for drill-and-practice that were already in workbooks for programmed instruction were transferred to the computer. Instead of turning pages in a book, a pupil could move from one screen to the next. In effect, the computer was being used for the kinds of things that books or flash cards, which cost much less, can do as well or even better. Although children enjoyed the novelty of using a computer, there was no gain in instructional power or purpose. Fortunately, we have now moved beyond drill-and-practice to explore exciting new ways that the computer can be used as a means of enhancing teaching and learning. That is what this chapter is about.

HARDWARE

This section is for readers who have had little opportunity to work with computers and are not familiar with all of the terms and pieces of equipment. The term *hardware* refers to computers and all the machines and gadgets, called *peripherals* and *attachments,* that may be attached to them, including printers, LCD panels, modems, television monitors, and others (all defined in the following paragraphs). What runs on the machines is software.

You will probably have little choice in the kinds or number of computers that are available to you. The most common computer in elementary schools has been the Apple 2E, but it is being replaced by a version of the MacIntosh, a faster and more powerful machine made by the same company that made the Apple 2E. Some schools have computers run on MS-DOS (Microsoft Disk Operating System, a brand name of software that runs the hardware), which are either IBM personal computers (PCs) or others that are similar. There are important differences between the kinds of computers, but most people find that once they have learned to use one kind of computer, it is not hard to learn to use a different kind.

Computers have built-in internal hard drives that can hold a very large amount of information. Programs, such as one for word processing, or files that are used over and over are stored on the hard drive. Disks, called *floppy disks* even though they are not floppy, hold much less information. They are inserted into a computer port so that the program on the disk can run on the computer.

An *LCD panel* is a device that is attached to a computer and placed over an overhead projector. It allows the user to project what is shown on the computer just as one usually projects whatever is placed on the overhead projector. Using the LCD panel, the whole class can see what is on the computer screen and, of course, the program can run just as if it were not being projected. Another way to do this, but one that is not quite as satisfactory, is to hook the computer up to a television monitor so that the television monitor displays what is on the computer screen. A special device is required to make the connection, but the cost is reasonable. If you shudder at the idea of having to make these connections yourself, you will probably be able to find someone in your school who is adept at this sort of thing and is more than willing to help with the hardware.

A *modem* is a piece of equipment that connects the computer to a telephone line and thus opens up the possibilities of telecommunication, including sending and receiving e-mail messages and gaining access through the Internet to the Worldwide Web. It is also possible to have computers hooked up directly to a line, in which case a modem is not necessary. This is called having the computer hard wired and is more convenient than having a modem but is more expensive and not yet common in schools.

Probes, or sensors, are devices that can be attached to computers and used to collect various kinds of data that go directly into the computer. There are probes that are sensitive to temperature, sound, light, and other variables. As the probe collects data on temperature changes, for example, the data can be shown as a graph on the computer screen. In a microcomputer-based laboratory (MBL), these devices take the place of other means of collecting data.

There are three basic kinds of printers: dot matrix, ink jet, and laser. The dot matrix printer was widely used when small computers first became available, and you may find that it is the only kind available in your school. This printer is noisy, and the print is somewhat hard to read. It is far from ideal, but it may be what you have to work with. Ink jet printers are immeasurably better and are adequate for use in the classroom. Laser printers are better still, but they are more expensive and may not be the best way to spend the funds that are available.

If your school has a computer lab or a number of computers in a resource center, the computers may be networked and connected to a server. This means that all the computers are connected to one computer that serves all of the others. When a program is put in the server, all the computers connected to the server have access to the program. In somewhat similar fashion, a number of computers are often connected to one printer so that all the computers can use the printer, although the printer only prints from one computer at a time.

Newer and larger computers may include a CD-ROM player. Multimedia software packages require a combination of hardware that usually includes a CD-ROM player, a videotape player, and perhaps other equipment.

MANAGING YOUR RESOURCES

Cooperative Learning on the Computer

Cooperative group work is as beneficial and effective when pupils are using computers as it is in other kinds of classroom activities. Sitting by oneself in front of a computer can be lonely and frustrating; when a problem arises, there is no one to turn to for help, and a child's attention span may be very short. When children work within cooperative groups on a computer, the benefits are social as well as cognitive; they learn to share an object that they all want to get their hands on, and they learn from each other as they work together to solve problems or produce a product.

A very practical reason for teaching students to cooperate is that you will not have enough computers for children to work alone, even if that were advisable. It has been suggested that at some time in the future all children should have a computer at their own desk; however, that is not likely to happen, and we don't think it's a good idea.

Setting up cooperative groups to work on a computer is similar to setting up such groups for other activities, as explained in Chapter 10. In assigning pupils to groups, try to compose groups that include children of different abilities and experience. If your pupils have already worked in cooperative groups, remind them that

◆ An individual is successful only if the group is successful.

◆ Each student is responsible to help others learn. Students should ask for help from the group when needed so that they will learn.

◆ They will receive guidelines and help in developing the social skills needed for group work.

◆ Each will be assigned a specific role, and they will alternate between roles. One pupil will read the problem and try to explain it to the others, one will control the mouse (and/or use the keyboard), one will remind everyone to stay on task when they go off onto tangents, and there may be a recorder.

As in other situations, you will have to monitor the group and be available for help if needed. Since you will probably also be needed elsewhere, you may have to rearrange the group members if one or more groups seem particularly contentious or nonproductive.

The One-Computer Classroom

A teacher with twenty-five pupils and one computer may think that little can be done except to let children take turns playing games as a reward for finishing their work or assigning a low-achieving student to a drill-and-practice program. Dublin, Pressman, Barnett, Corcoran, and Woldman (1994), in their book, *Integrating Com-*

A group of pupils use the computer while classmates are engaged in other tasks.

puters in Your Classroom, suggest a number of practical ways to take advantage of just one computer in your classroom. Some of their suggestions follow:

◆ By using an LCD screen with the overhead projector or by connecting the computer to a television monitor, you can display the computer screen to the whole class. You can run software as a way to introduce a new topic or to present information and ideas that pupils will use in subsequent activities. You can demonstrate how to use tool software such as word processing as you would in a direct instruction lesson.

◆ If your classroom has a number of learning centers, you can add a computer center, cycling small groups of students through a computer center while the rest of the class is engaged in other activities. If your class is doing independent investigations, there may be several groups who can use the computer to advantage. Those groups can take turns using the one computer, or you might have one period each day in which groups of children carry out assignments at the various learning centers.

◆ A single computer can be used as a peer tutoring tool. Children who have had an opportunity outside of class to learn how to use particular software can help classmates acquire the new skill. Having teams of two students introduce other teams of two students to a piece of new software provides benefits to both teams.

◆ If your school has a collection of computers in a central place, such as a resource center or a computer lab, you can introduce a topic or a skill to the whole class on your classroom computer so that your students are ready to work on their own, in pairs, or in groups when they go to the computer center. Pupils can ask questions, clear up confusion, perhaps come up to the computer, and make entries that everyone can see. They can then use their time on the computers to best advantage, which is important because time on the computers is always limited for any one class.

◆ If you can secure the resources for telecommunications, this is an obvious and excellent way to use one computer in your classroom. This opens up the possibility for your pupils to send and receive messages from children all over the country as well as other parts of the world. Your pupils can become part of exciting scientific investigations as they collect data and share it with other pupils across the country.

Later in this chapter, the "Unit on Stars" shows how Ms. Oldhand used one computer in a unit on astronomy.

The Multiple-Computer Classroom

The ideas suggested for the single-computer classroom are applicable in a classroom that has two or three computers, but it becomes easier to integrate computers into your teaching as more become available.

◆ If the classroom has three computers and twenty-four pupils, it's possible for everyone to get time on the computer in one period. In groups of four, half the class works at the computers for half the period, then they switch with the other half who have been working on some other activity.

◆ Two computers, with different software installed, can be used to set up two computer centers, perhaps one for math and one for science. A computer in a learning center can be moved and connected to an LCD panel or television monitor and used for whole-class teaching whenever the teacher wants to use it in that way.

Computers in a Resource Center or Computer Lab

In most schools, individual classrooms do not have computers; the computers are all installed in a resource center or computer lab. So this is probably the situation you are most likely to find. However, teachers are recognizing the difficulty of true integration of computers into the curriculum when all the computers are down the hall somewhere, and they can only take pupils at certain times under conditions set by someone else. Here are some suggestions for maximizing benefits of this arrangement:

◆ Plan ahead with the person in charge of the computers so that software appropriate for your curriculum is available at the time you need it.

◆ Assign cooperative groups of two to four children, not individuals, to each computer.

◆ Monitor the class carefully to keep pupils on task. There are many distractions and attractions in a resource center or computer lab.

CURRICULUM-RELATED SOFTWARE

Once you're familiar with the hardware available in your school, your main concern will be with software. While you will probably have little choice in the kind or amount of hardware you have, you may be able to participate in decisions about the purchase of software and how it is used. When teachers refer to *software,* they often restrict the meaning to certain types of instructional programs, but the term actually includes both curriculum-related software and software tools.

Curriculum-related software is designed to teach content or skills related to one or more areas of the curriculum. Some of the main types of software are described next.

Informational Programs or Tutorials

The best informational programs or tutorials present information or concepts in a way that the teacher cannot reproduce with a blackboard and textbook. By using graphics, making it possible to find almost instant answers to questions and performing calculations that would be impossible for the teacher, these programs can be effective tools of instruction. An example is *Sky Travel* (no date), described in a later section.

Simulations

Real-life experiences are simulated so that the user has the sensation of "being there" and manipulating variables or, in some cases, tools. The opportunity to interact with the computer makes these programs different from, and more useful than, films or videos on similar subjects. *Operation Frog* (no date) is an example.

Problem-Solving Software

Early examples of problem-solving software, such as *The Factory* (no date), presented problems that require general problem-solving skills. Programs are now available that present problems on topics in science and that are also more open ended than the older programs. For example, *Botanical Garden* (Kimball & Donoghue, no date) lets pupils experiment with environmental conditions to find the conditions that a given plant needs for maximum growth. With *Build a Circuit* (no date), pupils can put together the elements of a circuit and the computer will tell them whether the circuit will work.

Problem Embedded in Narrative

Some useful programs pose a problem in the context of an adventure or expedition with many factors to take into account. An early example of this type of software is *The Oregon Trail* (no date), designed for social studies. The user makes decisions that the leader of a wagon train would have had to make throughout the westward journey. The objective is survival of the pioneers as they face one problem after another along the way to Oregon. A newer program, *Ecosystems* (Bank Street College of Education, no date), which focuses on science and is designed for grades 4 to 8, also poses the problem of survival but in a different context. Students are challenged to survive on an island, using only the resources found on the island and without disrupting the island's ecosystem. Both programs are interactive. They force the user to make decisions, and each decision has consequences for survival.

Drill-and-Practice

Programs for drill-and-practice, which have been more widely used in math than in science, are not recommended. They are intended to help students learn basic facts, such as the multiplication table, by repetition and rote memory. In our view, they have no place in an inquiry-based science program.

◆ MS. OLDHAND INTEGRATES SOFTWARE INTO THE CURRICULUM

Ms. Oldhand had wanted a computer in her classroom for a long time, so she was very excited when she learned in August that she was actually going to get one. Right away, she started planning science units for the fall and looking through software catalogues to find reasonably-priced programs that would add something special to her science units. She soon realized that she needed a way to project the computer screen so that the whole class could see it. She made a good case to her principal, who knew she was a conscientious and creative teacher, and he was able to find the funds for an LCD panel. An outline of one of Ms. Oldhand's units follows:

A UNIT ON STARS

NSE STANDARD

Objects in the sky: The sun, moon, and stars all have properties, locations, and movements that can be observed and described (National Research Council, 1996, p. 134).

GRADE LEVELS: 4 AND 5

STUDENT OBJECTIVES

Ms. Oldhand took these cognitive objectives from *Benchmarks* (American Association for the Advancement of Science, 1993, p. 63):

1. Know that the pattern of stars in the sky stays the same, although they appear to move across the sky nightly and different stars can be seen in different seasons.
2. Know that stars are like the sun, some being smaller and some larger, but so far away that they look like points of light.

Ms. Oldhand added an affective objective of her own:

3. Develop awareness of the vastness and mystery of the universe beyond our solar system.

Ms. Oldhand's pupils had experience in earlier grades of observing the moon at night and in the daytime. They had learned that the earth travels around the sun and the moon travels around the earth, and they had learned something about the planets. This unit was designed to take the pupils out of our solar system into the universe beyond.

Ms. Oldhand asked how many pupils had looked at the stars at night and what they thought about as they looked up into the night sky. She asked them to imagine that they were all on an island, with no land in sight and no communication with the rest of the world except for messages that came over a radio. The messages had predictable patterns, but they were otherwise unintelligible. No one knew where they came from or what they meant. She explained that this was not unlike the situation of people long ago as they looked up at the stars and wondered what they were, where they were, and what meaning they had.

Ms. Oldhand led a discussion about what could be learned by just looking up at the night sky. Pupils said that they could see that some stars are brighter than others and that stars are in different places at different times. Some pupils could find the North Star and knew that it was always in the same place, near the Big Dipper. They talked about the invention of the telescope and the more recent Hubble telescope.

After this discussion, the pupils did a series of hands-on activities to help them understand, first, that the movement of the earth makes it appear that the stars are traveling across the sky and, second, how scientists measure distances in space. They also learned that some objects that appear to be stars are actually planets in our solar system, and they learned how to distinguish planets from stars. Finally, they used sky maps to identify constellations, and each group chose a constellation to study and draw.

Now it was time to get ready for a special star-gazing field trip that Ms. Oldhand had planned with parents. Before the children arrived, Ms. Oldhand connected the computer to the LCD panel and loaded *Sky Travel* (no date) into the computer. This program has many features, but the one that Ms. Oldhand brought up on the screen was the "Sky Window," a module that charts hundreds of stars and shows dozens of constellations. It shows the heavens at any chosen time and place. Ms. Oldhand chose the time and place of the field trip, and there appeared on the screen what the children would see when they looked up at the night sky. Ms. Oldhand brought first one and then another constellation into the center of the screen. When she chose one star in a constellation, the computer gave information about that star. (If Ms. Oldhand had a printer, she could have printed the images on the screen.) Since Ms. Oldhand had been careful to see that all groups chose a constellation that would be visible at the designated time and place, all of the children could check their information and maps with what was on the screen. At the end of the period, Ms. Oldhand told them that she would leave the program on the computer and keep a flexible schedule for two days remaining before the field trip so that groups could use the program in between other work.

They were lucky to have good weather on the night of the field trip, and all the groups were able to find their constellations and identify the stars they had studied. They found that they could see much more in the sky than they had seen before, because now they knew what to look for.

Ms. Oldhand knew that she had barely touched the surface of *Sky Travel,* and she made a note to herself to tell other teachers how easy it was to use and how much the children learned from it. She also decided that she would find additional uses for this software in the future.

Now that she had a computer in her classroom and she had used one piece of software successfully, her thoughts raced to other curriculum-related software that she could integrate into the units she would teach on electricity, ecosystems, and weather. She had also heard of a software simulation of the dissection of a frog (*Operation Frog,* no date) that might be a good choice for her sixth graders. She had a lot of homework to do to find software that would make her science program more meaningful for her pupils.

SOFTWARE TOOLS

In contrast to the curriculum-related programs, software tools are not tied to any subject area or to problem solving and can be used in a multitude of ways by both pupils and teachers. The main categories are described next.

Word Processors

Word processors are the familiar programs that allow you to produce text or writing on the computer. There are simple programs that are easy for children to use and others that are more complex but allow more flexibility and creativity. (Children often learn these programs more easily than adults.)

Graphics

Graphics programs allow children to make their own drawings and designs and use them alone or in combination with print.

Spreadsheets and Graphs

A spreadsheet is a large ledger sheet with rows and columns into which data can be entered and stored. The numbers of columns and rows can be adjusted to suit the data to be entered. With a few strokes on the keypad or clicks of the mouse, the data from a spreadsheet can be converted into a bar graph, a line graph, or a pie graph.

Database Programs

A database contains information, usually a large amount, that has been gathered and entered into a computer or on a disk in some organized way. Database software allows the user to search the database and extract whatever specific information may be needed.

◆ ### MS. OLDHAND'S PUPILS USE SOFTWARE TOOLS

Mr. Newman, who had now graduated and had a class of his own, dropped by to see Ms. Oldhand.

MR. NEWMAN: I came by to get some ideas from you about how to use the one computer that I have in my classroom.

MS. OLDHAND: Oh, there are lots of ways to use one computer. Come by after school, and I'll explain some of the ways we have used the computer in this room. Right now, those pupils over by the computer are getting out a newsletter.

MR. NEWMAN: That requires a printer, doesn't it? How did you manage that?

MS. OLDHAND: I learned about a program of small grants to teachers and applied for one of the grants. It's very competitive, but I received a grant that provided enough money for an ink jet printer and software for basic word processing, graphics, and spreadsheets. My pupils were ecstatic.

MR. NEWMAN: I'm beginning to understand that there's more to teaching than I thought.

MS. OLDHAND: We old-timers have learned to stay on the lookout for ways to get resources to improve our teaching.

When Ms. Oldhand received a printer and software and explained to her pupils some of the things that could be done, they decided that they would like to produce a newsletter to distribute in the school and to parents. Ms. Oldhand divided them into four groups of six pupils each, being careful to have mixed groups in terms of gender, ethnicity, ability, and any other variables among the pupils in her class. Since it was January when she received the equipment, she assigned each group to one of the months remaining in the school year. The tasks of producing a newsletter were divided up, and each group was told that they would have time to work on this project, when it was their turn while other pupils were engaged in other activities. The whole class decided, after much discussion, what the basic layout of the newsletter would be, but each month's content was left up to the group that was responsible. Ms. Oldhand found that some of her pupils were already very adept on the computer and that they caught on very quickly to the new user-friendly software. These children were able to teach others, and, with some initial instruction and continuous monitoring, all groups produced newsletters that surprised themselves as well as Ms. Oldhand.

Ms. Oldhand's pupils also learned to use spreadsheets and to make graphs. As they collected data in their investigations throughout the year, each cooperative group had a computer file, and the groups took turns entering data. Some children suggested writing lab reports on the computer, but Ms. Oldhand explained that if every group did this, it would take too much time. That would have to wait until they had more computers.

Ms. Oldhand's pupils are proud of their computer-generated poster.

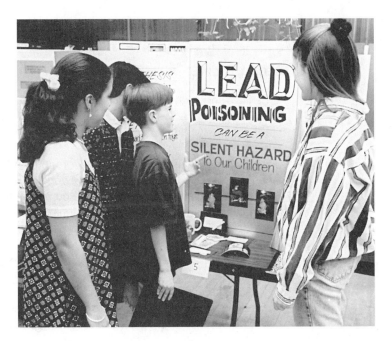

TELECOMMUNICATIONS

Telecommunications combine hardware and software to allow you and your pupils to reach out, beyond the classroom, to communicate with people all over the globe, through e-mail (electronic mail), and to find information about almost any imaginable subject through the Internet on the Worldwide Web. The hardware you need in addition to a computer are a modem and access to a telephone or a direct line, as explained earlier. Special software makes it possible for your computer to call a telephone number that puts you on-line and gives you access to the Internet.

OTHER WAYS TO TEACH WITH COMPUTERS

Microcomputer-Based Laboratory

Combinations of hardware and software, such as *The Bank Street Laboratory* (Bank Street College of Education, no date), are now available for elementary children to collect data on temperature, sound, light, and pressure and to see the data displayed on the computer screen. Data are collected by means of sensors, or probes, connected to the computer via an interface box that fits into the computer port. These devices have more frequently been used in middle schools and high schools where each pair of students works at a computer in a laboratory setting and the experiments involve more advanced science concepts and higher-level math. However, they can be used effectively in elementary grades as the following lesson outline shows.

LESSON OUTLINE: MIXING WATER AT DIFFERENT TEMPERATURES

The fifth- and sixth-grade teachers in Mr. Nicola's school each had one computer for a classroom and shared software. When it was Mr. Nicola's turn to have the MBL for two weeks, he designed an experiment using the temperature probe (thermistor).

He installed the software in the computer, attached the interface box, and tried it out to see that everything was working. Then he introduced MBL to the class by using an LCD panel with the computer to teach a modified direct instruction lesson on the use of the equipment to measure temperature. This included a demonstration in which he put the thermistor first into a beaker of hot tap water and then into a beaker of cold water; had individual pupils come up to the computer and take readings, which were then displayed; and asked and answered questions.

Then he explained that he would place the computer with the MBL in the science learning center and each cooperative group would have directions for carrying out an investigation and a series of questions to answer. Groups would circulate through the center as their work permitted over the following week. The materials at the learning center follow:

Three beakers, one set in a styrofoam jacket
A graduated cylinder
A stirring rod
A timer
Access to hot and cold water
(Hot tap water can be used, or a hot plate, set on low, can be used to keep
 water moderately hot.)

The directions were as follows: Measure a specified volume of cold water, pour it into one beaker, and take the temperature; then measure a specified volume of hot water, pour it into a beaker, and take the temperature. Carefully pour the water from the two beakers into the third beaker (the one insulated by the styrofoam jacket), place the probe in the beaker, and watch the computer screen as the temperature changes. Wait until the temperature stops changing (reaches equilibrium), then note the temperature and the time it took to reach that temperature.

Each group had directions to mix different volumes of water; for example, one group mixed 20 ml of cold water with 40 ml of hot water, while another group mixed 30 ml of cold water with 30 ml of hot water. When all groups had completed the assignment, Mr. Nicola put all of the data together, displayed it to the class, and asked what patterns could be seen. With his skillful questioning and allowing time for pupils to think, they learned that when water of two temperatures is mixed

- The final temperature is somewhere in between the starting temperatures.
- The final temperature is determined by two variables, (a) the beginning temperatures and (b) the volumes of the hot and cold water.

Mr. Nicola did not introduce the terms *heat capacity* or *heat energy* and did not explain that the mass rather than the volume is the operating variable. He used this as an introduction to a concept that would be studied later. *Benchmarks* (American Association for the Advancement of Science, 1993) supports this approach by recommending that "students need not come out of this grade span [3 to 5] understanding heat or its difference from temperature. . . . Computer labware probes and graphic displays that detect small changes in temperature and plot them can be used by students to examine many instances of heat exchange" (pp 83–84).

Multimedia Programs

Although the following two programs each require more resources than many schools are able to make available to elementary teachers (i.e., both the software and hardware are expensive), it is well to know about them. They are exciting programs that take advantage of the unique possibilities of technology to be used as an instructional tool. We hope that these programs will become available to teachers and children in many more classrooms in the future as their instructional value becomes recognized.

National Geographic Kids Network (1988–1997) is a telecommunications-based curriculum with an interdisciplinary approach to topics in science and social studies. There are units for grades 3 to 6 on trash and recycling, water quality, noise pollution, weather, acid rain, and others. All of the units run on National Geographic software (NGS), which includes tools for word processing, drawing pictures, making maps, and communicating with other children on the network. Each unit consists of sixteen class sessions scheduled in a specific eight-week period, during which each class is assigned to a research team of twelve to fourteen other classes from around the world. Children in your class can communicate with a scientist assigned to the unit and with children in all of the other classes in the team, some of whom will probably be from outside the United States. In the weather unit, for example, children set up observation stations and record data on temperature, cloud formations, and sky conditions each day. As they share these data with teammates around the world, they learn about weather conditions where their teammates live. They also develop scientific inquiry skills as they use this information to represent data on maps and graphs, look for patterns, and make predictions. Statistics come to life for both when a pupil in Miami and one in Moscow trade data on the weather they are experiencing in January.

Each unit is scheduled for a specific eight-week period to make it possible for all the classes on the team to communicate with each other while the unit is being taught. Curriculum materials for each unit include a teacher's guide, activity/lab sheets, and other classroom materials. Participation in this program requires that pupils have access to a computer that is connected to a telephone line in addition to the software and curriculum materials.

The Voyage of the Mimi (Bank Street College of Education, no date), developed at Bank Street College of Education for grades 4 to 8, is an interdisciplinary, theme-based series of lessons that use videotapes or videodisks, computer software, and print materials to present concepts and problems in science, social studies, language arts, and math. The twenty-six segments of the videotapes tell the story of a ship called the Mimi, her captain, his grandson, and a research team who go to sea to study whales. As exciting adventures at sea unfold, students learn about whales, about navigation, how to use maps, how to survive a shipwreck, and more. An important part of the program, and what makes it inquiry-based, is that the software requires students to use the information and skills they have learned in order to solve problems encountered on the voyage. Two pieces of software are available: One provides simulations where students use science and mathematics to locate treasure, avoid hurricanes, and rescue whales, while the other explores concepts of ecology and challenges students to live for a year on an island without disrupting the ecosystem. A free video that introduces the program and shows how one group of teachers have used it is available.

One advantage of a multimedia program such as *Voyage of the Mimi* is that all of the pupils in a class can watch the video at one time. Then, depending on how many computers you have, children can take turns, in groups, to follow up on the computer. If you are using a computer lab, instead of having computers in your classroom, the pupils can watch the video in class and then work in groups at computers in the lab.

The Worldwide Web

The Worldwide Web is a global information system that can be entered from the Internet. It provides access to information about almost every imaginable subject from all over the world and offers the opportunity to place information on the Web by setting up a homepage with its own address. Learning to navigate the Web takes time and patience, both for you and your pupils.

The Internet can be integrated into the curriculum by using it as a source of information; that is, children find information on curriculum-related topics and use it as data for investigations or information for reports. It can also be integrated into the curriculum by having children participate in building a small part of the Internet themselves. Fifth and sixth graders in schools with access to the Internet are setting up their own Web pages, which include e-mail addresses, so that those who know their Web address can communicate via e-mail.

MAKING THE COMPUTER WORK FOR YOU

What most teachers look forward to least is averaging grades at the end of a marking period. Now you can make this chore a thing of the past by setting up a spreadsheet for each subject, or for each class if you are a special science teacher and teach different classes. Once the spreadsheet is set up, you enter a grade for each pupil every time you give a quiz or a test or assess a project or portfolio. Grades can be weighted by entering one grade more than once; that is, a project grade will count more than a short quiz, so the grade is weighted appropriately. With a click of the mouse, the computer will average all the grades. If you need to change a grade, the computer will give you a new average immediately. The spreadsheet lets you know when a pupil is falling behind and gives you a basis for feedback to pupils and their parents at any time. Programs with special features for teachers are available, but any spreadsheet program will work.

The computer can help you plan units and lessons, either with special software designed for teachers or with a more general program. You can create a template for lesson plans that makes planning simpler. As ideas for lessons and units come to mind, they can be filed and retrieved with much greater ease and certainty than can be achieved by most of us with notebooks, file cards, and manila folders. As you explore the possibilities, you will become more aware of the power and utility of the computer to help you with creative planning as well as with paperwork.

◆ SUMMARY

The computer has become an important, almost an essential, tool for teaching. The challenge to teachers is to use it to help meet instructional goals rather than using it as something extra that is not integrated into the curriculum.

While teachers may have little choice in the available hardware, which consists of computers and the many kinds of equipment that can be attached to them, they can decide how to use what is available. Options for integrating the computer into instruction are available whether the teacher has a one-computer classroom, has a multiple-computer classroom, or is in a school where all computers are concentrated in one spot. In all of these situations, assigning cooperative learning groups to work together on the computer is preferable to having children work individually on a computer.

Software, the programs that run on computers, can be classified into two categories, curriculum-related software and tool software. Curriculum-related software includes tutorials, simulations, problem solving, narrative adventures, and drill-and-practice. All of these except drill-and-practice can be integrated into an inquiry-based science program. The main categories of tool software are word processors, graphics programs, and spreadsheets. These are productivity tools that children use to produce text, pictures, graphs, and combinations of all of these in reports, stories, booklets, analysis of data, and large displays for science fairs or other presentations.

Other ways that the computer can be integrated into the curriculum are the microcomputer-based laboratory (MBL) and such multimedia programs as *The National Geographic Kids Network* (1988–1997) and *The Voyage of the Mimi* (Bank Street College of Education, no date). These tend to be more costly than software alone and thus not as widely available. The same is true of telecommunications, which require access to a telephone line as well as other equipment. Where available, this opens up the possibility of children's communicating with other children in this country and abroad via e-mail and of accessing the Worldwide Web.

The computer can work for teachers as well as for pupils by serving as an automated grade book that averages grades and as a means of making planning easier and more systematic.

◆ ACTIVITIES FOR THE READER

1. Order the free video introducing *The Voyage of the Mimi* (Bank Street College of Education, no date) from Sunburst Communications (see "Resources" for the address). Give a brief report to the class.

2. Obtain a catalog from William Bradford Publishing Company (see "Resources" for the address), and choose a software program to preview without charge. Develop a lesson plan using the software.

3. If you have a computer skill that your classmates lack, arrange to give a workshop for your classmates, teaching them the skill.

◆ QUESTIONS FOR DISCUSSION

1. Discuss the advantages and disadvantages of having all computers in one place as opposed to having them dispersed into classrooms.

2. How can you use a computer to meet the special needs of children with hearing disabilities, sight disabilities, or emotional problems?

3. Would you ever use a computer for drill-and-practice? Explain your answer.

4. What can a teacher do to compensate for the fact that some children have computers at home, while others have no access to a computer at all?

◆ REFERENCES

American Association for the Advancement of Science. (1993). *Benchmarks for science literacy.* New York: Oxford University Press.

Bank Street College of Education. (no date). *The Bank Street laboratory* [Computer program]. Pleasantville, NY: Sunburst Communications.

Bank Street College of Education. (no date). *Ecosystems* [Computer program]. Pleasantville, NY: Sunburst Communications.

Bank Street College of Education. (no date). *The voyage of the Mimi* [Computer program]. Pleasantville, NY: Sunburst Communications.

Build a circuit [Computer program]. (no date). Pleasantville, NY: Sunburst Communications.

Dublin, P., Pressman, H., Barnett, E., Corcoran, A., & Woldman, E. (1994). *Integrating computers in your classroom. Elementary education.* New York: HarperCollins.

The factory [Computer program]. (no date). Pleasantville, NY: Sunburst Communications.

Kimball, A., & Donoghue, D. (no date). *Botanical garden* [Computer program]. Pleasantville, NY: Sunburst Communications.

Merriam-Webster. (1995). *Merriam-Webster's collegiate dictionary* (10th ed.). Springfield, MA: Author.

National Geographic kids network [Computer program]. (1988–1997). Washington, DC: Educational Services, National Geographic Society.

National Research Council. (1996). *National science education standards.* Washington, DC: National Academy Press.

Operation frog [Computer program]. (no date). Jefferson City, MO: Scholastic, Inc.

Oregon trail [Computer program]. (no date). Jefferson City, MO: Scholastic, Inc.

Sky travel [Computer program]. (no date). Acton, MA: William K. Bradford.

◆ RESOURCES

Education Resources (1550 Executive Drive, Elgin, IL 60123) is the source for *Oregon Trail.*

Educational Services, National Geographic Society (P.O. Box 98018, Washington, DC 20090-8018) is the source for *National Geographic Kids Network.*

Scholastic, Inc. (P.O. Box 7502, Jefferson City, MO 65102), is the source for *Operation Frog* and many other useful programs.

Sunburst Communications (101 Castleton Street, P.O. Box 10, Pleasantville, NY 10570 [800-321-7511]). *Botanical Garden, The Bank Street Laboratory,* and *The Voyage of the Mimi* are a few of the software packages available from this source.

William K. Bradford (16 Craig Road, Acton, MA 01720 [800-421-2009]). *Earth Clock, Science Search Series* (using a database), and *Sky Travel* are available from this source.

Index

343